Classic Furniture

Meubles de Style

Klassische Möbel

Publisher • Éditeur • Herausgeberin
Ana María Valdós

Publishing Director • Directeur d'édition• Verlagsleiter
Nacho Asensio

Editing • Rédaction • Redaktion
Anna Jolis

Design and layout • Composition et maquette • Design und Layout
Miguel Ángel Palleiro

Translation • Traduction• Übersetzung
S.A.M. (english)
Elisabeth Bonjour Ruiz de Gopegui (français)
Rita Mattutat und Douglas Yacoub (deutsch)

Production • Production • Produktion
Juanjo Rodríguez Novel

Editorial Project: Books Factory
e-mail: books@booksfactory.org

Published by: Atrium Internacional de México, S.A. de C.V.
Fresas nº 60 (Colonia del Valle)
03200 México D.F. MÉXICO

Tel: +525 575 90 94
Fax: +525 559 21 52
e-mail: atriumex@prodigy.net.mx
www.atriumbooks.com

ISBN: 84-95692-27-9
Legal Deposit: B-36457-2002

Printed in Spain
Grabasa, S.L.

Projet éditorial: Books Factory
e-mail: books@booksfactory.org

Publication: Atrium Internacional de México, S.A. de C.V.
Fresas nº 60 (Colonia del Valle)
03200 México D.F. MÉxICO

Tél: +525 575 90 94
Fax: +525 559 21 52
e-mail: atriumex@prodigy.net.mx
www.atriumbooks.com

ISBN: 84-95692-27-9
Depôt légal: B-36457-2002

Imprimé en Espagne
Grabasa, S.L.

Verlagsprojekt: Books Factory
e-mail: books@booksfactory.org

Herausgegeben von: Atrium Internacional de México, S.A. de C.V.
Fresas nº 60 (Colonia del Valle)
03200 México D.F. MÉXICO

Telf: +525 575 90 94
Fax: +525 559 21 52
e-mail: atriumex@prodigy.net.mx
www.atriumbooks.com

ISBN: 84-95692-27-9
Depot gesetzlicher Pflichtexemplare: B-36457-2002

Druck in Spanien
Grabasa, S.L.

Classic Furniture

Meubles de Style

Klassische Möbel

Contents

Index

Inhaltsverzeichnis

Introduction

Like in any other artistic manifestation carried out by the hand of man, such as clothes or decoration, our first information about the furniture of the most remote civilizations comes fundamentally from stone inscriptions and paintings, which give an approximate idea of shape and proportion, but not of their details and construction. From these study sources, a certain hedonistic attitude towards life can easily be deduced – always tied to the privileged social classes – which will introduce the taste for beautiful things in objects of daily use.

The furniture, understood as a usual element, is a good example of this premise. In it, man combines its technical aspect with an artistic load, giving it a meaning which manifests the spirit of an age. In fact, the item of furniture can be understood as a work tool through which man exalts his ideal essence, whether it be individual or collective.

This same quest for the pleasure of the beautiful, for the well-made, from the second half of the 20th Century onwards, caused some eccentric English aristocrats, moved by the heyday of romanticism which was so preponderant in the past, became interested in old furniture which up until then had been discarded.

Inheriting an old piece was only well regarded if it showed the rank of one's ancestors; if not, anyone who had to decorate their house opted for new objects which they acquired to show their social and economic category.

As we have said, in the 19th Century, romanticism was articulated through bygone desires and wishes which boost the reevaluation of what we today call antique pieces. In the beginning, by means of auctions, original objects were sought. Soon they were not enough to satisfy the growing demand of the eccentrics, who organized themselves to continue rummaging in old farmhouses or rural inns in search of furniture with evident rough aftertaste, although subject to the so highly valued antique tradition. When these sources ran out, there was no alternative but to recreate the furniture according to the old style, motivating the impulse of a new commercial sector prepared to satisfy the desires of the well-off bourgeoisie. For that reason, as has occurred in other areas of creation by man, in the middle of the 19th Century in France and England, catalogues and magazines were published and distributed with illustrations of said productions. This material has contributed enormous to elucidate, in this day and age, specific aspects of antique furniture and has likewise helped us to understand what were the causes which unleashed such devotion.

The 19th Century was a century of great political, social, cultural and technical changes. Between 1820 and 1830, liberal revolutions exploded in Europe which consolidated the triumph of Romanticism in the artistic field and in bourgeois society. In the middle of this panorama of political and social turbulence, the highest and most powerful classes tried to reinstate the customs of the Old Regime.

Through furniture and subject to the ideological instructions of romanticism, the new hegemonic class tried to reinstate

a present based on an imaginary and escapist reality which tried to emulate the old regime. The result was the birth of a lively trade in beautiful pieces from the 18th Century. Conditioned by these preferences, the industry articulated, then, a production of contemporary furniture under the inspiration and the styles of the 18th Century, with which interest grew in France about antique furniture, providing it did not go beyond the styles of the 18th Century.

The original pieces which, as we have said, were auctioned, were usually in a middling state of conservation which led to them being restored. This activity led to the discovery that many of them had the names of the furniture makers, the cabinet maker or the manufacturers engraved on them, and this led to a hazardous study directed towards the more or less objective history of furniture, which in turn led to overcrowding at the turn of the century in the taste for collecting antique pieces, to the point where its commercialization increased to the detriment of the more up-to-date furniture. In addition, this led to a conceptual change in interior decoration, in which eclecticism and heterogeneity were allowed and in which furniture, often in a poor state, was given a new treatment, by being included in spaces different to the originals or by giving them an apparently displaced meaning.

Evidently, this preoccupation for all that which surrounds the human being in domestic spaces is not absolutely generalized, but restricted to a certain social sector, and within this sector, often to a well-defined consumer. If in the beginning we usually associate it with those people who are considered sensitive to the fine arts, often we realize that this is insufficient to define them as a group. In fact, furniture gives detailed information about the idiosyncrasy of an individual.

The primary objective of the publication of this book is to offer, to both professionals and the general public, a large gathering of materials, which are presented systematically structured in four large sections (Introduction, Basic Furniture, Classical Furniture and its Styles and Basic Glossary), in order to open before the eyes of the reader a wide panoramic overview of modern manufactured classical furniture in its most interesting versions.

With the explanations which accompany them, always precise and systematic and specifically tailored to each subject or section, and the manner of exposing their elements, both literary and graphic, our readers are presented with a true guide which is easy to consult and highly useful.

Classical furniture is a subject which is always up to date, which easily raises passions in people who give it a try. With this book, we hope to achieve two apparently contradictory aims, but which are really complementary: to satisfy the need of those who want to know more and more about a subject which is already familiar to them, and to awaken or increase interest in those people who feel curiosity and eagerness for a subject whose discovery and study will undoubtedly arouse their enthusiasm.

Introduction

Comme toutes les manifestations artistiques crées par la main de l'homme , telles que le vêtement ou la décoration, les premières informations que nous avons au sujet du mobilier dans les civilisations les plus éloignées proviennent fondamentalement d'inscriptions rupestres et de peintures, qui nous donnent une idée approximatives de ses formes et de ses proportions, mais pas du détails et de la construction. A partir de cette source d'information, il est facile de déduire que l'homme avait à une idée assez hédoniste de la vie –toujours en relation avec les couches sociales privilégiées- et tendait à appliquer le goût pour les belles choses dans les objets quotidiens.

Le meuble, compris comme élément d'usage quotidien, est un bon exemple de cette théorie. L'homme tend à conjuguer en lui l'aspect technique avec une forte charge artistique, tout en lui donnant un sens particulier de l'esprit d'une époque. De fait, le meuble peut être interprété comme un outil qui permet à l'être humain d'exalter son essence idéale, particulière ou collective.

La recherche du plaisir dans tout ce qui est beau pour les choses bien faites, et poussés par la montée du romanticisme si en vogue dans le passé provoquent chez quelques excentriques aristocrates à partir de la seconde moitié du XIX ème en Angleterre, l'apparition d'un grand intérêt pour les meubles anciens qui jusqu'à maintenant étaient complètement négligés.

Hériter un meuble ancien n'était bien considéré que si l'on pouvait démontrer le rang de nos ancêtres ; dans le cas contraire, tous ceux qui désiraient décorer leur maison devaient opter pour l'acquisition de nouveaux objets à travers lesquels il était possible de confirmer la catégorie sociale et économique.

C'est un fait qu'en plein XIX ème siècle, le romanticisme s'articule à partir de la nostalgie et le désir vétustes qui provoquent la revalorisation de ce que nous dénommons aujourd'hui des pièces d'antiquaires. Au début, les objets originaux étaient les plus recherchés à travers les ventes aux enchères. Mais bientôt, ceux-ci devenus insuffisants par rapport à la demande, les plus excentriques s'organisèrent pour continuer à fouiller dans les vieilles fermes et auberges rurales à la recherche de meubles d'aspect nettement plus rude, mais tellement appréciée par leur tradition ancienne. Une fois épuisée cette ressource, il ne restait que la solution de re-créer des meubles selon le style ancien, provoquant le décollage d'un nouveau secteur commercial disposé à satisfaire les besoins d'une riche bourgeoisie. C'est pour cela que vers la moitié du XIX ème siècle en France et en Angleterre, tout comme dans d'autres secteurs de la création, la publication et divulgation de catalogues et de revues avec des illustrations de pièces fabriquées est devenu un fait habituel. Ce matériel a énormément contribué à nous éclairer de nos jours certains aspects concrets du mobilier ancien et à comprendre quelles fut la raison qui provoqua un tel dévouement.

Le XIX ème siècle fut un siècle de grands bouleversements politiques, sociaux, culturels et techniques. Entre 1820 et 1830 éclatèrent toute une série de révolutions libérales qui consolidèrent le triomphe du Romanticisme dans le domaine artistique et celui de la bourgeoisie sociale. Au centre de ce paysage de turbulences politiques et sociales, les classes les plus aisées et prépondérantes tentèrent la restauration des coutumes de l'ancien régime.

À travers le mobilier, et soutenus par les directrices idéologiques du Romanticisme, la nouvelle classe hégémonique essaya d'instaurer un présent imaginaire et fuyant qui prétendait émuler l'ordre ancien. Le résultat fut la naissance d'un commerce dynamique de belles pièces du XVIII ème siècle. Conditionnée par cette prédilection, l'industrie commença à produire des meubles contemporains inspirés dans le style du XVIII ème ce qui provoqua en France un croissant intérêt pour le meuble ancien sans jamais dépasser les limites du style du XVII ème.

Les pièces originales, comme il a été signalé auparavant, étaient habituellement vendues aux enchères dans un état de conservation plutôt moyen d'où la nécessité de les restaurer. Cette activité permis la découverte que sur certaines avaient été gravé le nom de l'artisan, de l'ébéniste, ou du fabriquant et provoqua une étude hasardeuse de l'histoire plus ou moins objective du meuble, ainsi qu'elle massifia pendant le passage d'un siècle à l'autre, le goût pour le collectionnisme de pièces anciennes jusqu'au point d'augmenter sa commercialisation en détriment des meubles contemporains. Ceci entraîna par conséquence un changement conceptuel de la décoration d'intérieur où l'éclectisme et l'hétérogène était à présent permis, et où l'on conféra un nouveau traitement a des meubles souvent en mauvais état en les plaçant dans des endroits originaux ou en leur donnant un sens tout à fait surprenant. C'est évident que la préoccupation pour tout ce qui entourait l'être humain et son foyer n'était pas de l'intérêt général, et était réservée à un secteur social déterminé et à un type de consommateur bien défini. Si en principe on avait tendance à l'associer aux personnes soit disant sensibles aux Beaux Arts , cela n'était pas suffisant pour en former un groupe déterminé. De fait, les meubles donnent une information très détaillée de la nature de l'individu.

L'objectif principal de cet ouvrage est d'offrir, tant aux professionnels comme au public en général, un important apport de matériel structuré en quatre grands chapitres (Introduction, Les meubles de base, Les meubles classique, ses différents styles et son lexique de base), dans le but présenter aux yeux du lecteur, une vision le plus vaste possible sur le meuble classique de fabrication moderne dans toutes ses différentes versions.

Cet ouvrage est un manuel facile à consulter et d'une grande utilité grâce aux explications toujours précises, systématiques et spécifiques, appropriées à chaque thème ou chapitre, aussi bien littéraire que graphique, et à la manière d'exposer les éléments.

Le meuble classique est un thème de perpétuelle actualité qui passionnent facilement les amants de ces objets. Notre désir est d'atteindre deux objectifs précis et complémentaires bien que contraposés avec la parution de ce livre : satisfaire le besoin d'en savoir plus sur un thème déjà familier, et réveiller ou augmenter l'intérêt pour une matière dont la découverte et l'étude enthousiasmera sans aucun doute les plus curieux .

Einleitung

Wie bei jeder anderen künstlerischen Betätigung des Menschen –wie Z. B. der Schneiderkunst oder der Dekoration– liefern uns Steininschriften und Malereien erste Informationen über das Mobiliar der ältesten Kulturen. So erhalten wir eine vage Vorstellung von der Form und den Größenverhältnissen, erfahren aber nichts über die Einzelheiten oder die Herstellungsweise. Geht man von diesen Forschungsquellen aus, läßt sich leicht eine sicherlich hedonistische – immer den privilegierten Klassen vorbehaltene - Lebenshaltung ableiten, die versuchte, den Geschmack an schönen Dingen in die alltäglichen Gebrauchsgegenstände einfließen zu lassen.

Das Möbel - in seiner Funktion als Gebrauchsgegenstand - ist ein gutes Beispiel für diese Prämisse. Im Möbel bringt der Mensch technische Aspekte mit künstlerischem Schaffen in Einklang und verleiht ihm eine Bedeutung, die vom Zeitgeist seiner Epoche geprägt ist. In der Tat kann man das Möbel als Werkzeug betrachten, mittels dessen der Mensch sein ideales Wesen verherrlicht – sei es individuell oder kollektiv.

Diese vergnügte Suche nach dem Schönen und dem gut Gemachten hat zur Folge, daß sich in der zweiten Hälfte des 19. Jh. in England einige exzentrische Aristokraten – angeregt durch die Blütezeit der Romantik, die die Vergangenheit verherrlichte - für das antike Möbel interessieren, das bis dato verschmäht wurde.

Das Erben eines antiken Möbelstückes wurde nur gut angesehen, wenn man damit die gesellschaftliche Stellung seiner Vorfahren unter Beweis stellen konnte; war dies nicht der Fall, entschied sich jeder bei der Einrichtung seines Hauses für den Erwerb neuer Objekte, mittels derer er seine soziale Klasse und Kaufkraft zu verstehen gab.

Wie bereits erwähnt, war die Romantik des 19. Jh. von einer Melancholie und Sehnsucht nach vergangenen Zeiten geprägt, die die Aufwertung dessen förderte, was wir heute Antiquitäten nennen. Anfangs suchte man auf Auktionen nach Originalstücken. Bald reichte dieses Angebot nicht mehr aus, um die wachsende Nachfrage der Exzentriker zu befriedigen, die systematisch alte Bauernhöfe und Landgasthäuser auf der Suche nach Möbeln durchstöberten, die zwar etwas roh wirkten, aber doch der so geschätzten alten Tradition entsprachen. Als diese Quellen versiegten, blieb nichts anderes übrig, als Möbel im alten Stil nachzubauen, was einen neuen Wirtschaftszweig in Schwung brachte, der die Wünsche des vermögenden Bürgertums befriedigen sollte. Deshalb wurden – wie dies auch in anderen Bereichen des menschlichen Schaffens der Fall ist – Mitte des 19. Jh. in Frankreich und England Kataloge und Zeitschriften mit Illustrationen der besagten Produktionen veröffentlicht und in Umlauf gebracht. Dieses Material hat sehr dazu beigetragen, daß man heutzutage konkrete Aspekte des antiken Möbels aufdecken kann, und es hilft zu verstehen, welche die Gründe waren, die eine solche Hingabe entfesselten.

Das 19. Jh. war ein Jahrhundert der großen politischen und sozialen Umbrüche und der technischen und kulturellen Neuerungen. Zwischen 1820 und 1830 brachen in Europa liberale Revolutionen aus, die den Triumph der Romantik im Bereich der Kunst und beim Bürgertum festigten. Inmitten dieses Panoramas politischer und sozialer Umbrüche versuchten die obersten und mächtigsten Klassen, die Bräuche des Ancien Régime wiedereinzuführen. Mittels

des Mobiliars und den ideologischen Richtlinien der Romantik folgend, war die neue herrschende Klasse bestrebt, eine Gegenwart zu schaffen, die auf einer imaginären, fluchtartigen Wirklichkeit beruhte, die die alte Ordnung wiederherstellen sollte. Daraus entstand ein reger Handel mit schönen Stücken des 18. Jh. Diesen Vorlieben folgend, produzierte die Industrie zeitgenössische Möbel, die von den Stilrichtungen des 18. Jh. inspiriert waren. Dadurch wuchs in Frankreich das Interesse an antiken Möbeln, solange die Stilrichtungen nicht über das 17. Jh. hinausgingen.

Die Originalstücke, die – wie bereits erwähnt – versteigert wurden, befanden sich normalerweise in einem mittelmäßigen Zustand, was dazu führte, daß sie restauriert wurden. Dabei entdeckte man, daß auf vielen Stücken die Namen der Möbelbauer, Kunsttischler oder Fabrikanten eingraviert waren, und dies ermöglichte eine gewagte Untersuchung, die auf eine mehr oder weniger objektive Geschichte des Möbels abzielte; diese wiederum machte um die Jahrhundertwende herum den Geschmack am Sammeln antiker Stücke zu einem Massenphänomen. Die Kommerzialisierung ging so weit, daß sie sich nachteilig auf die neueren Möbel auswirkte. Dies brachte auch eine Veränderung in der Konzeption der Innendekoration mit sich: Eklektizismus und Heterogenität waren erlaubt und den oft in schlechtem Zustand erhaltenen Möbeln wurde eine neue Behandlung zuteil, indem man sie an anderen Orten als die Originale aufstellte und ihnen eine augenscheinlich veränderte Bedeutung zukommen ließ. Natürlich kann diese Besorgnis um alles, was Bestandteil der häuslichen Umgebung des Menschen ist, nicht verallgemeinert werden, sondern bleibt auf eine bestimmte soziale Schicht und innerhalb dieser wiederum oft auf einen ganz bestimmten Konsumententyp beschränkt. Wenn man dieses Interesse in einem ersten Versuch mit Menschen in Verbindung bringt, die offen für Kunst sind, erkennt man oft, daß dies nicht ausreicht, um sie als Gruppe zu definieren. In der Tat geben die Möbel detailliert über den Charakter eines Individuums Auskunft.

Das Hauptanliegen dieses Buches ist es, sowohl Spezialisten als auch dem allgemeinen Publikum eine wichtige Sammlung von Material vorzulegen, das systematisch in 4 große Kapitel aufgegliedert wurde (Einleitung, Die wichtigsten Möbelstücke, Das klassische Möbel und seine Stilrichtungen und die Grundbegriffe), um dem Leser einen breiten Überblick über das klassische Möbel moderner Herstellung in seinen interessantesten Varianten zu geben. Die begleitenden Erklärungen, die stets präzise, systematisch und dem jeweiligen Thema oder Absatz angepaßt sind, sowie die Anordnung der literarischen und grafischen Elemente machen dieses Buch zu einem einfachen, äußerst nützlichen Nachschlagewerk. Das klassische Möbel ist und bleibt ein aktuelles Thema, das jeden begeistert, der es mag. Mit diesem Buch sollen zwei auf den ersten Blick widersprüchliche, aber in Wirklichkeit komplementäre Ziele erreicht werden: Es soll einerseits den Wissensdurst jener stillen, die mit dem Thema bereits vertraut sind und ihre Kenntnisse vertiefen wollen. Andererseits soll es bei aufgeschlossenen und neugierigen Lesern das Interesse für ein Thema wecken, dessen Entdeckung und Erforschung sie ohne Zweifel begeistern wird.

Le Meuble dans l'histoire

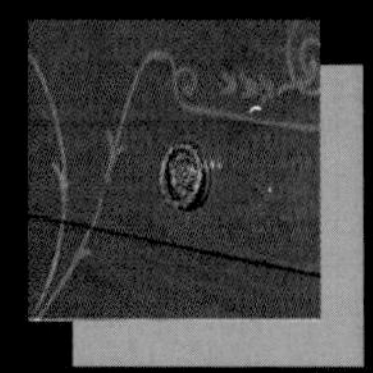

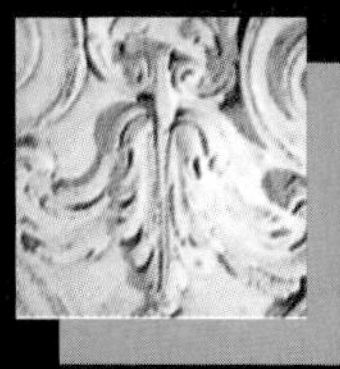

Die Geschichte des Möbels

Furniture in History

Le Meuble dans l'histoire

Die Geschichte des Möbels

The first structure conceived by artists for human comfort is the bed, whose function is to distribute our body weight on a horizontal plane. The mattress, however, did not appear until the Neolithic Period (7,000-6,000 CE), arising only in sedentary groups.

Another element in the future bed, the mattress, was placed on the ground or on the floor, and later raised on stones or legs to avoid attacks from insects. Slowly, the mattresses were complemented by headboards, backs, canopies, and other sorts of structures.

In the Middle Ages, the area of the house where the bed was placed was also used at other hours of the day to de-

Le lit, dont la fonction principale est de distribuer sur un plan horizontal tout le poids du corps, représente la premiè-re structure crée par l'homme

1

dans le but d'obtenir un certain confort. Le matelas, par contre n'apparaîtra pas avant le Néolithique (7000-6000) et uniquement dans les groupes sédentaires.

Die erste vom Menschen entworfene Struktur, die seiner Bequemlichkeit dienen sollte, ist das Bett, dessen Funktion darin besteht, das Körpergewicht auf eine horizontale Fläche zu verteilen. Die Matratze hingegen trat erst im Neolithikum (7000-6000 v. Chr.) in Erscheinung und war nur bei seßhaften Völkergruppen zu finden.

Ein weiteres Element des zukünftigen Bettes, das Unterbett, wurde anfangs auf den Boden und später auf Steine oder Bettfüße gelegt, um sich gegen die Insekten zu schützen. Nach und nach wurden die Unterbetten durch Kopfteile, Rückenlehnen, Baldachine und andere Strukturen ergänzt. Im Mittelalter wurde der Ort, an dem das Bett

1 - 2

Details, Lancaster fireplace and library

Détails d'une cheminée et librairie Lancaster

Ausschnitt Kamin und Bücherschrank Lancaster.

1

2

pp. 16-17
Paneling (Melarca).
Boiserie (Melarce).
Boiserie (Melarca).

1.
Paneling (Arin y Embil).
Boiserie (Arin et Embil).
Boiserie (Arin y Embil).

2.
Library paneling (Mariano García).
Librairie en boiserie (Mariano Garcia).
Bücherschrank Boiserie (Mariano García).

3.
Paneling (Muebles Calvo).
Boiserie (Meubles Calvo).
Boiserie (Muebles Calvo).

4.
Paneling (Muebles Calvo).
Boiserie (Muebles Calvo).
Boiserie (Muebles Calvo).

3

4

1 - 2

Details, paneling 3.

Détails de boiserie 3.

Ausschnitt Boiserie 3.

velop different activities, such as sharing meals or resting. It is not until the lower Middle Ages that castles and palaces

1

begin to organize the bed as an exclusive space.

With the development of the bourgeois way of life, in the eighteenth century, the alcove will appear, ideated as a small pavilion separated off into a corner of the room as a kind of prelude to the modern bedroom. Today's equipment attempts, above all, to be functional, practical, and comfortable.

The chair, from ancient times, took on an individual significance that would not leave it subordinated to its first function. The chair presents a highly complex structure when it comes to being adapted to the driving forces and functional needs of the human race, and it has been the subject of detailed studies. Following this path, the modern designs almost always procure a combination of comfort and ergonomics.

The third main furniture structure to come out of the human mind is the table, which will appear after the bed and the chair. The table, thus,

L'autre élément qui composera le lit est le sommier, qui était tout d'abord situé par terre pour s'élever à posteriori sur des cailloux ou des pattes et éviter ainsi l'attaque des insectes. Petit à petit, des éléments tels que des têtes de lit, dossiers, baldaquins et d'autres structures sont devenus les compléments des sommiers.

Au Moyen Age, on utilisait aussi le lit pendant différentes heures de la journée pour y développer d'autres activités comme les repas ou le repos. C'est à l'arrivée du Moyen Age que l'on commença à organiser le lit comme un pavillon exclusif.

L'alcôve, comprise comme un petit pavillon séparé dans un coin de la pièce et comme précurseur de la chambre à coucher moderne, apparaît au XVIII ème siècle avec le développement de la bourgeoisie. Mais c'est en plein XIX ème que le lit reçoit sa forme définitive selon le concept moderne. Dans l'équipement actuel, l'important est surtout d'être fonctionnel, pratique et confortable au maximum.

La chaise, depuis l'antiquité, a une signification individuelle qui ne la subordonne pas à sa première fonction. Il est très difficile d'adapter la complexité de la structure de la chaise aux nécessités motrices et fonctionnelles de l'être humain et ceci fut l'objet d'une étude détaillée. Suivant cette théorie, le design moderne tente toujours de conjuguer commodité et ergonomie.

La table est la troisième structure imaginée par l'hom-

stand, tagsüber für verschiedene Aktivitäten genutzt, wie z. B. Essen oder Ausruhen. Erst im Spätmittelalter wurde das Bett in den Schlössern und Palästen zu einer ausschließlichen Ruhestätte. Mit dem Aufstreben des Bürgertums trat im 18. Jh. der Alkoven in Erscheinung, ein kleiner Nebenraum, der von einer Ecke des Raumes abgetrennt wurde und als Vorgänger des modernen Schlafzimmers betrachtet werden kann. So erhielt das Bett im 19. Jh. seine definitive Form nach unserer modernen Auffassung. Bei der heutigen Ausstattung achtet man darauf, daß das Bett funktional, praktisch und bequem ist.

2

Der Stuhl hat sich eine individuelle Bedeutung zu eigen gemacht, die ihn nicht seiner primären Funktion unterordnet. Der Stuhl hat eine sehr komplexe Struktur, da er den motorischen und funktionalen Bedürfnissen des Menschen angepaßt wird, und wurde in detaillierten Studien untersucht. Das moderne Design folgt dieser neuen Richtung und versucht fast immer, Bequemlichkeit und Ergonomie zu verbinden.

Die dritte vom Menschen entworfene Möbelstruktur ist der

3

3.

Paneling of oak and walnut veneer (Viuda Hurtado).

Boiserie en racine de chêne et rainurée en noyer (Viuda Hurtado).

Boiserie aus Eiche, mit Nußbaum furniert (Viuda Hurtado).

4.

Detail, fireplace cornice.

Détail d'une corniche de cheminée.

Ausschnitt Kaminsims.

pp. 22-23.

Paneling (Nova Serenissima).

Boiserie (Nova Serenissima).

Boiserie (Nova Serenissima).

4

1.

General view of table and dining room with chairs veneered in walnut and rosewood (Carpanelli).

Vision générale d'une table de salle à manger et chaises contreplaquées en racine de noyer et palissandre (Carpanelli).

Gesamtansicht von Eßtisch und Stühlen aus Nußbaum und Palisander, furniert.(Carpanelli).

2.

Chair in myrtle veneer (Carpanelli).

Chaise contreplaquée en racine de myrte (Carpanelli).

Stuhl aus Myrtenholz, furniert (Carpanelli).

2

3

3.

Detail, chair back 2. Inlaid work.

Détail d'un dossier de chaise 2. Ornementation en marqueterie

Ausschnitt Rückenlehne Stuhl 2. Intarsienverzierung

1.

Extendable table with combination mirror panel and inlaid work (Carpanelli).

Table extensible avec tablette en combinaison avec le miroir et la marqueterie (Carpanelli).

Ausziehbarer Tisch. Tischplatte mit Spiegel und Intarsien (Carpanelli).

1

will be born of the need to carry out precision activities. Its first form is that of a simple plank balanced on the knees or legs of its users who, at the same time, carry on their activities from the ground or floor. From the fourteenth and fifteenth centuries, the table was assigned different functions. Aside from being the place where meals were taken, tables developed into forms better adapted to sedentary work: desks or other models, like consoles. The austerity of medieval homes continued to the time of the birth of bourgeois

me, mais qui n'apparut qu'après le lit et la chaise. La table naquit du besoin de réaliser des travaux de précision. Elle s'articula d'abord comme une simple tablette d'appuy soutenue directement par les genoux de l'usager, qui de son coté continua à développer ses activités en contacte directe avec le sol. C'est à partir des XIV ème et XV ème siècles que l'on commença à assigner à la table différentes fonctions. En plus du fait d'y manger, les tables prirent des formes adaptées au travail sédentaire comme le secrétaire ou d'autres

Tisch, der zeitlich nach dem Bett und dem Stuhl in Erscheinung trat. Der Tisch entstand aus der Notwendigkeit, Präzisionsarbeiten durchzuführen. Anfangs war der Tisch ein einfaches Stützbrett, das direkt auf die Knie des Benutzers gelegt wurde, der sich selbst bei der Ausführung seiner Tätigkeiten in direktem Kontakt mit dem Boden befand. Ab dem 14. und 15. Jh. wurden dem Tisch verschiedene Funktionen zugewiesen. Zusätzlich zum Eßtisch entstanden Formen, die dem Arbeiten im Sitzen angepaßt waren, wie der Schreibtisch, oder andere Modelle wie z. B. die Konsol-

2

3

2.

Extendable center table with floral and rhombic motifs (Carpanelli).

Table extensible avec tablette centrale aux motifs de fleurs et de losanges (Carpanelli).

Ausziehbarer Tisch. Der mittlere Teil der Platte ist mit Blumenmotiven und Rauten verziert. (Carpanelli).

1

1.

Dining room integrated with different elements (Muebles Canella).

Salle à manger formée par divers éléments (Meubles Canelle).

Mit verschiedenen Elementen ausgestattetes Eßzimmer (Muebles Canella).

2.

Display case in Madrona veneer (Muebles Canella).

Vitrine en placage de Madrona (Muebles Canella).

Madrona Vitrine, furniert (Muebles Canella).

3.

Détail d'une vitrine 2.

Détail d'une vitrine 2

Ausschnitt Vitrine 2.

2

3

1

2

1 - 2.

Armchair and chair (Muebles Canella).

Fauteuil et chaise (Meubles Canella).

Sessel und Stuhl (Muebles Canella).

3.

Display case in mahogany (Muebles Pérez Benau).

Vitrine en palme d'acajou (Meubles Perez Benau).

Vitrine aus Mahagoniholzverbindung (Muebles Pérez Benau).

3

4.

Detail, display case 3 moldings.

Détail des moulures de la vitrine 3.

Ausschnitt Leiste der Vitrine 3.

1

2

1.

Detail, sideboard handles (Picture's).

Détail de manettes du buffet (Picture's).

Ausschnitt Griffe der Anrichte (Picture's).

2.

Detail, chair back (Picture's).

Détail d'un dossier de chaise (Picture's).

Ausschnitt Rückenlehne des Stuhls (Picture's).

3.

Dining room with different elements (Picture's).

Salle à manger formée par divers éléments (Picture's).

Eßzimmer mit verschiedenen Elementen (Picture's).

3

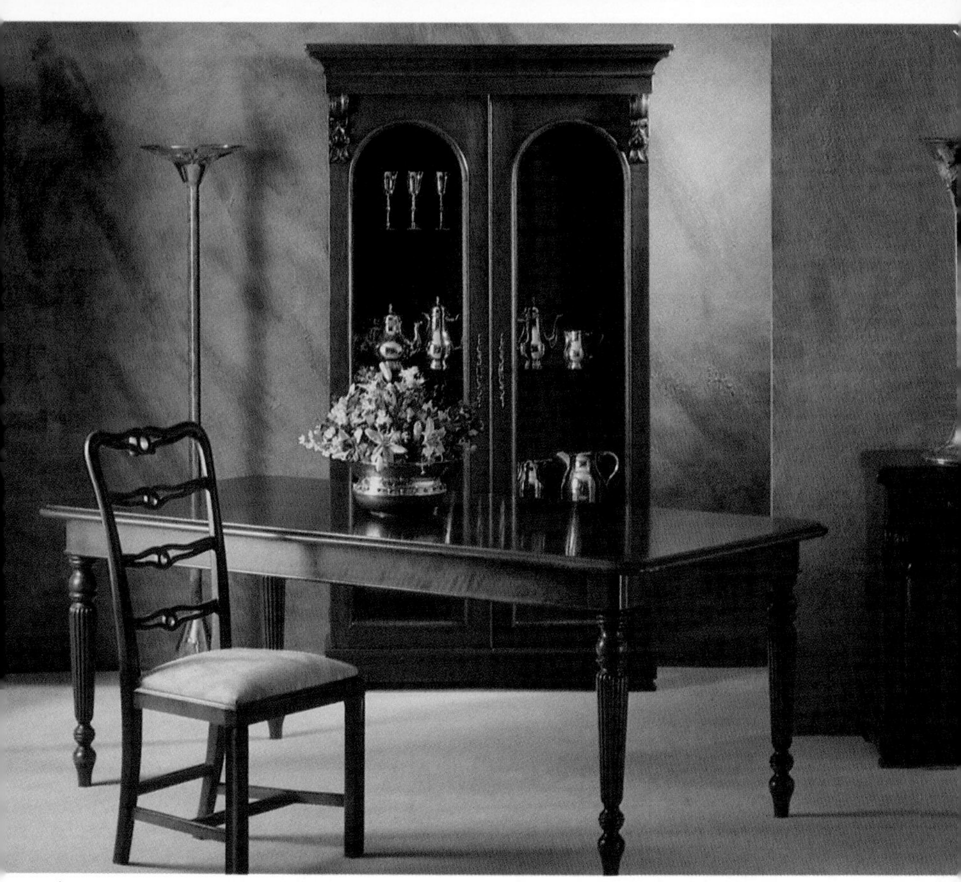

1

lifestyles, when signs of greater comfort and luxury were introduced.

The last of the basic furniture structures is the container, the origin of which must be the box, chest, or hall seat of medieval times.

The first container is the luggage trunk or chest fashioned from a section of tree trunk hollowed out and with one of its parts used as lid. Onto this cover or lid hinges

modèles, comme les tables auxiliaire. L'austérité moyenâgeuse continua jusqu'à l'éclosion du mode de vie bourgeois, tout en introduisant des touches de commodité et de luxe.

Le bahut fut le premier container : celui-ci est le résultat du fait de couper un tronc d'arbre, de le vider de son intérieur et utiliser la partie coupée comme couvercle. Avec le temps, ce couvercle fut fixé avec des gons et des charnières pour

tische. Die Nüchternheit der mittelalterlichen Heimstätten blieb solange bestehen, bis das Aufblühen bürgerlicher Lebensarten Merkmale von Bequemlichkeit und Luxus mit sich brachte.

Die letzte der grundlegenden Möbelstrukturen ist das Aufbewahrungsmöbel, dessen

Ursprung in den mittelalterlichen Kästen, Truhen und Schranktruhen zu suchen ist.

Das erste Aufbewahrungmöbel ist die Truhe, die daraus ent-

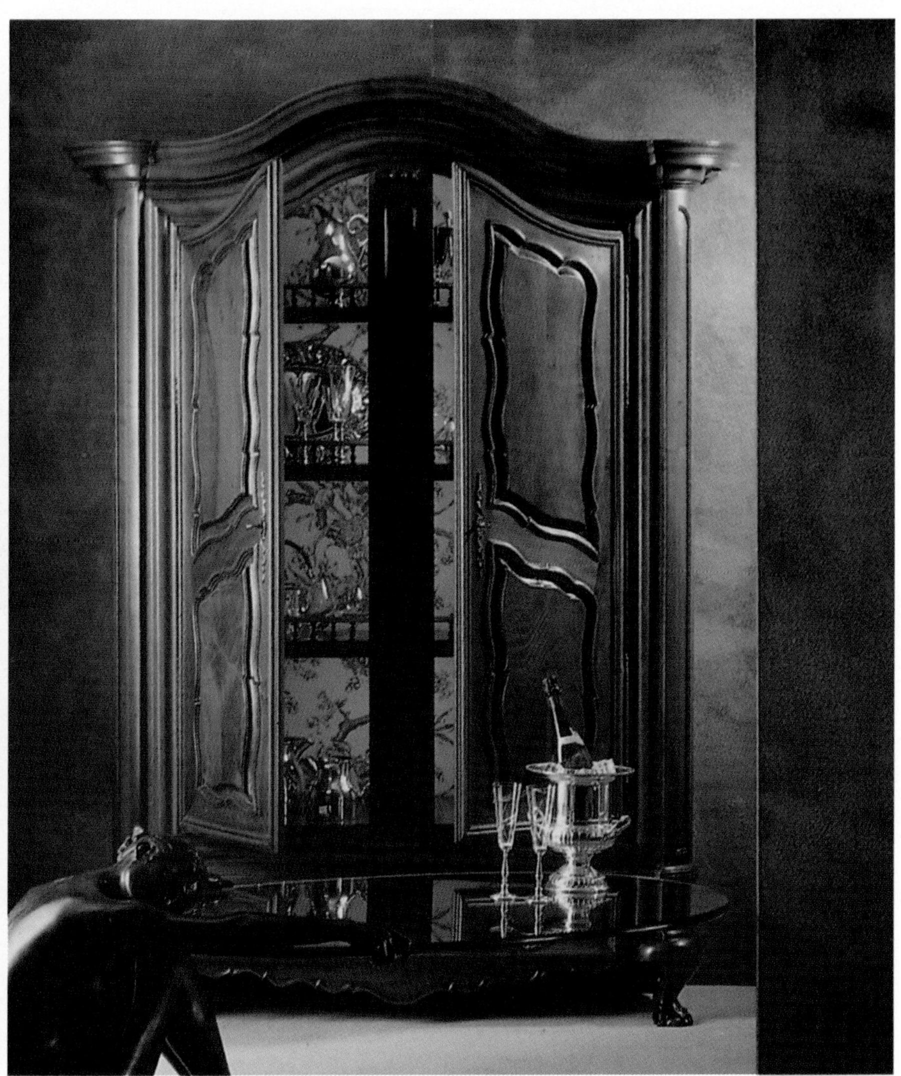

2

1.

Delibes display case, Principado dining room table, Coruña chair, Victorian style (Varo-Valentí).

Vitrine Delibes, table à manger Principado, chaise Coruña, inspirées du style Victorien (Varo-Valenti).

Vitrine Delibes, Eßtisch Principado, Stuhl Coruña, vom viktorianischen Stil inspiriert (Varo-Valentí).

2.

Navarra cocktail cabinet, Marieta table (Varo-Valentí).

Meuble bar Navarra, table Marieta (Varo-Valenti).

Bar-Schrank Navarra, Tisch Marieta (Varo-Valentí).

1

2

1.

Sycamore display case (Hijos de R. Baixauli).

Vitrine en bois de sycomore (Hijos de R. Baxauli)).

Vitrine aus Sykomore (Hijos de R. Baixauli).

2.

Sycamore display case (Hijos de R. Baixauli).

Vitrine en bois de sycomore (Hijos de R. Bauxali).

Vitrine aus Sykomore (Hijos de R. Baixauli).

3.

Regency style display case in birch and veneered walnut, ash, olive, and boxwood (More San).

Vitrine d'inspiration Régence en bois de hêtre et chape de noyer, frêne olivé et rainurée en buis (More San).

Vom Régencestil inspirierte Vitrine aus Buche, furniert mit Nußbaum und Esche und Filets aus Buchsbaum (More San).

3

1

1.

Veneered display case (Muebles Lino).

Vitrine contreplaquée en sapelli (Meubles Lino).

Furnierte Vitrine aus Pomelí de Sapely (Muebles Lino).

2.

Sycamore display case (Hijos de R. Baixauli).

Vitrine en bois de sycomore (Hijos de R. Baixauli).

Vitrine aus Sykomore (Hijos de R. Baixauli).

2

would soon be attached, thus bringing into existence a robust and highly functional piece. From there, all kinds of variations would come about, giving rise to multiple container-furnishings: credencia,

obtenir une pièce robuste et fonctionnelle. A partir d'ici, la possibilité de créer toutes sortes de variations autour du meuble caisson devint enfin une réalité : crédence, crédence à deux portes, armoires et se-

stand, daß man einen Baumstamm zerteilte, ihn aushöhlte und den zuvor abgetrennten Teil als Deckel verwendete. Dieser Deckel wurde bald mit Hilfe von Scharnieren und Gelenken befestigt, so daß ein robustes und

1

2

3

1 - 2.
Detail, inlaid work of display case 3.
Détail de marqueterie de la vitrine 3.
Ausschnitt Intarsien der Vitrine 3.

3.
Display case, front view (Carpanelli).
Vitrine. Vue frontale (Carpanelli.
Vitrine. Vorderansicht (Carpanelli).

1.
Library (Arthur Brett and Sons).
Bibliothèque (Arthur Brett & Sons).
Bücherschrank (Arthur Brett and Sons).

2.
Display case (Titchmarsh and Goodwin).
Vitrine (Titchmarsh and Goodwin).
Vitrine (Titchmarsh and Goodwin).

2

1.

Art Deco sideboard in ash with solid cherry wood columns and ebony fillets. Art Deco armchair (Annibale Colombo).

Buffet Art Déco en racine de frêne, cerisier et ébène, avec partie centrale positionnable et fauteuil Art Déco en racine de frêne entrelacé rainuré en ébène (Annibale Colombo).

Art Decó Anrichte aus Esche mit Säulen aus massivem Kirschbaumholz und Filets aus Ebenholz. Art Decó Lehnstuhl (Annibale Colombo).

2.

Art Deco desk-dressing table in ash, cherry, and ebony with reclining center piece and Art Deco armchair in ash latticed with ebony fillets (Annibale Colombo).

Secrétaire Art Déco en racine de frêne, les colonnes sont en cerisier massif avec incrutations d'ébènes. (Annibale Colombo)

Art Decó Toilettentisch aus Esche, Kirsche und Ebenholz mit aufklappbarem Mittelteil und Art Decó Lehnstuhl aus Esche mit verarbeiteten Filets aus Ebenholz (Annibale Colombo).

p. 46.

George III armchair in oak. Original piece (Antigüedades Fortuny).

Fauteuil en chêne Jorge III. Pièce originale (Antiquités Fortuny).

Sessel aus Eiche Georg III. Originalstück (Antigüedades Fortuny).

p. 47.

William IV English reading chair in mahogany and latticework (1830). Original piece (Antigüedades Fortuny).

Fauteuil de lecture anglais en acajou et cannage Guillaume IV (1830). Pièce originale (Antiquités Fortuny).

Englischer Lesesessel aus Mahagoni und Geflecht, Wilhelm IV. (1830). Originalstück (Antigüedades Fortuny).

1

p. 48 Chair. Original piece (Antigüedades Fortuny).

Chaise. Pièce originale (Antiquités Fortuny).

Stuhl. Originalstück (Antigüedades Fortuny).

p. 49 French armchair, Directoire style (1800). Original piece (Angüedades Fortuny).

Canapé français style Directoire (1800). Pièce originale (Antiquités Fortuny).

Französischer Lehnstuhl im Directoirestil (1800). Originalstück (Antigüedades Fortuny).

1.

Writing desk, front view: The detailed cabinetwork creates silken reflections in a play of chiaroscuro, achieved through the small mother-of-pearl moles inlaid in root triangles (Carpanelli).

Vue frontale du secrétaire : le travail précis d'ébénisterie craie des reflets soyeux dans un jeu de clair-obscur réussi grâce aux petits points en huître perlière incrustés en triangles de racine (Carpanelli).

Vorderansicht des Sekretärs. Die präzise Tischlerarbeit schafft weiche Reflexe in einem Kontrastspiel aus Hell und Dunkel. Dieser Effekt wird mit Hilfe der kleinen Perlmuttelemente erreicht, die in Dreiecke eingearbeitet wurden. (Carpanelli).

2.

Cylindrical writing desk with elm root rolltop of classical inspiration (Carpanelli).

Secrétaire cylindrique avec volets en racine d'orme d'inspiration classique (Carpanelli).

Klassisch inspirierter zylindrischer Sekretär mit Rolladen aus Ulmenholz. (Carpanelli).

1.

French style bedroom: close-up of the bed in solid walnut (Melarca).

Chambre à coucher de style français : premier plan du lit réalisé en noyer massif (Malarca) .

Schlafzimmer im französischen Stil: Großaufnahme des Bettes aus massivem Nußbaumholz. (Melarca).

2.

French style bedroom: close-up of the dressing table-writing desk with mirror in solid walnut (Merlarca).

Chambre à coucher de style français : premier plan de la commode secrétaire avec miroir réalisée en noyer massif (Melarca).

Schlafzimmer im französischen Stil: Großaufnahme Sekretär-Kommode mit Spiegel aus massivem Nußbaumholz. (Melarca).

1

2

1.

English headboard in olive veneer and inlaid work (García Requejo).

Tête de lit anglaise en chape d'olivier et marqueterie (Garcia Requejo).

Englisches Kopfteil eines Bettes, furniert mit Olivenbaumholz und Intarsien.

2.

Sketch of night table 1.

Détail de table de nuit 1.

Skizze Nachttisch 1

3.

Chiffonier in olive veneer and inlaid work (García Requejo).

Chiffonnier en chape d'olivier et marqueterie (Garcia Requejo).

Chiffonniere, furniert mit Olivenbaumholz und Intarsien (García Requejo).

3

1.

Andromeda model bedroom including headboard, night tables, and dresser in elm root, inlaid work and boxwood fillet (Caler Tol).

Chambre à coucher modèle Andromeda formée par tête de lit, table de nuit et commode en chape de racine d'orme, marqueterie et rainuré en buis (Caler Tol).

Schlafzimmer Modell Andrómeda, bestehend aus Kopfteil, Nachttischen und Kommode aus furniertem Ulmenholz, Intarsien und Filets aus Buchsbaumholz. (Caler Tol).

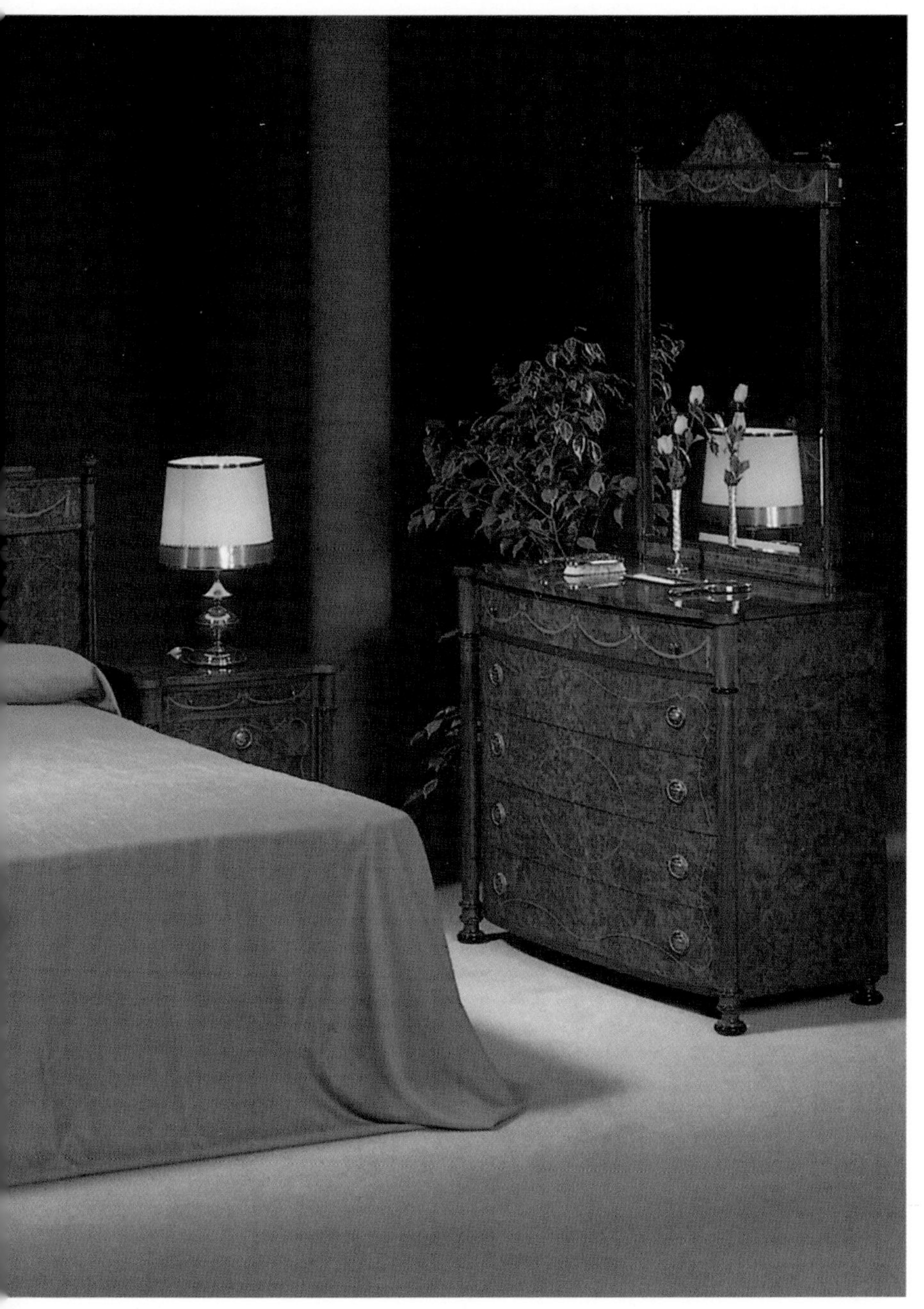

1.

Bedroom with headboard, night tables, writing desk, armchair, and chair (Picture's).

Chambre à coucher formée par tête de lit, table de nuit, secrétaire, fauteuil et chaise (Picture's).

Schlafzimmer, bestehend aus Kopfteil, Nachttischen, Sekretär, Sessel und Stuhl (Picture's).

pp. 60-61.

1.

Office with dual purpose table-desk, library-display case, and low library (Indumoble).

Bureau formé par table écritoire, librairie vitrine et librairie basse (Indumoble).

Arbeitszimmer, bestehend aus Schreibtisch, Büchervitrine und kleinem Bücherschrank.(Indumoble).

2.

Armchair (Indumoble).

Détail d'un fauteuil (Indumoble).

Skizze Sessel (Indumoble).

3.

Library display case (Indumoble).

Librairie vitrine (Indumoble).

Büchervitrine (Indumoble).

1

credenca de dos cuerpos, armario or secrétaire.

Comfortable furniture such as the bench came into existence and developed into other more complex and luxurious forms. The medieval bench adopted into the home comes from the choir benches of churches. From the seventeenth century on new forms would evolve such as the settee or the divan. When the European bourgeoisie began to increase its power, other paral-

crétaire. Quant aux meubles confort, le banc est le modèle à partir duquel d'autres formes plus complexes et confortables ont été développées. Les foyers ont adopté les bancs médiévaux procédant des sièges de chorale d'église. Les nouvelles formes comme le canapé ou le divan sont originaires du XVII ème siècle.

Quand la bourgeoisie européenne vu augmenter son pouvoir, d'autres parallèlement favorisérent l'apparition de

funktionales Möbelstück entstand. Von diesem ausgehend konnte man jegliche möglichen Varianten bauen, aus denen vielfältige Aufbewahrungsmöbel entstanden: Kredenz, zweiteilige Kredenz, Schrank oder Sekretär.

In Bezug auf die Sitz- und Liegemöbel wurden, ausgehend von der Bank, komplexere und bequemere Formen entwickelt. Die mittelalterliche Bank der Wohnhäuser ist von den Sitzen der Kirchenchöre abgeleitet. Ab dem 17. Jh. entstanden neue Formen, wie

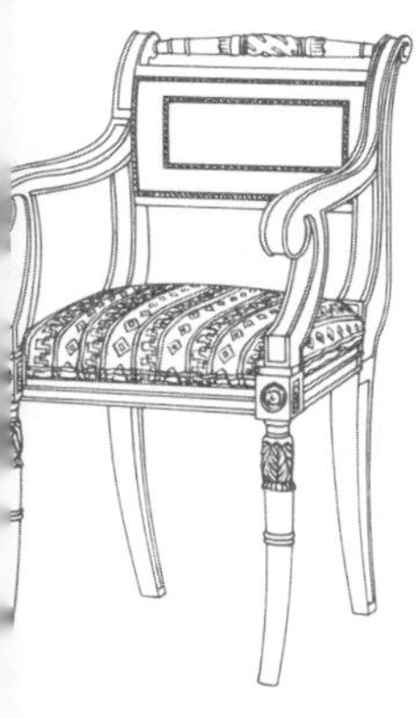

3

1

2

1.

Detail, writing desk drawers .

Détail d'écritoire 2.

Ausschnitt Schubladen des Schreibtisches 2.

2.

Writing desk in lemon wood, ebony, rosewood, and olive root (Carpanelli).

D'écritoire en citronnier, ébène, palissandre, racine d'olivier et bois de rose (Carpanelli).

Schreibtisch aus Zitronenbaum, Ebenholz, Palisander, Olivenbaumholz und Bois de rose. (Carpanelli).

p. 64.

Detail, office desk drawers in yew on English Regency lines (Picture's).

Détail du tiroir de la table de bureau anglais d'inspiration Régence réalisée en yew (Picture').

Detalhe do gavetão de mesa de Ausschnitt Schubladen des Bürotisches, vom englischen Regency-Stil inspiriert, aus Eibenholz. (Picture's).

p. 65.

Writing desk on English Regency lines (Picture's).

Bureau bas anglais d'inspiration Régence.

Niedriger Bureau oder Canterano, vom englischen Regency-Stil inspiriert. (Picture's).

1

2

1.

Desk-dresser with olive and ash veneer work (Caler Tol).

Commode écritoire avec finitions en chape de frêne olivé (Caler Tol).

Kommode-Schreibtisch, nachbehandelt mit Eschenfurnier. (Caler Tol).

2.

Detail of the inside of writing desk 3.

Détail intérieur de bureau 3.

Ausschnitt Innenteil des Bureau 3.

3.

Writing desk with Spanish walnut veneer finishings (Caler Tol).

Bureau: écritoire librairie avec finitions en chape de noyer espagnole (Caler Tol).

Bureau: Schreibtisch-Bücherschrank, nachbehandelt mit spanischem Nußbaumfurnier.(Caler Tol).

3

1

2

lel uses were proposed that gave rise to the appearance of new furniture forms. Hence, the rigid, overlarge Renaissance and baroque armchairs were opposed the first padded easy chairs as still greater comfort began to be sought.

nouveaux modèles de meubles. Ainsi, après les rigides et immenses fauteuils Renaissance et Baroque, naquirent les premiers grands fauteuils capitonnés qui recherchaient un plus grand confort.

das Canapé oder der Diwan. Als die europäische Bourgeosie ihre Macht ausbaute, schlug man weitere Parallelen vor, die das Erscheinen neuer Möbelarten förderten. So begann man, den strengen und großen Sesseln der Renaissance und des Barocks die ersten gepolsterten Lehnsessel entgegenzustellen, die auf eine größere Bequemlichkeit abzielten.

1.

Walnut writing desk (García Requejo).

Bureau bas en noyer (Garcia Requejo).

Canterano aus Nußbaum (García Requejo).

2.

Writing table (Picture's).

Écritoire bureau bas (Picture's).

Schreibtisch-Canterano (Picture's).

3.

Wales model console table and mirror (Zadise Muebles Auxilares).

Console et miroir modèle Gales, de Zadise Meubles Auxiliaires.

Konsoltisch und Spiegel Modell Gales, von Zadise Muebles Auxiliares.

3

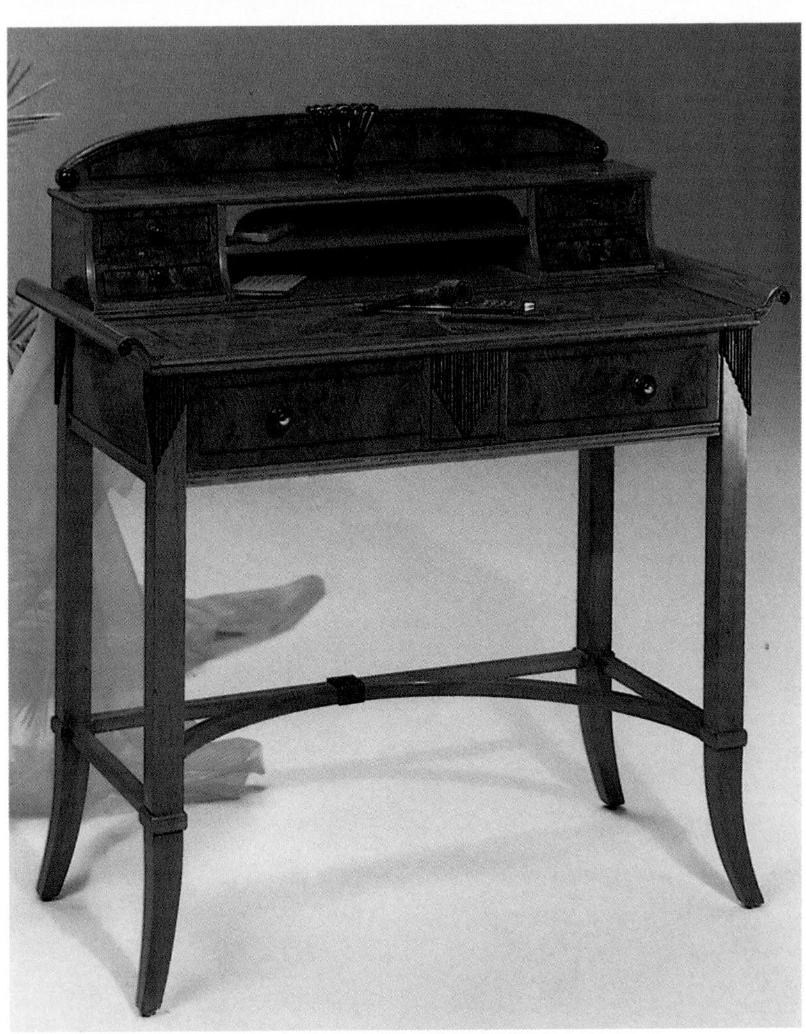

1.

Duma writing desk in Brazilian mahogany and elm veneer, Art Deco style (Conceptes).

Écritoire Dumas en acajou du Brésil et chape de racine d'orme style Art Déco. (Conceptes).

Schreibtisch Dumas aus brasilianischem Mahagoni und furniertem Ulmenholz im Art Decó Stil. (Conceptes).

2.

Writing desk with wooden top (Muarva).

Ecritoire avec couvercle de bois (Muarva).

Schreibtisch mit Holzabdeckung (Muarva).

pp. 72-73

Portillo writing desk (Acanto).

Bureau Portillo (Acanto).

Bureau Portillo (Acanto).

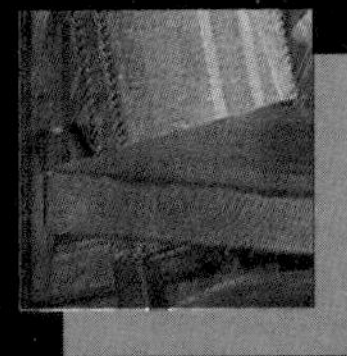

Classical Furniture and its different Styles

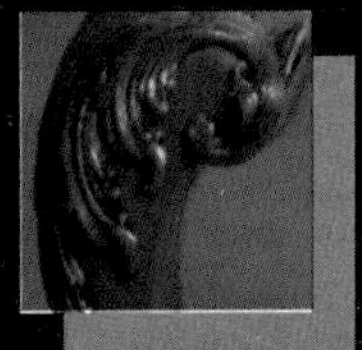

Le Meuble Classique et ses différents Styles

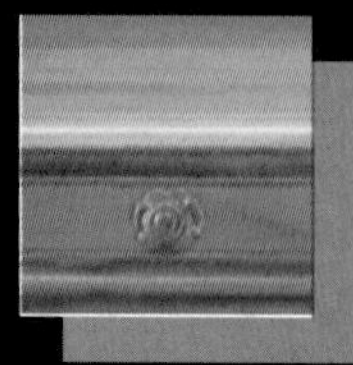

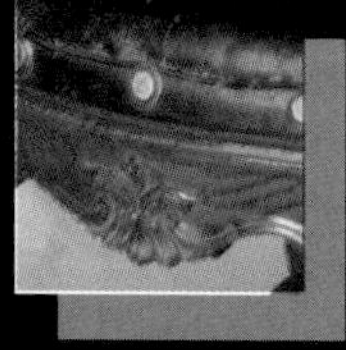

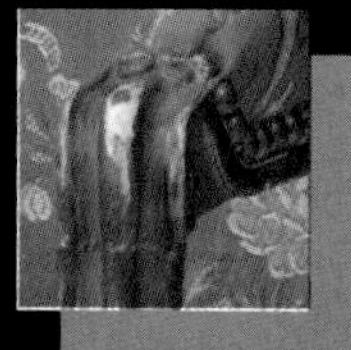

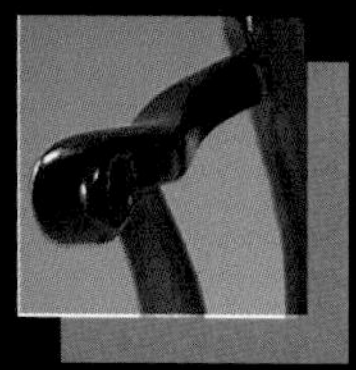

Das klassische Möbel und seine Stilrichtungen

The Renaissance

Le style Renaissance

Renaissance

The Renaissance
Louis XIII
Le style Renaissance
Le style Louis XIII
Renaissance
Louis XIII

The transition from the Renaissance to the baroque period will begin in Italy but then take on great force in France, above all toward its end. The style of this time is known as Louis XIII (finalizing in 1643).

After a time of great austerity and sobriety marked by the Spanish court, the pieces of this style began their bid to adapt themselves to larger spaces with better lighting, spaces that also enjoyed greater comfort. The ornamentation will have a certain flexibility close to that of the baroque but will be structurally more reminiscent of the Renaissance.

In the Louis XIII style, oak or walnut were much used.

La transition entre le style Renaissance et le Baroque est originaire d'Italie, mais c'est en France que celle-ci acquit sa grande force, surtout durant la dernière période. Le style de cette époque est connus comme le style Louis XIII et il se termina en 1643.

Après une période de grande austérité et de sobriété marquée par la Court d'Éspagne, les pièces de ce style tentent de s'accommoder à des espaces plus amples et mieux illuminés, tout en jouissant de plus de confort. L'ornementation est d'une flexibilité très proche du Baroque même si la structure rappelle le style Renaissance.

Dans le style Louis XIII on utilise le chêne et le noyer.

Der Übergang von der Renaissance zum Barock hatte seinen Ursprung in Italien, gewann aber in Frankreich große Bedeutung, vor allem im letzten Zeitabschnitt. Der Stil dieser Epoche, der als Louis-treize-Stil bekannt ist, endet 1643.

Nach einer Zeit, die von der Strenge und Nüchternheit des spanischen Hofes gekennzeichnet war, versuchte man, die Möbel des besagten Stiles an größere und besser belichtete Räume anzupassen und ihnen mehr Bequemlichkeit zu verleihen.

Der Reichtum der Verzierungen nähert sich bereits dem Barock an, wenn die Ornamente auch von ihrer Struktur her an die Renaissance erinnern. Im Louis-treize werden Eichenholz und Nußbaumholz verwendet.

1.

Louis XIII style room with Rousseau library in solid oak (Simon Bigart).

Salle style Louis XIII formée par bibliothèque Rousseau en chêne massif (Simon Bigart)

Raum im Louis-treize-Stil, bestehend aus Bücherschrank Rousseau aus massiver Eiche.(Simon Bigart)

1.

Louis XIII Bescos table in solid beech (Simon Bigart).

Table Bescos Louis XIII en hêtre massif (Simon Bigart).

Tisch Bescos im Louis-treize-Stil aus massiver Buche (Simon Bigart).

2.

Louis XIII canopy bed in solid beech (Simon Bigart).

Lit Louis XIII avec baldaquin en hêtre massif (Simon Bigart).

Louis-treize-Bett mit Baldachin aus massiver Buche (Simon Bigart).

1.

Library furniture in oak. Note the wooden lamps with geometrical patterns.

Meuble bibliothèque en chêne. À remarquer la formation de plafonds de bois assemblés en dessins géométriques.

Bücherschrank aus Eiche. Auffallend sind die Täfelungen aus verleimten, geometrisch angeordneten Hölzern.

2.

Small oak wood cupboard.

Meuble type coffret en chêne.

Möbelstück aus Eiche, ähnlich einer Anrichte.

3.

Lasanc Louis XIII hall seat of solid oak (Simon Bigart).

Banc coffre de Lansac style Louis XIII en chêne massif (Simon Bigart)

Sitztruhe von Lasanc im Louis-treize-Stil (Simon Bigart).

The Baroque Period

Le style Baroque

Barock

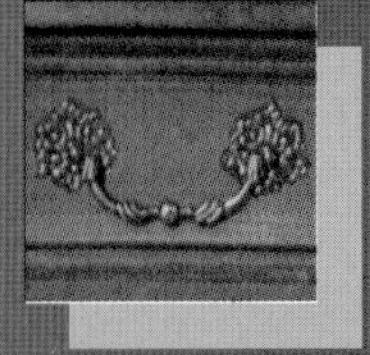

The Baroque Period

Louis XIV

Le style Baroque

Le style Louis XIV

Barock

Louis XIV.

With the Louis XIV style we enter the high French baroque period. This gives rise to a style that is majestic, solemn, pompous, rich, heavy, and eminently regal–all in accordance with feelings of grandeur and the eagerness for the ostentation of power shown by Louis XIV from the time he acceded to the throne in 1643. This style will culminate, from the second half of the eighteenth century, in the Louis XV style.

The harmonious ornamentation of the Louis XIV style is subject to three defining codes:

On atteint la plénitude du Baroque français sous le style Louis XIV, avec un air majestueux, solennel, exagéré, riche, lourd et royal, en accord avec les sentiments de grandeur et le désir de faire une démonstration de pouvoir tout à fait caractéristique du roi Louis XIV depuis sa montée sur le trône. Le sommet de ce style sera atteint à partir de la deuxième moitié du XVIII ème siècle avec le style Louis XV. L'ornementation harmonieuse du style Louis XV est sujette à trois clés qui la définisse comme la sy-

Mit dem Louis XIV gelangt der französische Barock zur Blütezeit und gibt den Weg frei für einen majestätischen, pomphaften, prunkvollen, reichen, schwerfälligen und überaus königlichen Stil, der mit dem Größenwahn und der Prunksucht, welche der König Louis XIV. seit seiner Thronbesteigung im Jahr 1643 an den Tag legte, durchaus in Einklang stand. Dieser Stil fand in der 2. Hälfte des 18. Jh. im Louis XV seinen Höhepunkt. Den harmonischen Ornamenten des Louis XIV liegen drei charakteristische Merkmale zugrunde: die Symmetrie, der Gebrauch von vergolde-

1.

Louis XIV style room with table, dresser, and corner unit.

Salle style Louis XIV formée par table, commode et meuble d'angle.

Raum im Louis-quatorze-Stil, bestehend aus Tisch, Kommode und Eckschrank.

1.

Louis XIV sacristy (made by Kahn Frères).

Vitrine sacristie Louis XIV (Mobilier réalisé par Kahn Fréres).

Sakristei-Vitrine Louis XIV. (Mobiliar durchgeführt von Kahn Frères).

2.

Dual bodied Louis XIV piece in solid wild cherry wood.

Meubles de deux corps Louis XIV en bois de cerisier sylvestre massif.

Zweiteiliges Louis-quatorze Möbel aus massivem Wildkirschbaumholz.

symmetry, the use of gilt wood, and the inclusion of motifs from ancient Rome.

From the origins of this style, carving disappears and is replaced by brass inlays and gilt bronze. The wavy lines that take precedence are visible in the double S-shaped curves of the feet of the furniture or the

métrie, l'utilisation de bois doré et l'inclusion de motifs inspirés de la Rome antique.

Depuis le commencement du style Louis XIV, la taille disparaît et celle-ci est remplacée par de timides applications en bronze et par des ondulations favorisées par des pattes doublement courbées

tem Holz und die Einbeziehung von Motiven aus dem alten Rom. Seit den Anfängen des Louis XIV verschwand das Schnitzwerk. An seine Stelle traten dezente Bronzeapplikationen und Wellenformen, die durch die geschwungene S-Form der Tisch– und Stuhlbeine oder durch eine einfache mit geschnitzten Abbildungen des Akanthus ver-

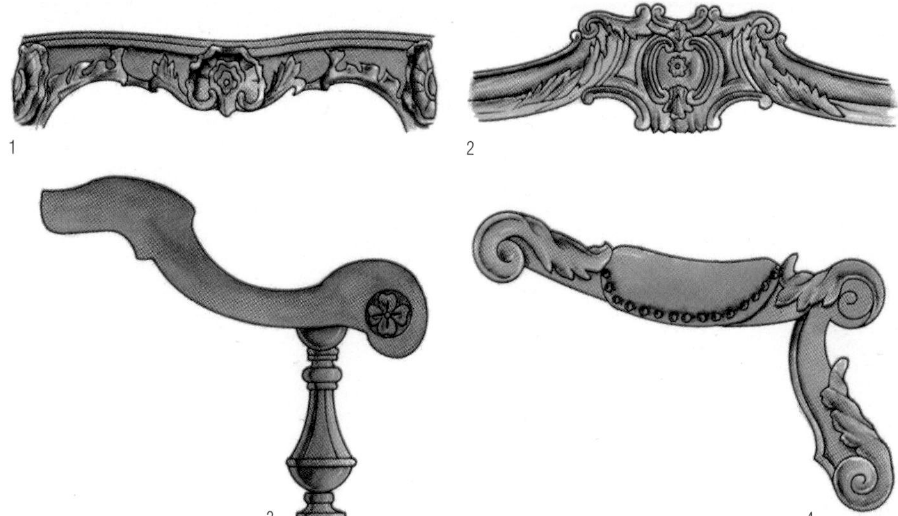

1 – 4:

Drawings of different types of backs and arms characteristic of the Louis XIV style.

Dessins de différents types de dossiers et accoudoirs caractéristiques du style Louis XIV.

Zeichungen von verschiedenen Arten von Rücken– und Armlehnen, charakteristisch für den Louis-quatorze-Stil.

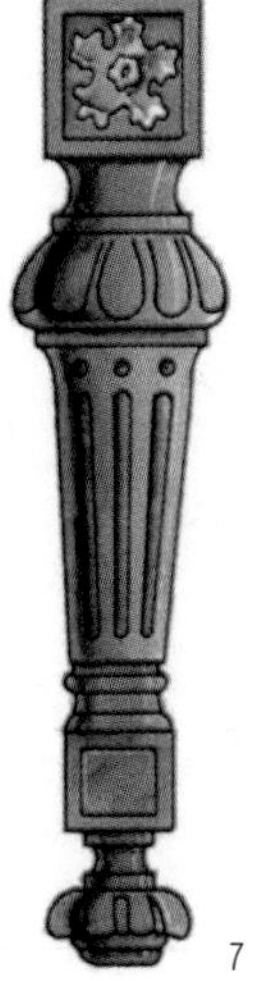

5 – 7:

Different types of feet in pieces of furniture where the curve, while restrained, is still appreciable.

Différents types de pattes où l'usage de la courbe est encore modéré.

Verschiedene Arten von Tisch- und Stuhlbeinen. Man sieht die Verwendung von Kurvenlienien, die noch nicht sehr ausgeprägt sind.

8.

Dining table, inspired on a seventeenth-century model.

Table à manger inspirée d'un modèle du siècle XVII.

Eßtisch, inspiriert von einem Modell aus dem 17. Jh.

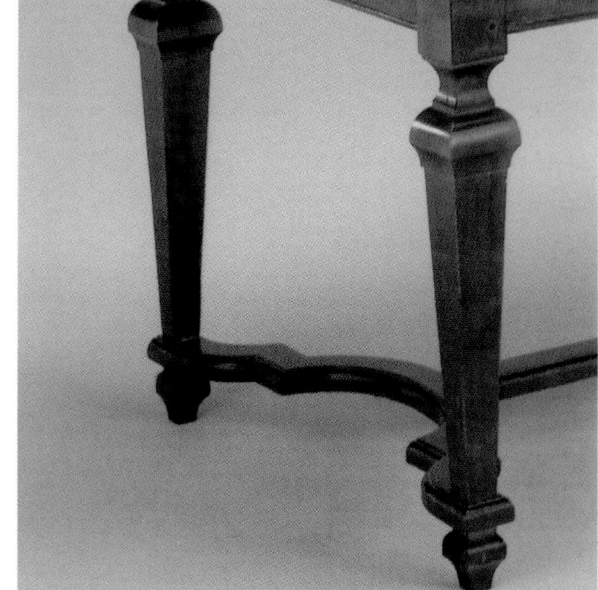

9.

Detail, pedestal and casement (8).

Détail d'une colonnade et d'une chambrane 8.

Ausschnitt kegelstumpfförmiges Tischbein und Keilsteg 8.

1.

Faithful copy of a dresser from the end of the seventeenth century (in wild cherry wood, made by L'Hermine).

Fidèle copie d'une commode de la fin du XVII ème siècle en bois de cerisier sylvestre (Mobilier réalisé par L'Hermine).

Getreue Nachahmung einer Kommode Ende des 17. Jh. aus Wildkirschbaumholz. (Mobiliar durchgeführt von L'Hermine).

2.

Louis XIV style salon with low table, sideboard, display case, and cabinet.

Mobilier de salon style Louis XIV formé par table base, buffet, vitrine et cabinet.

Raummobiliar im Louis-quatorze-Stil, bestehend aus niedrigem Tisch, Anrichte, Vitrine und Cabinet.

sweeping lines with lightly sculpted acanthus leaves.

From a structural point of view, the Louis XIV style pieces show great pomp and weight. The ancient Roman motifs –small heads, trophies, garlands– combined with other stricter elements –conch shells, animal talons and, preeminently, the radiant sun– are governed by symmetry along the perpendicular and horizontal axes. The lines of these pieces get lost in the rigidity of their construction and the static containment of the classical conception, bringing about serpentine forms still somewhat broken up by more restrained features.

en forme de S invertie ou par une sobre ondulation avec de légères tailles en feuilles de chapiteau.

Du point de vue de la structure, les meubles de style Louis XIV son lourd et pesants, et les motifs de la Rome antique –petites têtes, trophées, guirlandes–, combinés avec d'autres plus strictes –coquillages, griffes d'animaux, et surtout le soleil levant–, sont subordonnés à la symétrie par rapport à l'axe horizontal vertical . Seule la ligne des meubles oublie la raideur et la contention statique du classique, provocant l'apparition de courbes encore retenues.

zierte Wellenbewegung erreicht wurden.

Vom strukturellen Gesichtspunkt aus gesehen, sind die Möbel des Louis XIV groß und schwerfällig. Die Motive aus dem alten Rom –kleine Köpfe, Trophäen, Zierkränze–, die mit weiteren strengeren Motiven kombiniert werden, wie z. B. Muscheln, Klauen und –dem vorherrschenden Element– der strahlenden Sonne, wurden gemäß einer auf vertikalen und horizontalen Linien basierenden Symmetrie angeordnet. Die Form der Möbel entfernt sich von der Steifheit und starren Unbeweglichkeit des klassischen Stils und bringt neue Formen hervor, die von –noch– zurückhaltenden Wellenbewegungen unterbrochen werden.

1.

Louis XIV writing table (Geka).

Table écritoire Louis XIV (Geka).

Schreibtisch Louis-quatorze (Geka).

1

2

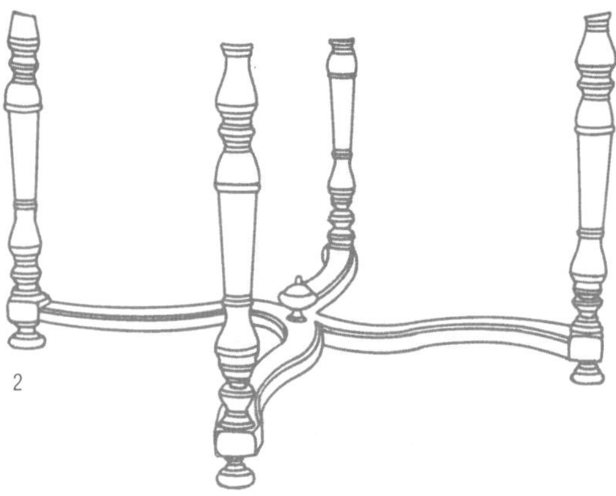

1.
Louis XIV round table.
Table ronde Louis XIV.
Runder Louis-quatorze-Tisch.

2.
Sketch of detail in table in 1, above.
Détail de chambrane table 1.
Skizze Keilsteg des Tisches 1.

3.

Sketch of squared table, a variation of the Louis XIV style.

Détail d'une table carrée, variation de chambranes de style Louis XIV.

Skizze quadratischer Tisch, Keilsteg-Variante des Louis-quatorze-Stils.

4.

Louis XIV style chair with high back and serpentine curves (Geka).

Chaise Louis XIV avec un long dossier et des boulonnes ondulées (Geka).

Louis-quatorze-Stuhl mit hoher Rückenlehne und wellenförmigen Querstreben (Geka).

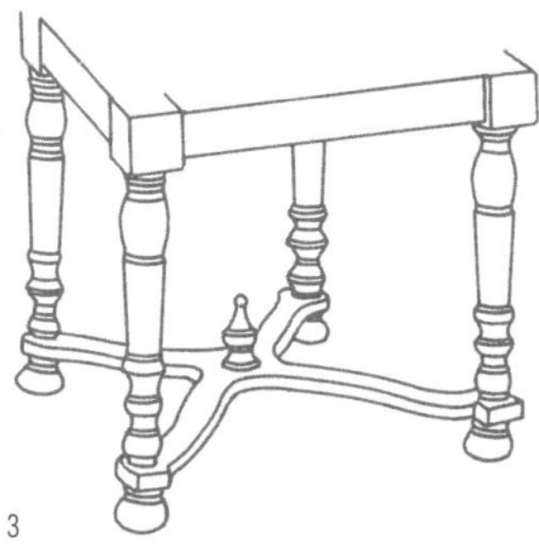

3

4

5

5.

Louis XVI style gaming table with parquet top (Faisser et Plata).

Table de jeu avec tablier en parquet de style Louis XIV. (Faïsse et Plata).

Spieltisch mit Parkett im Louis-quatorze-Stil. (Faïsse et Plata)

Baroque

William and Mary

Le style Baroque

Le style Guillaume et Marie

Barock

Wilhelm und Maria

This style emerged in England around 1668. It is typified by shapes and features that arose and found favor with the bourgeoisies in France and Flanders.

In England, the baroque period would suppose a clearly bourgeois financing.

In the William and Mary style we find the flourishing of what had once been important elsewhere: the Jacobin style.

This style in England will establish the model for the period's classical furniture and, from then on, its influence will begin to be decisive on the Continent.

As regards materials, there is a noteworthy use of walnut as the style is initiated.

Ce style émerge en Angleterre vers l'an 1668 et possède des formes et des particularités provenant de France et des Flandres qui gagnèrent aussitôt le cœur de la bourgeoisie.

En Angleterre, le Baroque représente la consolidation d'un caractère clairement bourgeois. Le style Guillaume et Marie comporte la naissance d'un fait d'important : le style jacobin.

Ce style marquera en Angleterre la norme à suivre dans le mobilier classique, et, à partir de là son influence sera décisive dans tout le continent.

Quant au matériel utilisé, c'est le noyer que l'on remarque en premier lieux.

Dieser Stil tritt in England ca.1668 in Erscheinung und zeichnet sich durch Formen und Merkmale aus, die aus Frankreich und Flandern stammen. Dieser neue Stil findet beim Bürgertum viel Anklang. In England nimmt der Barock eine klar spießbürgerliche Form an. Der Wilhelm und Maria Stil bringt das Aufblühen eines Stils mit sich, der bereits von Wichtigkeit ist: der Jakobinerstil. Dieser Stil setzt in England den Maßstab für klassische Möbel und von nun an wird sein Einfluß entscheidend in Europa. Unter den verwendeten Materialien, sticht anfangs das Nußbaumholz hervor.

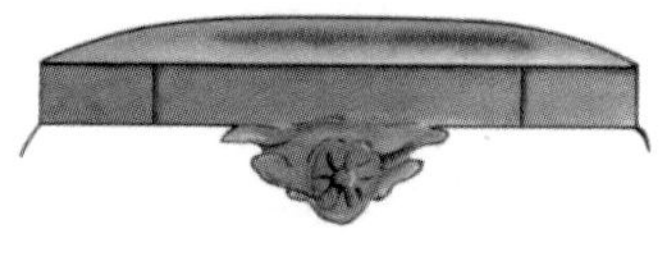

1.

Writing table of seventeenth-century inspiration in solid walnut and wild cherry.

Table écritoire d'inspiration XVII ème siècle en noyer et cerisier sylvestre massif.

Vom 17. Jh. inspirierter Tisch/Schreibtisch aus massivem Nußbaumholz und massivem Wildkirschbaumholz.

2 - 5:

Drawings of the feet of different pieces of furniture with lathed elements, characteristic of the William and Mary style.

Dessins de pattes avec éléments tournoyés, caractéristiques du style Guillaume et Marie.

Zeichnungen von Tisch- und Stuhlbeinen mit gedrechselten Elementen, charakteristisch für den Stil Wilhelm und Maria.

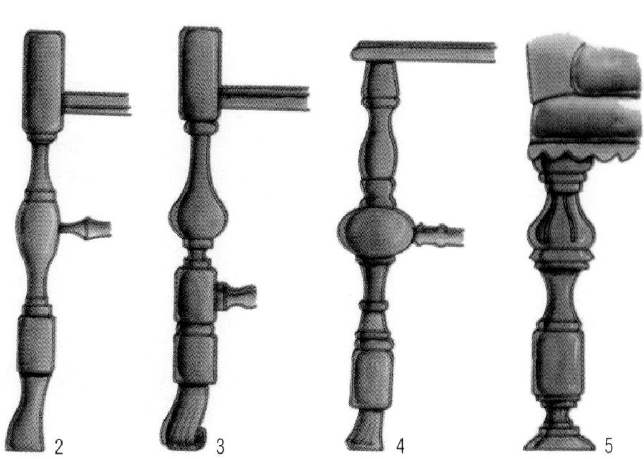

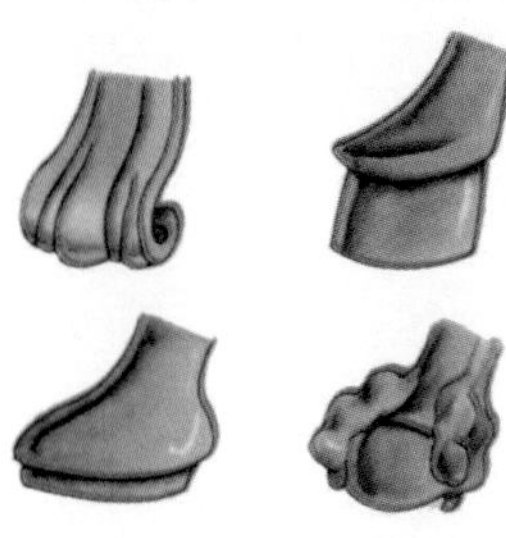

1.

Different types of ornaments on the feet.

Différents types d'ornementation de pattes.

Verschiedene Arten von Verzierungen von Tisch- und Stuhlbeinen.

2.

Telephone table inspired on the seventeenth century in solid walnut (Tradition).

Table téléphone d'inspiration XVII ème siècle en noyer massif (Tradition).

Vom 17. Jh. inspirierter Telefontisch aus massivem Nußbaumholz (Tradition).

Baroque

Queen Anne

Le style Baroque

Le style Reine Anne

Barock

Queen Ann

The baroque style par excellence was introduced into England from 1712 in the version called Queen Anne. It would produce pieces of a lineal cut, eminently logical and distinctive.

In spite of the fact that Anne's reign lasted from 1702 to 1714, the style that bears her name continued until 1720.

One of the most innovative characteristics here is the substitution of oak for walnut. Furniture-makers took advantage of the wood's qualities and potentials by making it more clearly displayed in their pieces.

Le style Baroque par excellence, apparaît en Angleterre à partir de 1712 sous le nom de style Reine Anne, et produit des pièces avec une structure linéale principalement logique et spécifique.

Malgré que son règne se prolongea de 1702 à 1714, le style Reine Anne demeura jusqu'en 1720.

Une des caractéristiques les plus innovantes est la substitution du chêne par le noyer. En profitant de toutes ses qualités et possibilités, les pièces présentent un aspect encore plus spectaculaire.

Der Barock par exellence tritt in England ab 1712 in Form des sogenannten Queen-Ann-Stils in Erscheinung, der Möbelstücke mit einer geradlinigen, überaus logischen und andersartigen Struktur hervorbringt. Obwohl die Herrschaft der Königin Ann auf den Zeitraum von 1702 bis 1714 beschränkt war, dehnte sich der Queen-Ann-Stil bis ins Jahr 1720 aus. Eine der bahnbrechendsten Neuerungen ist die Verwendung des Nußbaumholzes, das an Stelle des Eichenholzes tritt. Man machte sich die Qualitäten des Materials zunutze und schöpfte alle Möglichkeiten aus, die dieses Holz bot, um noch herrlichere Stücke zu kreieren.

1.

Queen Anne trumeau (or jamb) in walnut and Ferrara walnut; molding in solid walnut (Annibale Colombo).

Trumeau style Reine Anne en racine de noyer de Ferrara, avec des moulures de bois de rose massif (Annibale Colombo).

Trumeau Queen Ann aus Nußbaumholz und Nußbaumholz aus Ferrara, Leisten aus massivem Rosenholz (Annibale Colombo).

1 - 2.

Chair backs, rounded and feminine, highly characteristic of the Queen Anne style.

Dossiers de chaises aux formes arrondies et féminines, si caractéristiques du style Reine Anne.

Rückenlehnen mit gerundeten und femininen Formen, charakteristisch für den Queen- Ann-Stil.

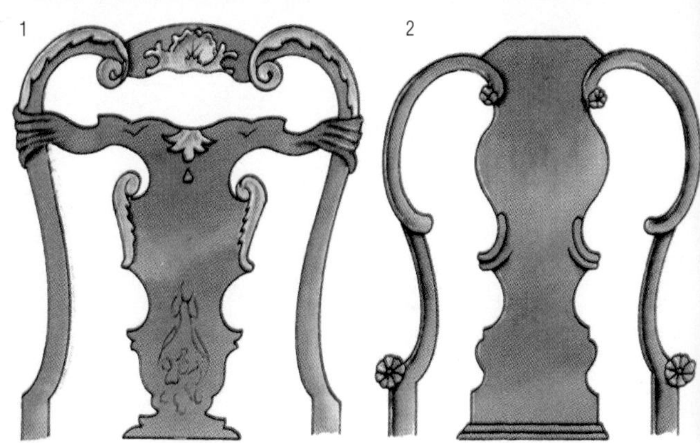

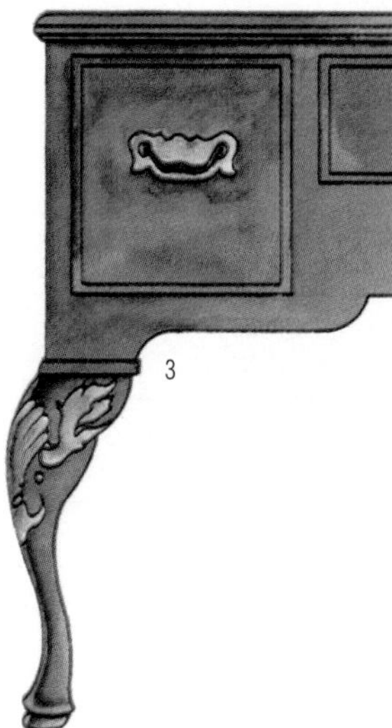

4 - 5 - 6.

These curved feet in the cabriolet style resume the dynamic philosophy of the Queen Anne style.

Les pattes courbée de manière cabriolée résument la philosophie dynamique du style Reine Anne.

Die geschwungenen Tisch- und Stuhlbeine im Cabriolé-Stil spiegeln die dynamische Philosophie des Queen-Ann-Stils wider.

7.

Queen Anne writing table in birch with old English lacquer, Chinese paintings in gold, and relief on a cracked background. An English style with Oriental influences (Fernando Guanter).

Bureau écritoire Reine Anne en bois de hêtre, laqué à l'ancienne en rouge anglais, peintures chinoises en or et reliefs sur fond craquelé. Style anglais d'inspiration orientale (Fernando Guanter).

Bureau-Schreibtisch Queen Ann aus Buchenholz mit antiker Lackierung in englischem Rot, chinesischen Malereien aus Gold und Reliefs auf geteiltem Hintergrund. Englischer Stil mit orientalischem Einfluß. (Fernando Guanter).

3.

Drawing of a foot of a writing desk. The finish is highly stylized.

Dessin d'une patte d'écritoire, avec finition très stylisée.

Zeichnung eines Schreibtischbeines, sehr stilisiert nachbehandelt.

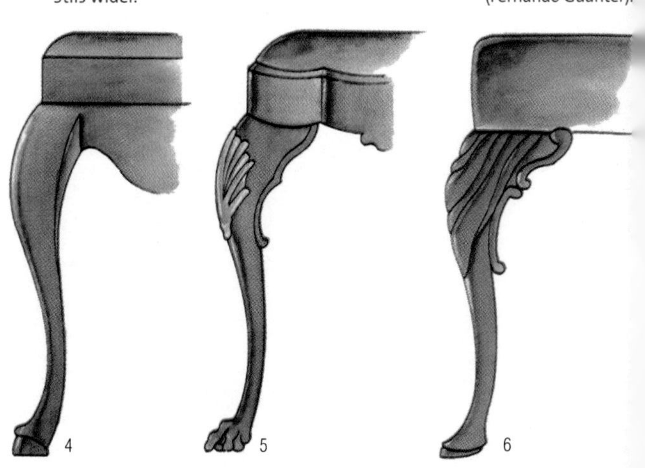

7

1.

Rectangular Queen Anne table of olive wood (Enebro).

Table triangulaire Reine Anne, olivier (Enebro).

Rechteckiger Queen-Ann-Tisch, Olivenbaumholz (Enebro).

2.

Writing desk tending toward the Queen Anne style.

Bureau bas librairie de tendance Reine Anne.

Canterano-Bücherschrank, Tendenz Queen Ann.

Baroque
Regency style
Le style Baroque
Le style Régence
Barock
Régence

The Regency style falls within the period of the French high baroque, appearing in the transition period between the kings Louis XIV and Louis XV.

What characterizes the Regency style involves more the structure of the furniture pieces themselves than their specifically ornamental aspects. The rigid conception of the Louis XIV artifact is softened and more rounded forms appear. The curve takes precedence over the straight line; in consequence, austerity gives way to sensuousness.

Le style Régence s'inscrit pleinement dans la période du Baroque français et apparaît pendant la période de transition entre les rois Louis XIV et Louis XV.

Ce qui définit le mieux le style Régence est plus la structure du meuble en soi que son aspect spécifiquement ornementale. La conception rigide du meuble Louis XIV s'adoucie et des formes arrondies apparaissent. La courbe s'impose aux lignes droites et par conséquence l'austérité laisse sa place à la sensualité.

Der Régencestil wird dem französischen Barock zugeordnet und trat in der Übergangszeit zwischen den Königen Louis XIV. und Louis XV. auf.

Die charakteristischen Elemente des Régencestils stützen sich eher auf die Struktur der Möbel an sich und weniger auf die Ornamente.

Die starre Konzeption der Louisquatorze-Möbel tritt immer mehr in den Hintergrund und wird von runderen Formen abgelöst.

Die geschwungenen Formen verdrängen die geraden Linien und infolgedessen läßt die Strenge der Weichheit den Vortritt.

1.

Chair. Original piece (Antigüedades Fortuny).

Chaise. Pièce originale (Antiquités Fortuny).

Stuhl. Originalstück (Antigüedades Fortuny).

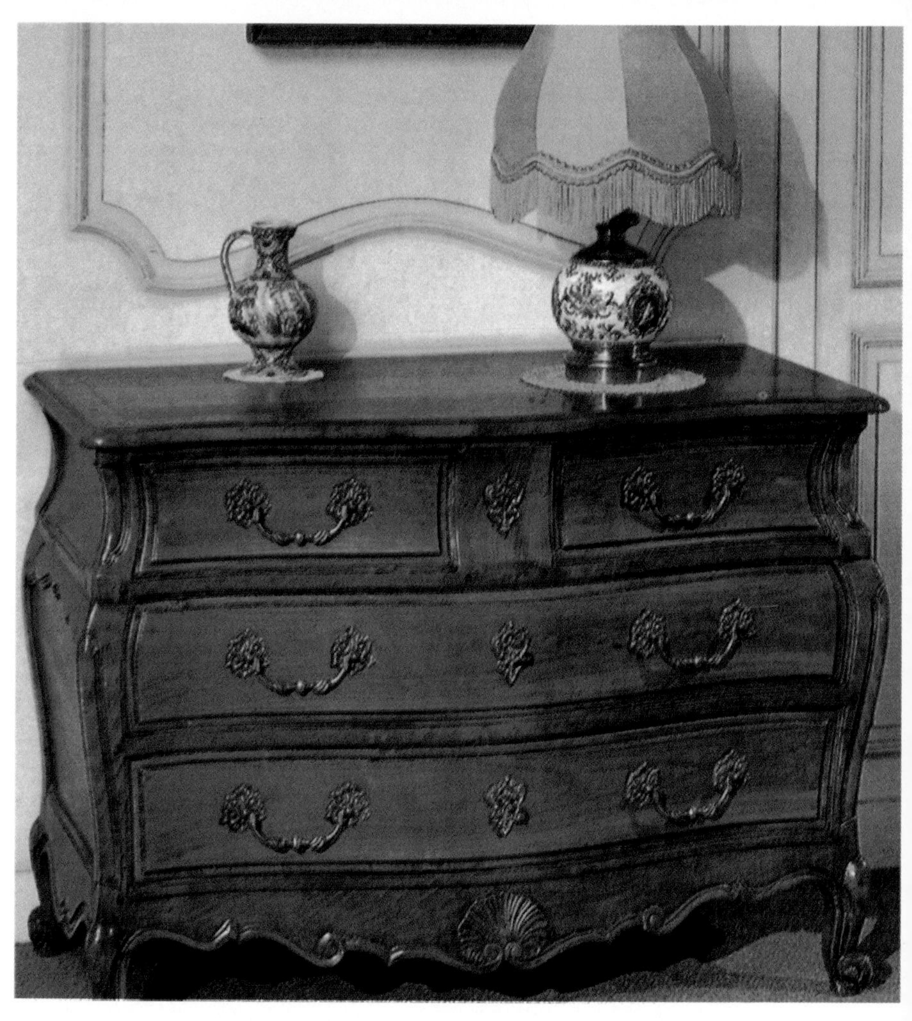

1.

Potbellied chest of drawers.

Commode ventrue.

Gewölbte Kommode.

2.
Sketch of chest 3.
Détail console 3.
Skizze Konsoltisch 3.

3.
Leones chest in mahogany and black lacquer (Fidel Bautista-Época).
Console Leones réalisée en acajou et laque noire (Fidel Bautista-Época).
Konsoltisch mit Löwenmotiv aus Mahagoni und Schwarzlack (Fidel Bautista-Época).

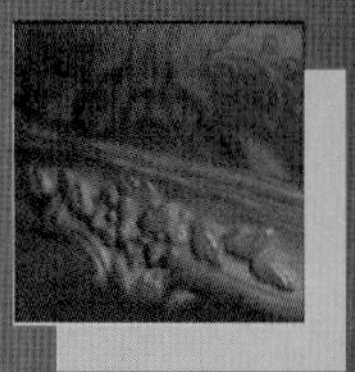

Rococo Style

Le style Rococo

Rokoko

Rococo Style
Louis XV

Le style Rococo
Le style Louis XV

Rokoko
Louis XV

Following the baroque period, which had dominated the scene until the first half of the eighteenth century, the emergence of liberal forms began subsiding to give rise to a decadent age represented by the rococo. The most genuine French rococo is represented by the Louis XV style, which will appear as a clearly determined phenomenon.

Thus, under the name of this king a furniture style will come to be recognized, situated between the years 1735 and 1770. It coincides with an age of seclusion and intimacy, with an abundance of rooms and small

Après le Baroque qui avait dominé la première moitié du XVIII ème siècle, l'éclosion des formes libres commence à perdre du terrain pour laisser sa place à une époque décadente durant laquelle le style Rococo eut la principale autorité. Le style Rococo le plus authentique en France est représenté par le style Louis XV et celui-ci apparaît comme un phénomène bien déterminé.

Sous le nom de Louis XV on reconnaît un style de mobilier que l'on peut situer entre les années 1735 et 1770. Il correspond à une période de grande réflexion et intimité avec une importante

Nach der Epoche des Barock, der bis zur ersten Hälfte des 18. Jh. vorherrschte, räumt das Aufbrechen liberaler Formen einer dekadenten Epoche den Platz ein, für die der Rokoko-Stil beispielhaft ist.

Der unverfälschte Rokoko wird in Frankreich durch den Louis-quinze-Stil verkörpert, der als genau festgelegtes Phänomen in Erscheinung trat.

Hinter dem Louis-quinze-Stil verbirgt sich ein Möbelstil, der dem Zeitraum zwischen den Jahren 1735 bis 1770 zugeordnet wird.

Diese Zeit geht einher mit einer Lebensart, die von Zurückgezogenheit und Intimität, dem Überfluß von Räumen und kleineren Gemä-

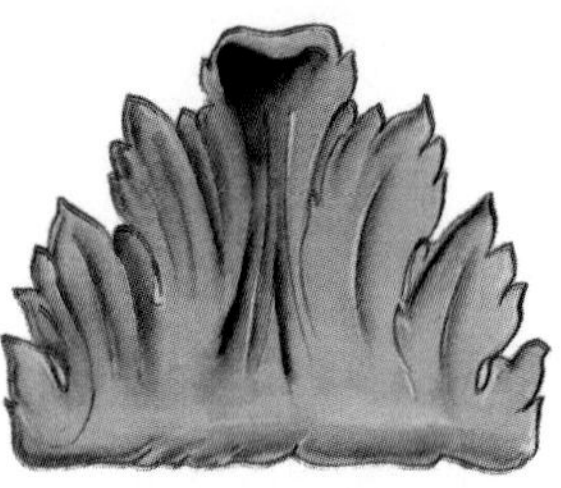

1.

Cabinet with marble top (Muarca).

Entre-deux avec couvercle de marbre (Muarca).

Wandschränkchen mit Marmorplatte (Muarca).

1

2

1 - 2.

Sketch of foot and detail of the door ornamentation of the previous piece.

Détail de patte et d'ornementation de porte de la page précédente.

Skizze Schrankfuß und Ausschnitt Türverzierung der vorherigen Abbildung.

nooks in palaces and the houses of nobles. This will also condition the dimensions of the furniture, the size of which determines the main difference in regard to the creations of the previous period.

From the conceptual point of view, Louis XV style offers no great novelties, but those characteristics the baroque had brought with it reach their greatest expression with rococo. This is true to the extreme

quantité de pièces et de salles de petite taille existant dans les palais et nobles demeures. Ce fait détermine ainsi la dimension des meubles car la taille marque la principale différence avec les créations de l'époque antérieure.

Du point de vue conceptuel, le style Louis XV offre une grande quantité de nouveautés, et les caractéristique apportées par le style Baroque atteignent le sommet de leur représentation avec le style Rococo, jusqu'au point de

chern in Palästen und Herrschaftshäusern geprägt war. Diese Umstände beeinflussen auch die Größe der Möbel, deren Ausmaße das wesentliche Unterscheidungsmerkmal zu den Möbeln der vorangegangenen Epoche darstellen.

Vom konzeptuellen Gesichtspunkt aus gesehen, bietet der Louis-quinze-Stil keine großen Neuheiten, aber jene Stilmerkmale, die im Barock entstanden waren, gelangten im Louis-quinze zu ihrem Höhepunkt. Dies ging so weit, daß

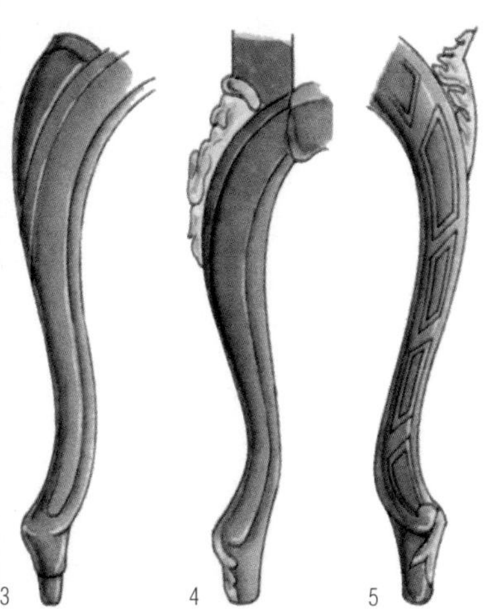

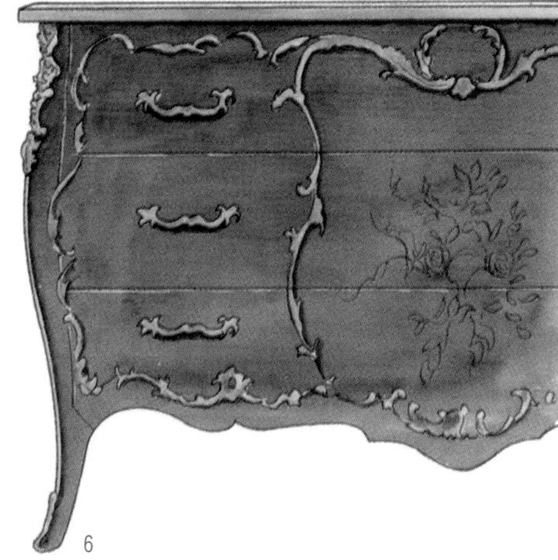

3 - 5.

In the Louis XV style, the cabriole leg decisively returned to fashion.

La patte cabriolée apparaît fortement sous le style Louis XV.

Im Louis-quinze-Stil werden die Tisch- und Stuhlbeine im Cabriolé-Stil bestimmend.

6.

Drawing of the front of a piece decorated with vegetal motifs.

Dessin frontal d'un meuble décoré avec des motifs végétaux.

Zeichnung der Vorderseite des Möbels, mit Pflanzenmotiven verziert.

7

7.

Drawing of the back, where the fiddle-shaped contraction of the curves may be appreciated.

Dessin de dossier ou on apprécie la concentration de courbes –dossier en violon– rétréci au centre.

Zeichnung der Rückenlehne, auf der das Zusammenziehen der Wellenform zu erkennen ist – Violinné-Rückenlehne, die in der Mitte zusammengedrückt ist.

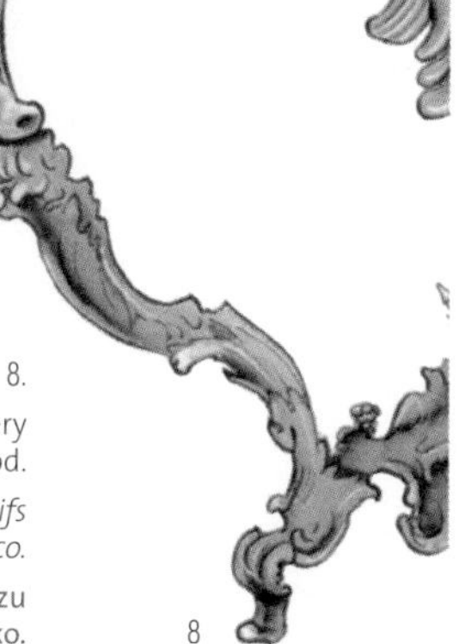

8.

Drawing showing vegetal motifs, very common in the rococo period.

Dessin ou on observe des motifs végétaux, si habituels avec le Rococo.

Zeichnung, auf der Pflanzenmotive zu sehen sind, sehr verbreitet im Rokoko.

1

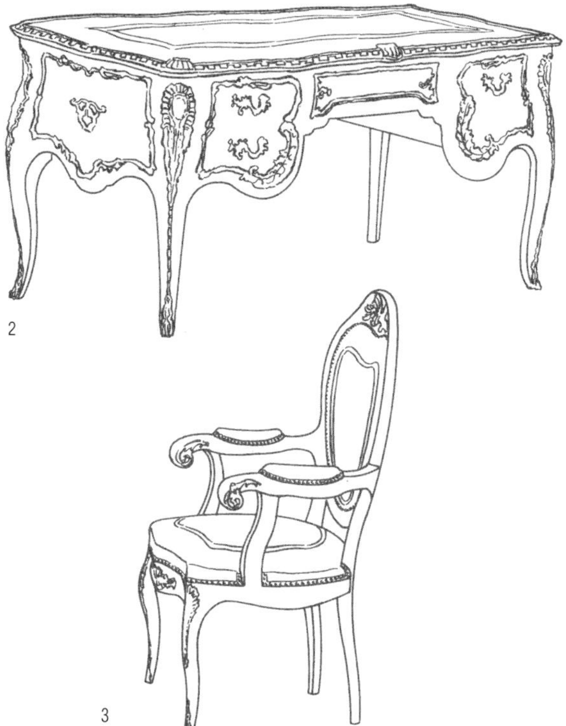

2

3

4

1.

Bookcase sketch.

Détail d'un librairie.

Skizze Bücherschrank.

2.

Sketch of armchair.

Détail d'un fauteuil.

Skizze Sessel.

3.

Sketch for a writing table.

Détail d'une table écritoire.

Skizze Tisch/Schreibtisch.

4.

French style office complex (Muarva).

Ensemble de bureau de style français (Muarva).

Büroeinrichtung im französischen Stil (Muarva).

1

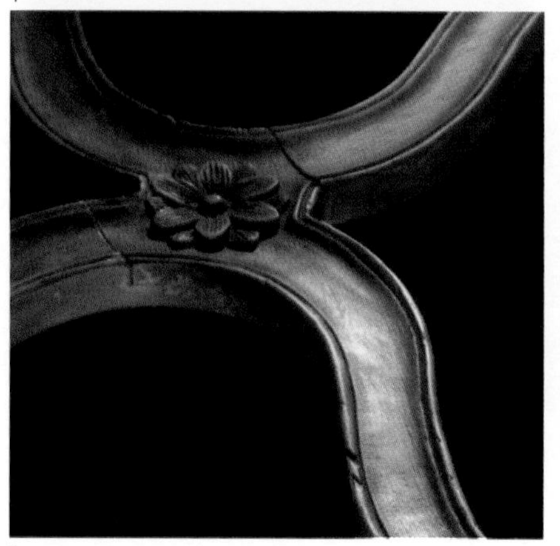

2

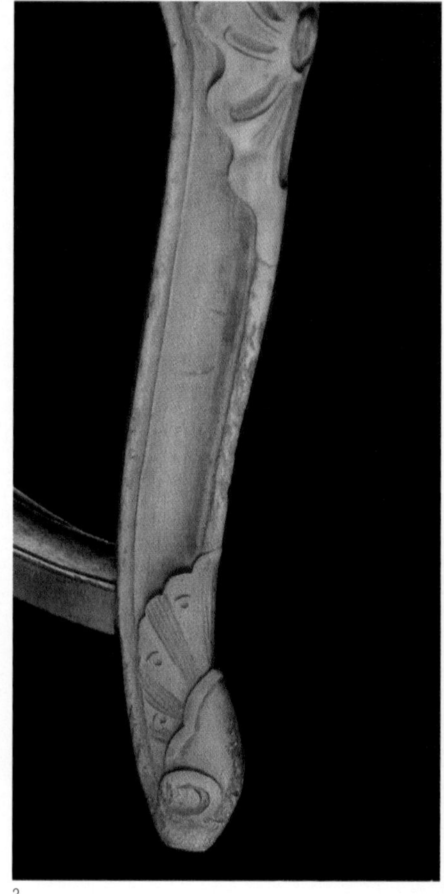

3

1.

Detail, assembly of 4.

Détail d'assemblage postérieur 4.

Ausschnitt hinteres Verbindungsstück 4.

2.

Detail, stretcher assembly 4.

Détail d'union de chambrane 4.

Ausschnitt Verbindung Keilsteg 4.

3.

Detail, carved leg of 4.

Détail de patte taillée 4.

Ausschnitt geschnitztes Stuhlbein 4.

4.

Perronneau Louis XV armchair (Mailfert Amos).

Fauteuil Perronneau Louis XV (Mailfert Amos).

Sessel Perronneau Louis XV. (Mailfert Amos).

4

1

2

3

1.

Detail of ornamentation 4.

Détail de pinacle de dossier 4.

Detalhe do ornamento superior das costas de 4.

2.

Detail of arm in 4.

Détail de bras 4.

Ausschnitt Armlehne 4.

3.

Detail, ornamental upright 4.

Détail d'ornementation montante 4.

Ausschnitt Ornament Strebe 4.

4.

Rigaud Louis XV armchair (Mailfert Amos).

Fauteuil Rigaud Louis XV (Mailifert Amos).

Sessel Rigaud Louis XV. (Mailfert Amos).

1

1.

Louis XV chair molding in lacquered birch.

Chaise moulure Louis XV en hêtre laqué.

Louis-quinze-Stuhl mit Leisten aus lackiertem Buchenholz.

2.

"Marquesa" Louis XV gondola chair in carved birch (Bonora).

« Marquise » gondole Louis XV en hêtre sculptée (Bonora).

Gondel «Marquesa» Louis XV. aus geschnitzter Buche (Bonora).

of making the terms rococo and Louis XV synonymous with contrived and exaggerated. In the Louis XV style, the curves that were timidly introduced earlier become convulsed until the final emergence that leads to a determined dynamic of asymmetry.

The Louis XV style is graceful and dynamic. The exuberance of the rounded forms, achieved through the inclusion of orna-

parler de lui ou de style Louis XV comme un synonyme de surchargé et d'exagération. Dans le style Louis XV les courbes, timidement introduites durant l'étape précédente, sont secouées jusqu'à l'explosion finale qui débouche vers un dynamisme traduit par l'asymétrie.

Le style Louis XV possède un caractère gracile et dynamique. L'exubérance des formes arrondies, obtenues grâce l'inclusion

man den Rokoko oder den Louis-quinze-Stil mit überladen und übertrieben gleichsetzt.

Im Louis-quinze-Stil wurden die von seinem Vorgänger noch zaghaft angedeuteten geschwungenen Linien derart verzerrt, daß dieser Stil letztendlich in einen von der Asymmetrie bestimmten Dynamismus mündete.

Der Louis-quinze-Stil weist grazile und schwungvolle Merkmale auf. Die runden Formen enstehen

2

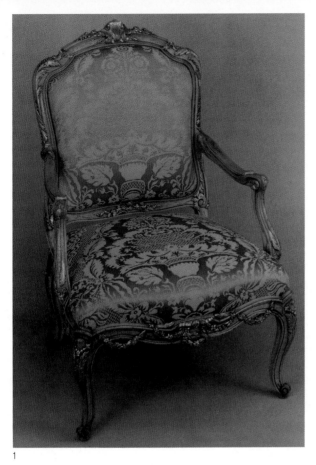

1

1.

Chair with cabriole legs termed à la reine (1770) in carved wood with copper gilt. Transition style between Louis X and Louis XVI (Bonora).

Fauteuil cabriolé à la Reine (1770) en bois sculpté et doré au cuivre. Style transition entre Louis XV et Louis XVI (Bonora).

Sessel Cabriolé à la reine (1770) aus geschnitztem Holz, verkupfert. Übergangsstil zwischen Louis XV. und Louis XVI. (Bonora).

2.

Armchair (Balzarotti).

Fauteuil (Balzarotti).

Sessel (Balzarotti).

mental motifs in inlaid work, carried out in exotic woods, such as lignum vitaes, rosewood, bois de roi, or lemon wood, as well, of course, as the bronzes, all of these fully dominate the structures of the furniture pieces. They give rise, then, to graceful pieces, vital, happy, with a tectonic character not infrequently giving the sensation of being the victim of bankruptcy and insolence.

de motifs ornementaux en marqueterie, réalisés moyennant des bois exotiques, comme la plaquemine, le bois de rose ou le bois de roi, ou le citronnier, et des bronzes, qui dominent complètement la structure des meubles, et crée des pièces amusantes, gaies et pleines de vie ou son caractère tectonique donne l'apparence d'être une victime du délabrement et de la déchirure.

durch die Einbeziehung von Intarsienverzierungen aus exotischen Holzarten, wie z. B. Guajakholz, Palisander, Bois de roi oder Limonenbaumholz, und Bronze, und sind beim Bau der Möbel sehr bestimmend. Der Überfluß an runden Formen bringt einige anmutige, lebendige und heitere Möbel hervor, deren tektonische Merkmale oft den Eindruck von Zerbrechlichkeit und Brüchigkeit hervorrufen.

1

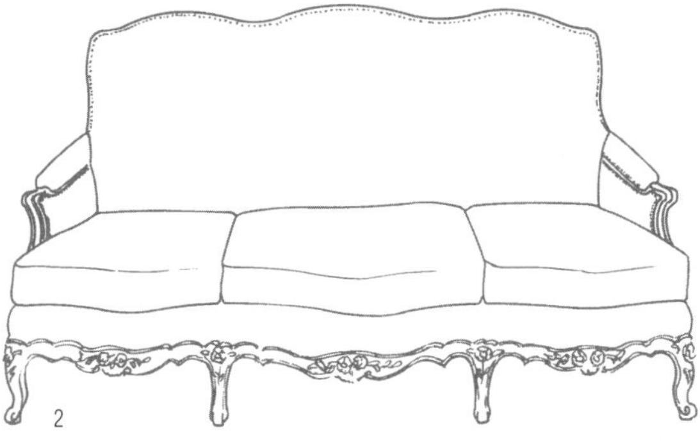

2

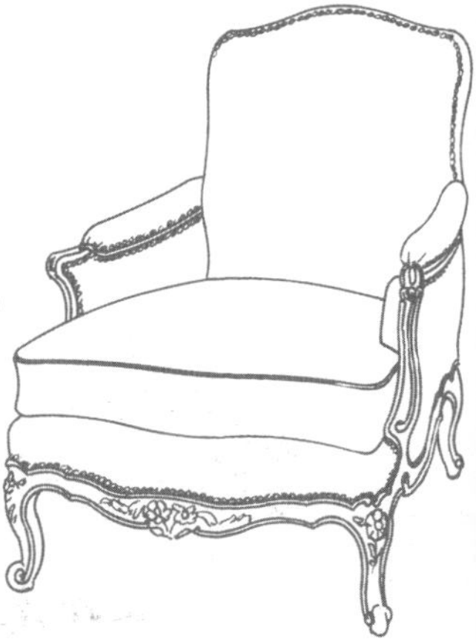

3

1.

Iranian settee seating three.

Canapé Iran de trois places.

Dreisitziges Canapé Iran..

2.

Sketch of settee in 1.

Détail de canapé 1

Skizze Canapé 1.

3.

Sketch of bergère in 4.

Détail de bergère 4.

Skizze Bergere 4.

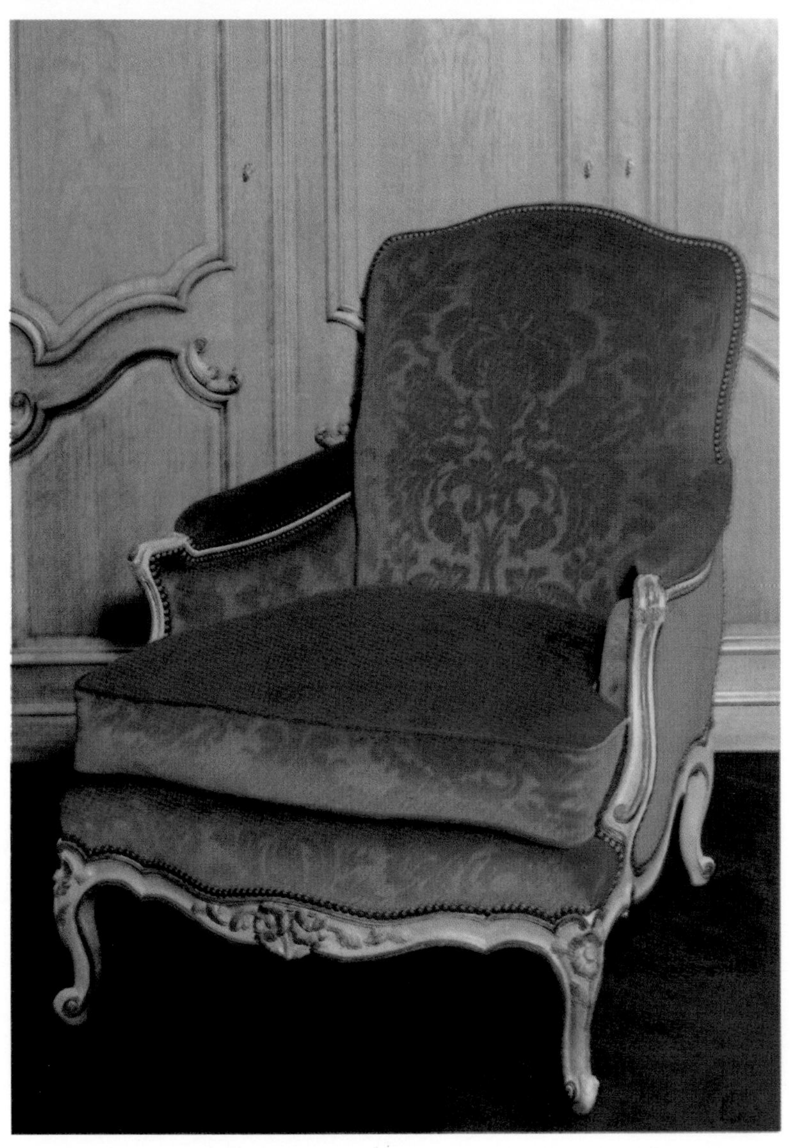

4.

Iranian bergère.

Bergère Iran.

Bergere Iran.

1

3

1.

"Quatre Saisons" settee for 2 (M. Bart).

Canapé Quatre Saisons de deux places (M. Bart).

Zweisitziges Canapé Quatre Saisons (M. Bart)..

2.

Sketch of the settee in 1.

Détail de canapé 1.

Skizze Canapé 1.

3.

Sketch, armchair 4.

Détail de fauteuil 4.

Skizze Sessel 4.

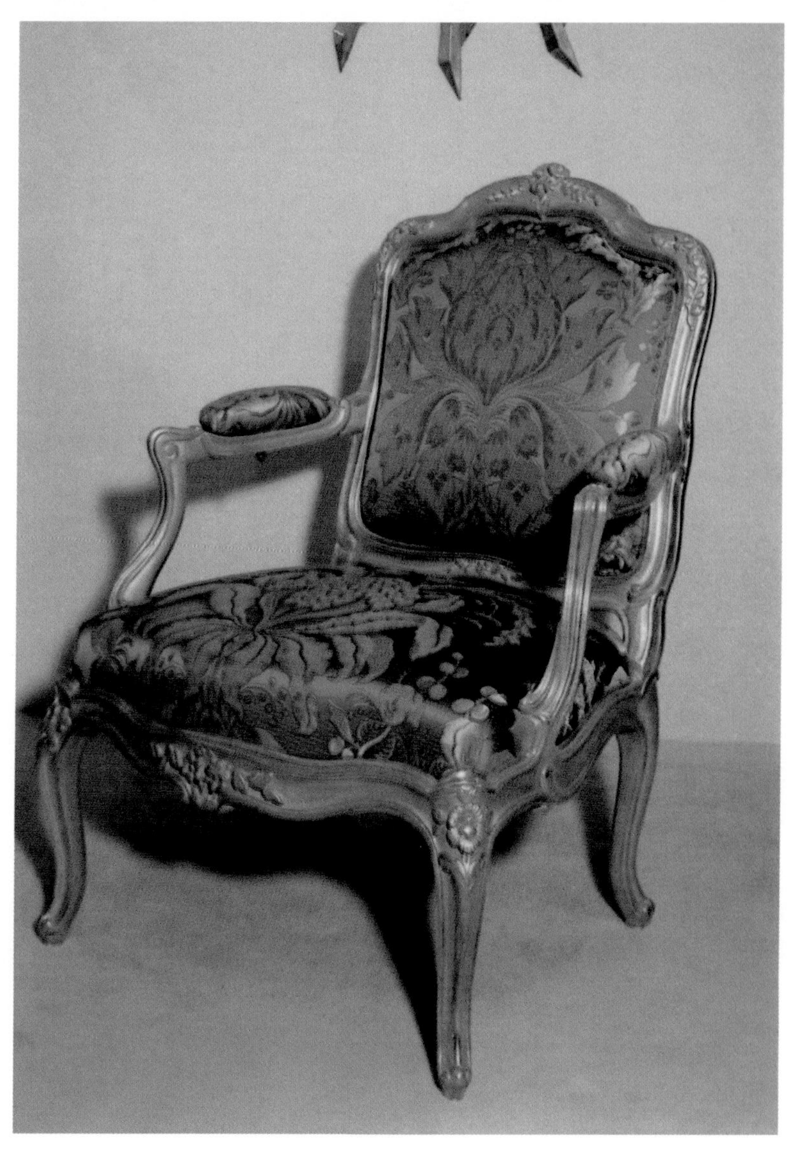

4.
"Quatre Saisons" armchair (M. Bart).
Fauteuil Quatre Saisons (M. Bart).
Sessel (M. Bart).

1.

Louis XV Meridienne sofa (Style et Confort).

Méridienne Louis XV (Style et Confort).

Méridienne Louis XV. (Style et Confort).

2.
Louis XV Meridienne sofa (Style et Confort).
Méridienne Louis XV (Style et Confort)
Méridienne Louis XV. (Style et Confort).

1.

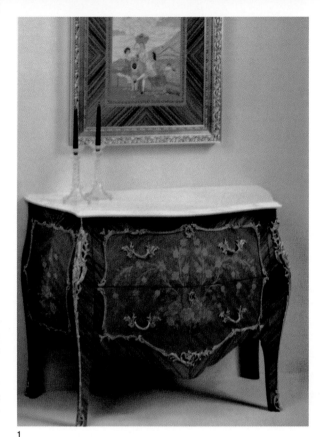

Louis XV potbellied dresser (Creaciones Royal).

Commode ventrue Louis XV (Créations Royal).

Bauchige Kommode Louis XV. (Creaciones Royal).

2.

Sketch of 1.

Détail de commode 1.

Skizze Kommode 1.

3.

Dresser with marble top (Creaciones Muarva).

Commode avec couvercle en marbre (Créations Muarve).

Kommode mit Marmorplatte (Creaciones Muarva).

1

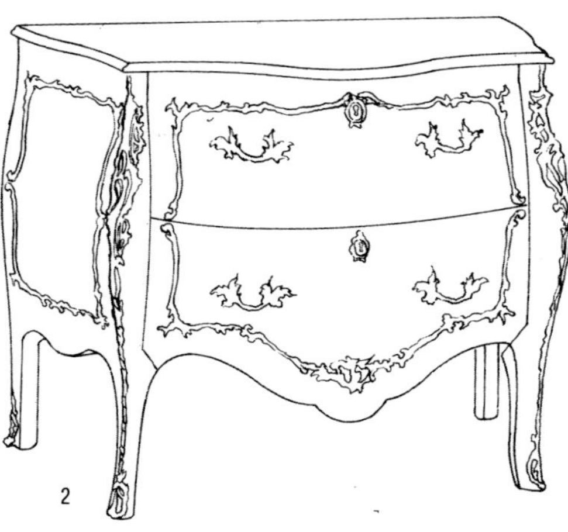

2

3

1

2

1.

Louis XV dresser (Craman-Lagarde).

Commode Louis XV (Craman-Lagarde).

Kommode Louis XV. (Craman-Lagarde).

2.

Detail, filleted ornamental corner dresser 1.

Détail de damasquinés ornementales de coin de commode 1.

Ausschnitt verzierte Eckleiste Kommode 1.

ransitional Louis XV-Louis XVI dresser (Craman-Lagarde).
ommode Transition Louis XV-Louis XVI (Craman-Lagarde).
ommode Übergangszeit Louis XV. – Louis XVI (Craman-Lagarde).

etail, central floral motif of 4.
étail de motif floral central 4.
usschnitt Blumenmotiv des Mittelteils 4.

4

1

1.

Louis XV dresser in solid wild cherry (Style Meuble).

Commode Louis XV en bois de cerisier sylvestre massif (Style Meuble).

Louis-quinze-Kommode aus massivem Wildkirschbaumholz (Style Meuble).

2.

Detail, handles of dresser 4.

Détail de manettes de commode 4.

Ausschnitt Griffe der Kommode 4.

3.

Detail, keyhole of dresser 4.

Détail de trou de serrure de commode 4.

Ausschnitt Schüsselloch der Kommode 4.

4.

Louis XV style dresser in solid wild cherry.

Commode Louis XV en cerisier sylvestre massif (Kahn Frères).

Louis-quinze-Kommode aus massiver Wildkirsche (Kahn Frères).

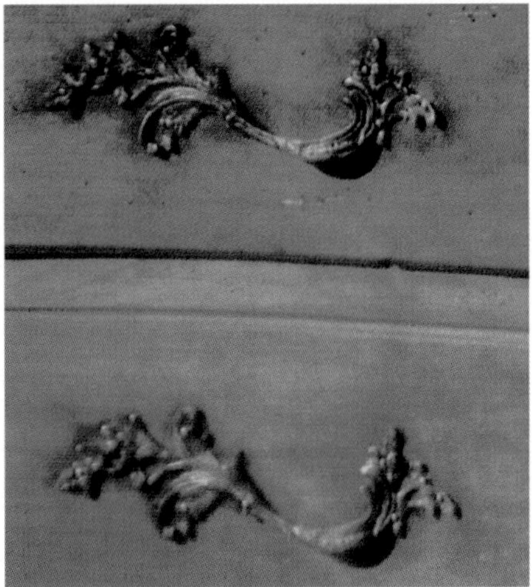
2

3

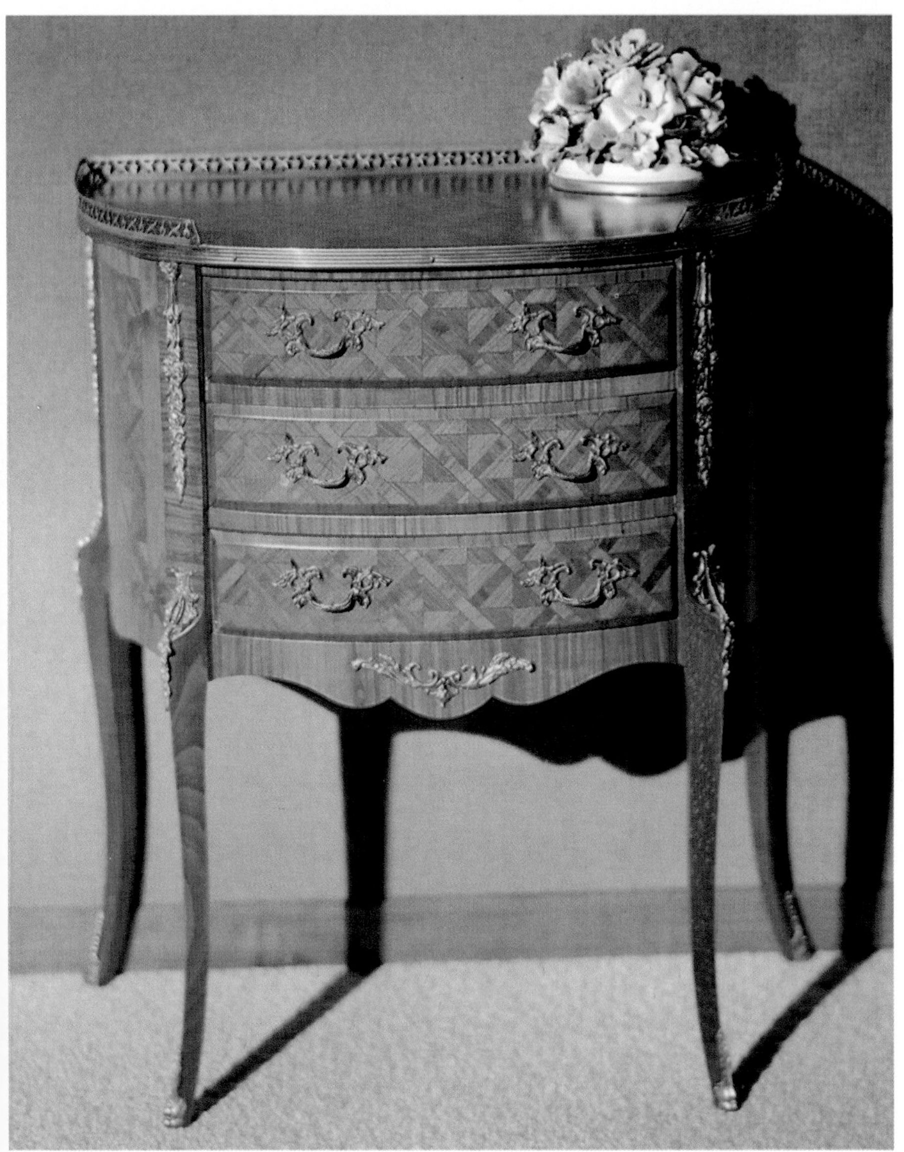

1.

Louis XV credence in solid wild cherry (Kahn Frères).

Crédence Louis XV en cerisier sylvestre massif (Kahn Frères).

Louis-quinze-Kredenz aus massiver Wildkirsche (Kahn Frères).

2.

Semi-circular rosewood dresser and brass gallery.

Commode demi circulaire en palissandre et balustre en laiton.

Halbrunde Kommode aus Palisander Galerie aus Messing.

1

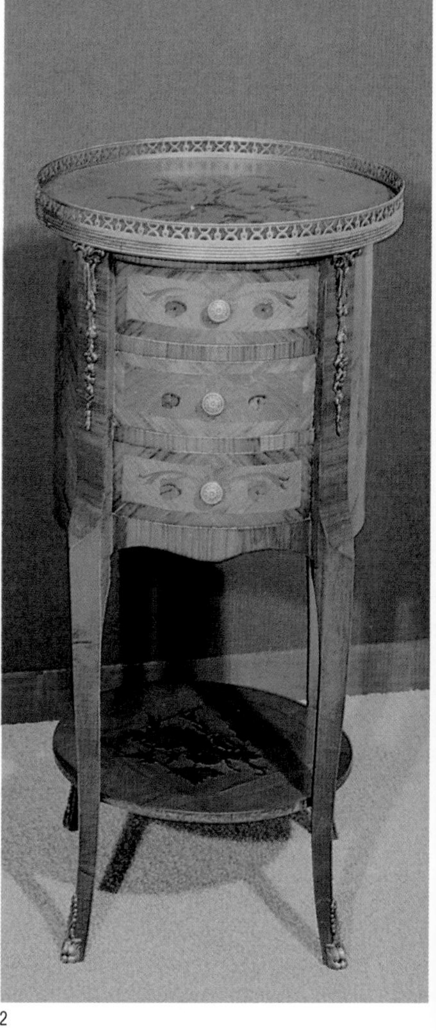

2

1.

Oval cabinet in rosewood with brass gallery.

Commode ovale en palissandre et balustre en laiton.

Ovale Kommode aus Palisander mit Galerie aus Messing

2.

Circular table in rosewood.

Table auxiliaire circulaire en palissandre et balustre en laiton.

Runder Beistelltisch aus Palisander mit Galerie aus Messing.

3

4

5

3.

Detail, drawers and brass gallery in 2.

Détail de tiroirs et balustre en laiton 2.

Ausschnitt Schubladen und Galerie aus Messing 2.

4.

Kidney side table in rosewood and gallery in brass.

Table auxiliaire en forme d'haricot en palissandre et balustre en laiton.

Nierenbeistelltisch aus Palisander mit Galerie aus Messing.

5.

Side tables in rosewood and galleries in brass (Fratelli Cattaneo).

Tables auxiliaires en palissandre et balustre en laiton (Fratelli Cattaneo).

Beistelltische aus Palisander mit Galerie aus Messing. (Fratelli Cattaneo).

1

2

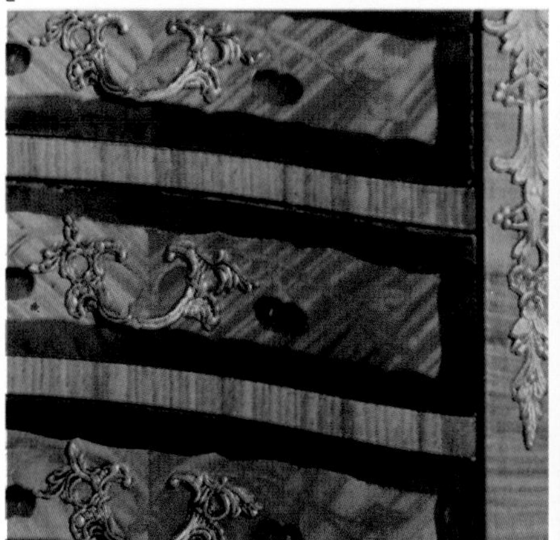

3

1. Kidney-shaped side table in rosewood and gallery in brass.
   Table auxiliaire en forme d'haricot en palissandre et balustre en laiton.
   Nierenbeistelltisch aus Palisander mit Galerie aus Messing.

2. Kidney-shaped side table in rosewood and gallery in brass.
   Table auxiliaire en forme d'haricot en palissandre et balustre en laiton.
   Nierenbeistelltisch aus Palisander mit Galerie aus Messing.

3. Detail, inlaid work and handles of 2 (Fratelli Cattaneo).
   Détail de marqueterie et manettes 2 (Fratelli Cattaneo).
   Ausschnitt Intarsien und Griffe 2 (Fratelli Cattaneo).

4.
Louis XV style oval bedside lamp in lignum vitaes (Style Meuble).
Chevet ovale Louis XV en bois de plaquemine (Style Meuble).
Ovaler Chevet Louis XV. Aús Guajakholz (Style Meuble).

1

2

3

1.

Chair with fluted legs.

Chaise avec pattes en forme de tronc conique rainuré.

Stuhl mit kegelstumpfförmigen, kannelierten Stuhlbeinen.

2.

Armchair with fluted legs.

Fauteuil avec pattes en forme de tronc conique rainuré.

Sessel mit kegelstumpfförmigen, kannelierten Stuhlbeinen.

3.

Louis XV low chiffonier table, Topeño model (Bonora).

Petite table chiffonnière Louis XV, Modèle Topeño (Bonora).

Chiffoniere-Tischchen Louis XV., Model Topeño (Bonora).

4.

Display case with inlaid work, upholstered in gold damask (Muarva).

Vitrine avec marqueterie tapissée en broché doré (Muarva).

Vitrine mit Intarsien, ausgekleidet mit goldfarbenem Damast (Muarva).

1.

Detail, ornamental work on the display case on the preceding page.

Détail d'ornementation de vitrine de la page préceédente.

Ausschnitt Verzierung der Vitrine, vorherige Seite.

2.

Sketch of the display case on the preceding page.

Détail de vitrine de la page précédente.

Skizze Vitrine, vorherige Seite.

3.

Curved display case inspired on the Louis XV style.

Vitrine courbée d'inspiration Louis XV (Imper Styl).

Vitrine aus gebogenem Holz, inspiriert vom Louis-quinze. (Imper Styl).

1

2

1.

Louis XV corner cabinet with inlaid work, brass ornamentation, and decorative fabric.

Meuble en coin Louis XV décoré avec marqueterie,bronzes et tissus..

Louis-quinze-Eckschrank, dekoriert mit Intarsien, Bronze und Stoffen.

2.

Louis XV display case with inlaid work, brass, and decorative fabrics.

Vitrine Louis XV décorée avec marqueterie, bronzes et tissus.

Louis-quinze-Vitrine, dekoriert mit Intarsien, Bronze und Stoffen.

3.

Transitional display case with inlaid work, brass, and decorative fabrics (Creaciones Royal).

Vitrine transition décorée avec marqueterie, bronze et tissus (Créations Royal).

Vitrine aus der Übergangszeit, dekoriert mit Intarsien, Bronze und Stoffen. (Creaciones Royal).

3

Rococo

Chippendale

Le style Rococo

Le style Chippendale

Rokoko

Chippendale

Chippendale is the first style to be designated by the name of the artist who created it. It is also the one that personalizes the rococo style in England, a style that will discover new modes of expression in the manufacture of furniture.

The Chippendale style constitutes the first part of the Georgian style, a period that is situated between 1714 and 1830.

Thomas Chippendale was a solemn cabinetmaker who knew how to open up to foreign influences, interpret them, and provide returns through his own personal vision. Born in Otley, Yorkshire in 1718, Chippendale was a famous artist who worked

C'est le premier style reconnu par le nom de l'artiste qui le créa, et celui qui personnalisa le style Rococo en Angleterre. C'est le style qui réussit à trouver de nouvelles voies d'expression dans la fabrication de meubles.

Le style Chippendale constitue la première époque du style Georgien, une période que l'on peut situer entre 1714 et 1830.

Chippendale fut un ébéniste solennelle qui su recevoir des influences extérieures, les interpréter et les renvoyer au continent avec sa propre vision des choses. Thomas Chippendale (Otley, Yorkshire h. 1718-Londres 1779), fut un artiste célèbre qui

Das Chippendale wurde als erste Stilrichtung nach dem Namen des Künstlers benannt, der ihn kreierte, und verkörperte den Rokokostil in England - ein Stil, dem es gelang, neue Ausdrucksformen in der Möbelherstellung zu finden.

Das Chippendale bestimmt die erste Epoche des georgischen Stils, eine Periode, die dem Zeitabschnitt zwischen 1714 und 1830 zugeordnet wird.

Chippendale war ein großartiger Kunsttischler, der es verstand, sich fremden Einflüssen gegenüber zu öffnen, sie zu interpretieren und diese eigene Interpretation auf kratvolle Art und Weise nach Europa zurückgab.

Thomas Chippendale (geb. 1718 Otley, Yorkshire – gest. 1779 London)

1.
Armchair and chair, in mahogany (Arthur Brett & Sons).
Fauteuil et chaise en acajou (Arthur Brett et Soon).
Sessel und Stuhl aus Mahagoni (Arthur Brett & Sons).

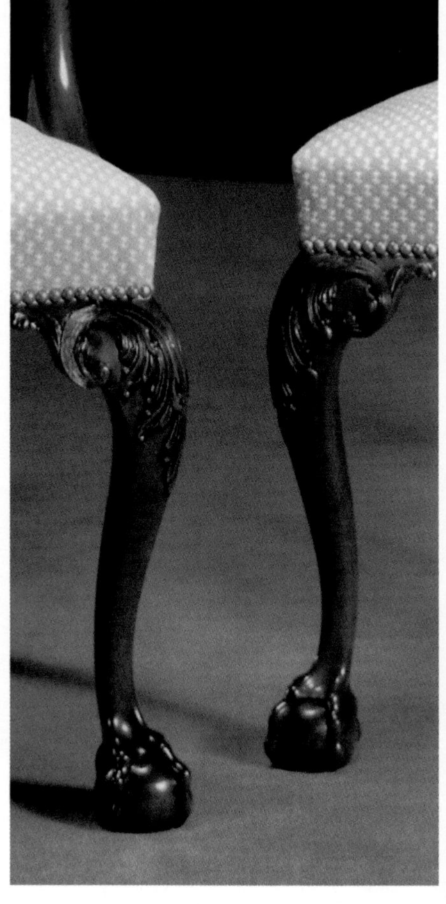

1.

Detail of the back of the chair shown on the preceding page.

Détail de dossier de chaise de la page précédente.

Ausschnitt schaufelförmige Stuhlrückenlehne, vorherige Seite.

2.

Detail of the ornamentation on the feet of the chair shown on the preceding page.

Détail d'ornementation de pattes de chaise de la page précédente.

Ausschnitt Verzierung des Stuhlbeins, vorherige Seite.

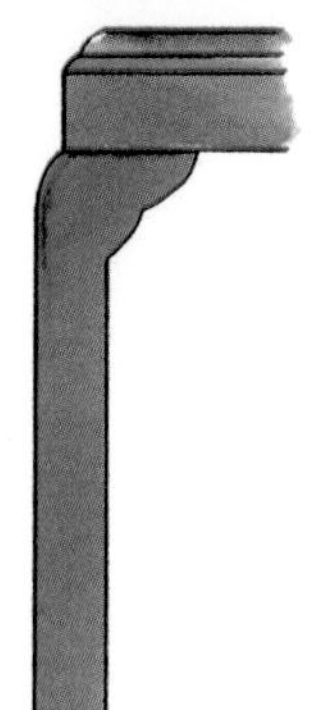

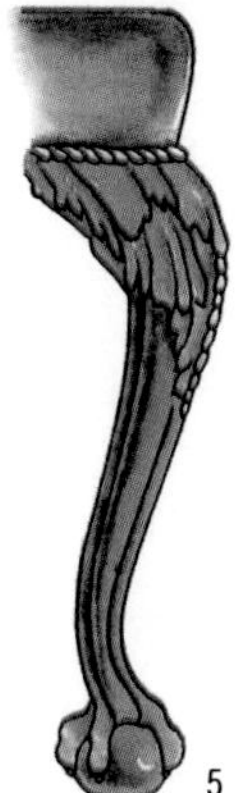

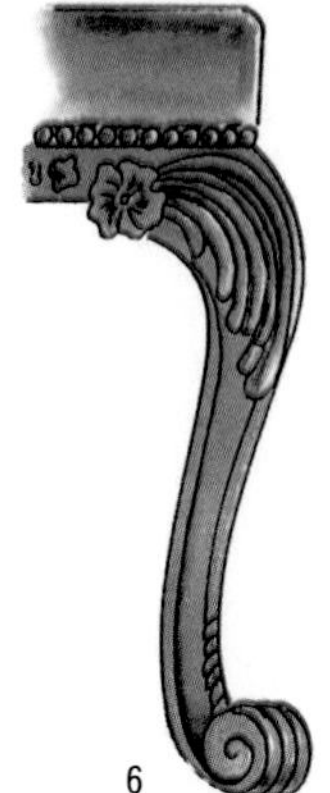

3 - 6.

The feet of Chippendale chairs are of two types: cabriole style, in the form of a talon or of a scroll (5 and 6), or squared off, in a more evolved form (3 and 4).

Les pattes des chaises Chippendale peuvent être de deux sortes : cabriolées avec une patte en forme de griffe ou de torsade (5 et 6), ou avec la rectitude du carré, sous une forme plus évoluée (3 et 4).

Es gibt zwei Arten von Chippendale-Stuhlbeinen: Cabriolé mit Greifenklaue oder Volute (5 und 6) oder mit der quadratischen Gerade, in einer weiterentwickelten Form (3 und 4).

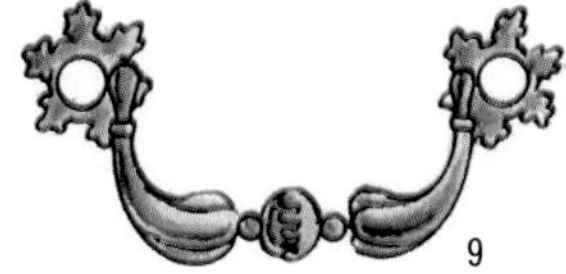

7.

Drawing of a piece with a pediment, a good evocation of the baroque style.

Dessin de meuble dont la finition en forme de fronton, bien que peut somptueux, évoque le mieux le style Baroque.

Zeichnung eines Möbels, dessen giebelförmiger Aufsatz, wenn auch wenig auffällig, eher an den Barockstil erinnert.

8 - 10.

Drawing of handles with small decorative motifs.

Dessins de manettes avec petits motifs décoratifs.

Zeichnung Griffe mit kleinen dekorativen Motiven.

pp. 156-157.

Chippendale office table (Zamorano).

Table de bureau Chippendale (Zamorano).

Chippendale Bürotisch (Zamorano).

1

1.

Chippendale center table (Enebro).

Table de centre Chippendale (Enebro).

Chippendale Wohnzimmertisch (Enebro).

2.

Chippendale center table (Enebro).

Table de centre Chippendale (Enebro).

Chippendale Wohnzimmertisch (Enebro).

2

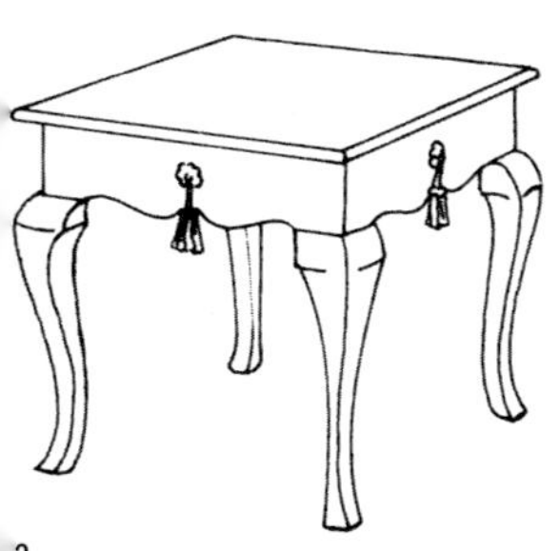

3.

Sketch of a square center table.

Détail de table de centre carrée.

Zeichnung quadratischer Wohnzimmertisch.

4.

Cabinet of semi-circular section (Indumueble).

Commode de plan demi circulaire (Indumueble).

Kommode mit halbrundem Aufbau (Indumueble).

or the British bourgeoisie and managed, with his collection of furniture, to attain a very high point between 1750 and 1770. He acquired great renown with the publication of The Gentleman and Cabinet-Maker's Director, which appeared in 1754. It contains a collection of furniture designs aimed at a very wide public and was long used as a complete catalogue of classical cabinetmaking. It constitutes an important compendium of this furniture maker's style. Chippendale died in London in 1779.

travailla pour la bourgeoisie anglaise et qui réussit à atteindre, avec sa collection de meubles, sa splendeur maximum entre 1750 et 1770. Il acquit une grande notoriété avec la publication de « The Gentleman and Cabinet Marker's Director », apparut en 1754, et qui contenait une collection de meubles destinée au grand publique. Cet ouvrage a été utilisé pendant longtemps comme un des plus complets catalogues d'ébénisterie classique et constitue le recueil du style Chippendale.

war ein berühmter Künstler, der für die englische Bourgeosie arbeitete und mit seiner Möbelsammlung zwischen 1750 und 1770 den Höhepunkt seines Ruhmes erreichte.

Er machte sich einen Namen mit der Veröffentlichung von The Gentleman and Cabinet Maker's im Jahre 1754, einer Sammlung von Designmöbeln, die für ein breites Publikum gedacht war. Diese Veröffentlichung wurde lange Zeit als vollständiger Katalog der klassischen Kunsttischlerei verwendet und stellt einen Leitfaden des Chippendale dar.

4.

Bookshelf (Arthur Brett & Sons).

Bibliothèque (Arthur Brett & Sons).

Bücherschrank (Arthur Brett & Sons).

1

2

3

1.- 3

Detail, bookshelf 4.

Détail de bibliothèque 4.

Ausschnitt Bücherschrank 4.

1

1.

Chippendale display case (Fernando Guanter).

Vitrine Chippendale (Fernando Guanter).

Chippendale Vitrine (Fernando Guanter).

2.

Chippendale Chinese chair in birch (Fernando Guanter).

Chaise Chinese d'influence orientale style Chippendale en hêtre (Fernando Guanter).

Stuhl Chinese, orientalischer Einfluß, im Chippendalestil aus Buchenholz a (Fernando Guanter).

3.

Chair and armchair in Chippendale style (Charles Barr).

Chaise et fauteuil style Chippendale avec dossier en forme de lacet (Charles Barr).

Stuhl und Sessel im Chippendalestil mit verschlungener Rückenlehne (Charles Barr).

2

3

1

2

1.

Chippendale double chair (replica).

Double chaise Chippendale (réplique).

Chippendale Stuhl, zweisitzig (Replikat).

2.

Chair and armchair (Furniture by Balmoral).

Chaise et fauteuil avec dossier en forme de lacet (Furniture by Balmoral).

Stuhl und Sessel mit verschlungener Rückenlehne (Furniture by Balmoral).

3.

Chippendale tea table with gallery (replica).

Table de thé Chippendale avec portique (réplique).

Chippendale Teetisch mit Abschlußstück (Replikat).

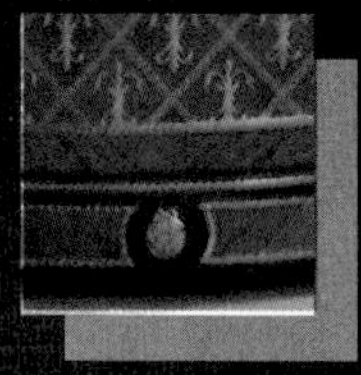

Neoclassicism

Le néoclassicisme

Neo-Klassizismus

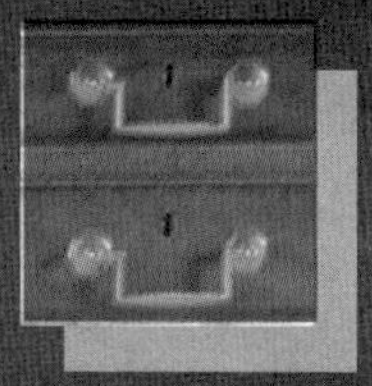

Neoclassicism
Louis XVI
Le néoclassicisme
Le style Louis XVI
Neo-Klassizismus
Louis XVI

Toward the middle of the eighteenth century, in France, with the style known by the name of the monarch Louis XVI, a reaction began against the dynamic and lack of control of the rococo style, translating into an exaltation of the ancient Greek-Roman styles. This opposition grew out of the discoveries of the archeological remains at Herculano and Pompeii, whose excavations were in full swing.

All of this would impact on the tastes of the time and give rise to the development of a style that tends to evoke these periods. Thus were preferences for straight lines imposed, and what had already

Vers la moitié du XVIII ème siècle en France, avec le style connu par le nom du roi Louis XVI, s'initie une réaction contre le dynamisme et le débordement du style Rococo, qui se traduit par une exaltation de l'antiquité gréco-latine. Cette opposition démarre à partir de la découverte des vestiges archéologiques d'Hercule et Pompée, dont les excavations étaient en plein essor.

Tout cela influençait sur les goûts du moment et provoqua le développement d'un style qui tendait à évoquer cette époque là. S'imposent alors la préférence pour la ligne droite et les idées qui avaient commencé à efflorer avec le style

Gegen Mitte des 18. Jh. entsteht in Frankreich mit dem Louis XVI. – nach dem Namen des Monarchen benannt – eine Bewegung gegen den Dynamismus und die Zügellosigkeit des Rokoko, die ihren Ausdruck in einer Verherrlichung der griechisch–römischen Antike findet.

Diese Gegenbewegung wurde von den Entdeckungen der archäologischen Reste von Herculaneum und Pompeji ausgelöst, deren Ausgrabungen ihren Höhepunkt erreichten.

Dies alles wirkt sich auf die derzeitigen Vorlieben aus und ermöglicht die Entwicklung eines Stils, der dazu neigte, jene Epochen wiede[r] wachzurufen. Daraus entsteht di[e] Vorliebe für gerade Linien und a[ll] das, was im Louis–qinze geschaffe[n]

1.
Louis XVI bookcase, lacquered and decorated.
Librairie Louis XVI laquée et décorée.
Louis-seize-Bücherschrank, lackiert und dekoriert.

1

2

3

begun with the Louis XV style again took root, while elements were incorporated whose simplicity made them perceivable as new.

Full-blown neoclassicism was the result. During this time, France continued to retain hegemony in furniture production and thus to set the

Louis XV s'implantent de plus en plus, tout en incorporant des éléments nouveaux par leur simplicité. C'est ainsi que l'on plonge directement dans le Néo-classicisme. Durant cette période, la France est toujours le centre hégémonique de production de meubles, et signale de ce fait la direction à

wurde, gewinnt immer mehr an Bedeutung. Gleichzeitig werden Elemente einbezogen, die durch ihre Einfachheit eine Neuheit darstellen.

So drang man vollends in die Epoche des Neo–Klassizismus ein. Während dieser Zeit behauptet Frankreich weiterhin seine Vormachtstellung in der Möbelherstellung und gibt somit ästhetische

1.

Detail of the highly ornamented bookcase on the previous page.

Détail de profusion ornementale de librairie de page précédente.

Ausschnitt üppige Verzierung des Bücherschranks, vorherige Seite.

2.

Detail of the ornamental crown of the corner furniture shown in 3.

Détail d'ornementation de pinacle de meuble en coin 3.

Ausschnitt Verzierung des Aufsatzes des Eckschranks 3.

3.

Louis XVI corner piece, lacquered and decorated

Meuble en coin Louis XVI laqué et décoré.

Louis-seize-Eckschrank, lackiert und dekoriert.

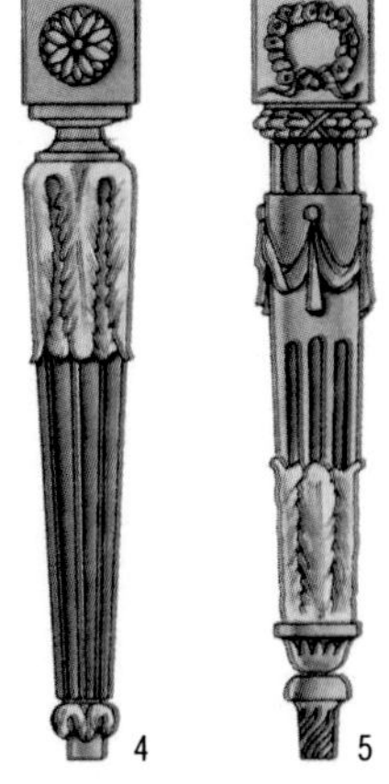

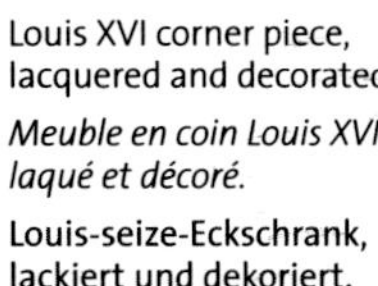

4 - 8.

Drawings for legs showing a prismatic form (tending toward truncated cones).

Dessins de pattes qui présentent une forme de prisme et qui tendent à une forme de tronc conique.

Zeichnung Tisch- und Stuhlbeine, mit prismatischen Formen, kegelstumpfförmige Tendenz.

9.

Drawing of a table leg using both curved and straight lines.

Dessin de pied de table où se mêlent la ligne courbée et la ligne droite.

Zeichnung Tischbein, Krümmung und Gerade gehen ineinander über.

10.

Drawing of richly carved stretchers crowned by chalices.

Dessin de chambranes richement taillées et couronnées par une coupe au croisement de celles-ci.

Zeichnung Keilsteg, mit reichem Schnitzwerk und aufgesetztem Kelch am Mittelpunkt.

1.
Sketch of a chair.
Détail de chaise.
Skizze Stuhl.

2.
Louis XVI style dining room, lacquered in blue and black. Included are: display case, sideboard, table, and chairs (Fratelli Radice).

Salle à manger style Louis XVI, laquée en noir et bleu, formée par divers éléments : vitrine, buffet, table, et chaises (Fratelli Radice).

Eßzimmer im Louis-seize-Stil, schwarz und blau lackiert, bestehend aus verschiedenen Elementen: Vitrine, Anrichte, Tisch und Stühle (Fratelli Radice).

aesthetic rhythms that would be in vogue and adopted by other countries according to their own idiosyncrasies.

With the Louis XVI style we move, as mentioned earlier, toward a revaluation of the classical way of living. The adaptation, however, will not be a strict one, breaking categorically with the preceding rococo style, but rather will suppose

suivre dans les coordonnés esthétiques qui doivent s'imposer et que les autres pays adoptent selon leur propre sensibilité. C'est avec le style Louis XVI que s'initie, comme signalé auparavant, la revalorisation de l'art de vivre classique, bien que l'adaptation ne soit pas si stricte, et qu'il ne rompe pas catégoriquement avec le style Rococo, mais qui suppose une

Richtlinien vor, die vorherrschend sein sollen und die die anderen Länder ihrem eigenen Wesen entsprechend anpassen.

Mit dem Louis XVI. beginnt, wie bereits erwähnt, eine Wiederaufwertung der – wenn auch nicht strikt übernommenen – klassischen Lebensart. Das Louis XVI. bricht nicht kategorisch mit dem Rokoko, sondern liefert seine ganz eigene Interpretation.

3.
Sketch of a sideboard.
Détail de buffet.
Skizze Anrichte.

1

1.

Louis XVI sofa (Gaëtan Lanzani).

Canapé Louis XVI (Gaëtan Lanzani).

Louis-seize-Sofa (Gaëtan Lanzani).

2.

Jacob chair à la reine (M. Bart).

Fauteuil Jacob à la Reine (M. Bart).

Sessel Jacob à la reine (M. Bart).

3.

Armchair and table in Louis XVI style (Mailfert Amos).

Fauteuil et table auxiliaire Louis XVI (Mailfert Amos).

Sessel und Beistelltischchen Louis XVI. (Mailfert Amos).

2

3

1.
Louis XVI dining room comprised of various elements (Creaciones Royal).

Salle à manger Louis XVI formée par divers éléments (Creaciones Royal).

Louis-seize-Eßzimmer, bestehend aus verschiedenen Elementen. (Creaciones Royal).

1

3

2

1.

Detail of the dining room on the previous page.

Détail de buffet de la page précédente.

Ausschnitt Anrichte, vorherige Seite.

2.

Sketch of the bookcase on the previous page.

Détail de vitrine de la page précédente.

Skizze Vitrine, vorherige Seite.

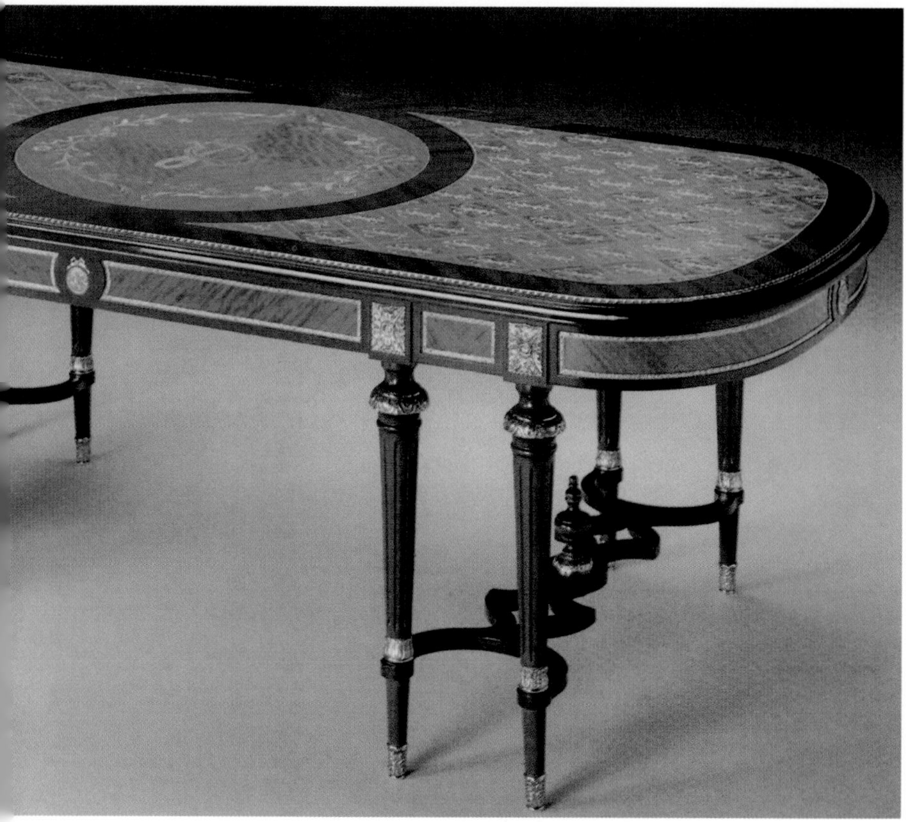

3.
Table (Creaciones Royal).
Table (Creaciones Royal).
Tisch (Creaciones Royal).

4.
Sketch of table.
Détail de table.
Skizze Tisch.

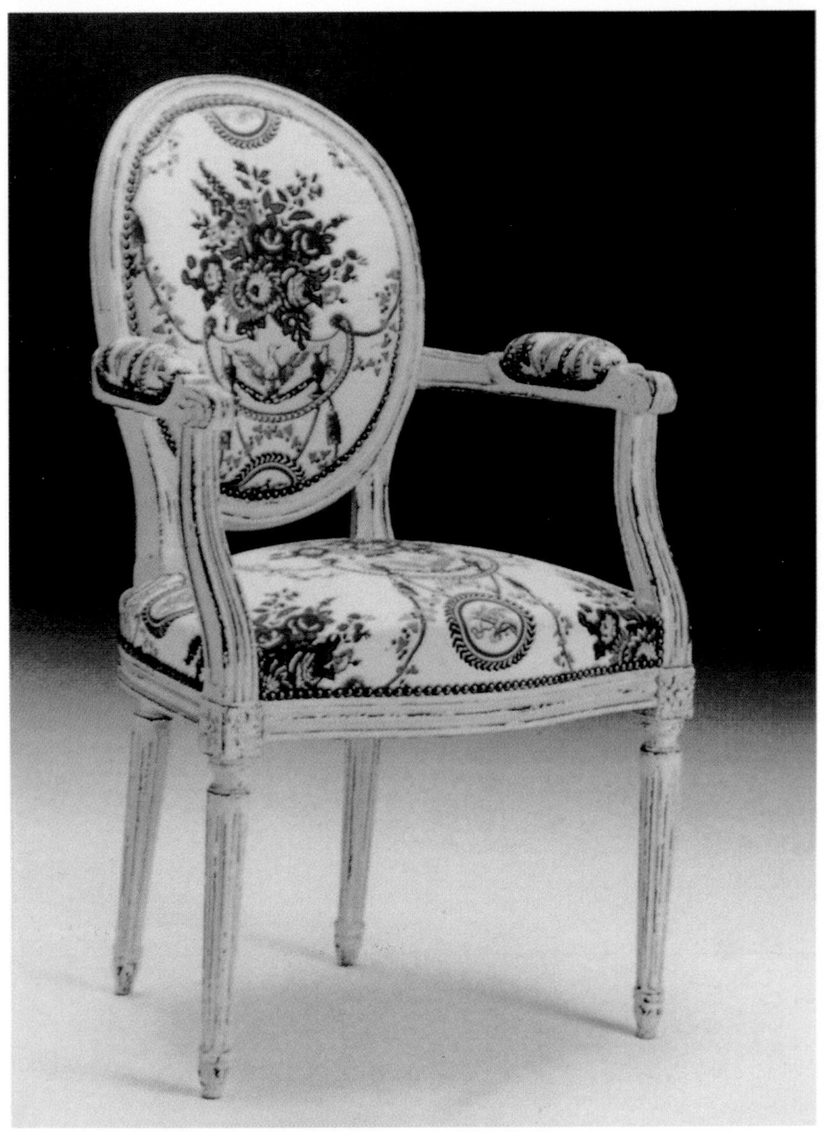

1.

Louis XVI medallion chair (Micheline Taillardat).

Fauteuil médaillon Louis XVI (Micheline Taillardat).

Louis-seize-Medaillonsessel (Micheline Taillardat).

2.

Louis XVI dressing table chair with radial mesh back (Bonora).

Chaise de chambre à coucher Louis XVI coiffeuse avec dossier en cannage radial (Bonora).

Zimmerstuhl Louis XVI, Coiffeuse mit Rückenlehne aus strahlenförmigem Geflecht (Bonora).

1.

Louis XVI armchair with molded birch back in medallion form (Bonora).

Fauteuil Louis XVI avec dossier en forme de médaillon en hêtre avec moulures (Bonora).

Louis-seize-Sessel mit Rückenlehne in Medaillonform, ausgekehltes Buchenholz (Bonora)

2.

Classical Louis XVI armchair with molded birch back in medallion form (Bonora).

Fauteuil Louis XVI avec dossier en forme de médaillon en hêtre avec moulures (Bonora).

Klassischer Louis-seize-Sessel mit Rückenlehne in Medaillonform, ausgekehltes Buchenholz (Bonora).

1.

Madame Du Deffand writing table, reproduction of a Louis XVI style model in wild cherry wood (L'Hermine-L'Ebénisterie Fraçaise).

Secrétaire Madame Du Deffand, reproduction d'un modèle Louis XVI en bois de cerisier sylvestre (L'Hermine-L'Ébénisterie Française).

Sekretär Madame Du Deffand, Reproduktion eines Louis-seize-Modells aus Wildkirschbaumholz (L'Hermine-L'Ebénisterie Française)

2.

Maurepas bonheur-du-jour, reproduction of a seventeenth-century model in wild cherry (L'Hermine-L'Ebénisterie Française).

Bonheur-du-jour Maurepas, reproduction d'un modèle du XVII ème siècle en bois de cerisier sylvestre (L'Hermine-L'Ébénisterie Française).

Bonheur-du-jour Maurepas, Reproduktion eines Modells des 17. Jh. aus Wildkirschbaumholz (L'Hermine-L'Ebénisterie Française).

1.

Louis XVI Marquesa sofa in carved birch (Bonora).

Sofa Marquise Louis XVI en hêtre sculptée (Bonora).

Sofa Marquesa Louis XVI., aus geschnitzter Buche. (Bonora).

2.

Louis XVI Marie Antoinette settee in carved and lacquered birch (Bonora).

Canapé Louis XVI Marie-Antoinette en hêtre sculptée et laquée (Bonora).

Louis-seize-Canapé Marie-Antoinette aus geschnitzter und lackierter Buche (Bonora).

3.

Dining room table and set of six chairs in the Louis XVI style.

Ensemble de table à manger et six chaises de style Louis XVI.

Eßzimmer im Louis-seize-Stil mit Eßtisch und sechs Stühlen..

3

an original interpretation. Thus, the Louis XVI style blends the lightness of the previous style with the serenity of the classical, in a highly eclectic fusion, and this makes it understandable as a transitional trend.

The furniture created during this period is worked in mahogany, a wood that had been irreplaceable in France since 1670.

As characteristics of this style, we might note that, in the structural aspect, the

interprétation originale. De cette façon, le style Louis XVI conjugue délicatement le style précédent avec la tranquillité su classique, en une fusion éclectique, qui doit être entendue comme une tendance de transition. Les meubles réalisés à cette époque sont fabriqués en acajou, bois incontournable en France depuis 1670.

Comme caractéristiques de ce style, il est important de signaler, dans l'aspect structurel que les meubles présente les éléments dans le sens vertical et

So verschmelzen die Zartheit des vorangegangenen Stils und die Gelassenheit der Klassik im Louis XVI. zu einer eklektizistischen Einheit. Deshalb muß diese Epoche als tendenzielle Übergangszeit betrachtet werden.

Die in diesem Stil hergestellten Möbel waren aus Mahagoni, eine in Frankreich seit 1670 unersetzliche Holzart.

Charakteristisch für diesen Stil ist – vom strukturellen Gesichtspunkt aus gesehen –, daß die Elemente der Möbel vertikal und horizontal angeordnet wurden. Den klar sicht-

1.
Louis XVI style headboard.
Tête de lit de style Louis XVI.
Kopfteil eines Bettes im Louis-seize-Stil.

2.
Louis XVI style chest of drawers (Mudeva).
Commode Louis XVI de Mudeva.
Louis-seize-Kommode, von Mudeva.

1

2

1.

Louis XVI style chair with medallion back in birch, upholstered in period fabric (Bonora).

Chaise Louis XVI avec dossier en médaillon de hêtre et tapissé avec tissu de l'époque (Bonora).

Louis-seize-Stuhl mit Medaillon-Rückenlehne aus Buche, mit zeitgenössischem Stoffbezug (Bonora).

2.

Louis XVI Marquise armchair in carved birch (Bonora).

Fauteuil Marquise Louis XVI en hêtre sculpté (Bonora).

Louis-seize-Sessel Marquesa aus geschnitzter Buche. (Bonora).

3.

Louis XVI armchair, lacquered and upholstered (Enebro).

Fauteuil Louis XVI tapissé et laqué (Enebro)

Louis-seize-Sessel, gepolstert und lackiert. (Enebro).

4.

Louis XVI bookshelf (Geka).

Librairie Louis XVI (Geka).

Louis-seize-Bücherschrank (Geka).

3

1.
Louis XVI chest of drawers (Geka).
Commode Louis XVI (Geka).
Louis-seize-Kommode (Geka).

2.

Louis XVI French chest of drawers in oak. Original piece (Antigüedades Fortuny).

Commode française Louis XVI en bois de chêne. Pièce originale (Antiquités Fortuny).

Französische Louis-seize-Kommode aus Eiche. Originalstück. (Antigüedades Fortuny).

3.

Detail, ornamental molding and metal frame of chest of drawers 2.

Détail de moulures ornementales et ferrage de commode 2.

Ausschnitt Ornamentleiste und Beschlag der Kommode 2.

1

1.

Table-bar with sliding top.

Table bar avec couvercle coulissant.

Tisch-Bar mit verschiebbarem Deckel.

2

2.

Low table-bar with drawer in the Louis XVI style.

Table bar avec tiroir inférieur style Louis XVI.

Niedrige Tisch-Bar mit Schublade im Louis-seize-Stil.

3.

Louis XVI room with low table-bar, cabinets, and console table (Atelier du Vendelais).

Salon Louis XVI avec table bar basse, armoires et console (Atelier du Vendelais).

Raum Louis XVI. Bestehend aus niedriger Tisch-Bar, Schränken und Konsoltisch (Atelier du Vendelais).

1.

Low chest of drawers in Louis XVI style

Commode basse Louis XVI.

Niedrige Louis-seize-Kommode.

2.

Louis XVI cabinet in a Normandy design (Atelier du Vendelais).

Armoire Louis XVI d'inspiration normande (Atelier du Vendelais).

Louis-seize-Schrank, normannisch inspiriert. (Atelier du Vendelais).

1

pieces are framed in straight, simple lines along all three axes with no loss whatever to fine craftsmanship. Curves and closed structures are abandoned. As an additional decorative trait, some corners bear ornamentation. The feet are prismatic and tend toward the truncated cone. On large surfaces, walnut veneer or that of exotic woods is used– mahogany, lignum vitaes, rosewood–except for the native woods whose varied coloration will be exploited to bring out the decorative potentials.

horizontal, sans éviter que ses points d'union paraissent évidents. On abandonne les formes recourbées et les structures fermées. On implante parfois dans certains coins des éléments ornementaux comme motif décoratif additionnel. Les pattes sont en forme de prisme et tendent à être en forme de tronc conique. Pour les grandes superficies les meubles son habituellement revêtues de bois exotiques –sapelli, palme d'acajou, bois de roi, plaquemine-, en plus de bois autochtones dont le coloris varié est exploité pour augmenter ses possibilités décoratives.

baren Verbindungsstücken wurde keine Bedeutung beigemessen.

Man kommt von den kurvenreichen Formen und den geschlossenen Strukturen ab. Einige Ecken werden mit zusätzlichen dekorativen Elementen versehen.

Die Tisch– und Stuhlbeine haben eine prismatische Form und neigen zu kegelstumpfförmigen Formen.

Man neigt dazu, die großen Oberflächen der Möbel mit Nußbaumholz oder exotischen Holzarten zu furnieren: Sapeli, Mahagoni, Bois de roi, Guajakholz. Ebenso verwendet man einheimische Holzarten, deren Farbvielfalt genutzt wird, um die Dekorationsmöglichkeiten auszuweiten.

2

1.

Louis XVI style low bookcase, Maurepas model in wild cherry.

Bibliothèque basse Louis XVI modèle Maurepas en bois de cerisier sylvestre.

Niedriger Louis-seize-Bücherschrank Modell Maurepas, aus Wildkirsche.

2.

Louis XVI style chest of drawers, Maurepas model in wild cherry (L'Hermine).

Commode Louis XVI modèle Maurepas en bois de cerisier sylvestre (L'Hermine).

Louis-seize-Kommode Modell Maurepas, aus Wildkirsche. (L'Hermine).

1

2

1.
Louis XVI style chest of drawers (G.C. Capelletti).
Commode Louis XVI (G.C.Capelletti).
Louis-seize-Kommode (G.C.Capelletti).

2.
Sketch of Louis XVI chest of drawers in 1.
Détail de commode Louis XVI 1.
Skizze Louis-seize-Kommode 1.

3

4

ouis XVI open chest of drawers
Maison François Daïdée).

ommode Louis XVI ouverte
Maison François Daïdée)

eöffnete Louis-seize-Kommode
Maison François Daïdée).

4.

Louis XVI closed chest of drawers
(Maison François Daïdée).

Commode Louis XVI fermée
(Maison François Daïdée).

Geschlossene Louis-seize-Kommode
(Maison François Daïdée).

1

2

1.

Louis XVI style gaming table.

Table de jeux style Louis XVI.

Spieltisch im Louis-seize-Stil.

2.

Sketch of a Louis XVI commode.(Creaciones Royal).

Détail de commode Louis XVI (Créations Royal).

Skizze Louis-seize-Kommode (Creaciones Royal).

3

3.
Extended Louis XVI gaming table.
Table de jeux Louis XVI déployée.
Ausgezogener Louis-seize-Spieltisch.

4

4.
Louis XVI closed chest of drawers. (Maison François Daïdée).
Commode Louis XVI fermée (Maison François Daïdée).
Geschlossene Louis-seize-Kommode (Maison François Daïdée).

1.

Maurepas bookcase in wild cherry-pure Louis XVI style.

Bibliothèque Maurepas en cerisier sylvestre de pure style Louis XVI.

Bücherschrank Maurepas aus Wildkirsche im reinen Louis-seize-Stil.

2.
Fontanelle display case in wild cherry in a transitional style.

Vitrine Fontenelle en cerisier sylvestre de style Transition.

Vitrine Fontenelle aus Wildkirsche im Übergangsstil.

1.

Louis XVI chest of drawers in wild cherry wood (Meubles Buffier).

Commode Louis XVI en cerisier sylvestre (Meubles Buffier)

Louis-seize-Kommode aus Wildkirsche (Meubles Buffier).

2.

Louis XVI style tripartite bookcase in solid wild cherry (Kahn Frères).

Librairie de trois corps Louis XVI en cerisier sylvestre massif (Kahn Frères).

Dreiteiliger Louis-seize-Bücherschrank aus massiver Wildkirsche (Kahn Frères).

1.

A chevet of hard masculine lines. More than ornamentation, the brass pieces are a simple structural element.

Chever de lignes dures et masculines, où les bronzes constituent, plus qu'un apport décoratif, un simple appuy structurel.

Chevet mit harten und maskulinen Linien. Die Elemente aus Bronze haben weniger eine dekorative Bedeutung, sondern sind bloße strukturelle Stütze.

2.

Louis XVI display case (Kahn Frères).

Vitrine Louis XVI (Kahn Frères).

Louis-seize-Vitrine (Kahn Frères).

Neoclassicism

Adam

Le Néoclassicisme

Le style Adam

Neo-Klassizismus

Adam-Stil

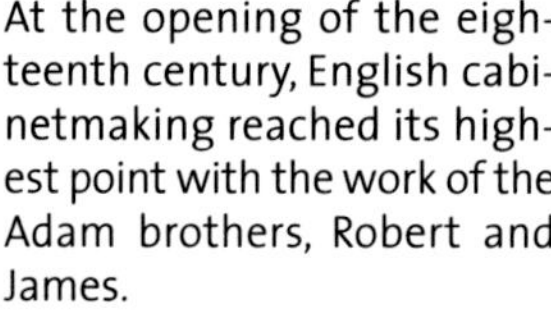

At the opening of the eighteenth century, English cabinetmaking reached its highest point with the work of the Adam brothers, Robert and James.

The family of Scottish architects and decorators into which they brothers were born derived its style from the ancient classic and Renaissance artists. Of William Adam's four children, Robert (1728-1792) and James (1730-1796) were the most renowned.

Their style very quickly extended itself throughout Europe. It was to inspire the designing arts up until the end of the Napoleonic Age.

Au début du XVIII ème siècle, l'ébénisterie anglaise atteint le sommet de sa gloire avec les frères Adam ou Adelphi, baptisés avec le nom de leur quartier. Les Adam étaient une famille d'architectes et de décorateurs écossais dont le style dériva vers l'Antiquité classique et la Renaissance. Fils de William Adam (1688-1748), entre les quatre frères, Robert (1728-1792) et James (1730-1796) ont été les plus représentatifs.

Son style s'étendit très tôt dans toute l'Europe, et inspirât l'art de la création jusqu'à la fin de l'époque Napoléonienne.

Zu Beginn des 18. Jh. erreicht die englische Kunsttischlerei mit den Gebrüdern Adam oder Adelphi, die nach ihrem Wohnviertel benannt wurden, seinen Höhepunkt.

Die Adams waren eine schottische Architekten- und Dekorateurfamilie, deren Stil auf die klassische Antike und die Renaissance zurückgeht. William Adam (1688-1748) hatte vier Söhne, von denen Robert (1728-1792) und James (1730-1796) die repräsentativsten waren.

Ihr Stil breitete sich sehr bald in ganz Europa aus und inspirierte die Design-Künste bis zum Ende der Epoche Napoleons

1

English style semicircular displa cabinet in mahogany (Arturo Peris)

Vitrine d'un demi point de styl anglais en acajou (Arturo Peris,

Halbrunde Vitrine aus Mahagon im englischen Stil (Arturo Peris)

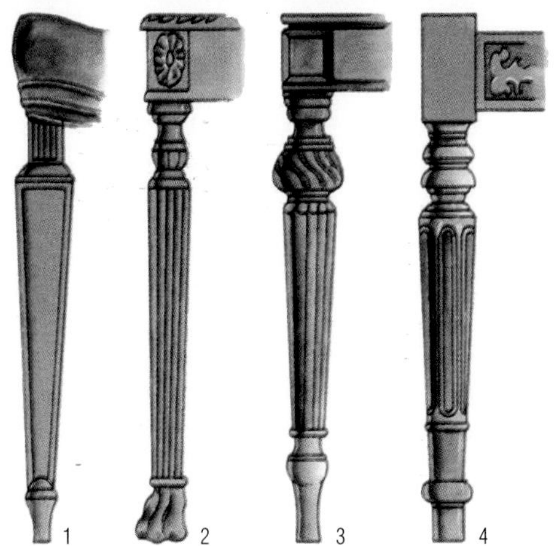

1 - 4.

Drawing of chair legs in the Adam style: straight-lined, prismatic, and fluted.

Dessin de pattes de chaises style Adam, droites, en forme de prisme, rainurées ou cannelées.

Zeichnung von Tischbeinen im Adam-Stil, gerade, prismatisch, mit Kannelierung oder Riffelung.

5.

The pieces created by the Adam brothers sought new structural lines.

Les meubles crées par les frères Adam recherchent de nouvelles lignes structurelles.

Die von den Brüdern Adam geschaffenen Möbel suchen nach neuen strukturellen Linien.

6.

Adam style furniture fall within classical lines, with the inclusion of subtle curves.

Les pièces de style Adam contiennent des lignes classiques avec l'inclusion de légères lignes courbées.

Die Stücke des Adam-Stils beschränken sich auf die klassischen Linien, unter Einbeziehung weicher Kurven.

7.

Drawing of a table where the truncated cone shape and the disappearance of flutes may be appreciated.

Dessin d'une table où l'on apprécie la patte en forme de tronc conique et la disparition de la chambrane.

Zeichnung eines Tisches. Auffällig sind die kegelstumpfförmigen Tischbeine und die fehlenden Keilstege.

8.

Display case with two doors from the Byron collection showing a rare combination of walnut with boxwood fillets (Viuda Hurtado).

Vitrine d'exposition de deux portes de la collection Byron en noyer et liséré de buis (Viuda Hurtado).

Ausstellvitrine mit zwei Türen aus der Kollektion Byron unter knapper Verwendung von Nußbaum und Filets aus Buchsbaum. (Viuda Hurtado).

1.

Two-door display case with beveled sides (Arturo Terrádez).

Vitrine de deux portes et cotés chanfreinés (Arturo Terrádez).

Vitrine mit zwei Türen und abgeschrägten Seiten (Arturo Terrádez).

2.
Semi-circular display case (Arturo Terrádez).

Vitrine de demi point (Arturo Terrádez).

Halbrunde Vitrine (Arturo Terrádez).

Neoclassicism
Hepplewhite
Le Néoclassicisme
Le style Hepplewhite
Neo-Klassizismus
Hepplewhite

This style takes its name from that of George Hepplewhite, one of the greatest cabinetmakers of the eighteenth century. Hepplewhite was also a cabinetmaker who knew how faithfully to interpret the concepts introduced by the Adam brothers.

In Hepplewhite, we find the most eclectic proponent of English neoclassicism. After his death, a book containing his designs and the costs of realizing them was published, with the corresponding scandal.

The furniture that he designed reaches an unmistakable exquisiteness, obtained by way of a highly simple structure and carefully tended proportions. Subtle curves are introduced, distancing the pieces from the coldness of the Adam style.

Ce style reçoit le nom de George Hepplewhite, un des plus grands ébénistes du XVIII ème siècle, et qui su interpréter de manière fidèle les propos introduits par les frères Adam.

Hepplewhite fut le personnage le plus éclectique du néoclassicisme anglais. Après sa mort, un livre avec ses créations et les coûts de production correspondants fut publié. Le mobilier crée par Heppelwhite acquit un représentatif goût exquis, obtenu grâce à une structure d'un grande simplicité et à des proportions très soignées où de douces courbes sont introduites pour éloigner la froideur des frères Adam.

Dieser Stil ist nach George Hepplewhite benannt, einem der größten Kunsttischler des 18. Jh., der es verstand, sehr getreu die Entwürfe der Adam-Brüder zu interpretieren.

Hepplewhite war der eklektischste Vertreter des englischen Neo-Klassizismus. Nach seinem Tod veröffentlichte man ein Buch mit seinen Entwürfen, den Kosten der Herstellung und der entsprechenden Wertfeststellung.

Das von Hepplewhite geschaffene Mobiliar war von unverwechselbarer Vortrefflichkeit, die er durch sehr einfache Strukturen und sehr sorgfältig gewählte Größenverhältnisse erreichte. Er entfernt sich von der Kühle der Adam-Brüder, indem er weiche Rundungen in seine Strukturen einfügt.

sk (Caler Home).
itoire (Caler Home).
ıreibtisch (Caler Home).

1.
Writing table (Eduardo Terrádez).
Secrétaire (Eduardo Terràdez).
Secrétaire (Eduardo Terrádez).

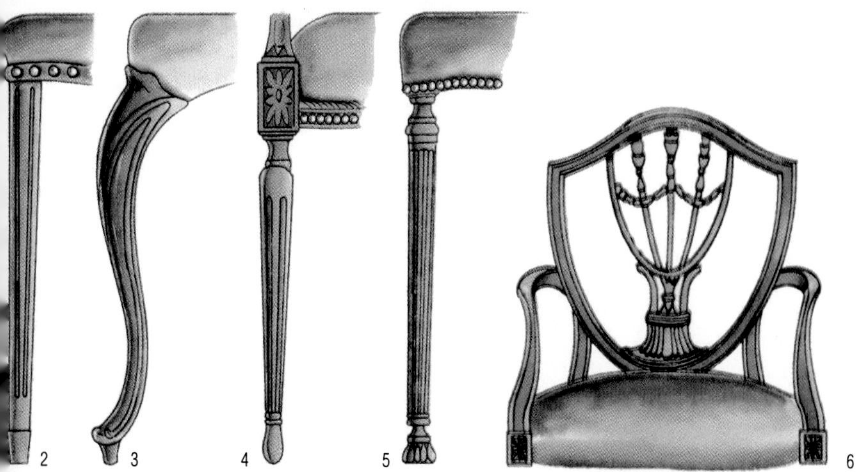

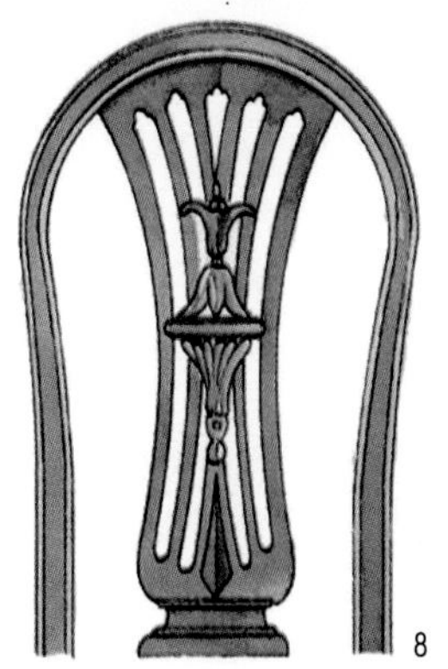

5.

ıwing of legs in the shape of truncated cones that ng about an agreeable outward curvature, ıracteristic of the Hepplewhite style.

ssin de pattes en forme de tronc conique qui prennent gracieuse courbature vers l'extérieur, actéristiques du style Hepplewhite.

chnung kegelstumpfförmige Stuhlbeine, die eine nutige, nach außen ausgerichtete Rundung chreiben, charakteristisch für den Hepplewhite-Stil.

wing of a backrest in the form of a shield.

sin de dossier avec partie postérieure en forme usson.

chnung hintere Rückenlehne in Form eines opens.

7.

The upper part of the display cases show very delicate moldings.

Il existe, dans le corps supérieur des vitrines, des moulures très délicates.

Im oberen Teil der Vitrinen befinden sich einige sehr zarte Abschlußleisten.

8.

Drawing of an oval chair back.

Dessin de dossier de chaise de forme ovale.

Zeichnung ovalförmige Rückenlehne.

1

2

3

4

1.

Carlto's Home writing desk in walnut with sycamore inlays.

Écritoire Carlo's Home en bois et loupe de noyer et incrustation de sycomore.

Schreibtisch Carlto's Home, aus Holz und Lupe aus Nußbaumholz mit Verzierungen aus Sykomore.

2.

Chair and armchair in the Hepplewhite style with chevron back.

Chaise et fauteuil de style Hepplewhite avec dossier en épis.

Stuhl und Sessel im Hepplewhite-Stil mit ährenförmiger Rückenlehne.

3.

Chair and armchair in a Hepplewhite rural style.

Chaises et fauteuils style Hepplewhite rurale.

Stuhl und Sessel im ländlichen Hepplewhite-Stil.

4.

Chair and armchair with ribbon back.

Chaise et fauteuil avec dossier en lacet.

Stuhl und Sessel mit schlaufenförmiger Rückenlehne

5.

Hepplewhite collection chairs (Becara).

Chaise collection Hepplewhite (Becara).

Stühle Hepplewhite-Kollektion (Becara)..

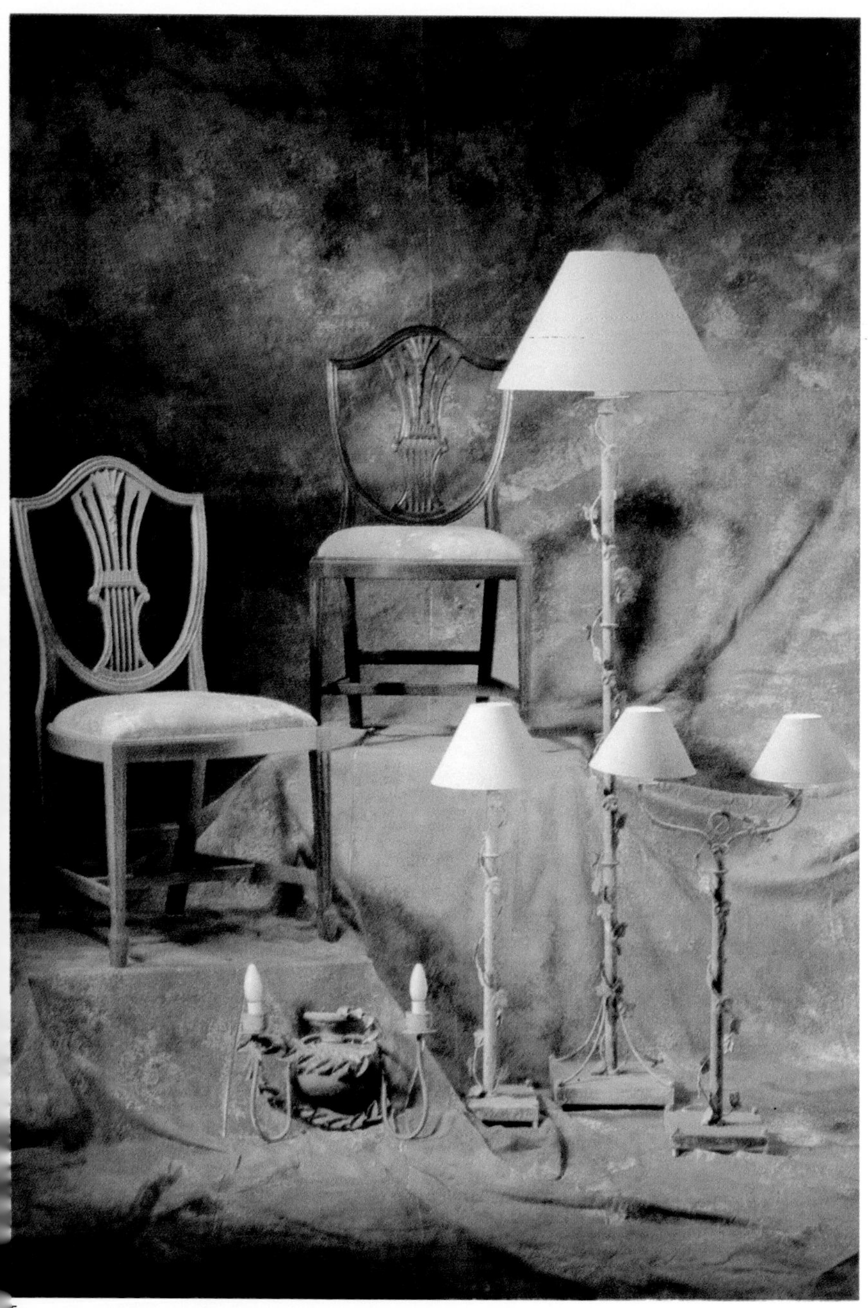

Neoclassicism
Sheraton

Le néoclassicisme
Le style Sheraton

Neo-Klassizismus
Sheraton

Sheraton is another great cabinetmaker who, along with Hope, characterized the second half of the Neoclassical movement.

Thomas Sheraton (1751-1806) showed a great knowledge of the possibilities and degree of resistance of wood. He also advocated the use of the least amount of wood possible in making his pieces, creating a collection of original furniture. The specimens were light, stylized, and they marked a true milestone. Sheraton managed to adapt the forms of artisanal production to the new factory manufacturing introduced by the Industrial Revolution in order to mass produce furniture.

Sheraton fut aussi un grand ébéniste et aux cotés de Hoppe, marqua le caractère de la seconde étape du Néoclassicisme.

Thomas Sheraton (1751-1806) prouva sa profonde connaissance des possibilités et du degré de résistance du bois. Il plaida aussi pour l'utilisation de la moindre quantité possible de bois, et créa ainsi une collection de pièces originales, très légères et stylisées, qui eurent un grand succès. Sheraton tenta d'adapter les formes de la production artisanale à la nouvelle fabrication manufacturée introduite par la Révolution Industrielle, dans le but de produire des meubles en série.

Sheraton ist ein weiterer großer Kunsttischler, der gemeinsam mit Hoppe den zweiten Abschnitt der neo-klassizistischen Epoche bestimmte.

Thomas Sheraton (1751-1806) bewies große Kenntnisse der Möglichkeiten und Widerstandsfähigkeit des Holzes.

Auch setzte er bei der Herstellung seiner Möbel möglichst wenig Holz ein und schuf eine Kollektion von sehr leichten und stilvoll gestalteten originellen Stücken, die einen wahren Meilenstein darstellten.

Sheraton versuchte, die handwerklichen Produktionsmethoden der neuen fabrikmäßigen Herstellung anzupassen, die von der industriellen Revolution eingeleitet wurde, um Möbelstücke in Serie zu produzieren.

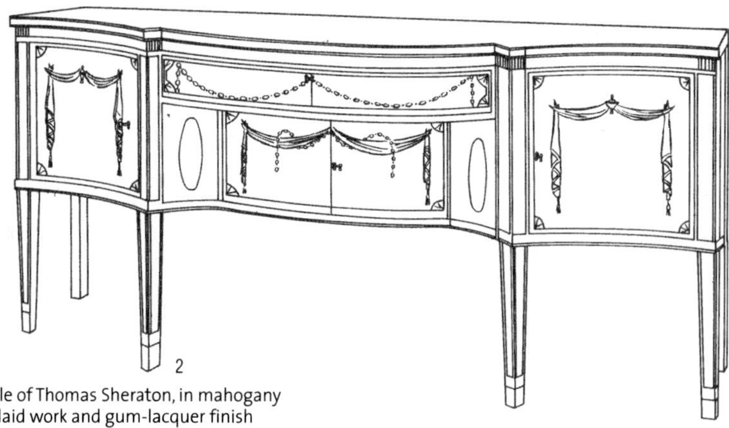

ꞁdeboard in the style of Thomas Sheraton, in mahogany ꞁth lemonwood inlaid work and gum-lacquer finish ꞁdel Bautista-Época).

ffet dressoir style Sheraton en acajou avec marqueterie en ronnier et finition en gomme laquée (Fidel Bautista-Época).

ffet-Anrichte im Sheraton-Stil aus Mahagoni mit ːarsien aus Zitronenholz, mit Schellack nachbehandelt. ꞁdel Bautista-Época).

2.

Sketch of the sideboard in 1.

Détail de buffet dressoir 1.

Skizze Buffet-Anrichte 1.

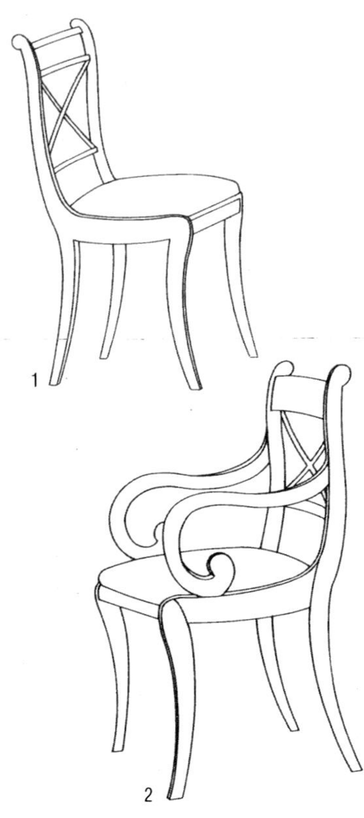

1.

Sketch of a chair.

Détail de chaise.

Skizze Stuhl.

2.

Sketch of a chair.

Détail de fauteuil.

Skizze Sessel.

3.

Sheraton dining room (Caler Home).

Salle à manger Sheraton formé par divers éléments (Caler Home).

Sheraton Eßzimmer, bestehend aus diversen Elementen (Caler Home).

3

2 - 4.

Different types of legs with the common characterist of being turned and of narrow section.

Différents types de pattes avec la caractéristique commune d'être toutes tournoyé avec de fines sections.

Verschiedene Arten von Stuhl- und Tischbeinen, allesamt gedrechselt und mit feingliedrigen Bestandteilen.

1.

Drawing of a Sheraton piece where the predominance of the straight lines may be easily appreciated.

Dessin de meuble Sheraton où l'on apprécie clairement la prépondérance de la ligne droite.

Zeichnung Sheraton Möbel, auf der man deutlich das Vorherrschen der geraden Linien sehen kann.

ne Sheraton back is linear and severe, although at mes it has a certain movement imparted by the ıbtle twisting of the upper parts.

s dossiers Sheraton sont d'une orthogonalité sévère, en que parfois on leur donne du mouvement oyennant le tournoiement subtil des pinacles.

ie Sheraton Rückenlehnen sind streng rechtwinklig, owohl sie manchmal von Bewegungen aufgelockert erden, die durch leichte Verdrehungen der oberen iste hervorgerufen werden.

6.

Sheraton writing table in mahogany (Fernando Guanter).

Table écritoire Sheraton en acajou (Fernando Guanter).

Sheraton Tisch/Schreibtisch aus Mahagoni (Fernando Guanter).

1.

English neoclassical dining room with a table in Sheraton's style.

Salle à manger Néoclassique anglaise avec table style Sheraton.

Englisches neo-klassizistisches Eßzimmer mit Tisch im Sheraton-Stil.

2.

Sheraton style mahogany table with inlays.

Table en acajou style Sheraton avec des rainures en marqueterie.

Mahagonitisch im Sheraton Stil mit Intarsien-Filets.

3.

Sheraton style cabinet and mirror in Brazilian mahogany (Caler Home).

Commode et miroir style Sheraton réalisés en acajou brésilien (Caler Home).

Kommode und Spiegel im Sheraton-Stil aus brasilianischem Mahagoni (Caler Home).

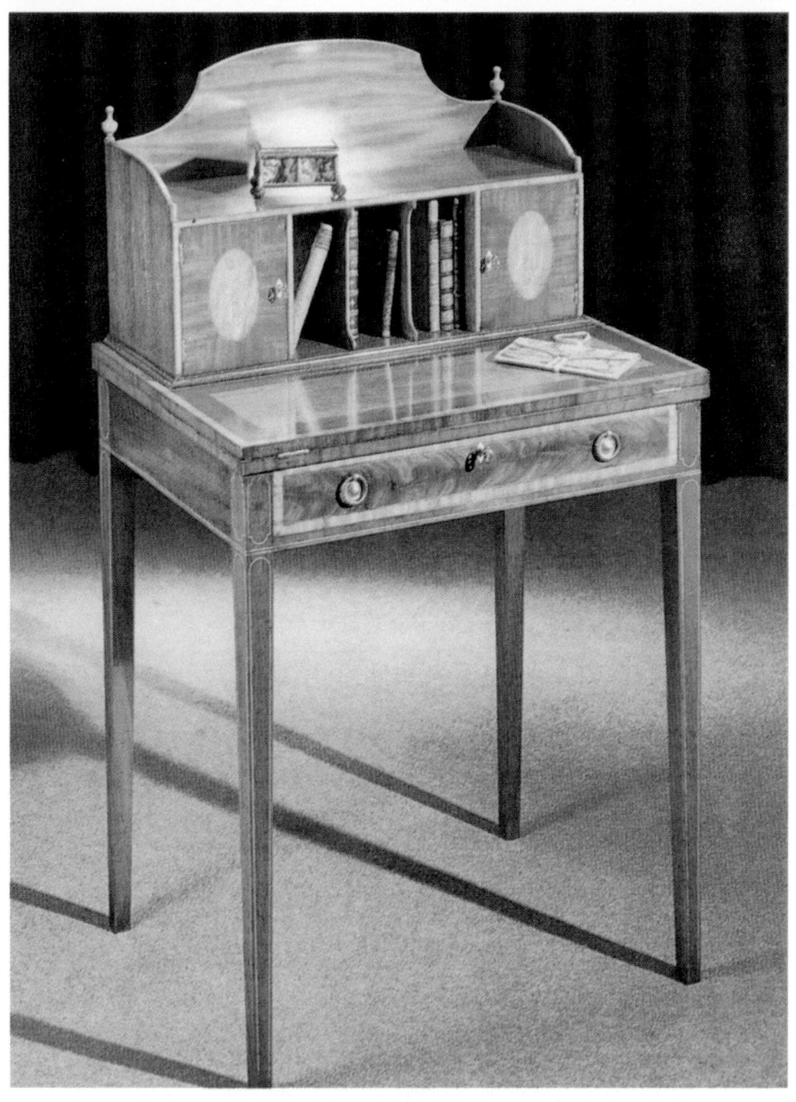

1.

Bonheur-du-jour in the Sheraton style. Satinwood and mahogany marquetry.

Bonheur-du-jour style Sheraton en satinwood et marqueterie d'acajou.

Bonheur-du-jour im Sheraton-Stil aus Seidenholz mit Intarsien aus Mahagoni.

2.

Oval table of the Sheraton type with circular inlaid work and collapsible top.

Table à café ovale type Sheraton avec marqueterie circulaire et dessus abattable.

Ovaler Kaffeetisch Sheraton-Typ mit kreisförmigen Intarsien und kippbarem Oberteil.

Neoclassicism
Regency
Le Néoclassicisme
Le style Regency
Neo-Klassizismus
Regency

Between the end of the eighteenth and the beginning of the nineteenth centuries there appeared in England a group of artists whose works taken together make up the so-called Regency style. Within this designation it is customary to distinguish two periods (1793-1820 and 1820-1835).

The pieces in this style are marked by the showiness and majesticality conferred by the exotic woods in which they are realized. Generally, it is a question of woods like American maple, amboina, and elm root. These are light-toned woods, with prominent veins and knots.

One of the main representatives of the first period is Thomas Hope (1769-1830), who was inspired in his

Entre la fin du XVIII ème et le début du XIX ème siècle, apparurent en Angleterre un groupe d'artistes dont les œuvres constituèrent le dénommé style Regency, où l'on y distingua deux périodes différentes (1793-1820 et 1820-1835).

Les meubles de ce style se caractérisent par la somptuosité et magnificence données par les bois exotiques avec lesquels il ont été réalisés. Il s'agit généralement de bois comme l'érable américain, l'emboise et la racine d'orme, de tons clairs, de veines prépondérantes et des loupes éclatantes.

Un des principaux représentants de la première période fut Thomas Hoppe (1769-1830), qui

Zwischen dem Ende des 18. Jh. und dem Anfang des 19. Jh. tritt in England eine Gruppe von Künstlern in Erscheinung, deren Werke den sogenannten Regency-Stil formen, innerhalb dessen man zwei Perioden unterscheidet (1793-1820 und 1820-1835).

Die Möbel dieser Stilrichtung zeichnen sich durch ihre Pracht und Herrlichkeit aus, die ihnen die exotischen Holzarten, aus denen sie erschaffen wurden, verleihen.

Verwendet werden im allgemeinen amerikanischer Ahorn, Rüster und Ulmenholz, in hellen Schattierungen, mit klaren Holzfasern und auffälligen Vorsprüngen.

Einer der wichtigsten Vertreter der ersten Periode ist Thomas Hoppe (1769-1830), der von der Epoche der

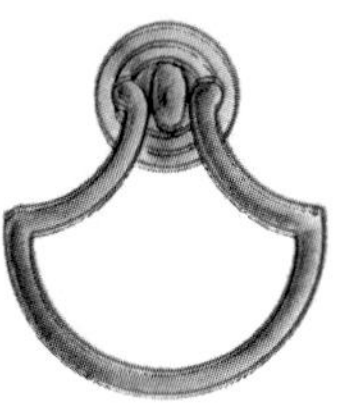

1.

English Regency style bookcase in lignum vitae wood. Original piece (Antigüedades Fortuny).

Bibliothèque anglaise style Regency en bois de plaquemine. Pièce originale (Antigüedades Fortuny)

Englischer Bücherschrank im Regency Stil aus Guajakholz. Originalstück (Antigüedades Fortuny).

1.

Detail, cube joint.

Détail de cube d'assemblage.

Ausschnitt Verbindung.

2.

English Regency style writing table in mahogany, lignum vitae, satinwood, and tin mounts (Arthur Brett & Sons).

Écritoire style Regency anglais en acajou, palissandre, bois satinés et attaches en laiton (Arthur Brett & Sons).

Englischer Schreibtisch im Regency-Stil aus Mahagoni, Palisander, Seidenholz und Messingbeschlag (Arthur Brett & Sons).

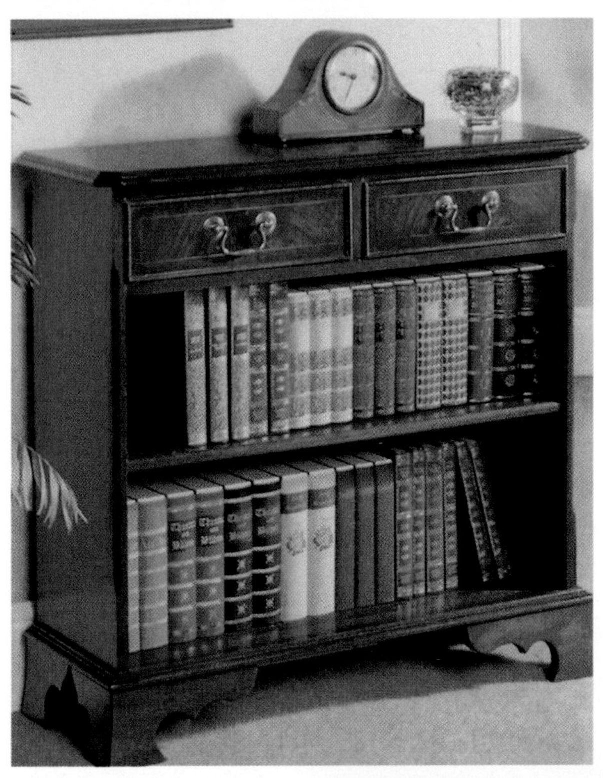

1.

Open bookcase with two drawers (Balmoral).

Bibliothèque ouverte de deux tiroirs (Balmoral).

Offener Bücherschrank mit zwei Schubladen (Balmoral).

2.

Walnut cabinet (Arthur Brett & Sons).

Commode en noyer (Arthur Brett & Sons).

Kommode aus Nußbaum (Arthur Brett & Sons).

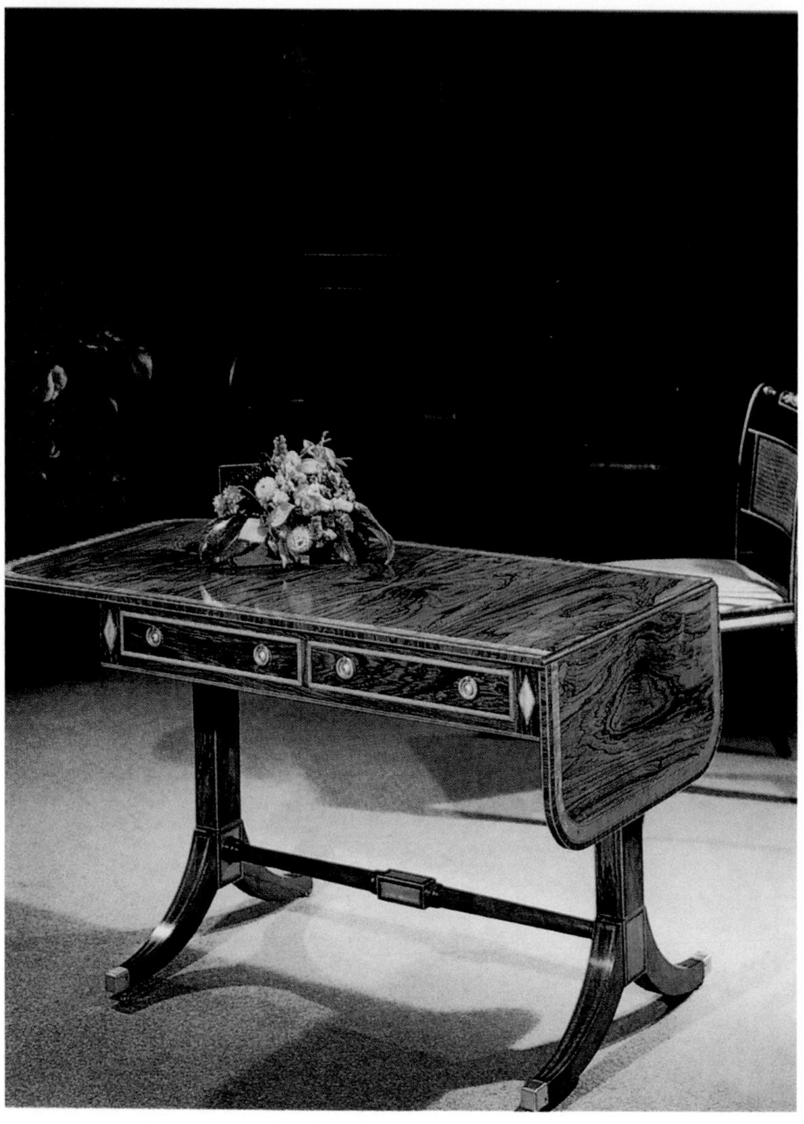

3.

Regency style table in lignum vitae wood with satinwood marquetry (Arthur Brett & Sons).

Table style Regency en palissandre avec marqueterie en satinwood (Arthur Brett & Sons)

Tisch im Regency-Stil aus Palisander mit Intarsien aus Seidenholz (Arthur Brett & Sons).

1.

Walnut bookcase with lignum vitae inlaid work of seventeenth-century inspiration.

Librairie en acajou avec marqueterie en palissandre d'inspiration XVIII ème.

Mahagonibücherschrank mit Intarsien aus Palisander, inspiriert vom 18. Jh.

2.

Detail of marquetry and doweling reminiscent of the Gothic (Arthur Brett & Sons).

Détail de marqueterie et baguettes de réminiscences gotiques (Arthur Brett & Sons).

Ausschnitt Intarsien und Leisten, die an die Gotik erinnern (Arthur Brett & Sons).

3.

English roll-top desk in satinwood (1840). Original piece (Antigüedades Fortuny).

Bureau anglais à volets en bois de satinwood (1840). Pièce originale (Antigüedades Fortuny).

Englisches Rolladen-Bureau aus Seidenholz (1840). Originalstück (Antiguidades Fortuny).

1

2

1.

Mahogany English roll-top desk in George III style (1880). Original piece.

Bureau anglais à volets en acajou style George III (1880). Pièce originale.

Englisches Rolladen-Bureau aus Mahagoni im Stil Georg III. (1880). Originalstück.

2.

Interior detail of a desk: drawers and pigeonholes.

Détail intérieur de bureau : gavettes et casiers.

Ausschnitt Innenteil des Bureaus: Schublädchen und Fächerschränkchen.

3

4

3.

English desk in mahogany wood (1800). Original piece.

Bureau anglais en acajou (1800). Pièces originale.

Englisches Bureau aus Mahagoni (1800). Originalstück.

4.

Detail, bottom part of desk: pigeonholes (Antigüedades Fortuny).

Détail inférieur de bureau : mur de casiers (Antigüedades Fortuny).

Ausschnitt unterer Teil des Bureaus: Trennwand Fächerschränkchen (Antiguidades Fortuny).

1.

Office of Regency inspiration (Picture's).

Officine anglaise d'inspiration Regency (Picture's).

Arbeitszimmer, inspiriert vom englischen Regency (Picture's).

2

3

2.

English Regency office in walnut (1800). Original piece (Antigüedades Fortuny).

Table de bureau anglaise en acajou style George III (1800). Pièce originale (Antigüedades Fortuny).

Englischer Bürotisch aus Mahagoni im Stil Georg III. (1800). Originalstück (Antiguidades Fortuny)

3.

Detail, edge of office desk.

Détail d'angle de table de bureau.

Ausschnitt Ecke des Arbeitstisches.

1

work by the classical periods of ancient civilizations (Egypt, Greece, and Rome). This author and designer did not make furniture, he adapted for it classical motifs or those inspired on the classical period. Hope conceived an ex novo kind of furniture, the synthesis of the aforementioned cultures, but in adaptations toward the modern sense.

The second period of neoclassicism is characterized by an interpretation in the English manner of work carried out in France to that time. These pieces would be very plain, even austere.

s'inspirât de l'époque classique antique (Egypte, Grèce, Rome). Cet ébéniste ne construisait pas ses meubles mais il leurs adaptait des motifs classiques ou inspirés de l'époque classique. Hoppe réalisât un meuble «ex nuovo» synthèse de ces cultures, mais adapté aux sentiments modernes.

La seconde période est caractérisée par une interprétation anglaise des créations faites en France à cette époque là. Il s'agit de meubles très sobres, presque austères.

klassischen Antike (Ägypten, Griechenland und Rom) inspiriert ist.

Dieser Kunsttischler kreiert nicht seine eigenen Möbel, sondern paßt klassische oder von der klassischen Epoche inspirierte Motive an.

Hoppe schafft ein alt-neues Möbel, eine Synthese aus jenen Kulturen, aber er paßt es dem modernen Stil an.

Bestimmend für die zweite Periode ist eine englische Interpretation der damaligen französischen Ausführungen.

Es handelte sich um sehr schmucklose, ja sogar strenge Möbel.

2

1.

Low desk inspired by the English Regency period (Picture's).

Bureau bas ou pupitre anglais d'inspiration Regency (Picture's).

Niedriges Bureau oder Canterano, vom englischen Regency inspiriert (Picture's).

2.

Regency bookcase table (1820) in lignum vitae. Original piece.

Table bibliothèque Regency de 1820 en bois de plaquemine. Pièce originale.

Regency Lesetisch von 1820 aus Guajakholz. Originalstück.

3.

Detail, low table.

Détail de base de table.

Ausschnitt Unterkonstruktion des Tisches.

3

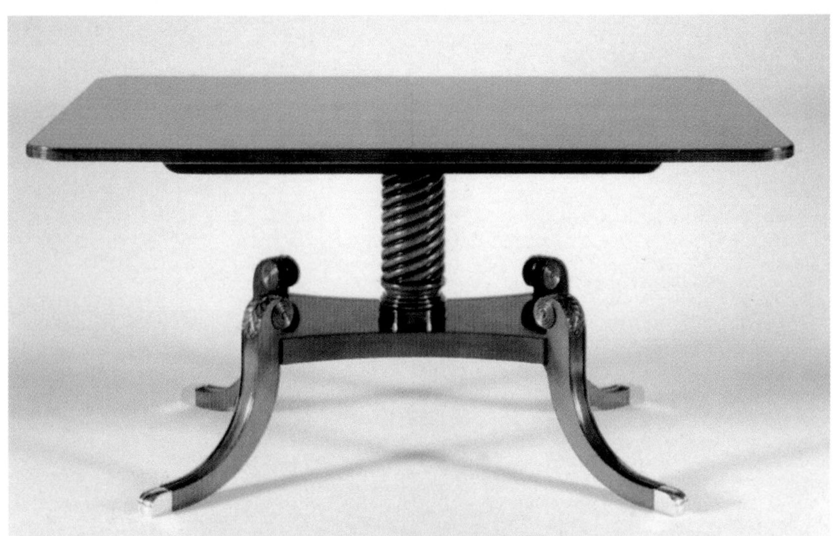

1

2

1.

English Regency table (Fernando Guanter).

Table anglaise Regency quadrangulaire (Fernando Guanter).

Englischer rechteckiger Regency Tisch (Fernando Guanter).

2.

English Regency table (Fernando Guanter).

Table Regency anglaise de fin de siècle (Fernando Guanter).

Englischer Regency Tisch, Ende des Jahrhunderts (Fernando Guanter).

3

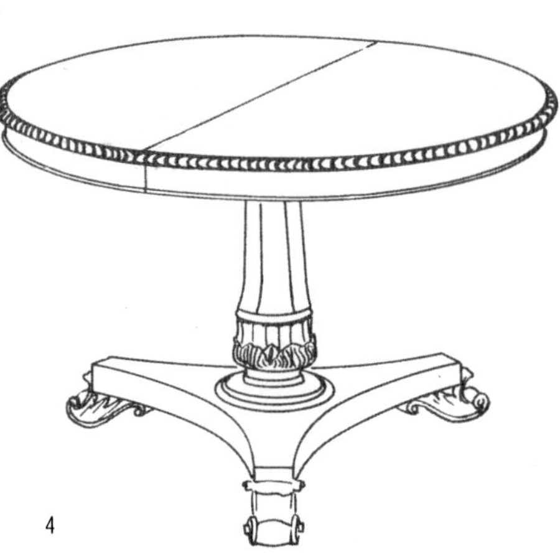

4

3.

Extendable table in the Regency style (Caler Home).

Table extensible style Regency (Caler Home).

Ausziehbarer Tisch im Regency Stil (Caler Home).

4.

Sketch of table shown in 3.

Détail table 3.

Skizze Tisch 3.

1

2

3

4

1.

Prince of Wales chair and armchair.

Chaise et fauteuil Prince de Galles

Stuhl und Sessel Prince of Wales.

2.

Chair and armchair with wheat ear back.

Chaise et fauteuil avec dossier en épis.

Stuhl und Sessel mit Ähren-Rückenlehne.

3.

Chair and armchair with fleur-de-lys back.

Chaise et fauteuil avec dossier Fleur de Lys.

Stuhl und Sessel mit Rückenlehne in Form einer Wappenlilie.

4.

Chair and armchair with upholstered back.

Chaise et fauteuil avec dossier tapissé.

Stuhl und Sessel mit gepolsterter Rückenlehne.

5

6

7

8

.
:hair and armchair with shield-shaped back (Heldense).
'haise et fauteuil avec dossier en forme d'écu. (Heldinse).
·tuhl und Sessel mit Rückenlehne in Form eines
Vappens (Heldense).

ieorge I chair in birch wood (Ferrando Guanter).
'haise George I en en bois de hêtre o (Ferrando Guanter).
tuhl Georg I. aus Buche (Ferrando Guanter).

7.
Chair and armchair with pitcher-shaped back.
Chaise et fauteuil avec dossier en forme de jarre.
Stuhl und Sessel mit Rückenteil in Vasenform.

8.
Regency chair.
Fauteuil Regency.
Regency Sessel.

Neoclasicism
Empire style
Le Néoclassicisme
Le style Empire
Neo-Klassizismus
Empire

The Empire style in France opened the last chapter of neoclassicism. It would last until 1815, although its influence would continue to be noted until around 1830.

With the irruption of this style, a set of strict rules with very precise and fixed principles was imposed. Cabinetmakers were thus left without any kind of freedom. From the conceptual point of view, the furniture will take on simple, serene forms, geometrical forms that are dominated by straight lines. The symmetry will be exaggerated and the framework of solid pieces in the form of cubes or prisms. The result was a majestic, solemn style

Le style Empire marqua en France le dernier chapitre du Néoclassicisme et dura jusqu'en 1815 bien que son influence continua jusqu'à peut près 1830.

C'est avec l'irruption du style Empire que s'imposa une norme très stricte avec des principes très précis et fixes qui ne permettait aux ébénistes aucun type de liberté. Du point de vue conceptuel, le mobilier adopta des formes simples, sereines et géométriques, dominées par la ligne droite, la symétrie exagérée et les structures massives, cubiques ou en forme de prisme. On obtint ainsi un style majestueux et solennelle.

Das Empire eröffnet in Frankreich das letzte Kapitel des Neo-Klassizismus und dauert bis 1815, obgleich sein Einfluß bis nahezu 1830 bemerkbar ist.

Mit dem Beginn des Empire werden sehr strikte Normen mit sehr präzisen und starren Prinzipien auferlegt, welche den Kunsttischlern keinerlei Kreativität lassen.

Vom konzeptuellen Gesichtspunkt aus gesehen nahm das Mobiliar einfache, gelassene und geometrische Formen an, die von geraden Linien, übertriebener Symmetrie und massiven, kubischen und prismatischen Strukturen bestimmt waren. Dadurch enstand ein majestätischer und festlicher Stil.

Empire style bookcase in solid wood with inlaid work in cherry wood (Giemme)

Bibliothèque style Empire en bois massif et marqueterie en cerisier (Giemme)

Bücherschank im Empire-Stil aus massivem Holz und Intarsien aus Kirschbaumholz (Giemme)

1

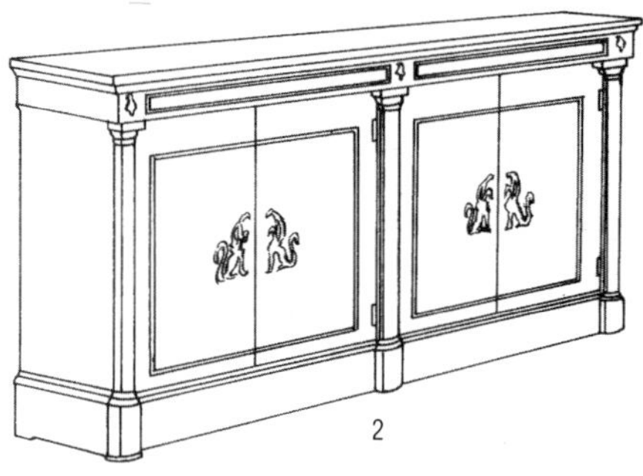

2

3

4

1.

Sketch of a bookcase.

Détail de librairie.

Skizze Bücherschrank.

2.

Sketch of a cupboard.

Détail de buffet.

Skizze Anrichte.

3.

Sketch for an office table.

Détail de table de bureau.

Skizze Arbeitstisch.

4.

Empire style office in birch wood, walnut veneer, and orange wood marquetry (Vicente Ramón Gil).

Bureau style Empire fabriqué en bois d'hêtre, chape de palme de noyer et marqueterie en bois d'oranger (Vicente Ramón Gil).

Arbeitszimmer im Empire-Stil aus Buche, Furnier Nußbaum und Intarsien aus Orangenbaumholz (Vicente Ramón Gil).

1 - 2.

Drawings of stretchers in a table. The ornamental work is in the ancient tradition so appreciated in the Empire style.

Dessin de supports de table où l'on voit des motifs ornementaux de tradition ancienne, si du goût de l'époque.

Zeichnungen von Tischstützen auf denen Schmuckmotive der Antike zu sehen sind, die dem Geschmack der Zeit entsprechen.

1

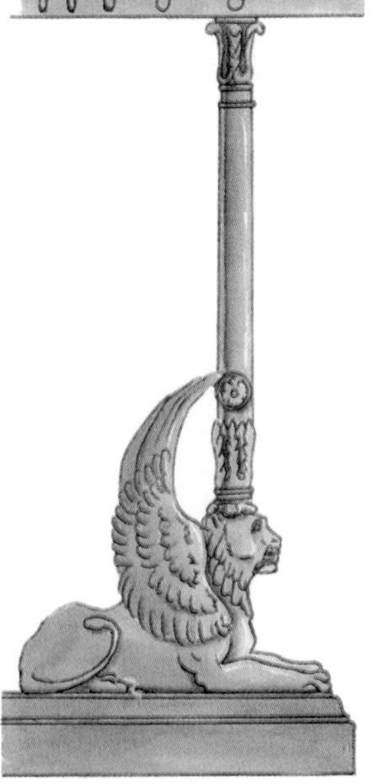

2

3

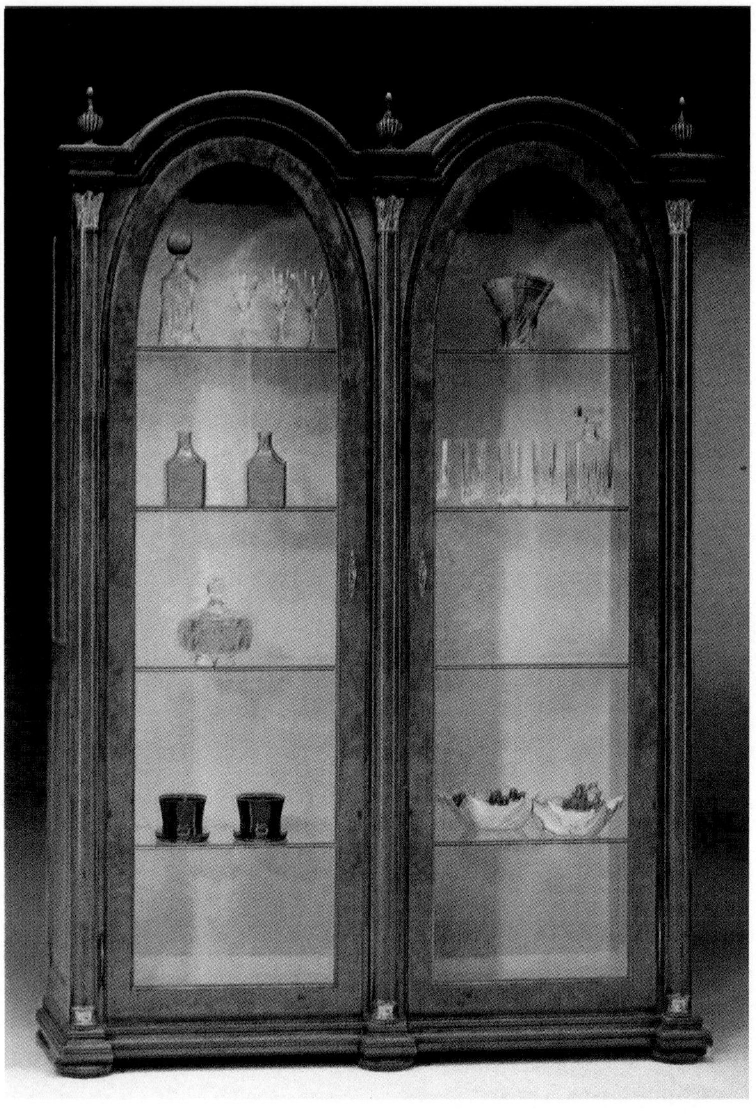

1.

Empire style display case in ash root veneer.

Vitrine style Empire en contreplaqué de racine de frêne olivé.

Vitrine im Empire-Stil aus, furniert mit Eschenholz.

2.

Writing table in the Empire style in patinaed ash wood veneer.

Commode écritoire style Empire en contreplaqué de frêne olivé patiné.

Schreibtisch-Kommode im Empire-Stil, poliertes Furnier aus Eschenholz.

4

Empire style writing desk (1810)
in lignum vitae

Bureau anglais Empire (1810)
en bois de plaquemine

Englisches Bureau im Empire-Stil
(1810) aus Guajakholz

1

2

3

1.

Detail, brass mounts and fillets 4.

Détail d'attaches et incrustations en laiton 4.

Ausschnitt Beschläge des Filets aus Messing 4.

2.

Detail, inside drawers of 4.

étail de gavettes intérieures 4.

Ausschnitt Innenseite Schubfächer 4.

3.

Detail, side desk of 4.

Détail latéral de bureau 4.

Ausschnitt Seitenteil Bureau 4.

1.

Ornamental drawing of a sphinx.

Dessin ornemental qui représente une éphigie.

Zeichnung Ornament, das eine Sphinx zeigt.

1

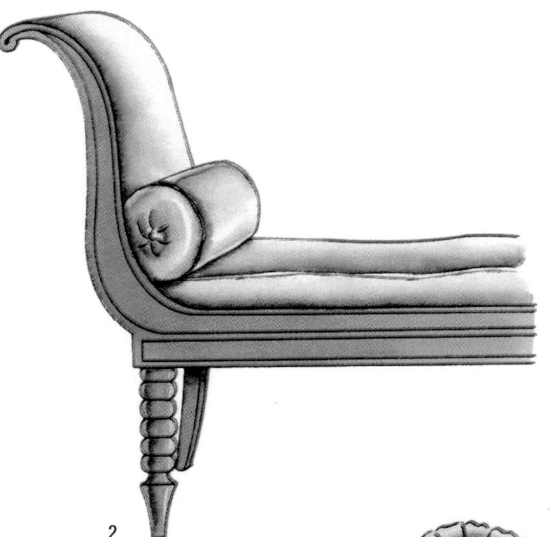

2

2.

Two armchairs. In section, these pieces are carefully proportioned prisms but for the turned front legs.

Les fauteuils présentent des sections en formes de prisme très proportionnées, à l'exception de certaines pattes de devant, de forme tournoyée.

Die Sessel zeigen sehr gleichmäßige und prismatische Teile, mit Ausnahme einiger gedrechselter vorderer Sesselbeine.

3

4

3 - 6.

In the Empire style, ornamentation uses elements from the Classical Age in Egypt, Greece, and Rome adapted to the reality of the eighteenth century.

Dans le style Empire, on utilise pour l'ornementation des éléments empruntés des époques classiques (Egypte, Grèce et Rome) adaptés à la réalité du XVIII ème siècle.

Beim Empire verwendet man bei der Verzierung Elemente, die den klassischen Epochen entnommen wurden (Ägypten, Griechenland und Rom) und der Wirklichkeit des 18. Jh. angepasst wurden.

5

6

mpire style dresser in solid wild herry wood (Kahn Frères).

Commode style Empire en cerisier sylvestre massif (Kahn Frères).

Kommode im Empire-Stil aus massiver Wildkirsche (Kahn Frères).

1

2

3

4

1.

Bergère with Egyptian touches (Gilles Nouilhac).

Bergère de réminiscences égyptiennes (Gilles Nouilhac).

Bergere, die an ägyptische Elemente erinnert (Gilles Nouilhac).

2.

Armchair with gondola-shaped back (Jacinto Usán).

Fauteuil avec dossier en gondole (Jacinto Usan).

Sessel mit Gondel-Rückenlehne (Jacinto Usán).

- 4.

hair and armchair in the Empire style with gondola-shaped acks. Reproduction of a model from 1800-1810 (Jacinto Usán).

haise et fauteuil de style Empire avec dossier en gondole. production d'un meuble de 1800-1810 (Jacinto Usán).

uhl und Sessel im Empire-Stil mit Gondel-Rückenlehne. produktion eines Modelles von 1800 – 1810 (Jacinto Usán).

5.

French chaise-longue in Empire style (1830). Original piece (Antigüedades Fortuny).

Chaise longue française se style Empire (1830). Pièce originale (Antigüedades Fortuny).

Französische Chaiselongue im Empire-Stil (1830). Originalstück (Antigüedades Fortuny).

1

1.

Empire style armchair by Colombo Mobili.

Fauteuil style Empire, de Colombo Mobili.

Lehnsessel im Empire-Stil, von Colombo Mobili.

2

2.

Empire style piece by Colombo Mobili.

Meubles style Empire, de Colombo Mobili.

Möbelstück im Empire-Stil, von Colombo Mobili.

3

3.
Empire style dining room table by Colombo Mobili.
Table de salle à manger style Empire, de Colombo Mobili.
Eßtisch im Empire-Stil, von Colombo Mobili.

1

2

3

1.

Cajonera estilo Imperio, de Colombo Mobili.

Meuble à tiroirs style Empire, de Colombo Mobili.

Sakristeischrank im Empire-Stil, von Colombo Mobili.

2.

Armchair in a nineteenth-century French style by Colombo Mobili.

Console style Empire, de Colombo Mobili.

Konsoltisch im Empire-Stil, von Colombo Mobili.

3.

French style armchair of nineteenth-century design by Colombo Mobili.

Fauteuil de style français du XIX ème siècle, de Colombo Mobili.

Sessel im französichen Stil des 19. Jh., von Colombo Mobili.

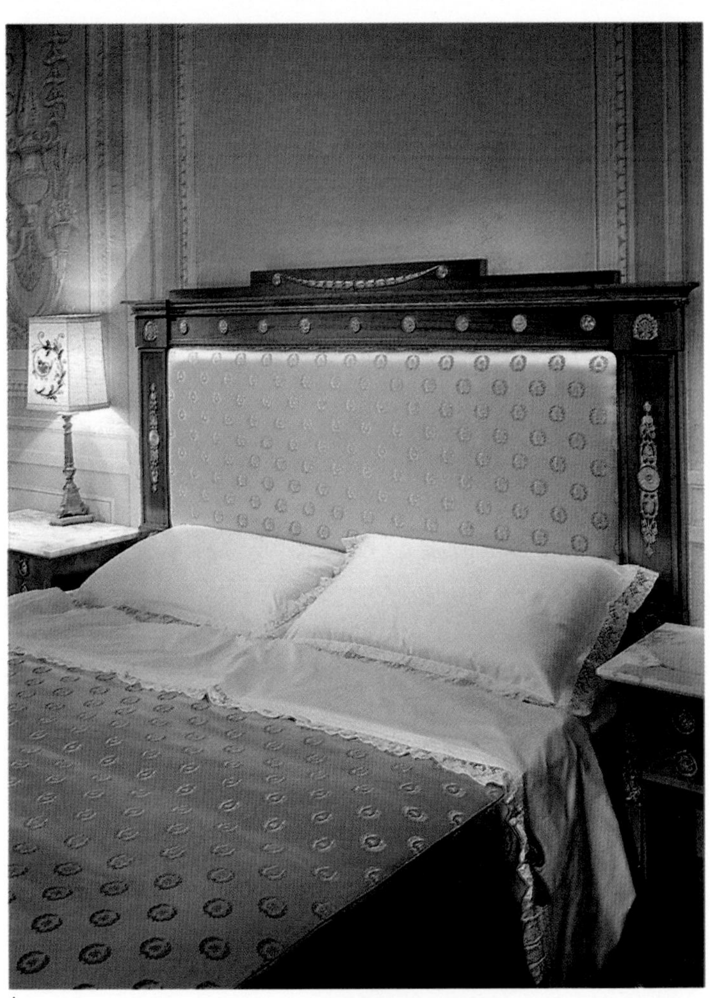

4

4.

Empire style headrest by Colombo Mobili.

Tête de lit style Empire, de Colombo Mobili.

Kopfteil im Empire-Stil, de Colombo Mobili.

1

2

1.

Empire style dining room by Soher.

Salle à manger style Empire, de Soher.

Eßzimmer im Empire-Stil, von Soher.

2.

Empire style piece by Colombo Mobili.

Meubles à tiroirs style Empire, de Colombo Mobili.

Sakristeischrank im Empire-Stil, von Colombo Mobili.

3

3.
Empire style salon suite by Mariner.
Ensemble de salon style Empire, de Mariner.
Wohnzimmereinrichtung im Empire-Stil, von Mariner.

Eclecticism
L'Eclectisme
Eklektizismus

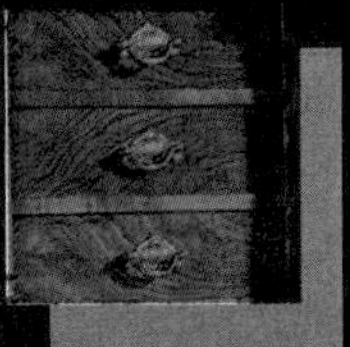

Eclecticism
The Victorian Age
L'Eclectisme
Le style Victorien
Eklektizismus
Viktorianischer Stil

The Victorian style appeared in England in the second half of the nineteenth century.

The furniture of this time will respond to reinterpretations, hybridization, mixtures, combinations, or approximations of previous styles. No single style will develop from this.

Thus, the Victorian style seen as a good exponent of the eclecticism of which we are speaking supposes an attempt to reconcile the bourgeois character of contradictory movements. Its pieces are therefore the result of a great amalgam of trends, be it gothic or baroque or a whole conflation of styles, characteristics, elements, and tendencies.

Le style Victorien apparut en Angleterre dans la seconde moitié du XIX ème siècle. Le meuble de cette époque correspond à une réinterprétation, hybrides, mélanges combinaisons ou approximations aux styles précédents et qui de ce fait n'a pas sa propre identité.

Le style Victorien, en tant que représentant de l'éclectisme dont nous parlons, est la tentative de concilier le caractère bourgeois de modes contradictoires. Ses pièces sont donc le résultat d'un important amalgame de tendances, parfois gotiques, parfois baroques, tout un mélange de styles, caractères, éléments et tendances.

Der viktorianische Stil tritt in der zweiten Hälfte des 19. Jh. in England in Erscheinung.

Das Möbel dieser Epoche entsteht aus Neuinterpretationen, Hybriden, Mischformen, Kombinationen und Annäherungen an vorhergegangene Stilrichtungen, ohne daß ein eigenständiger Stil zustande kommt.

Der viktorianische Stil ist ein gutes Beispiel für den Eklektizismus. Er versucht, die widersprüchlichen Modeerscheinungen auf spießbürgerliche Art zu versöhnen. Die Stücke sind das Ergebnis einer Vielfalt von Tendenzen, mal gotisch, mal barocker Art. Sie sind ein Mischmasch aus Stilen, Merkmalen, Elementen und Tendenzen.

1.

Victorian style dining room suite combined with black tones.

Ensemble de salle à manger style Victorien combiné avec des tons en noir.

Eßzimmergruppe im viktorianischen Stil, Kombination mit Schwarztönen.

Habit de Bouquetiere.

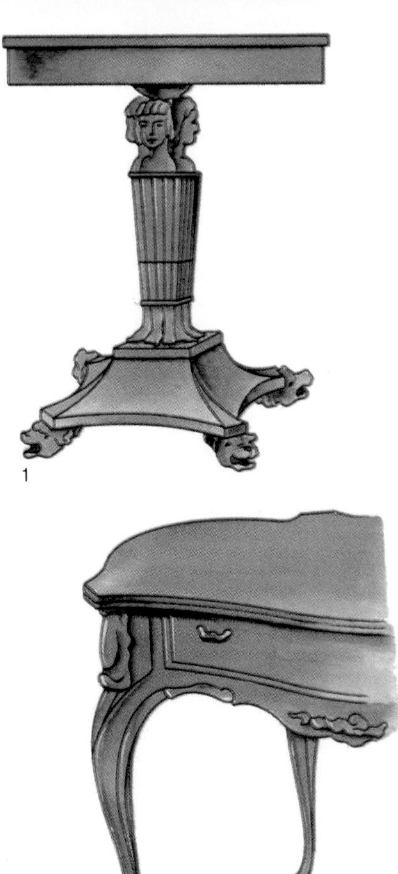

1

2

3

1 - 2.

Drawings of different types of table legs in the Victorian style.

Dessins de différents types de pattes de table de style Victorien.

Zeichnungen verschiedener Arten von Tischbeinen, viktorianischer Stil.

3.

Victorian extendable table (Caler Home).

Table Victorienne extensible (Caler Home).

Ausziehbarer viktorianischer Tisch (Caler Home).

1

2

3

4

1 - 3.

The eclecticism of this style makes it a conglomerate of different trends that lacks personality.

L'Éclectisme de ce style fait de lui un congloméré de différentes tendances avec un grand manque de personnalité.

Der Eklektizismus macht aus diesem Stil eine Anhäufung von verschiedenen Tendenzen, zeigt aber mangelnde Eigenständigkeit.

eproduction of a Victorian dining
oom in solid walnut with silver
nounts (Melarca).

*eproduction de salle à manger
ictorienne en noyer massif avec
ttaches en argent (Melarca).*

**eproduktion eines viktorianischen
ßzimmers aus massivem Nußbaum
it Silberbeschlägen (Melarca).**

1

2

1.

Reproduction of a Victorian dining room in solid walnut with silver mounts (Melarca

Reproduction de salle à manger Victorienne en noyer massif avec attaches en argent (Melarca).

Reproduktion eines viktorianischen Eßzimmers aus massivem Nußbaum mi Silberbeschlägen (Melarca).

2.

Victorian writing table in mahogany veneer (Blanch).

Écritoire Victorien contreplaqué en palme d'acajou (Blanch).

Viktorianischer Schreibtisch, Furnier aus Mahagoniholzverbindung (Blanch).

3

3.

Two Victorian tables (Enebro).

Écritoire Victorien contreplaqué en palme d'acajou (Enebro).

Zwei viktorianische Beistelltische (Enebro).

4.

Sketch of a Victorian table.

Détail de table Victorienne auxiliaire.

Skizze viktorianischer Beistelltisch.

5.

Sketch of a Victorian table.

Détail de table Victorienne auxiliaire.

Skizze viktorianischer Beistelltisch.

1

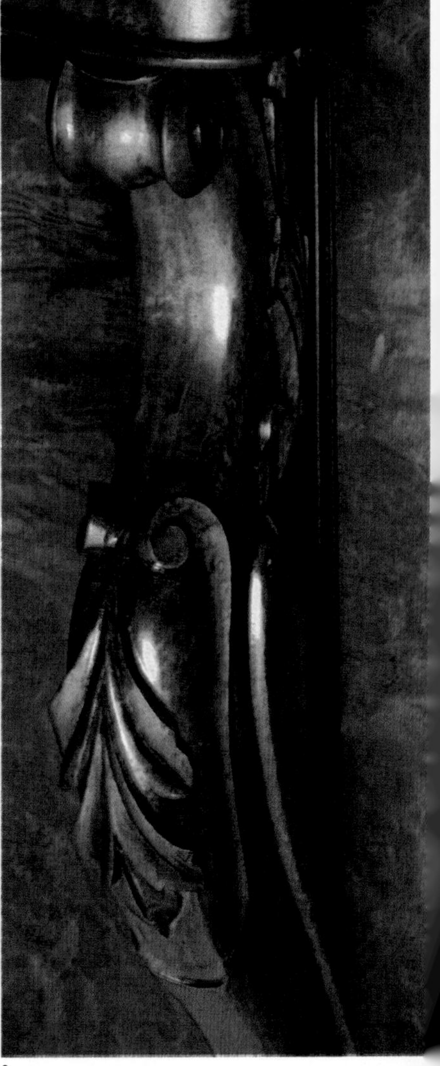

2

1.

Drawing of a piece from the first half of the Victorian Age. Curved lines predominate. The furniture from this time are richly padded, upholstered, and in general highly adorned.

Dessin de meuble de la première étape Victorienne où dominait la ligne courbe. Ce sont des meubles enrichis avec des matelassés, des tapissés et des galons.

Zeichnung eines Möbels aus der ersten viktorianischen Epoche, bei dem die Rundung hervorsticht. Die Möbel sind mit Polsterungen, Bezügen und Galonen versehen.

2.

Detail, desk in 3.

Détail d'écritoire 3.

Ausschnitt Schreibtisch 3.

3.

Reproduction of a Victorian style writing table (Caler Home).

Reproduction d'écritoire de style Victorien (Caler Home).

Reproduktion eines Schreibtisches im viktorianischen Stil. (Caler Home).

3

Eclecticism

Isabelline style

L'Éclectisme

Le style Isabelle II

Eklektizismus

Isabelinisch

The Isabelline style is a part of what we call eclecticism. It takes shape basing itself on characteristics borrowed from other periods, its name coming from its development in Spain throughout the long reign of Isabel II.

In alluding to the Isabelline style, it is impossible to avoid thinking of a style that is an intermixture, certainly bourgeois, and very much without an identity that is really its own.

This style has a first stage that is characterized by an imitation of the Empire style, but where the decorative use of brass has been lost and there is a kind of degeneration at work. This includes those references

Le style Isabelle II se situe dans ce que l'on appelle l'Éclectisme. Il se forme à base de caractéristiques empruntées d'autres époques. Il se développe d'où son nom en Espagne durant le royaume d'Isabelle II.

Quand on parle de ce style, il est impossible d'éviter de penser à un style mélangé, très bourgeois et sans personnalité.

La première partie de cette époque est une imitation du style Empire, après suppression des applications décoratives en bronze pour dériver vers une dégénération de celui-ci, et avec l'inclusion de références communes au Directoire qui avaient peut de relation avec le monde classique (le Classicis-

Der isabelinische Stil wird dem sogenannten Eklektizismus zugeordnet.

Der isabelinische Stil basiert auf Merkmalen, die anderen Epochen entnommen wurden.

Dieser Stil entwickelt sich in Spanien im Laufe der Herrschaft von Isabel II.

Spricht man von diesem Stil, denkt man unweigerlich an einen gemischten und sicherlich spießbürgerlichen Stil ohne eigene Identität.

Der erste Zeitabschnitt dieses Stils ist durch die Imitation des Empire-Stils gekennzeichnet. Die dekorativen Applikationen aus Bronze verschwinden und der Empire-Stil wird entartet, indem man ihn später mit typischen Elementen des Directoire vermischt,

1.
Birch wood writing table, Isabelline model (Muebles Pérez Benau).
Bureau en hêtre, modèle Isabelle II (Muebles Pérez Binau).
Arbeitszimmer aus Buche, isabelinisches Modell (Muebles Pérez Benau).

1

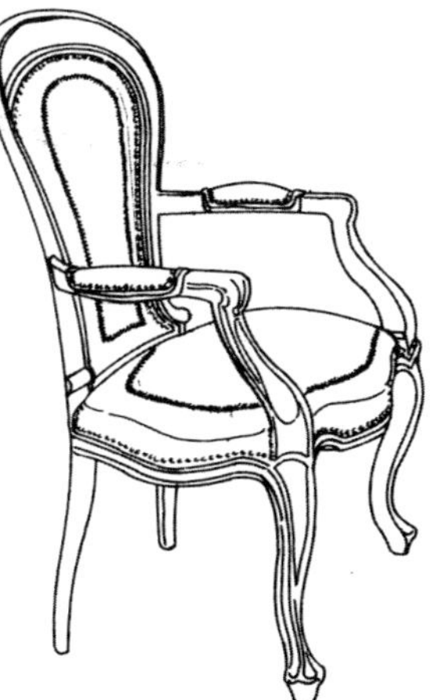

2

1.

Birch wood writing table, Isabelline model (Muebles Pérez Benau).

Table écritoire en hêtre, modèle Isabelle II (Muebles Pérez Binau).

Schreibtisch aus Buche, isabelinisches Modell (Muebles Pérez Benau).

2.

Sketch of the upholstered chair in 1.

Détail de fauteuil tapissé 1.

Skizze gepolsterter Sessel. 1.

3.

Round table with an upholstered surface (Muebles Pérez Benau).

Table ronde avec superficie tapissée (Muebles Pérez Binau).

Runder Tisch mit überzogener Platte (Muebles Pérez Benau).

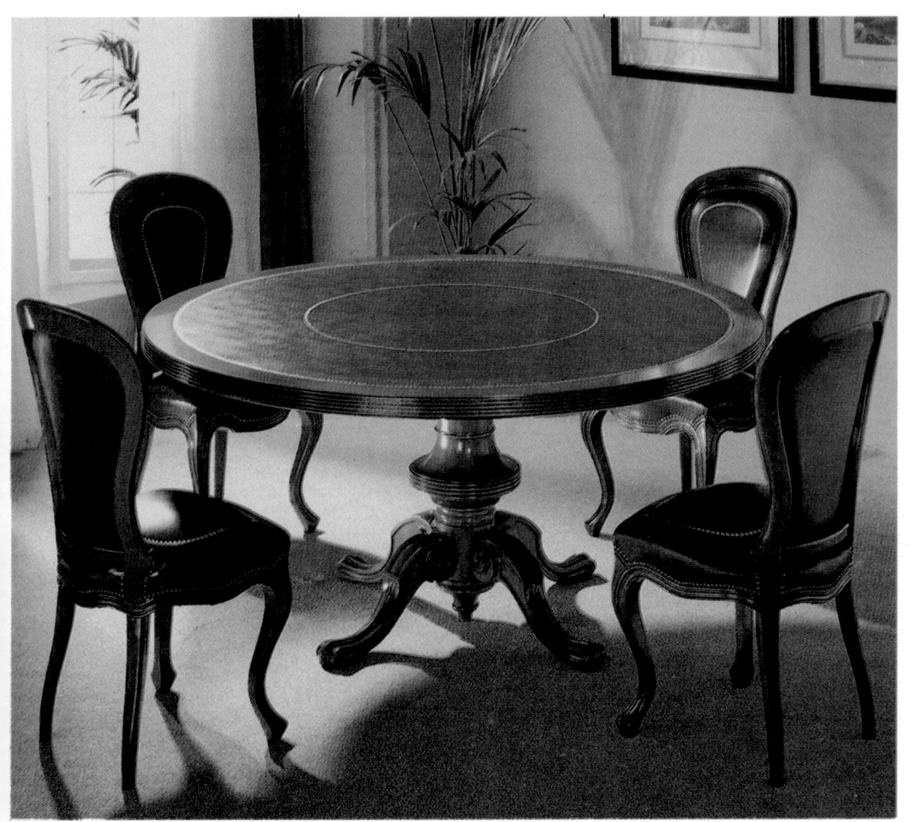

3

common to the Directoire with few links to the classical world (Etruscan classicism), such as swans and dragons.

The pieces in this second movement have solid framing materials and are cubic, with simple forms. In a third period, Isabelline style will prefer a revival of the models of the Louis: the cabriole leg will again gain great force, as will the long curve and the generously proportioned frame.

me étrusque) comme les cygnes et les dragons.

Les pièces de la seconde étape son caractérisées par leur aspect massif, cubique et de profiles simples. Durant la troisième période le style Isabelle II revient vers la répétition des modèles des différents Louis, ce qui entraîne le retour en force de la patte cabriolée, de grandes courbes, de généreuses structures ventrues.

die am wenigsten mit der klassischen Welt (Etruskischer Klassizismus) verknüpft waren, wie z. B. Schwäne und Drachen.

Die Stücke dieses zweiten Zeitabschnittes sind massiv, kubisch und haben einfache Formen.

In einer dritten Periode mündet der isabelinische Stil in eine Wiederbelebung der Modelle der Louis-Stilrichtungen und plötzlich tauchen Tisch– und Stuhlbeine im Cabriolé-Stil, großzügig geschwungene Linien und ausgeprägte Wölbungen auf.

1

1.

Isabelline model office in birch wood (Muebles Pérez Banau).

Bureau modèle Isabelle II réalisé en hêtre (Muebles Pérez Binau).

Arbeitszimmer aus Buche, isabelinisches Modell (Muebles Pérez Benau).

2 - 3.

Drawing of chair legs that show different styles, as is characteristic of the Isabelline piece.

Dessin de pattes de chaise qui conjuguent différents styles, si caractéristiques du meuble Isabelle II.

Zeichnung von Tischbeinen, die verschiedene Stile vereinen, charakterstisch für das isabelinische Möbel.

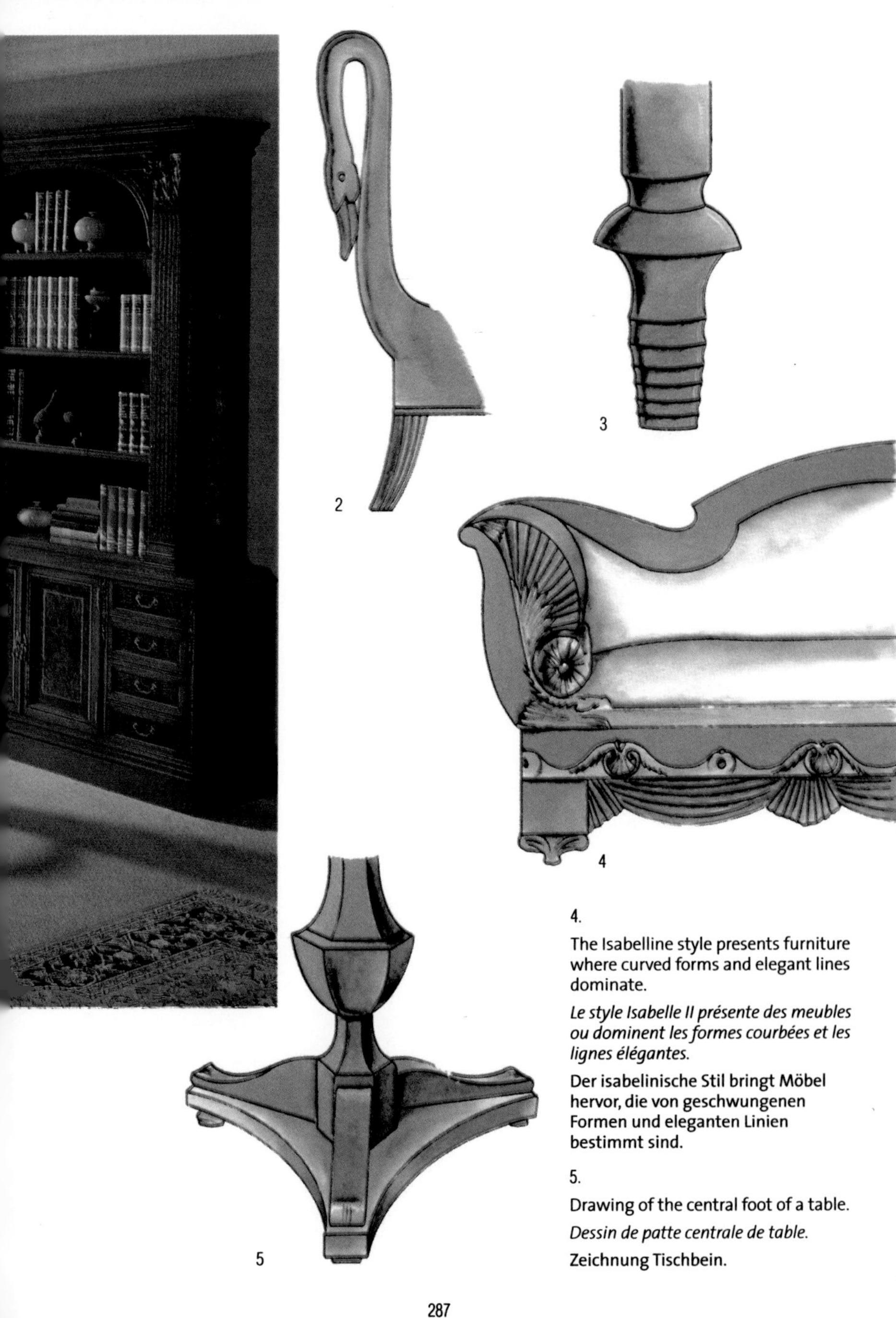

4.

The Isabelline style presents furniture where curved forms and elegant lines dominate.

Le style Isabelle II présente des meubles ou dominent les formes courbées et les lignes élégantes.

Der isabelinische Stil bringt Möbel hervor, die von geschwungenen Formen und eleganten Linien bestimmt sind.

5.

Drawing of the central foot of a table.

Dessin de patte centrale de table.

Zeichnung Tischbein.

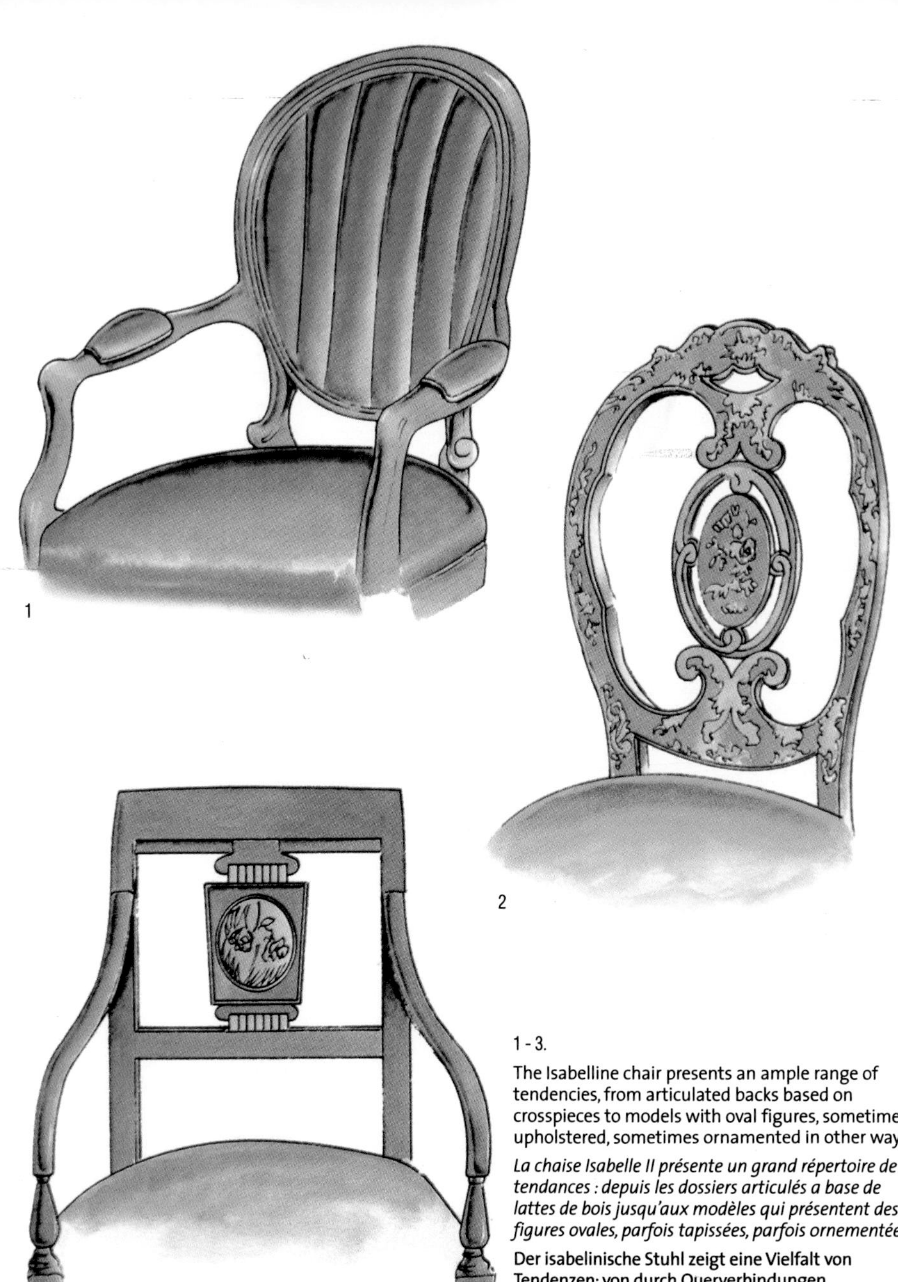
1
2
3

1 - 3.

The Isabelline chair presents an ample range of tendencies, from articulated backs based on crosspieces to models with oval figures, sometimes upholstered, sometimes ornamented in other ways.

La chaise Isabelle II présente un grand répertoire de tendances : depuis les dossiers articulés a base de lattes de bois jusqu'aux modèles qui présentent des figures ovales, parfois tapissées, parfois ornementées.

Der isabelinische Stuhl zeigt eine Vielfalt von Tendenzen: von durch Querverbindungen gegliederten Rückenlehnen bis hin zu ovalförmigen Modellen, manchmal gepolstert, manchmal verziert.

4

5

4.

Armchair in walnut veneer (Artes Moble).

Fauteuil en plaque de noyer (Artes Moble).

Sessel, nußbaumfurniert. (Artes Moble).

5.

Armchair in walnut veneer (Artes Moble).

Fauteuil en plaque de noyer (Artes Moble).

Sessel, nußbaumfurniert. (Artes Moble).

6.

Armchair in walnut veneer (Artes Moble).

Fauteuil en plaque de noyer (Artes Moble).

Sessel, nußbaumfurniert. (Artes Moble).

6

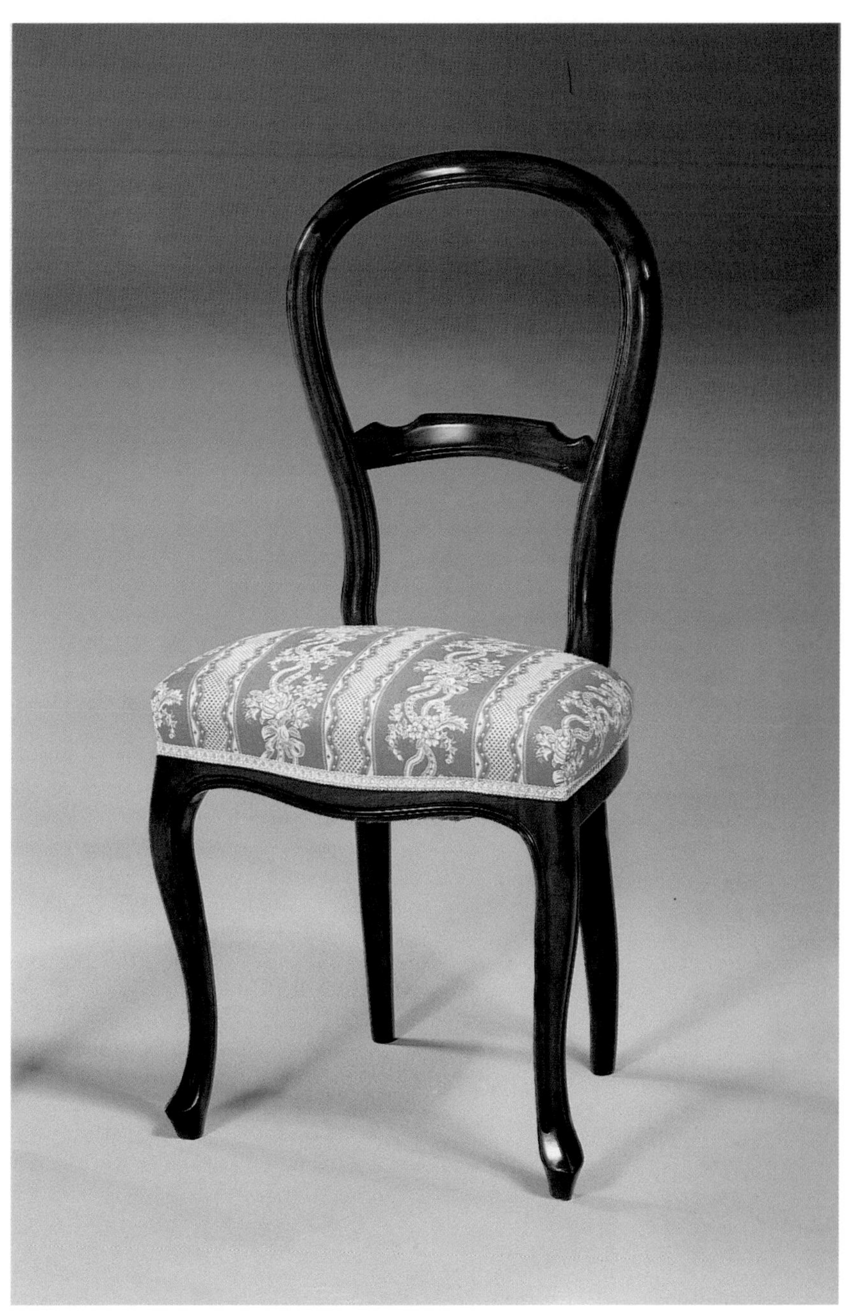

p. 290.

Isabelline armchair (Zamorano).

Fauteuil Isabelle II (Zamorano).

Isabelinischer Sessel (Zamorano).

p. 291.

Isabelline armchair (Zamorano).

Chaise Isabelle II (Zamorano).

Isabelinischer Stuhl (Zamorano).

1.

Isabelline bedroom (Zamorano).

Chambre à coucher Isabelle II (Zamorano).

Isabelinisches Schlafzimmer (Zamoraπno).

Eclecticism

Biedermeier style

L'Éclectisme

Le style Biedermeir

Eklektizismus

Biedermeier

The Biedermeier style arose in Vienna, although it's headquarters is often given as Germany since it was in the latter country that it took root and came to have a special relevance.

The Beidermeier style began around 1830, a phenomenon eminently of the prosperous middle class and of English influence that would purge the decorative excesses of the French Empire style.

Furniture in this new style would stand out for their solidity and their simple lines with generous padding-as well as their quest for domestic comfort.

Ce style surgit à Vienne, bien que certains attribuent ses origines en Allemagne puisque c'est là qu'il prit racine et acquit un prestige spéciale.

Le style Biedermeier date d'à peut près de 1830 et consiste en un style particulièrement bourgeois, d'influence anglais et où l'on dépure les excès décoratifs de l'Empire français.

Les meubles de style Biedermeier sont réputés par leur solidité et formes douces centrées en lignes rectangulaires, ainsi que par la recherche du confort domestique

Dieser Stil stammt aus Wien, obwohl man ihn oft Deutschland zuschreibt, da er dort heimisch wurde und eine besondere Bedeutung erlangte.

Der Biedermeierstil begann um 1830 und war ein außerordentlich spießbürgerlicher Stil. Er war durch englische Einflüsse geprägt und gab die übertriebenen Verzierungen des französischen Empire auf.

Die Biedermeier-Möbel stechen durch ihre Gediegenheit und ihre abgeschwächten rechteckigen Formen hervor und sollten häusliche Gemütlichkeit schaffen.

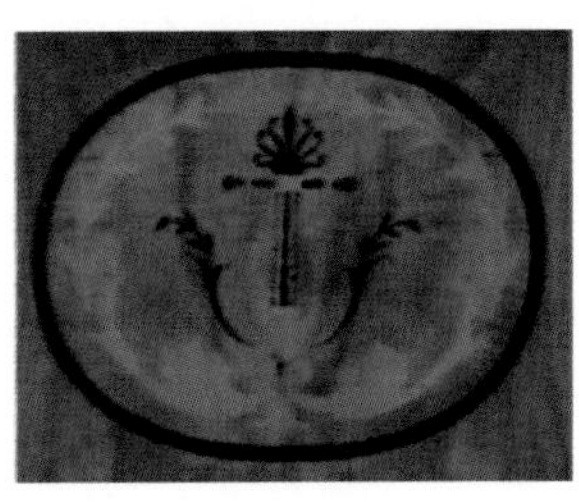

1.
Elche cupboard in cherry (Villa Garmelo).
Buffet Elche en cerisier (Villa Garmelo).
Anrichte Elche aus Kirschbaum (Villa Garmelo).

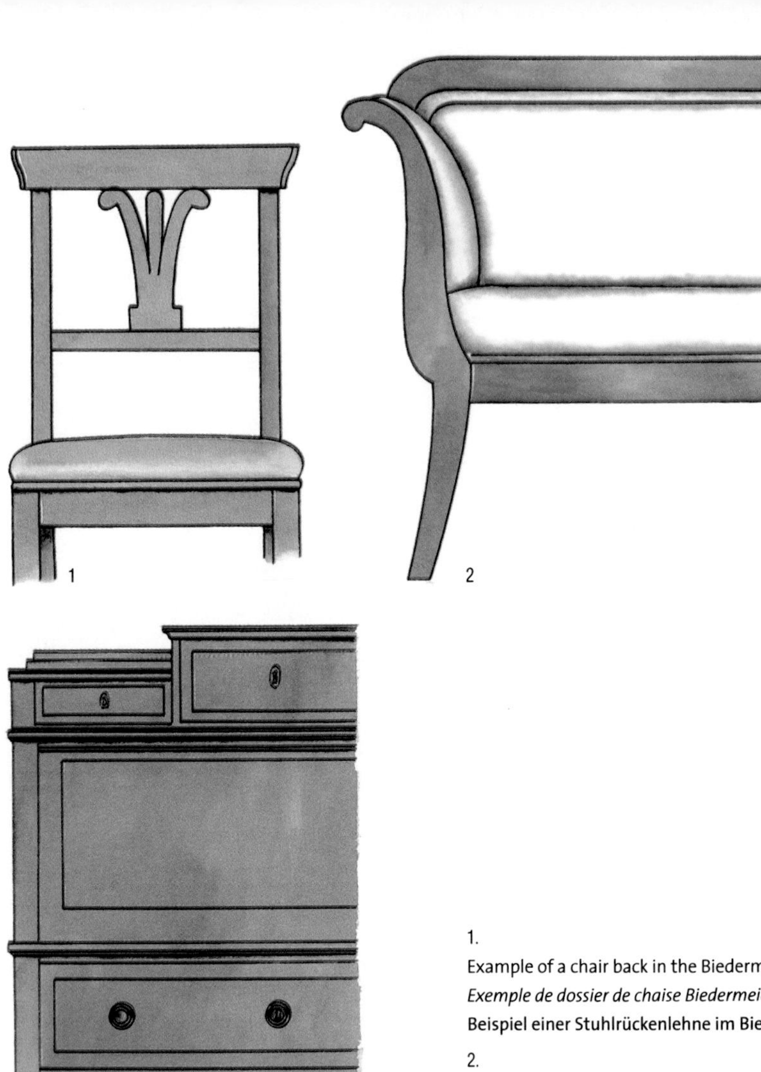

1.

Example of a chair back in the Biedermeier style.

Exemple de dossier de chaise Biedermeier.

Beispiel einer Stuhlrückenlehne im Biedermeierstil.

2.

Armchair with upholstered seat and back.

Fauteuil avec siège et dossier tapissés.

Sessel mit gepolsterter Sitzfläche und Rückenlehne.

3.

Biedermeier style: the straight line continues to dominate.

Meuble style Biedermeier où l'on peut démontrer que la ligne droite est toujours la figure prédominante.

Möbel im Biedermeierstil. Man sieht, daß die gerade Linie weiterhin vorherrschend ist.

4.

Table group in the Biedermeier style. The base is carved and the top is in walnut. The two chairs are in the same style, with upholstered seats and backs and filleted marquetry (Enegro-Mayfer y Mayfer-Tex).

Ensemble de table style Biedermeier avec base taillée et couvercle en noyer et deux chaises du même style avec sièges tapissés et dossier rainuré en marqueterie (Enebro-Mayfer e Mayfer-Tex).

Tischgruppe im Biedermeierstil mit geschnitztem Fuß und Platte aus Nußbaum und zwei Stühlen im gleichen Stil mit gepolsterter Sitzfläche und Rückenlehne mit Intarsien (Enebro-Mayfer e Mayfer Tex).

1.

Cologne cabinet in mahogany inspired on the Biedermeier style (Fidel Bautista-Época).

Table basse Köln réalisé en acajou, d'inspiration style Biedermeier (Fidel Bautista-Época).

Canterano Köln aus Mahagoni, inspiriert vom Biedermeierstil (Fidel Bautista-Época).

)resden writing desk in walnut
nspired on the Biedermeier style
Fidel Bautista-Época).

Écritoire Dresden realisé en noyer, d'inspiration style Biedermeier (Fidel Bautista-Época).

Schreibtisch Dresden aus Nußbaum, inspiriert vom Biedermeierstil (Fidel Bautista-Época).

1

2

3

1.

Chair in birch with fan-shaped back (Jacinto Usán).

Chaise en hêtre avec dossier en éventail (Jacinto Usán).

Stuhl aus Buche mit Rückenlehne in Fächerform (Jacinto Usán).

2.

Chair in birch with rectangular back (Jacinto Usán).

Chaise en hêtre avec dossier rectangulaire (Jacinto Usán).

Stuhl aus Buche mit rechteckiger Rückenlehne (Jacint Usán).

3.

Debra model display table in mahogany (Fidel Bautista-Época).

Table vitrine modèle Debra en acajou (Fidel Bautista-Época).

Tisch-Vitrine Modell Debra aus Mahagoni (Fidel Bautista-Época).

p. 300.

Writing desk in the Biedermeier style in cherry, walnut veneer, and different types of inlaid work (Fidel Bautista-Época).

Secrétaire style Biedermeier en bois de cerisier, plaque de noyer, marqueterie et incrustations.

Sekretär im Biedermeierstil, aus Kirschbaum, nußbaumfurniert, Intarsien und eingelegte Verzierungen.

p. 301.

Pigeonhole desk

Bureau casier.

Bureau-Fächerschrank.

5

4.

Chair and armchair in birch with lotus flower back. Reproduction of a model made around 1820 (Jacinto Usán).

Chaise et fauteuil en hêtre avec dossier en fleur de lys. Reproduction d'un modèle de 1820 (Jacinto Usán).

Stuhl und Sessel aus Buche in Form einer Lotusblüte. Reproduktion eines Modelles von ca. 1820 (Jacinto Usán).

5.

Biedermeier style chair (Geka).

Chaise style Biedermeier (Geka).

Stuhl im Biedermeier-Stil (Geka).

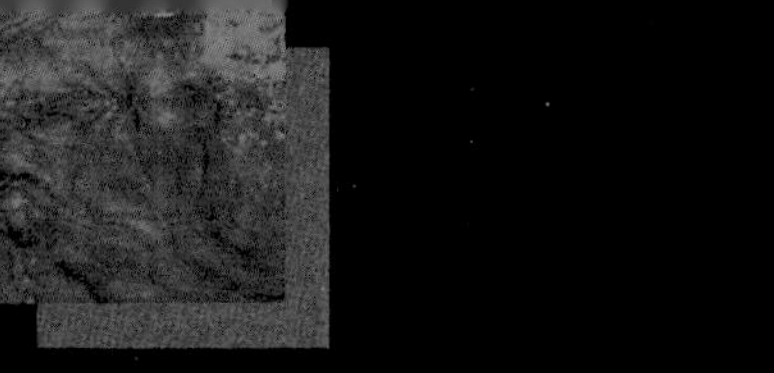

Types of wood

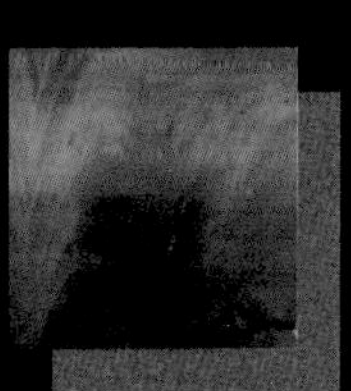
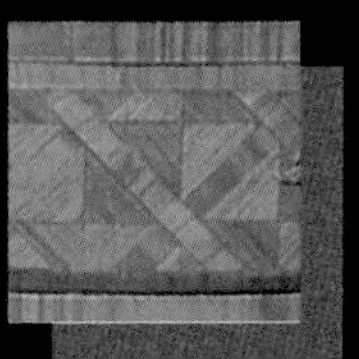
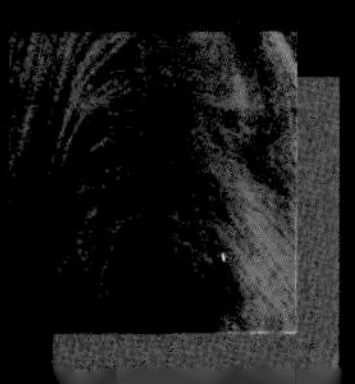

Différents types de bois

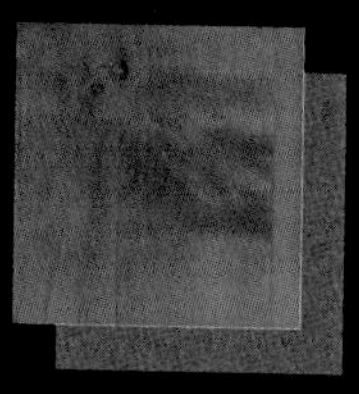

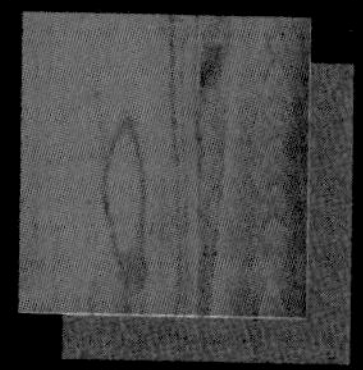

Holzarten

Wood is and has always been the basic material used in the making of furniture, something which comprises objects of daily use in our lives. There are many varieties of wood, although not all trees produce a material with the essential characteristics needed for woodworking and cabinetry. Here, we offer a selection that includes the woods that are used in furniture-making. Included is a list of the natural features of the wood, color, texture, and so on, and of the most frequent applications of the different types.

Le bois a été et est toujours le matériel fondamentale dans la réalisation d'un meuble, objet d'usage quotidien. Mais il est vrai que si la Nature nous offre une grande quantité de variétés, tous les arbres ne produisent pas un matériel aux caractéristiques essentielles pour pouvoir être travaillé dans l'art de l'ébénisterie. Nous offrons à continuation une sélection des bois les plus utilisés dans le monde du meuble, avec ses caractéristiques naturelles –couleur, texture, etc...– et ses applications les plus fréquentes.

Das Holz war und ist das wichtigste Material bei der Herstellung von Möbeln, die Gegenstände des täglichen Lebens sind. Nun, die Natur bietet uns viele Holzarten, wenn auch nicht jeder Baum ein Holz hervorbringt, das die notwendigen Eigenschaften besitzt, um in der Kunsttischlerei verwendet zu werden. Das folgende Kapitel enthält eine Auswahl jener Holzarten, die in der Möbelherstellung am meisten verwendet werden, und eine Beschreibung ihrer natürlichen Besonderheiten – Farbe, Textur, usw. – so wie die häufigsten Verwendungen.

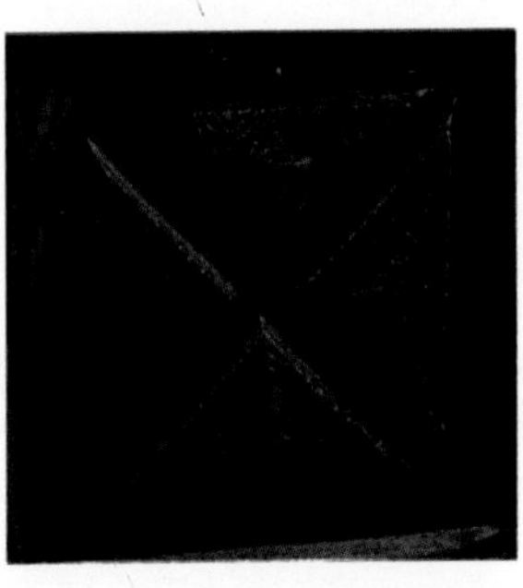

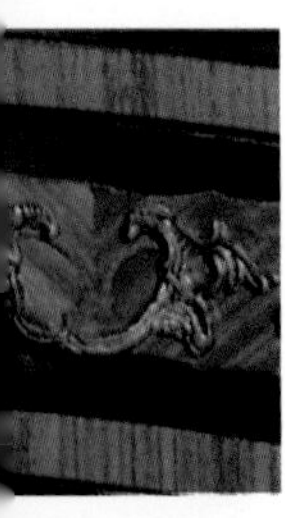
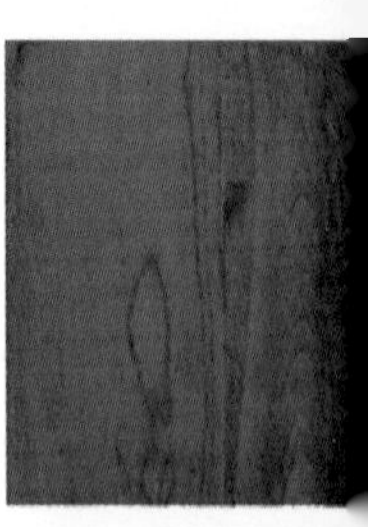

BIRCH. The tree thrives in the northern hemisphere and is very important in Canada, especially yellow birch. In the expansive woodlands of northern Europe, and in Asia, birch trees are also important. The sapwood has lustrous surfaces, a fine texture, and a rich white color. The duramen, or heartwood, has shades of reddish ivory or brownish yellow. It works well and has an excellent finish. Birch, unlike white oak, is not water-resistant. It is usually used more in plywoods than in solid pieces. At present, birch is used in house construction, in concealed frames in cabinetmaking, in parquet flooring, and in curved furniture pieces. The pulp is important in the manufacture of writing paper.

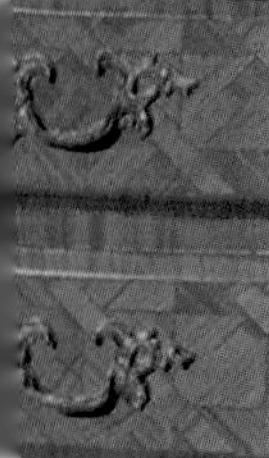

ACACIA CAVEN: *L'acacia caven provient du sud de Floride et d'îles de l'Inde occidentale, existant toutefois d'autres espèces moins intéressante en Afrique. L'acacia caven a un bois d'une couleur jaune doré ; la texture est fine et uniforme, avec un grain ondulé qui produit un dessin moucheté à l'aspect brillant et satiné. L'acacia caven sèche bien, il est assez dur mais se taille bien. Il était très utilisé au XVIII ème siècle par Adam, Sheraton et Hepplewhite dans la fabrication de meubles de luxe, bien qu'actuellement il soit peu fréquent. Sa plaque est utilisée en marqueterie et pour les incrustations, et massif, ce bois sert à la fabrication de petits objets travaillés et occasionnellement pour décorer les brosses et miroirs de boudoirs et autres ustensiles domestiques.*

ACAJOU: *L'acajou authentique, celui des meubles des années 1700, de Chippendale, Adam, etc... appartient à une vaste région qui s'étend depuis le*

AMARANT. Das Amarantholz stammt aus dem nördlichen Südamerika, vor allem aus Brasilien und Guayana. Kurz nach dem Schneiden ist das Holz bräunlich-gelb, aber sobald es mit Luft in Kontakt kommt, nimmt es ein glänzendes Purpurrot an und ist daher eines der farbschönsten kommerziellen Hölzer. Nach einer gewissen Zeit verwandelt sich das Purpur in einen ebenso schönen bräunlich-rötlichen Farbton. Die Faserung variiert je nach Spezie, von fein bis hin zu einer leicht groben Faserung. Das Amarantholz ist schwer und je nach Spezie hart, widerstandsfähig, zäh oder elastisch. Es trocknet schnell und behält dabei seinen Farbton; ist das Holz trocken, ist es auch haltbar. Es ist schwer zu schneiden und zu lackieren. Trotz seiner schönen Farbe verwendet man das Amarantholz selten zu dekorativen Zwecken, sondern verarbeitet es fast immer zu kleinen gedrechselten Gegenständen, wie Enden von Queues oder Platten für Einlegearbeiten. Die häufigste Verwendung findet das Amarantholz im Baugewerbe, bei der Konstruktion von

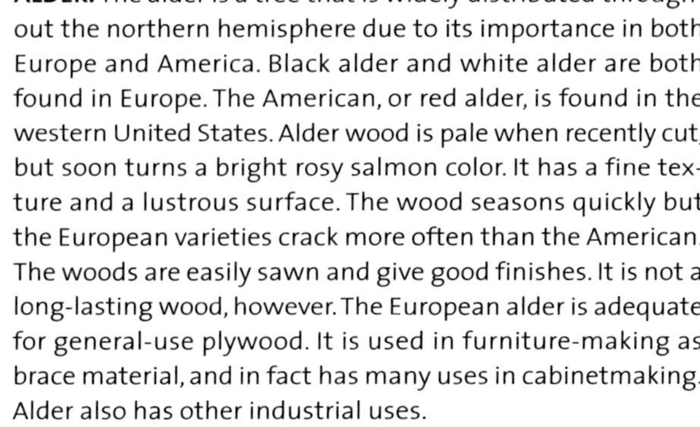

ALDER. The alder is a tree that is widely distributed throughout the northern hemisphere due to its importance in both Europe and America. Black alder and white alder are both found in Europe. The American, or red alder, is found in the western United States. Alder wood is pale when recently cut, but soon turns a bright rosy salmon color. It has a fine texture and a lustrous surface. The wood seasons quickly but the European varieties crack more often than the American. The woods are easily sawn and give good finishes. It is not a long-lasting wood, however. The European alder is adequate for general-use plywood. It is used in furniture-making as brace material, and in fact has many uses in cabinetmaking. Alder also has other industrial uses.

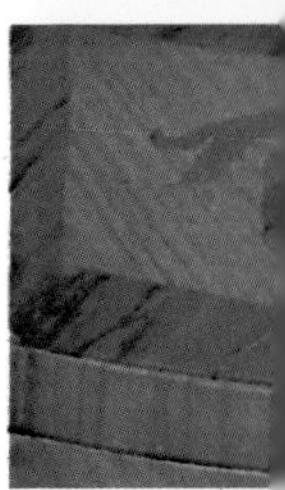

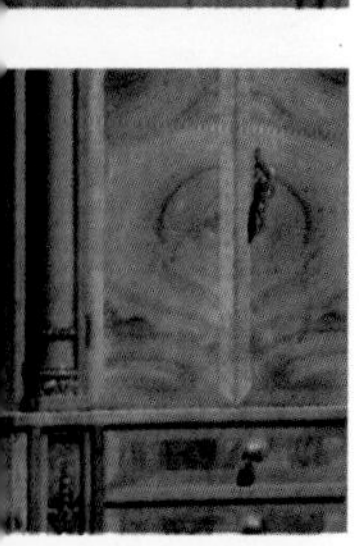

Mexique jusqu'au Honduras, comprenant aussi toutes les îles des Caraïbes, surtout l'acajou originaire du Venezuela. L'acajou américain est un produit importé en Europe par les Espagnoles depuis le XVI ème siècle depuis leurs colonies, mais son utilisation définitive comme bois principal dans la fabrication de meubles, grâce au coup de pouce donné par les ébéniste s comme Chippendale, Hepplewhite et Sheraton n'a pas lieu avant le XVIII ème siècle. Actuellement, il n'y a qu'une petite quantité d'acajou provenant de Cuba et c'est pour cela que maintenant la plupart des bois américains sont connus par leur pays d'origine comme le Brésil, le Pérou, le Venezuela, etc... L'acajou est de couleur rose clair bien qu'il devient plus foncé avec le temps, pouvant atteindre un ton rougeâtre variant entre moyen et très foncé. L'acajou de camomille de Cuba, est lourd et pesant, pendant que celui qui appartient au continent est plus léger et clair. C'est un bois généralement dur et compact, de grain fin et pressé, presque sans pores, et au longues veines.

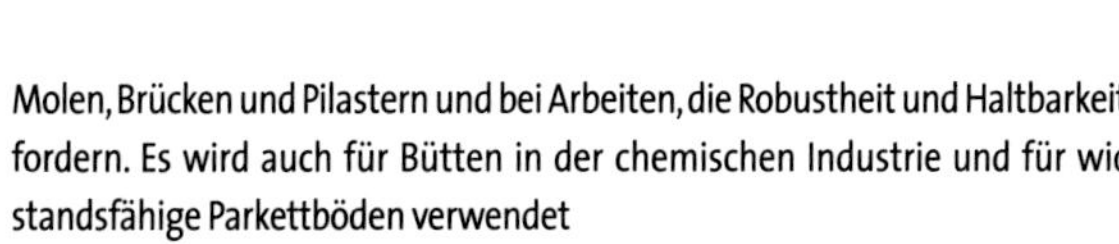

Molen, Brücken und Pilastern und bei Arbeiten, die Robustheit und Haltbarkeit erfordern. Es wird auch für Bütten in der chemischen Industrie und für widerstandsfähige Parkettböden verwendet

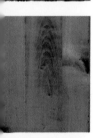

BIRKE. Die Birke ist in der nördlichen Hemisphäre zu finden, mit großer Häufigkeit in Kanada – vor allem die Gelbbirke -, auf den Ebenen Nordeuropas, vor allem auf Waldlichtungen, und in Nordasien. Das Birkenholz hat eine glänzende Oberfläche, eine feine perlweiße Faserung und ein weiß-rosa-elfenbeinfarbenes Kernholz oder ist gelb mit bräunlichem Kernholz. Es ist leicht zu bearbeiten und die Nachbearbeitung bietet keine Schwierigkeiten. Gleichzeitig liefert es bei rotierendem Abblättern hervorragendes Furnier. Unter Bedingungen, die die Fäulnis begünstigen, ist dieses Holz nicht beständig. Gewöhnlich wird es mehr als Furnierholz und nicht als Massivholz verwendet. Heutzutage wird es im Bauwesen, in Form ver-

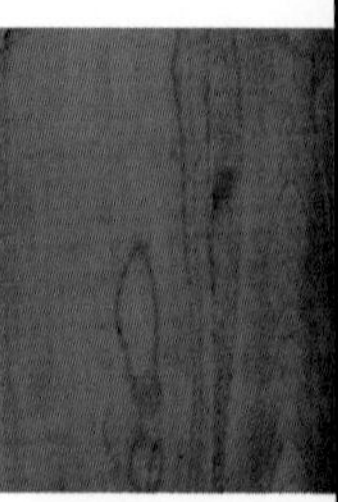

BOX. This wood comes from a number of different trees. It is hardwood, with a very fine and uniform texture and a pale yellowish color. One European species, found in some parts of Britain and of Spain, is widely distributed also in other parts of Southern Europe such as Turkey and Iran. There also exist other species in Asia and South Africa. Box is one of the commercial woods with the finest textures. The grain is fine, tight, and at times irregular. Because of its hardness, even when seasoned it hardly floats in water. Box must in fact be carefully dried because of its tendency to split. Once seasoned, however, it has excellent woodworking qualities. It works well, almost like ivory, in panels, when turned on a lathe, or carved. It is thus possible to decorate the wood in detail. Boxwood has a long history and was used in ancient

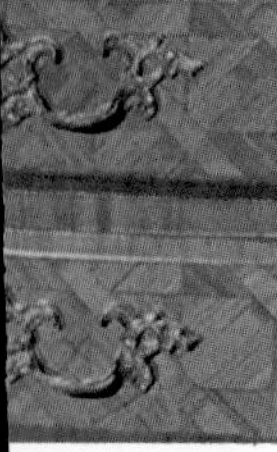

L'acajou américain sèche facilement, stable et facile à scier, polir et vernir, on obtient en conséquence une parfaite finition. L'acajou est un bois très utile dans le travail d'ébénisterie de grande qualité, les meubles de luxe, pour faire des reproductions, ainsi que pour les revêtements. À partir du XIX ème siècle, l'acajou africain est commercialisé afin de complémenter l'apport du véritable acajou américain. Cette variété, de couleur allant du rose pale au rougeâtre, est légère, maniable, permet aussi de bonnes finitions malgré son manque de résistance aux attaques de champignons d'humidité.

AMARANTE: *Le bois d'amarante provient de la zone septentrionale d'Amérique du Sud, spécialement du Brésil et de la Guyane. Coupé récemment ce bois a une couleur jaune grisâtre, mais devient d'un pourpre brillant au contacte de l'air, et est de ce fait apprécié par sa couleur. Au bout d'un certain temps, sa couleur propre s'éteint et il devient d'un ton marron rougeâ-*

steckter Stützelemente im Kunsttischlergewerbe, für Parkett und für Möbel aus gebogenem Holz verwendet. Sein Zellstoff ist im Bereich der Schreibpapierherstellung wichtig.

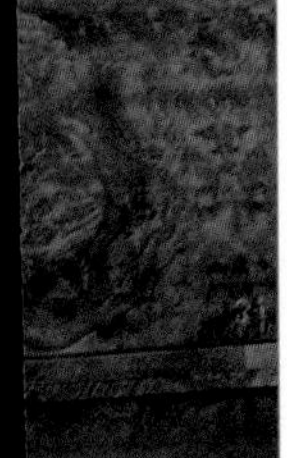

BOIS DE ROI. Der Bois de Roi ist ein in Brasilien und Europa beheimateter, violettfarbener Baum mit schwarzen, harten Fasern. Er ist sehr widerstandsfähig, gut schneidbar und neigt dazu, sich zu spalten. Da das Holz ziemlich leicht zu bearbeiten ist, wird es sowohl für Drechslerarbeiten als auch für Furniere verwendet.

BRASILHOLZ. Das Brasilholz stammt aus Amerika, genauer aus Brasilien und von den Antillen. Sein Holz ist rosa-lachsfarben. Es hat ein feines Kernholz und verschlungene Fasern und wird vorzugsweise für Intarsienarbeiten, in der Luxus-Kunsttischlerei und für ausgewählte Stücke in der Drechslerei verwendet.

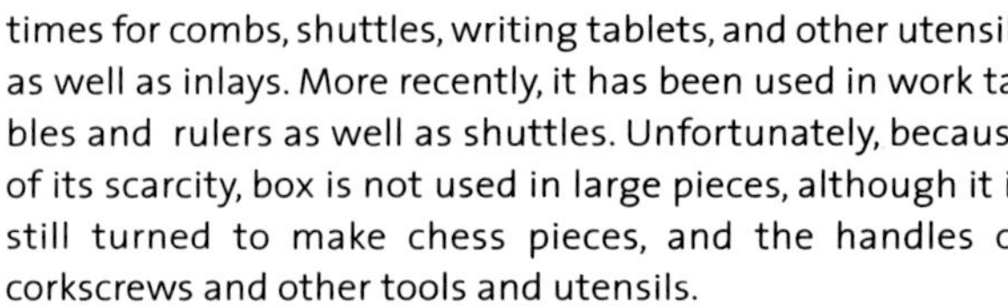

times for combs, shuttles, writing tablets, and other utensils as well as inlays. More recently, it has been used in work tables and rulers as well as shuttles. Unfortunately, because of its scarcity, box is not used in large pieces, although it is still turned to make chess pieces, and the handles of corkscrews and other tools and utensils.

MAHOGANY. Authentic mahogany, one of the woods used by Chippendale, Adam, and many others, is found in the area between Mexico and Honduras as well as all of the Caribbean islands. Venezuela is especially rich in commercial mahogany. American mahogany was imported to Europe from these lands by the Spanish, beginning in the sixteenth century, in colonial times. It was not, however, until the eigh-

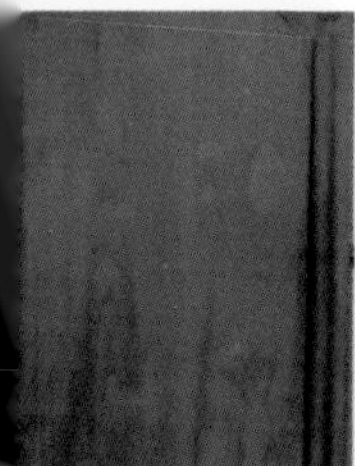
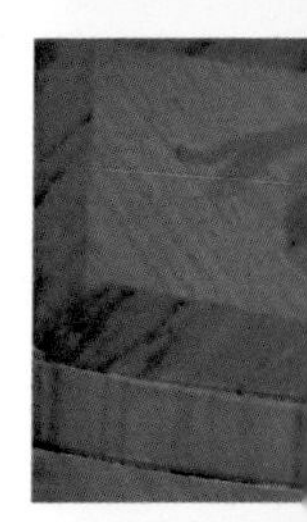

---

tre très beau. Le texture varie selon l'espèce, de fine à modérément épaisse. Le bois d'amarante est plus ou moins lourd selon les espèces,dure, résistante, tenace et élastique. Il sèche facilement, et se détériore difficilement ; un fois séché, il est de longue durabilité. Il est difficile à couper et à vernir. Malgré sa belle couleur, le bois d'amarante n'est utilisé que rarement comme effet décoratif, mais est presque toujours employé dans des petits objets travaillés, comme la pointe des sticks de billard, ou comme le bois de placage pour travaux d'incrustations. Il est plus fréquemment utilisé dans la construction lourde, tels que les quais, les ponts, les piliers et pour les travaux qui recherchent la solidité et la durabilité. Il sert aussi comme fût dans l'industrie chimique et pour former des estrades de grande résistance.

***AUNE:** L'aune est un arbre d'ample distribution dans tout l'hémisphère Nord, et l'importance de son bois va d'Europe aux États-Unis. L'aune noir et le blanc*

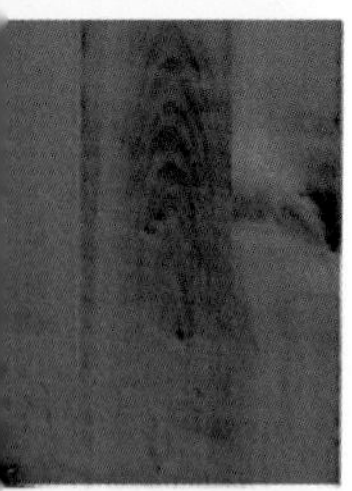

BUCHE. Das Buchenholz wächst in ganz Europa, aber das am meisten geschätzte Holz stammt aus den Bergen Jugoslawiens. Außerdem gibt es qualitativ hochwertige Spezien in den USA, in Japan, Chile und in der Antarktis. Seine weißliche Farbe verwandelt sich schnell in Rosa und sanftes Rot, sobald das Buchenholz unter Dampfeinfluß steht. Es hat relativ leicht erkennbare Jahresringe und vom Kern ausgehende Strahlen, die in der radialen Schnittfläche rechteckige Maserungen und in der tangentialen Schnittfläche braune Flecken ergeben. Typischerweise ist das Kernholz gerade. Es hat eine feine und gleichmäßige Textur und ist mittelschwer, das Gewicht kann jedoch variieren. Das Buchenholz trocknet schnell, aber es verbiegt sich leicht. Ist es einmal getrocknet, verändert es sich unter Feuchtigkeitseinfluß. Es läßt sich leicht nachbearbeiten und drechseln, obwohl es manchmal rissig werden kann. Das Holz wird für die Herstellung von Möbeln und vor allem für gedrechselte Haushaltsgegenstände verwendet, wie z. B.

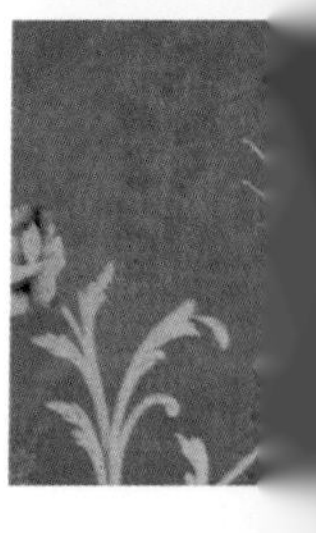

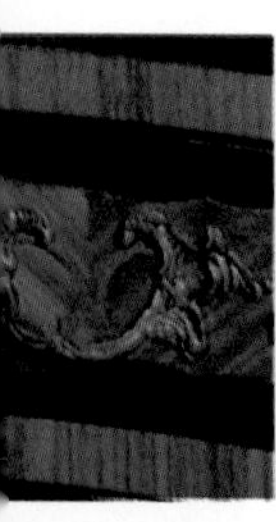
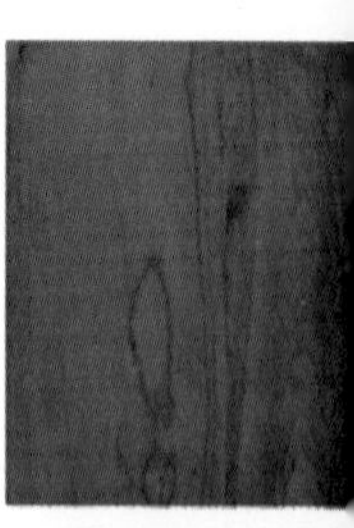

teenth century that mahogany began to be the main wood used in furniture-making, receiving its great impulse from cabinetmakers like Chippendale, Hepplewhite, and Sheraton. In our times, mahogany has become scarce and the wood continues to be classified by its country of provenance, Brazil, Cuba, Peru, Venezuela, etc. The color of mahogany is light red, although it darkens over time. It eventually becomes a reddish brown color, varying between very dark and medium tones. Cuban mahogany is dark and heavy; that from the continent is light in both weight and tone. It is generally hard and compact, with a fine tight grain, almost without pores, with prominent grain. American walnut is easily seasoned. It is stable, easy to saw, polish, and varnish, and thus gives an excellent finish. Mahogany is used in the finest cabinetry for

se trouvent en Europe ; l'aune américain, le rouge, en Amérique centrale. Le bois d'aune coupé récemment est de couleur pâle, mais en peut de temps il devient d'un ton brillant rose saumon. Il a une texture fine et une superficie brillante. Le bois d'aune sèche facilement, mais la variété européenne se rompt plus aisément que l'américaine. Ils se scient facilement et on obtient de meilleures finitions. Il ne dure pas. Le bois d'aune européen est recommandé pour le contreplaqué en général. On l'utilise pour faire des chaises bon marché, en ébénisterie commune et dans la petite industrie, pour l'envers des brosses, manches de balais, manches d'outils, jouets, etc...C'est un bois traditionnellement utilisé dans la construction de bras artificiels et roulements de l'industrie textile et la fabrication de charbon pour faire de la poudre.

BILINGA: *Il pousse en Afrique et aux Philippines, de couleur jaune clair, son bois est dur, compacte, avec un pore très serré. Il est facile à tra-*

Küchengerätschaften, Werkzeuggriffe und Bürsten. Es dient der Herstellung von beständigen Parkettböden im Hausbau.

BUCHSBAUM. Den Namen dieses blaßgelben Holzes, das von feiner gleichmäßiger Textur ist, tragen mehrere schwergewichtige Holzarten. Die europäische Spezie, die in einigen Gebieten Großbritanniens und Spaniens anzutreffen ist, ist im nördlichen Teil Europas sehr verbreitet; sogar in der Türkei und im Iran findet man Exemplare dieser Spezie. Außerdem existieren andere Spezien in Asien und in Südafrika. Das Holz ist einheitlich gemsfarben-gelb und gehört zu den kommerziellen Holzarten feinster Textur. Die Maserung ist fein, fest und manchmal unregelmäßig. Das Holz ist schwer und schwimmt auch nach dem Trocknen schwerlich im Wassser. Das Buchsbaumholz muß mit Vorsicht getrocknet werden, da es leicht rissig wird. Wenn es jedoch einmal trocken ist, hat es hervorragende Vorteile. Es

deluxe furniture, for reproductions, and for veneers. In addition to American mahogany, a variety began to be commercialized in the nineteenth century in Africa. This was for the purpose of complementing the shipments of the original American mahoganies. The African variety, a pale pink color, varying to reddish brown, is light, manageable, and also provides a good finish. It is, however, little resistant to fungal attacks.

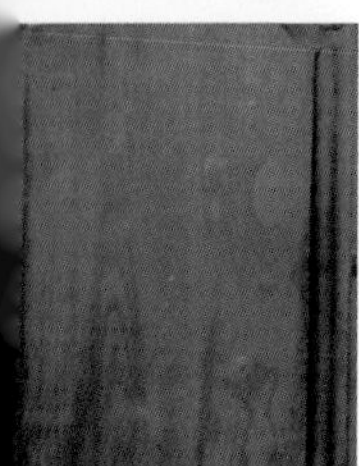

CHESTNUT. This wood grows especially well in deep earths rich in organic materials and with a minimum of clays. It is originally from the Eastern Mediterranean, but can also be found in Switzerland, Germany, and even in the south of England. It is light brown in color, with very visible growth rings,

---

vailler et à polir et on l'utilise spécialement pour faire des plaques et des revêtement.

BOIS DE ROI: *Le bois de roi est un arbre du Brésil et D'Europe, de couleur violette et avec des veines noires d'aspect dur. Il est très résistant mais a tendance à s'ouvrir ce qui provoque l'apparition d'échardes. Comme il est assez facile à travailler, on l'emploie pour faire des pièces confectionnées et des contreplaqués.*

BOIS DE ROSE: *Il provient d'Amérique du Sud, spécialement du Brésil et du Pérou. Il présente une couleur jaune blanchâtre et des veines fines et longues de couleur rose violacées. C'est un bois facile à travailler, qui permet une finition, un vernissage et se polie parfaitement. On l'utilise dans l'ébénisterie, l'artisanat et l'incrustation.*

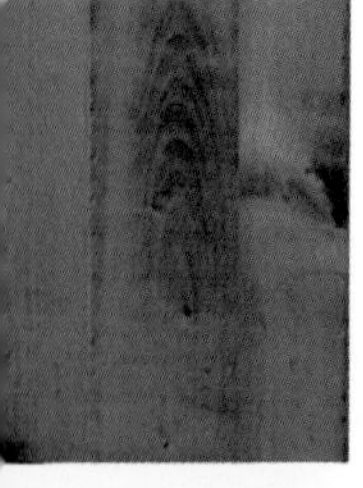

ist dann leicht wie Elfenbein zu verarbeiten, es ist für Schnitzereien, Drechslerarbeiten und Stiche geeignet und erlaubt ein großes Maß an Feinarbeit. Das Buchsbaumholz blickt auf eine lange Geschichte zurück. Früher verwendete man es zur Herstellung von Kämmen, Spinnmaschinen, Schreibtafeln, anderen Gebrauchsgegenständen und ebenso für Intarsienarbeiten. Später wurde das Holz zur Herstellung von Arbeitsblöcken, Linealen und Webstühlen verwendet. Wegen der Knappheit des Buchsbaumholzes wird es für das Drechseln kleiner Gegenstände, wie Schachfiguren, Korkenzieher, und vereinzelt für Werkzeuggriffe eingesetzt. Das amerikanische Mahagoniholz trocknet leicht, ist stabil, leicht zu sägen, polieren und lackieren und eignet sich dadurch perfekt zur Nachbearbeitung. Das amerikanische Mahagoniholz wurde seit dem 16. Jh. von den Spaniern aus ihren Kolonien nach Europa importiert, aber erst ab dem 18. Jh. wurde es dank des starken Einflusses von Kunsttischlern wie Chippendale, Hepplewhite und Sheraton zum wichtigsten Holz in der Möbelherstellung. Das Holz ist braun-rosafarben, obwohl

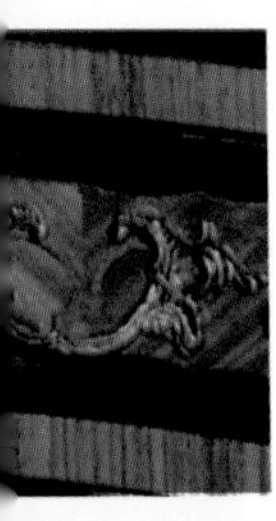
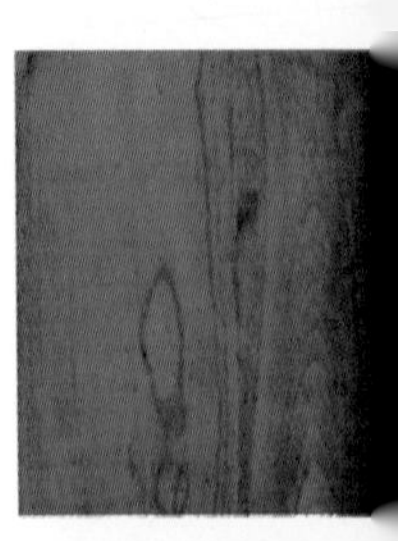

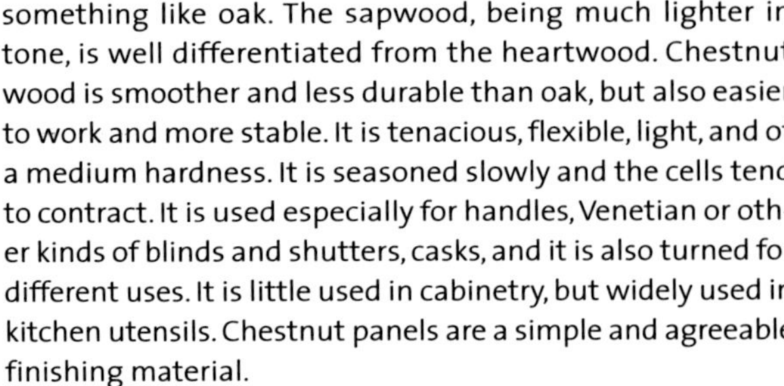

something like oak. The sapwood, being much lighter in tone, is well differentiated from the heartwood. Chestnut wood is smoother and less durable than oak, but also easier to work and more stable. It is tenacious, flexible, light, and of a medium hardness. It is seasoned slowly and the cells tend to contract. It is used especially for handles, Venetian or other kinds of blinds and shutters, casks, and it is also turned for different uses. It is little used in cabinetry, but widely used in kitchen utensils. Chestnut panels are a simple and agreeable finishing material.

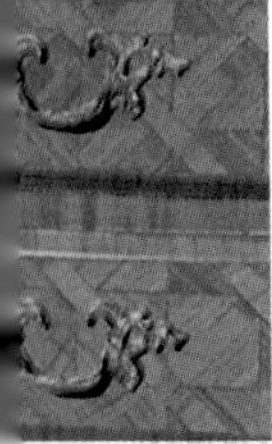

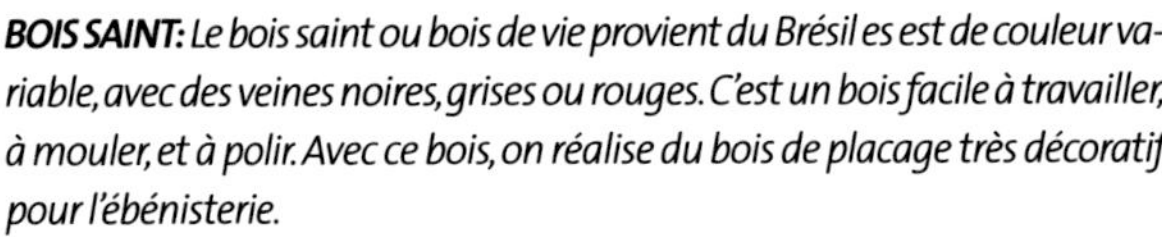

CEDAR. The name of cedar is given to different woods with an agreeable aroma from Central and South America, Europe, and the Middle East (Lebanon), as well as Africa (Alge-

---

BOIS SAINT: *Le bois saint ou bois de vie provient du Brésil es est de couleur variable, avec des veines noires, grises ou rouges. C'est un bois facile à travailler, à mouler, et à polir. Avec ce bois, on réalise du bois de placage très décoratif pour l'ébénisterie.*

BOULEAU: *C'est un arbre de l'hémisphère Nord, très important au Canada –spécialement le bouleau jaune-, dans les plaines de l'Europe septentrionale, surtout dans les clairs de forêts et en Asie boréale. Le bois de bouleau a une superficie brillante , une texture fine, de couleur blanchâtre et noyau blanc ivoire rosé, ou jaune et noyau grisâtre. Il est très facile à travailler et ne présente aucune difficulté dans la finition. Il s'exfolie par rotation donnant ainsi d'excellentes lamelles. Dans des conditions de putréfaction, il ne tient pas longtemps. Il est conseillé de l'utiliser comme bois contreplaqué plutôt que comme bois massif. Actuellement on l'utilise dans la construction d'im-*

es mit der Zeit dunkler wird und einen mahagoni-roten Farbton annimmt. Das Holz ist fein gemasert und hat dunkelbraune Öffnungen einher. Es ist ein empfindliches Holz, das gut getrocknet werden muß, da es leicht verbiegt. Es neigt zur Wurmstichigkeit und zu Verwitterungen im Freien. Es ist leicht zu sägen und kann sowohl manuell als auch maschinell exzellent verarbeitet werden. Beim Dämpfen wird die Qualität besser. Das Kirschbaumholz ist sehr dekorativ und wird bei der Herstellung von Möbeln, vor allem Stühlen, in der Luxus-Kunsttischlerei, sowie bei der Herstellung von Verkleidungen und Galvanplatten verwendet. Das Mahagoniholz ist hellrosa, aber es wird mit der Zeit dunkler und nimmt einen von halbdunkel bis dunkel rötlich-braunen Farbton an. Das kubanische Mahagoniholz des Manzanillobaums ist dunkel und schwer, während das des Kontinents leichter und heller ist. Normalerweise ist es hart und dicht, von feiner und dichter Textur, fast ohne Poren und hat lange Fasern. Das Mahagoniholz wird in der hochwertigen Kunsttischlerei für Luxusmöbel, Reproduktionen sowie für Holzverschalungen ver-

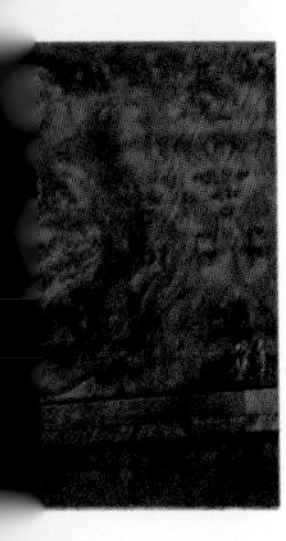

ria). It can be similar in color to mahogany, but it has a grainier texture, weighs less, and is resinous. It cures quickly, is very stable, and is also hard-wearing, able to resist both fungal attacks and termites. Because of its softness it works easily. The decorative aspect of cedar and the qualities mentioned earlier make it a much appreciated wood in furniture upholstery as well as the carving and finishing of luxury pieces. Cedar is also the traditional wood used in cigar boxes and humidors.

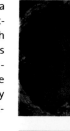

CHERRY. Cherry wood is found mostly in the Northern Hemisphere. North America has at least a dozen species, and a similar number exists in Europe, with perhaps even more in Eastern Asia. The wood of the cherry varies in color, but tends

---

meubles, dans les structures intérieures en ébénisterie, dans les assemblages à tenon et mortaise et dans les meubles courbés. La pulpe est importante dans la fabrication du papier à écrire.

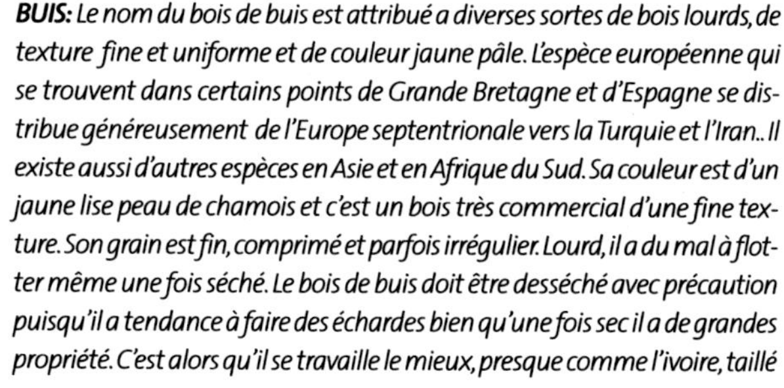

BUIS: *Le nom du bois de buis est attribué a diverses sortes de bois lourds, de texture fine et uniforme et de couleur jaune pâle. L'espèce européenne qui se trouvent dans certains points de Grande Bretagne et d'Espagne se distribue généreusement de l'Europe septentrionale vers la Turquie et l'Iran.. Il existe aussi d'autres espèces en Asie et en Afrique du Sud. Sa couleur est d'un jaune lise peau de chamois et c'est un bois très commercial d'une fine texture. Son grain est fin, comprimé et parfois irrégulier. Lourd, il a du mal à flotter même une fois séché. Le bois de buis doit être desséché avec précaution puisqu'il a tendance à faire des échardes bien qu'une fois sec il a de grandes propriété. C'est alors qu'il se travaille le mieux, presque comme l'ivoire, taillé*

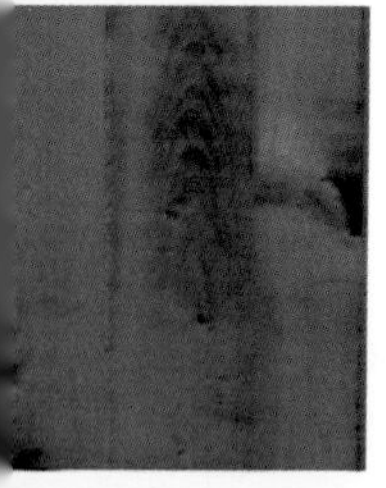

wendet. Neben dem amerikanischen Mahagoniholz kommerzialisierte man ab dem 19. Jh. das afrikanische Mahagoniholz, um den Handel mit echtem Mahagoniholz zu ergänzen. Die Farbe der PECHKIEFER ist gelblich-braun oder rötlichbraun. Sie hat gut sichtbare Jahresringe und stammt aus dem Süden der USA. Es ist die Kiefernart mit der größten Harzbildung, sie trocknet langsam und spaltet sich leicht. Das Holz ist fest, hart, resistent und schwer zu bearbeiten und wird deshalb in der Bauindustrie - also für große und schwere Konstruktionen - verwendet. Heutzutage ist dieses Material sehr selten. Die MONTERREY-KIEFER stammt aus Kalifornien und von der Insel Guadeloupe. Sie wird auch in Neuseeland, Australien, Chile und Südafrika angebaut. Das Kernholz ist braun-rosa. Bei den Jungkiefern ist das Splintholz hell. Es hat eine gleichmäßige Textur, unauffällige Jahresringe und Knorren, die bei der Bearbeitung rissig werden. Es ist nicht beständig. Es wird für die Herstellung von Kisten, Verpackungen, Bürsten und Besen verwendet. Ist die Qualität höher, verwendet man es auch im Möbelbau. Bei der Ab-

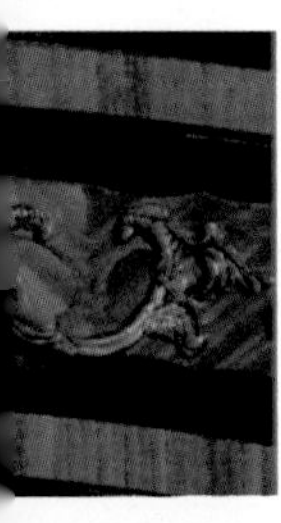
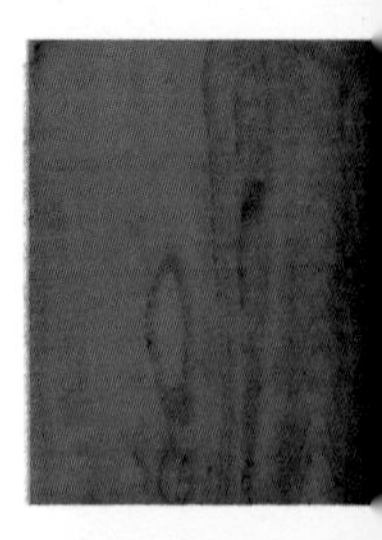

to rosy brown, darkening with time to ressemble mahogany. It is finely grained and pored. The delicate wood must be well seasoned as it tends to warp and is susceptible to woodworm and other alterations. It is easily sawn and can be worked manually or by machine, providing an excellent finished surface. Steaming improves its qualities. Cherry wood is highly decorative and used in furniture-making, above all in chairs. It is also used in deluxe cabinetmaking, in finishes, both solid and veneered.

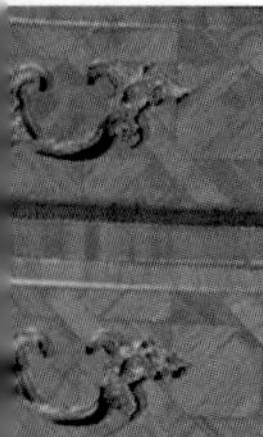

LEMON. The wood of the lemon tree comes from eastern India and from the isle of Sri Lanka. It is yellowish brown with a golden grain, thus providing great beauty in solid form or

---

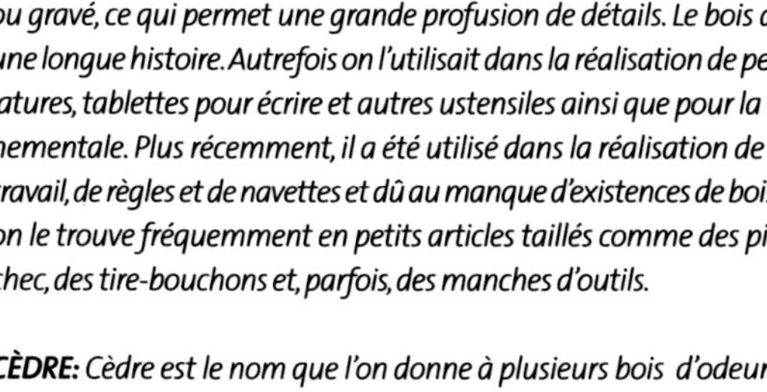

ou gravé, ce qui permet une grande profusion de détails. Le bois de buis a une longue histoire. Autrefois on l'utilisait dans la réalisation de peignes, filatures, tablettes pour écrire et autres ustensiles ainsi que pour la taille ornementale. Plus récemment, il a été utilisé dans la réalisation de blocs de travail, de règles et de navettes et dû au manque d'existences de bois de buis, on le trouve fréquemment en petits articles taillés comme des pièces d'échec, des tire-bouchons et, parfois, des manches d'outils.

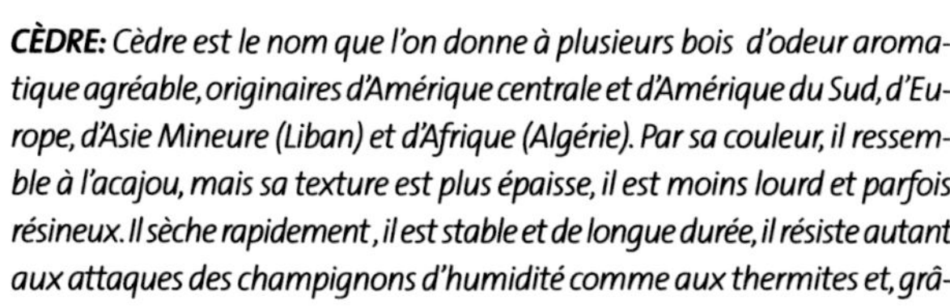

***CÈDRE:** Cèdre est le nom que l'on donne à plusieurs bois d'odeur aromatique agréable, originaires d'Amérique centrale et d'Amérique du Sud, d'Europe, d'Asie Mineure (Liban) et d'Afrique (Algérie). Par sa couleur, il ressemble à l'acajou, mais sa texture est plus épaisse, il est moins lourd et parfois résineux. Il sèche rapidement, il est stable et de longue durée, il résiste autant aux attaques des champignons d'humidité comme aux thermites et, grâ-*

tragung liefert die MONTERREY-KIEFER Furniere. Die WEYMOUTH-KIEFER oder KANADISCHE KIEFER ist ein leichtes und empfindliches Holz. Es ist blaßgelb oder beige und hat einen leichten Rosastich. Seine Textur ist fein und gleichmäßig. Es trocknet problemlos, ist stabil, wenig resistent, leicht zu bearbeiten und liefert exzellente Ergebnisse bei der Nachbearbeitung. In seiner teuersten und hochwertigsten Variante wird es im industriellen Modellbau verwendet und ist für feine Schnitzarbeiten geeignet. Es dient auch der Herstellung von Verkleidungen. Die GEMEINE KIEFER ist die am meisten kommerzialisierte Spezie. Sie wächst in Mitteleuropa und Zentralasien. Sie hat ein rötlich-braunes Kernholz und sehr ausgeprägte Jahresringe. Das Holz trocknet gut und ist stabil. Außerdem erlaubt es eine leichte und gute Verarbeitung sowie eine gute Nachbearbeitung. Es ist anfällig für Fäulnis. Das hochwertigere Holz der GEMEINEN KIEFER wird in der Luxus-Kunsttischlerei und im Möbelbau verwendet, während die einfachere Variante im Baugewerbe genutzt wird. Das Holz ist sehr wichtig für den Zellstoff, aus dem Ver-

in veneers. It is not difficult to carve. It is used in the furniture-making industry and in interior design and finishes.

EBONY. Ebony is found in different locations throughout the world, but black ebony, previously obtained in India and Sri Lanka, now comes from tropical Africa, for the most part. Along with African wenge, it is the darkest wood known, although it also has a dark brown form with black veins and one with gray or brown speckling. The grain is fine and tight, hard-wearing but easily worked. There is some difficulty in varnishing this wood. It is especially used in decoration and elegant interiors, in high-quality furniture, musical instruments, and in turned objects.

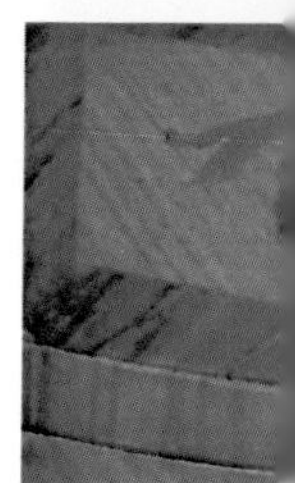

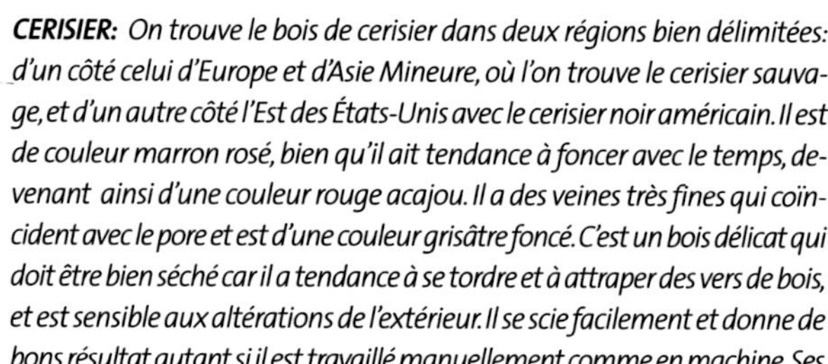

ce à sa mollesse, se travaille bien. Son aspect décoratif et les qualités nommées précédemment, font de lui un bois très apprécié pour contreplaquer des meubles, pour des tailles ou revêtements luxueux, et c'est aussi le bois traditionnelle des boites de cigares.

CERISIER: *On trouve le bois de cerisier dans deux régions bien délimitées: d'un côté celui d'Europe et d'Asie Mineure, où l'on trouve le cerisier sauvage, et d'un autre côté l'Est des États-Unis avec le cerisier noir américain. Il est de couleur marron rosé, bien qu'il ait tendance à foncer avec le temps, devenant ainsi d'une couleur rouge acajou. Il a des veines très fines qui coïncident avec le pore et est d'une couleur grisâtre foncé. C'est un bois délicat qui doit être bien séché car il a tendance à se tordre et à attraper des vers de bois, et est sensible aux altérations de l'extérieur. Il se scie facilement et donne de bons résultat autant si il est travaillé manuellement comme en machine. Ses*

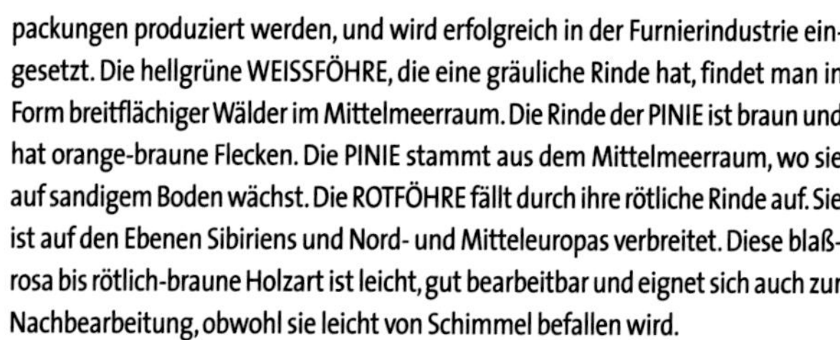

packungen produziert werden, und wird erfolgreich in der Furnierindustrie eingesetzt. Die hellgrüne WEISSFÖHRE, die eine gräuliche Rinde hat, findet man in Form breitflächiger Wälder im Mittelmeerraum. Die Rinde der PINIE ist braun und hat orange-braune Flecken. Die PINIE stammt aus dem Mittelmeerraum, wo sie auf sandigem Boden wächst. Die ROTFÖHRE fällt durch ihre rötliche Rinde auf. Sie ist auf den Ebenen Sibiriens und Nord- und Mitteleuropas verbreitet. Diese blaßrosa bis rötlich-braune Holzart ist leicht, gut bearbeitbar und eignet sich auch zur Nachbearbeitung, obwohl sie leicht von Schimmel befallen wird.

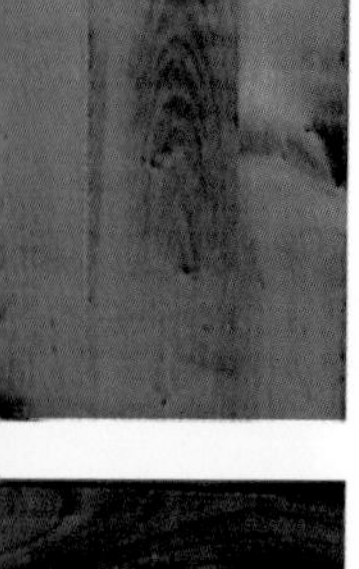

EBENHOLZBAUM. Das Ebenholz wächst in verschiedenen Gebieten der Erde, aber das schwarze Ebenholz, das früher aus Indien und Sri Lanka beschafft wurde, stammt heute größtenteils aus dem tropischen Afrika. Zusammen mit der afrikanischen Wenge ist es das schwärzeste der uns bekannten Holzarten; obwohl es auch eine dunkelbraune Variante mit schwarzer Maserung oder grauen oder brau-

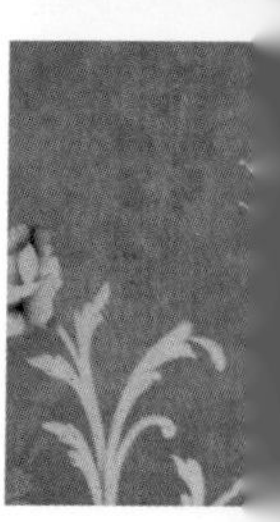

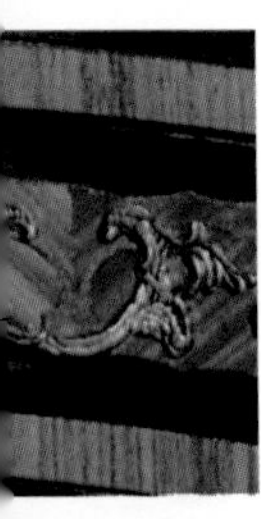
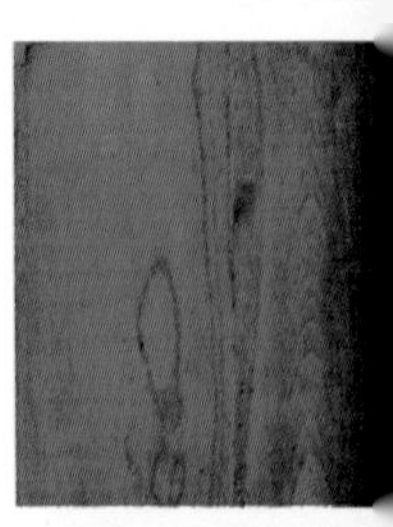

OAK. The hot zones of some tropical lands as well as those of the southern Mediterranean provide this wood. It wears extraordinarily well, and is beige or light brown. It is difficult to season since it warps and tends to crack. Strong, hard-wearing, hard to saw, and hard to work, it presents problems for a smooth finish. It is used in expensive furniture.

ESPINILLO. This wood comes from the south of Florida and the Caribbean islands. There are also other species of less interest in Africa. It is a golden yellow wood, of fine, uniform texture, with a wavy grain that produces a speckled pattern, and with a shiny, satiny lustre. The wood seasons well, is rather hard, and is easily turned on a lathe. It was much used in the eighteenth century by Adam, Sheraton, and Hepple-

---

qualités s'améliorent si il est vaporisé préalablement. Le bois de cerisier est très décoratif et il est utilisé dans la fabrication de meubles, surtout pour faire des chaises, dans l'ébénisterie de luxe, pour faire des revêtements et des plaques galvanisées.

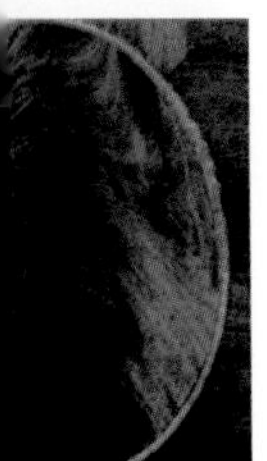

CITRONNIER: *Le bois de citronnier provient de la partie orientale de l'Inde et de l'île de Ceylan. Il est de couleur marron jaunâtre avec de veines dorées qui donnent au bois de placage une grande beauté. Il se taille sans difficultés. On l'emploie dans l'industrie du meuble, pour la décoration et pour contreplaquer.*

CHATAIGNIER: *Il pousse spécialement sur des terrains profonds, riches en matières organiques, pas trop argileux, et est originaire du territoire sous méditerranéen oriental, mais apparaît aussi en Suisse, en Allemagne, et au*

nen Tupfen gibt. Der Kern ist fein und gedrungen, sehr hart, aber das Holz läßt sich leicht bearbeiten, auch wenn es etwas schwierig zu lackieren ist. Es wird vor allem für Innenausstattungen, für Qualitätsmöbel, für Musikinstrumente und für Drechslerarbeiten verwendet.

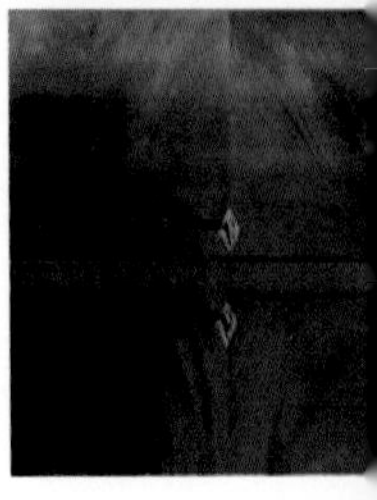

EICHE. Die Eiche ist weit verbreitet und in ganz Europa, in Asien, Nordafrika und Nordamerika anzutreffen. Am hochwertigsten sind die jugoslawische, die deutsche und die nordamerikanische Eiche. Man unterscheidet zwischen der braungelblichen, grob gefaserten WEISSEICHE, die in Europa, Japan und den USA wächst, und der rosafarbenen ROTEICHE, die in milden Gebieten der nördlichen Hemisphäre - vor allem in den USA und im Iran – zu Hause ist. Das Holz der WEISSEICHE ist für gewöhnlich stark, dicht, hart und beständig, so daß es deshalb manchmal ziemlich schwer zu bearbeiten ist. Letzteres Merkmal trifft auf die ROTEICHE zu, die weniger beständig ist. Heutzutage wird das Holz der WEISSEICHE weiterhin in

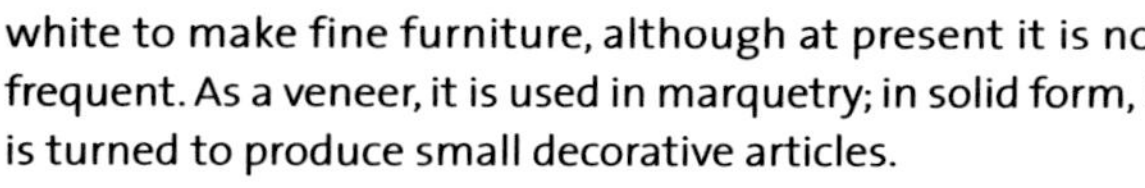
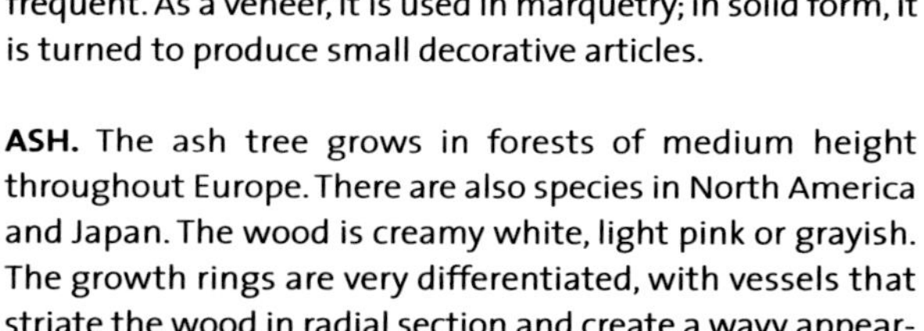

white to make fine furniture, although at present it is not frequent. As a veneer, it is used in marquetry; in solid form, it is turned to produce small decorative articles.

ASH. The ash tree grows in forests of medium height throughout Europe. There are also species in North America and Japan. The wood is creamy white, light pink or grayish. The growth rings are very differentiated, with vessels that striate the wood in radial section and create a wavy appearance when cut tangentially. The wood is very flexible and strong. It saws and machines easily for a good finish, and can be doubled without difficulty when steamed. It is not advisable to use ash for exterior facings unless it is specially treat-

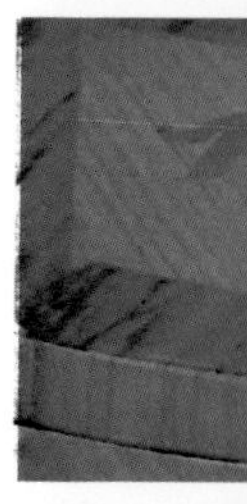

---

sud d'Angleterre. Il est de couleur marron clair avec des annaux de croissance bien visibles semblable au chêne. L'aubier se distingue parfaitement du coeur grâce à sa couleur beaucoup plus blanche. Le bois de châtaignier est plus doux et faible que celui de chêne et ainsi plus facile à travailler et plus stable. Il sèche lentement et ces cellules tendent à se contracter. Il est de longue durée. On l'emploie spécialement pour faire des manches, des persiennes, de l'artisanat et des tonneaux. On l'utilise peux en ébénisterie, mais souvent pour contreplaquer des portes de mobilier de cuisines. Les plaques de châtaigniers représentent un revêtement simple et agréable.

CHÊNE: *Les territoires de croissance du chêne sont très étendus et sont répartis dans toute l'Europe, en Asie, en Afrique septentrionale et en Amérique du Nord. Le plus réputé est le yougoslave, l'allemand, et celui d'Amérique du Nord. On peut faire la différence entre le chêne blanc, qui pousse en Europe,*

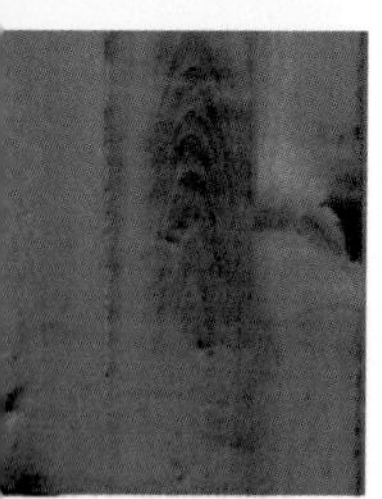

Bereichen verwendet, in denen Traditionalität, Beständigkeit und Gediegenheit gefragt sind. Das Holz wird viel im Möbelbau und in der Kunsttischlerei, für Verkleidungen und Parkett eingesetzt. Die ROTEICHE hingegen findet ihre häufigste Verwendung im Innenausbau – Verkleidungen, Parkett und Möbel. Da es wenig beständig ist, sollte es nicht im Bau, in der Tischlerei oder für äußere Konstruktionen verwendet werden. Es ist qualitativ minderwertiger als die WEISSEICHE.

EINGRIFFELIGER WEISSDORN. Der eingriffelige Weißdorn stammt aus dem südlichen Florida und von den Westindischen Inseln. Weitere, weniger bedeutsame Spezien findet man in Afrika. Das Holz des eingriffeligen Weißdorns ist goldgelb, hat eine feine und gleichmäßige Textur, einen wellenförmigen Kern, der ein geflecktes Muster ergibt, und einen schimmernden und satinierten Glanz. Das Holz des eingriffeligen Weißdorns trocknet gut und ist ziemlich hart, obwohl es sich gut drechseln läßt. Es wurde im 18. Jh. von Adam, Sheraton und Hepplewhite oft für

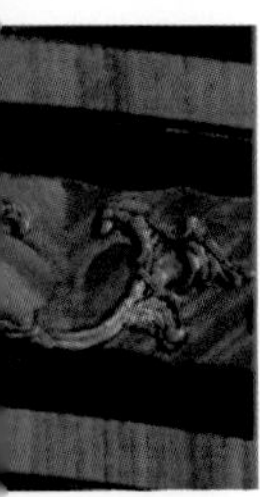

ed previously. Ash is mostly used in curved pieces and the root is much appreciated in cabinetry.

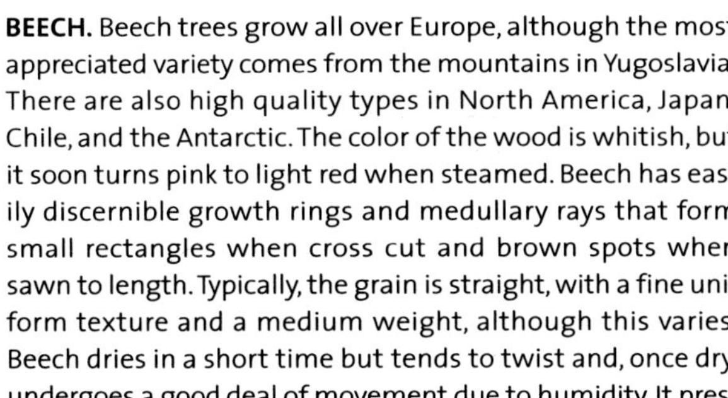

BEECH. Beech trees grow all over Europe, although the most appreciated variety comes from the mountains in Yugoslavia. There are also high quality types in North America, Japan, Chile, and the Antarctic. The color of the wood is whitish, but it soon turns pink to light red when steamed. Beech has easily discernible growth rings and medullary rays that form small rectangles when cross cut and brown spots when sawn to length. Typically, the grain is straight, with a fine uniform texture and a medium weight, although this varies. Beech dries in a short time but tends to twist and, once dry, undergoes a good deal of movement due to humidity. It pres-

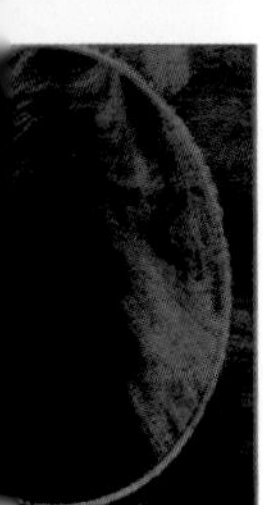

au Japon et aux Etats-Unis, de couleur gris jaunâtre et de texture épaisse, et le chêne rouge, produit dans les zones tempérées de l'hémisphère nord, spécialement aux Etats-Unis et en Iran, de couleur rosée. Le bois de chêne blanc est habituellement fort, dense dur et de longue durée, et de ce fait est assez difficile à travailler. Cette dernière caractéristique est commune au chêne rouge mais de moins longue durée. Actuellement, le bois de chêne blanc est toujours utilisé dans les ambiances qui représentent la tradition, durabilité et solidité. C'est un bois très utilisé pour la fabrication de meubles et s'emploie en ébénisterie, pur faire des revêtements et des planchers. D'un autre côté, l'usage le plus habituel donné au bois de chêne rouge sont les intérieurs -revêtements, planchers et meubles- et est peu recommandé pour faire des structures, en menuiserie ou constructions extérieures, car il est de courte durée. Sa qualité est inférieure à celle du chêne blanc.

die Herstellung von Luxusmöbeln verwendet, wird allerdings heutzutage kaum noch verarbeitet. Als Furnierholz wird es für Intarsien- und Holzeinlegearbeiten, und als Massivholz für kleine gedrechselte Gegenstände gebraucht. Gelegentlich dient es auch der Verzierung von Toilettenbürsten, Spiegeln und anderen Haushaltsgegenständen.

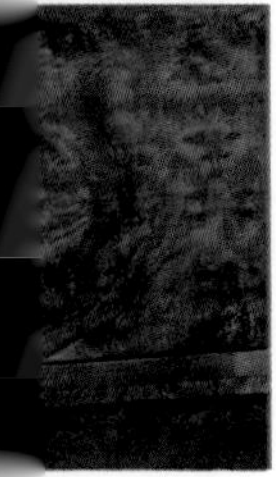

ERLE. Die Erle ist in der nördlichen Hemisphäre weit verbreitet und ist aufgrund seines Holzes sowohl in Europa als auch in Amerika sehr wichtig. Die weiße und die Schwarzerle wachsen in Europa; die amerikanische Roterle im Westen von Amerika. Kurz nach dem Schneiden ist das Holz von blasser Farbe, aber nach kurzer Zeit nimmt es einen glänzenden rosa-lachsfarbenen Farbton an. Die Faserung ist fein und die Oberfläche glänzend. Das Erlenholz trocknet schnell, aber die europäische Spezie bricht schneller als die amerikanische. Es ist leicht zuzuschneiden und eignet sich gut für die Nachbearbeitung. Es ist nicht beständig. Das Holz der europä-

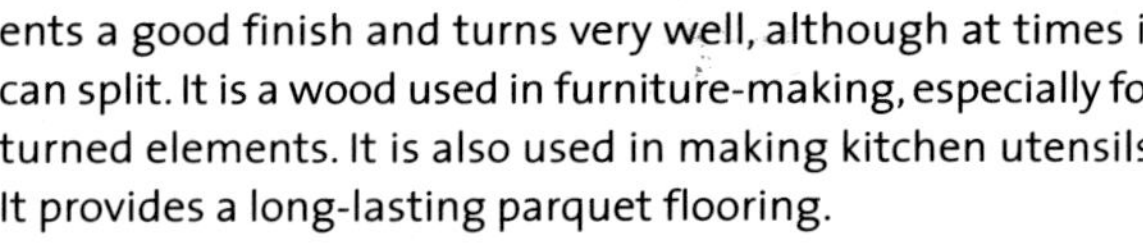

ents a good finish and turns very well, although at times it can split. It is a wood used in furniture-making, especially for turned elements. It is also used in making kitchen utensils. It provides a long-lasting parquet flooring.

JACARANDA. The jacaranda grows in the Americas (Brasil, Cuba), in Africa, and in Asia (India). It is blackish, with different dark tones. It is used in the highest quality cabinetry, for turned objects, and in the manufacture of musical instruments, especially pianos.

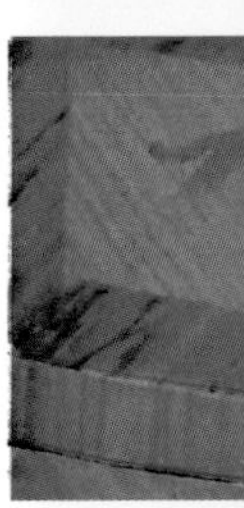

LIMONCILLO (aloma). This grows in Africa and in the Philippines. It is light yellow, a hard, compact wood with close

---

ÉBÈNE: *On trouve de l'ébène dans plusieurs coins du monde, mais l'ébène noir, que l'on obtenait autrefois en Inde et à Sri Lanka, provient dans l'actualité principalement d'Afrique tropicale. C'est avec le wenge africain le bois noir le plus connu, bien qu'in existe aussi en marron foncé avec des veines noires ou moucheté en gris ou grisâtre. Son grain est fin et serré, de grande dureté mais se travaille très facilement bien qu'il présente quelques difficultés lors du vernissage. On l'emploie spécialement pour la décoration d'intérieurs luxueux, pour faire des meubles de qualité, des instruments de musique et de l'artisanat.*

FRÊNE: *Le frêne pousse dans les bois d'Europe à une hauteur moyenne et on trouve des espèces similaires aux Etats-Unis et au Japon. Il est de couleur blanche fumée, légèrement rosé ou grisâtre. Les annaux de croissance sont très séparés les uns des autres par des vaisseaux qui forment des stries vei-*

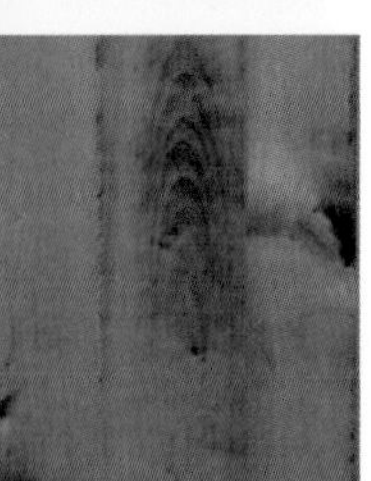

ischen Erle ist im allgemeinen für Furnierarbeiten geeignet. Es wird für einfache Stühle , im gewöhnlichen Tischlergewerbe und in der Kleinindustrie verwendet, ebenso für die Rückseite von Bürsten, Besenstiele, Werkzeuggriffe, Spielzeug usw. Das Holz wird traditionell für die Konstruktion von Armprothesen und Rollen in der Textilindustrie und in der Herstellung von Kohle für Schießpulver verwendet.

ESCHE. Die Esche wächst in halbhohen Wäldern in ganz Europa. Ähnliche Spezien findet man in den USA und in Japan. Es hat eine cremeweiße Farbe mit einem Rosa- oder Graustich. Die Jahresringe sind sehr gut zu erkennen und verfügen über Gefäße, die in der radialen Schnittfläche gefaserte Streifen und in der tangentialen Schnittfläche wellenförmige Streifen bilden. Es handelt sich um ein sehr elastisches und nachgiebiges Holz, das sich leicht sägen und maschinell ver- und nachbearbeiten läßt und beim Dämpfen leicht zu biegen ist. Es fault leicht und sollte nicht der freien Luft ausgesetzt werden, ohne daß es vorher behandelt wurde. Das

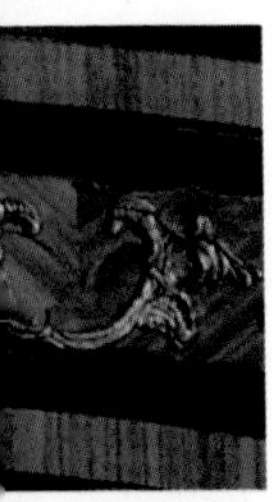

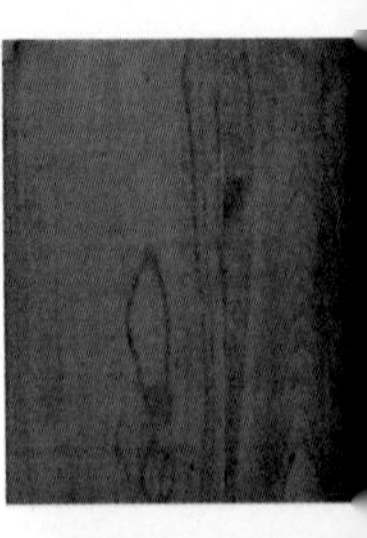

pores. It is easy to work and polish. It is especially used in inlays and veneers.

WALNUT. Although it originally comes from the Middle East, the common walnut is cultivated in all known temperate and warm regions of the Northern Hemisphere. The Spanish variety is the most appreciated but there is only a small cultivation. The black walnut tree (Juglans nigra) comes from the American woodlands and the common (sometimes called English) walnut (Juglans regia) grows from southeastern Europe to China. The wood of the common walnut is brownish gray, with almost black veins. Generally, its color is more variable than the black variety, which is typically reddish brown, uniformly dark. Walnut is a hardwood, homoge-

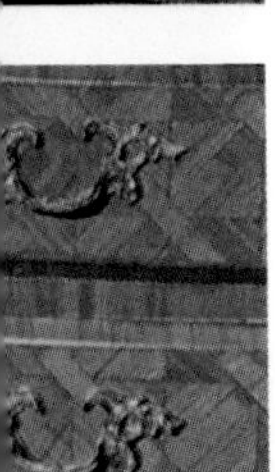

---

nées dans le sens radial et ondulées dans le sens tangentiel. C'est un bois de grande élasticité et ténacité, qui se scie et travaille en machine facilement, obtenant ainsi une bonne finition et pouvant être plié à la vapeur sans difficultés. Il est de courte durée et n'est pas recommandable à l'extérieur, à moins qu'il n'ait été traité spécialement auparavant. On utilise le frêne principalement pour faire des objets arrondis, et sa racine est très appréciée en ébénisterie.

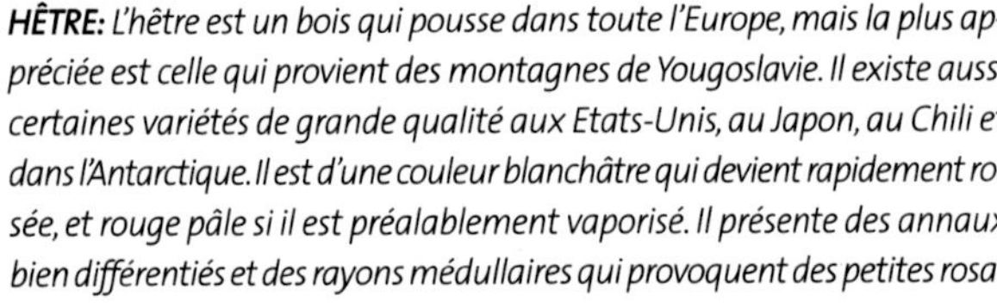

HÊTRE: *L'hêtre est un bois qui pousse dans toute l'Europe, mais la plus appréciée est celle qui provient des montagnes de Yougoslavie. Il existe aussi certaines variétés de grande qualité aux Etats-Unis, au Japon, au Chili et dans l'Antarctique. Il est d'une couleur blanchâtre qui devient rapidement rosée, et rouge pâle si il est préalablement vaporisé. Il présente des annaux bien différentiés et des rayons médullaires qui provoquent des petites rosa-*

Holz der Esche wird vorwiegend für runde Gegenstände verwendet und seine Wurzel wird in der Kunsttischlerei sehr geschätzt.

GUAJAK. Das Guajakholz stammt aus Brasilien. Es taucht in verschiedenen Farben auf, mit schwarzen, braunen und roten Maserungen. Es ist ein leicht zu bearbeitendes und formbares Holz, das leicht zu polieren ist. Aus diesem Holz werden sehr dekorative Furniere hergestellt. Es wird auch in der Kunsttischlerei verwendet. Heutzutage ist das aus Kuba stammende Mahagoniholz knapp. So wird auch die Mehrheit der amerikanischen Holzarten nach ihrem Herkunftsland – Brasilien, Peru, Venuzuela etc., - unterschieden.

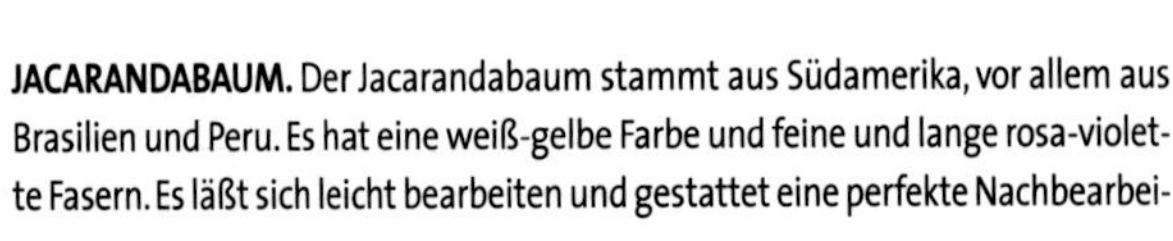

JACARANDABAUM. Der Jacarandabaum stammt aus Südamerika, vor allem aus Brasilien und Peru. Es hat eine weiß-gelbe Farbe und feine und lange rosa-violette Fasern. Es läßt sich leicht bearbeiten und gestattet eine perfekte Nachbearbei-

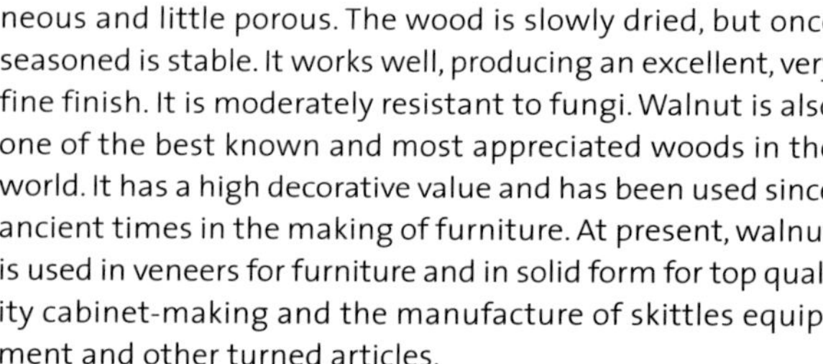

neous and little porous. The wood is slowly dried, but once seasoned is stable. It works well, producing an excellent, very fine finish. It is moderately resistant to fungi. Walnut is also one of the best known and most appreciated woods in the world. It has a high decorative value and has been used since ancient times in the making of furniture. At present, walnut is used in veneers for furniture and in solid form for top quality cabinet-making and the manufacture of skittles equipment and other turned articles.

OKUME. This African hardwood comes from the east coast, especially Gabon, Equatorial Guinea, the Democratic Republic of Congo (former Zaire), Cameroon, and the Republic of Congo. Okume is salmon pink without veins or patterns. It is

---

ce rectangulaires dans la section radiale et des petites taches grisâtres dans la section tangentielle. Habituellement, son grain est droit, sa texture fine et uniforme et son poids moyen bien que variable. L'hêtre sèche rapidement mais il a tendance à se tordre, et même une fois séché, il lui arrive de subir des mouvements dus à l'humidité. Il présente une bonne finition et se travaille bien, malgré qu'il ait tendance parfois à se fendre. On utilise ce bois pour fabriquer des meubles, surtout pour faire des objets d'usage domestique, comme des ustensiles de cuisine, des manches d'outils et des brosses. Il forme des panneaux domestiques de longue durée.

JARACANDA: *Le jaracanda pousse en Amérique (Brésil et Cuba), en Afrique et en Asie (Inde). Il est de couleur noirâtre, avec plusieurs tons qui tendent à foncer. Il est utilisé dans l'ébénisterie de luxe, pour réaliser des tailles et pour la fabrication d'instruments de musique, plus particulièrement des pianos.*

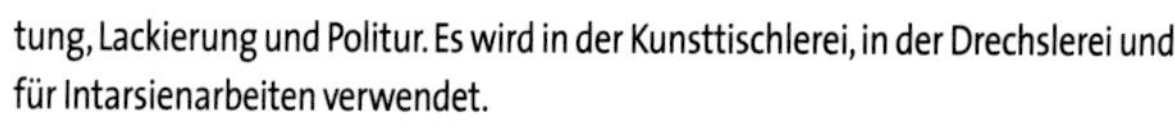

---

tung, Lackierung und Politur. Es wird in der Kunsttischlerei, in der Drechslerei und für Intarsienarbeiten verwendet.

JAKARANDABAUM. Der Jakarandabaum wächst in Amerika (Brasilien und Kuba), in Afrika und in Asien (Indien). Er hat eine schwärzliche Farbe, die aus verschiedenen, dunkler werdenden Nuancen besteht. Das Holz wird in der Fabrikation von Luxusmöbeln verwendet und dient der Herstellung von Drechslerarbeiten und Musikinstrumenten, vor allem Klavieren.

KASTANIE. Der Kastanienbaum wächst vor allem auf tiefen Böden, die reich an organischem Material sind und wenig Lehm enthalten, und kommt ursprünglich aus dem östlichen submediterranen Gebiet. Er ist aber auch in der Schweiz, in Deutschland und sogar im Süden von England zu Hause. Das Holz ist hellbraun und die Jahresringe sind wie bei der Eiche gut zu erkennen. Das Splintholz ist gut

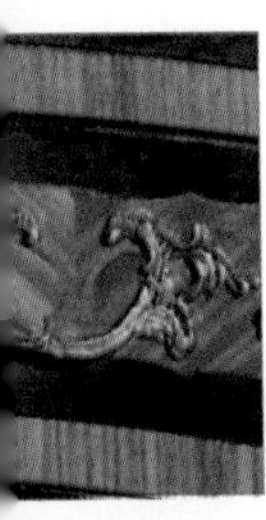
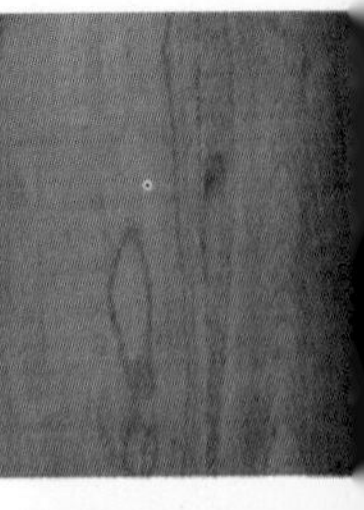
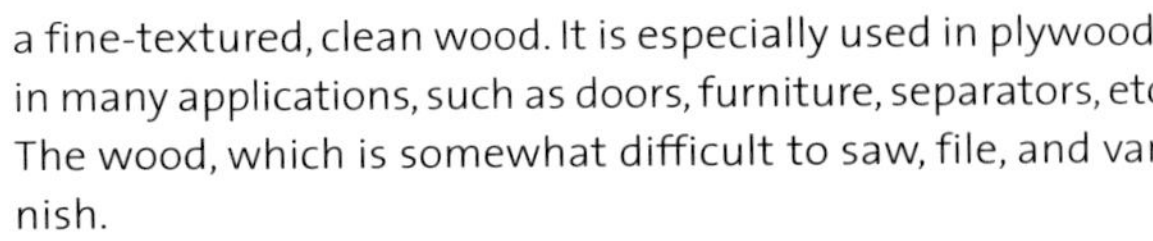

a fine-textured, clean wood. It is especially used in plywoods in many applications, such as doors, furniture, separators, etc. The wood, which is somewhat difficult to saw, file, and varnish.

OLIVE. Olive wood comes from the tree of the same name. It is cultivated in the Mediterranean countries and, by extension, in all the countries of southern Europe and North Africa where the climate allows. The wood's color is greenish ochre. It has brown veins distributed irregularly, and the surface is smooth. Olive wood dries slowly and has a certain tendency to fissure. It is rather difficult to saw, but works well both by hand and machine. It provides very smooth finishes and can be polished and stained. It is moderately resistant to fungi.

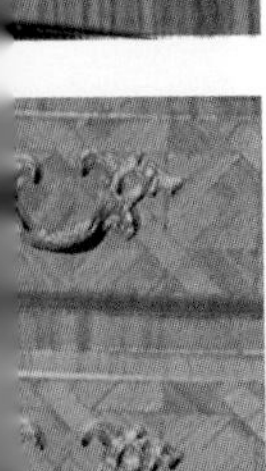

NOYER: *Bien qu'il provienne du Proche Orient, le noyer commun est cultivé dans toutes les régions tempérées et chaudes de l'hémisphère nord. La variété espagnole est une des plus appréciées mais la production est très limitée. Le noyer noir provient de l'Amérique boréale et le noyer blanc américain est en réalité une variété de la même famille du noyer. Le bois de noyer européen est d'un marron grisâtre, avec des veines presque noires et sa couleur est plus variable que celle du noyer américain, qui est typiquement marron rougeâtre, foncé et uniforme. C'est un bois dur, homogène et peu poreux. Le noyer est un bois qui sèche lentement, mais est très stable une fois sec. Il se travaille très bien, et présente une fine et excellente finition. Il est modérément résistant aux champignons. C'est un des bois les plus connus et appréciés au monde et possède une grande valeur décorative, étant utilisée depuis l'antiquité dans la fabrication de meubles. Actuellement, le noyer est utilisé sous forme de bois de placage dans la fabrication de meu-*

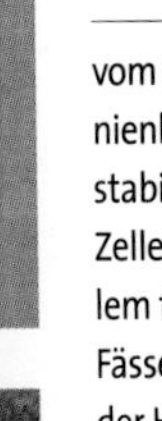

vom Kernholz zu unterscheiden, da es eine hellere Farbe hat. Das Holz des Kastanienbaums ist weicher und dünner als das der Eiche, ist leichter zu bearbeiten und stabiler. Es ist zäh, nachgiebig, leicht und mittelhart. Es trocknet langsam und die Zellen neigen dazu, sich zusammenzuziehen. Es ist sehr beständig. Es wird vor allem für die Herstellung von Griffen, Rolläden, gedrechselten Gegenständen und Fässern verwendet. In der Kunsttischlerei wird es selten verwandt, obgleich es oft der Herstellung von Küchenmöbeltüren dient. Die Furniere aus Kastanienbaumholz ergeben eine einfache und hübsche Verkleidung.

KIEFER. Es gibt viele Arten der Kiefer. Die Kiefer gehört zu den Holzarten mit der größten Harzbildung. Unter anderem sind die folgenden Spezien bekannt: Die PARANÁ-Kiefer stammt aus dem brasilianischen Bundesstaat Paraná. Das Holz ist beige-strohfarben und hat manchmal eine rote glänzende Maserung. Diese Spezie hat eine feine, gleichmäßige Textur ohne Jahresringe. Es ist schwer zu trok-

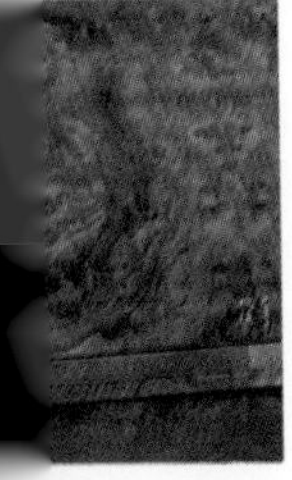
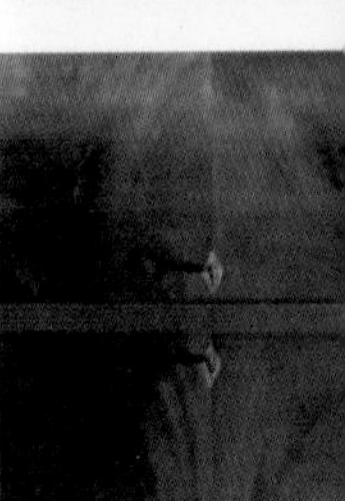

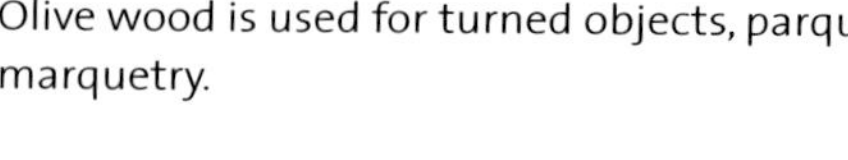

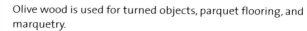

Olive wood is used for turned objects, parquet flooring, and marquetry.

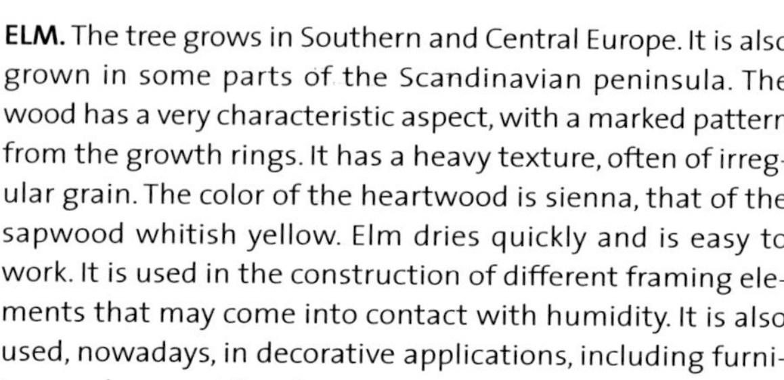

ELM. The tree grows in Southern and Central Europe. It is also grown in some parts of the Scandinavian peninsula. The wood has a very characteristic aspect, with a marked pattern from the growth rings. It has a heavy texture, often of irregular grain. The color of the heartwood is sienna, that of the sapwood whitish yellow. Elm dries quickly and is easy to work. It is used in the construction of different framing elements that may come into contact with humidity. It is also used, nowadays, in decorative applications, including furniture and parquet flooring.

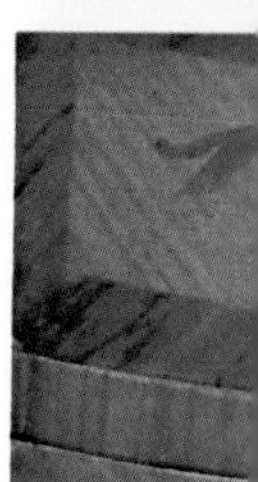
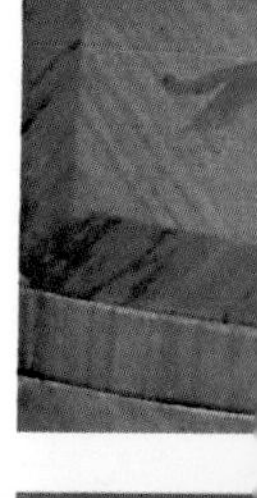

bles et comme bois massif, on l'emploie pour l'ébénisterie de luxe et dans la réalisation d'articles taillés.

OKUME: *L'okume se trouve en Afrique Occidentale spécialement au Gabon, Guinée Équatoriale, Zaïre, Cameroun et Congo. Il est de couleur rose saumon sans veines ni dessins à remarquer, de texture fine et nette. On l'emploie spécialement pour faire des plaques de contreplaqué et a de nombreuses applications telles que le revêtement de portes, fabrication de meubles, des cloisons, etc... C'est un bois assez compliqué qui présent des difficultés à être scié, poncé ou vernis.*

OLIVIER: *Le bois d'olivier s'obtient de l'arbre du même nom cultivé dans les pays méditerranéens et par extension, dans tous les pays du Sus de l'Europe et d'Afrique du Nord qui ont des hautes températures. Il est de couleur*

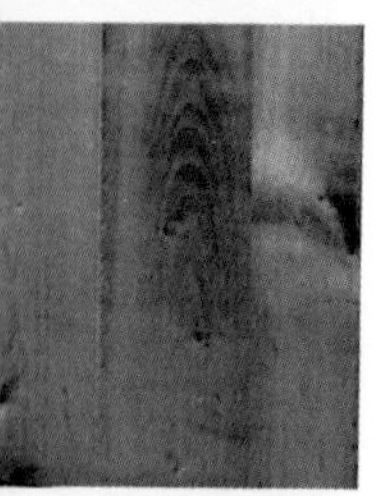

knen und sehr hart, aber es läßt sich trotzdem sowohl manuell als auch maschinell gut bearbeiten und erlaubt eine gute Nachbehandlung. Es ist nicht beständig. Es wird vor allem im Innenausbau, für die Herstellung weißer Möbel und für den Modellbau verwendet.

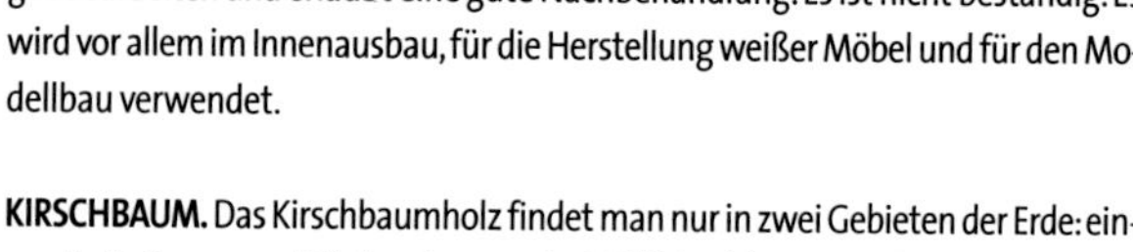

KIRSCHBAUM. Das Kirschbaumholz findet man nur in zwei Gebieten der Erde: einerseits in Europa und Kleinasien, wo der Wildkirschbaum wächst, und andererseits im Osten der Vereinigten Staaten, wo die amerikanische Schwarzkirsche beheimatet ist.

MAHAGONI. Das echte Mahagoniholz, das der Möbel des 700, des Chippendale, Adam-Stils etc. ist im Gebiet von Mexiko bis Honduras und auf den karibischen Inseln beheimatet. Man findet es vor allem in Venezuela, wo das kommerzielle Mahagoniholz ursprünglich herstammt.

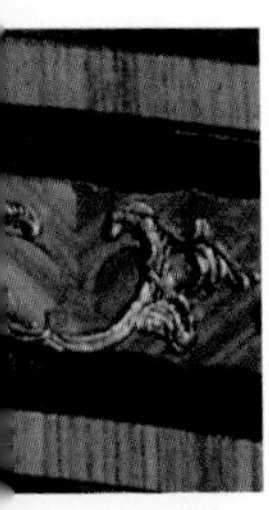

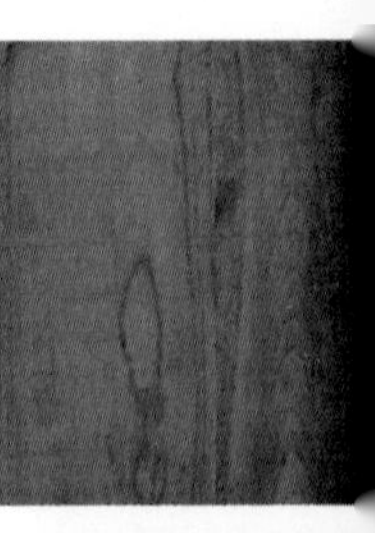

ROSEWOOD. The varieties of this very decorative wood have always been much coveted. At present, the commercial supply of rosewood is limited to two geographical points that determine two types of rosewood. We thus differentiate between Indian rosewood, with yellowish white sapwood and some pink tones and a much more intensely colored heartwood, from dark blue-violet to orange; and Rio de Janeiro rosewood, with the same color sapwood but a duramen that is orange with violet or black veins. The first type comes from India, Thailand, Indonesia, Sri Lanka, and Java; the second from Brasil and Argentina, principally. It is not a wood that is excessively difficult to dry or to work mechanically. This makes it easy to produce high quality veneers. Rosewood has

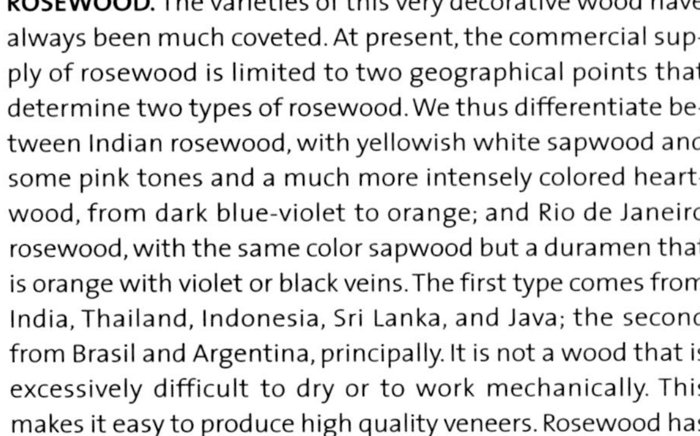

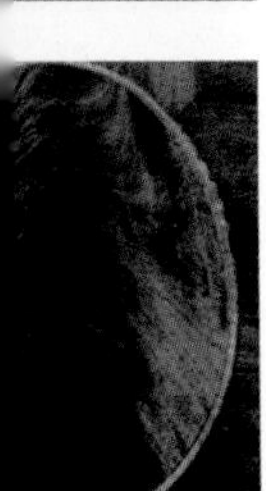

ocre verdoyant avec des veines grisâtres très irrégulières de fine superficie. Le bois d'olivier sèche lentement et a une certaine tendance à se fendre et à se fissurer. Il est assez difficile à scier, mais se travaille facilement à la main et en machine ; la finition est très fine et on peut le polir et le vernir. Il est modérément résistant aux champignons. Le bois d'olivier est utilisé dans les tailles, les incrustations, dans la réalisation de petits objets et détails,et aussi pour faire des planchers.

ORME: *Il pousse spécialement en Europe méridionale et centrale, et dans certains coins de la péninsule scandinave. Le bois d'orme a un aspect caractéristique, avec un dessin très marqué dus ses anneaux de croissance. Il a une texture grossière et souvent un grain irrégulier. Il est de couleur grisâtre rouge de Sienne ou rougeâtre avec l'aubier blanc jaunâtre. Il sèche rapidement et est facile à travailler. On l'utilise dans la construction de n'im-*

NUSSBAUM. Obwohl der Nußbaum ursprünglich aus dem Nahen Orient stammt, wird der gemeine Nußbaum in allen milden und warmen Gebieten der nördlichen Hemisphäre angebaut. Das spanische Nußbaumholz gehört zu den am meisten geschätzten Holzarten, aber es wird kaum produziert. Das schwarze Nußbaumholz stammt aus Nordamerika und der weiße Nußbaum ist in Wirklichkeit ein Hickory, obwohl er zur gleichen Gattung gehört wie der Nußbaum. Das europäische Nußbaumholz ist gräulich-braun und hat fast schwarze Fasern. Im allgemeinen variiert sein Farbton eher als der des amerikanischen Nußbaumholzes, das normalerweise rötlich-braun, dunkel und einheitlich ist. Es handelt sich um ein hartes und gleichmäßiges Holz mit wenigen Öffnungen. Das Nußbaumholz trocknet langsam; ist es jedoch einmal trocken, ist es ziemlich stabil. Es läßt sich sehr gut bearbeiten und liefert ein exzellentes und sehr feines Ergebnis bei der Nachbehandlung. Es ist mäßig resistent gegen Pilze. Es ist eine der weltweit bekanntesten und meist geschätzten Holzarten. Es hat einen hohen dekorativen Wert und wird

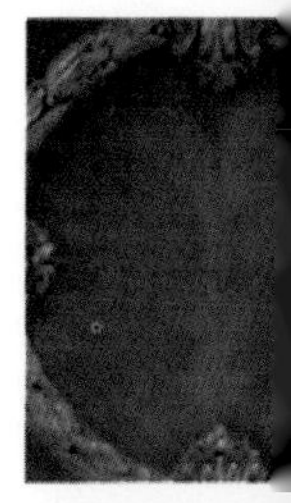

been highly prized for two centuries, used in quality cabinetry for the best furniture. It is also used in turned articles.

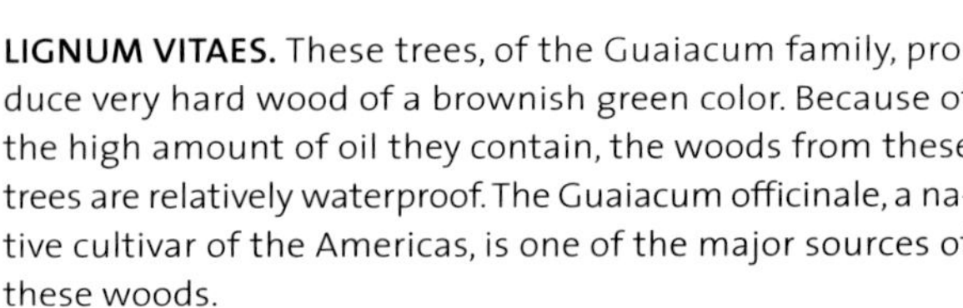

LIGNUM VITAES. These trees, of the Guaiacum family, produce very hard wood of a brownish green color. Because of the high amount of oil they contain, the woods from these trees are relatively waterproof. The Guaiacum officinale, a native cultivar of the Americas, is one of the major sources of these woods.

PINE. There are many varieties of pine tree, the source of one of the most resinous woods known. Some of these are: Parana, from the region of Brazil of the same name, a beige straw color with some bright red veining. This variety is of

---

porte quel élément structurale qui doit demeurer dans l'humidité, et de nos jours, on l'utilise dans la fabrication de meubles et de planchers de part sa qualité de bois très décoratif.

PALISSANDRE: *Le bois de palissandre, très décoratif, a toujours été très appréciée. Actuellement l'approvisionnement commercial de ce bois est centré vers deux zones géographiques qui déterminent deux types de palissandre différents. C'est pour cela que l'on marque la différence entre le palissandre d'Inde, à l'aubier blanc jaunâtre avec quelques tons rosés et un cœur de couleur très intense, qui va du violet bleuté foncé à l'orange, et le palissandre Rio, avec le même aubier et au cœur de couleur marron et veines allant du violacé au noir. La première variété pousse en Inde orientale, Thaïlande, Indonésie, Ceylan et Java ; la seconde au Brésil et en Argentine, principalement. Ce n'est pas un bois spécialement difficile à sécher ni à trai-*

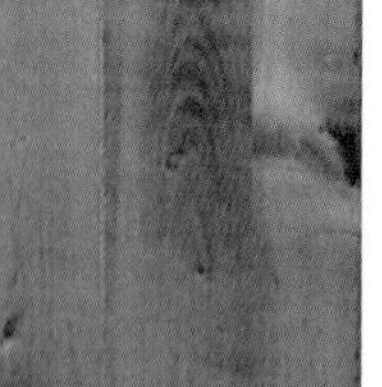

seit jeher im Möbelbau eingesetzt. Heutzutage wird das Nußbaumholz als Furnierholz für den Möbelbau und als Massivholz für die Herstellung von Luxusmöbeln, Treppenspindeln und anderen gedrechselten Gegenständen verwendet.

OKOUMÉ. Das Okouméholz findet man in Ostafrika, vor allem in Gabun, Äquatorialguinea, Zaire, Kamerun und im Kongo. Das Holz ist rosa-lachsfarben, ohne ausgeprägte Maserung oder Muster und ist von relativ zarter und reiner Textur. Es wird vor allem für Furnierplatten benutzt, findet aber eine Vielzahl von Verwendungsmöglichkeiten, wie z.B. Türverkleidungen, Möbelbau, Trennwände, etc. Es ist ein etwas störrisches Holz, das sich schwer sägen, abschleifen und lackieren läßt.

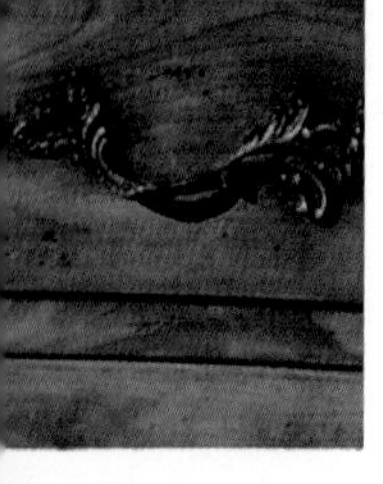

OLIVENBAUM. Das Olivenholz wird aus dem Olivenbaum gewonnen, der in den mediterranen Ländern kultiviert wird, dessen Anbau sich aber in alle südeuropä-

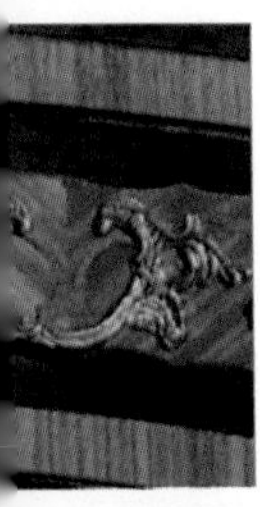
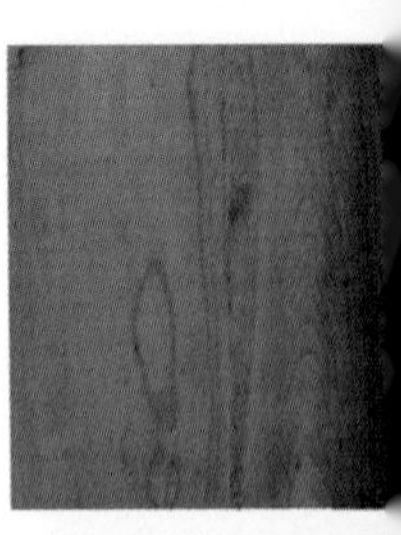

fine and uniform texture. It dries with difficulty and is very rigid. At the same time, it works well both manually and mechanically and gives a good finish. It is not long-lasting. It is mainly used in interior carpentry, for furniture in white, and in modeling. Rigid pine is a yellow or sienna color, with very notable growth rings. Its provenance is the U.S.A. This type of pine is one of the most resinous. It dries slowly and has a certain tendency to split. As the name implies, it is rigid, hard, resistant, difficult to work, and thus used in industrial construction, that is, in heavy structures. Today it is a very scarce material, however. Monterrey pine, from California and the Island of Guadalupe, is also grown in New Zealand, Australia, Chile, and South Africa. The heartwood is pinkish-brown and in young specimens the sapwood is very light. It has a uni-

---

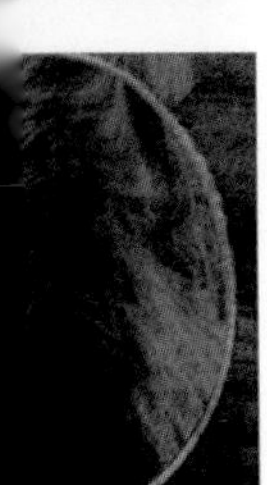

ter mécaniquement, ce qui permet d'obtenir du bois de placage de grande qualité. Le palissandre est un bois très apprécié depuis deux siècles, utilisée en ébénisterie de qualité pour la réalisation de meubles de luxe. On l'emplois aussi pour faire des articles taillés.

PAU BRASIL: *Il se trouve en Amérique, concrètement au Brésil et aux Antilles. C'est un bois de couleur rose saumoné, au grain fin et aux fibres entrelacées qui s'emploient de préférence pour l'incrustation, l'ébénisterie de luxe et des pièces sélectes d'artisanat.*

PIN: *Il existe une grande variété de pins, un des bois les plus résineux. On connaît, entre autres, les variétés suivantes: le pin Parana, provenant de l'état de Parana au Brésil, de couleur rouge paille beige avec des veines occasionnelles d'un ton rouge brillant. Cette variété de pin a une texture fine et*

ischen Länder und Afrika (Nord) ausdehnt, wo das Klima wärmer ist. Das Holz ist grünlich-ockerfarben und hat eine sehr unregelmäßige, braune Faserung und eine feine Oberfläche. Das Olivenholz trocknet langsam und neigt zu Rissen und Spalten. Es ist ziemlich schwer zu sägen, aber es läßt sich manuell und maschinell gut bearbeiten. Es liefert glatte Oberflächen und kann poliert und gefärbt werden. Es ist etwas anfällig für Pilzbefall. Man verwendet das Olivenholz für Intarsien, Drechselarbeiten, für die Herstellung kleiner und feiner Gebrauchsgegenstände und darüber hinaus für Parkettböden.

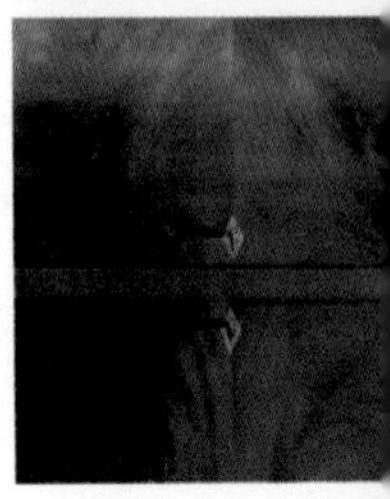

PALISANDER. Das äußerst dekorative Palisanderholz ist schon immer sehr begehrt gewesen. Heutzutage konzentriert sich der kommerzielle Handel auf zwei Gebiete, nach denen man zwei Arten von Palisanderholz unterscheidet. Das indische Palisanderholz hat ein gelblich-weißes Splintholz mit einem Rosastich und ein Kernholz mit sehr kräftigen Farben, die von dunklem Violett-blau bis Orange vari-

form texture with rings blending with wood and knots that cause it to crack when worked. It is not long-lasting. Its main use is in the production of boxes, packing material, brushes and brooms. The best-quality wood of this variety is also used in furniture-making. Monterrey pine can be used easily to make veneer. Weymouth (or Canadian) pine is a very light, delicate wood. It is pale yellow or beige in color, with a kind of pink tint. The texture is fine and uniform. It is not difficult to dry and it is stable. The resistance is minimal so that it works easily and gives an excellent finish. The most expensive type is used in industrial molding, this high-quality type allowing very detailed carving. Albar (or wild) pine is used for finishes and is the most commercialized variety of pine. It grows in Central Europe and Central Asia. The heart-

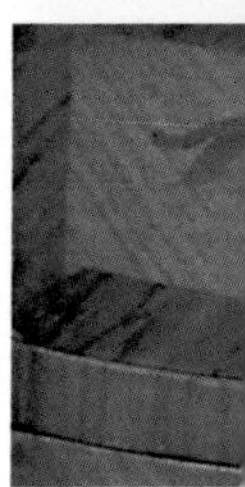
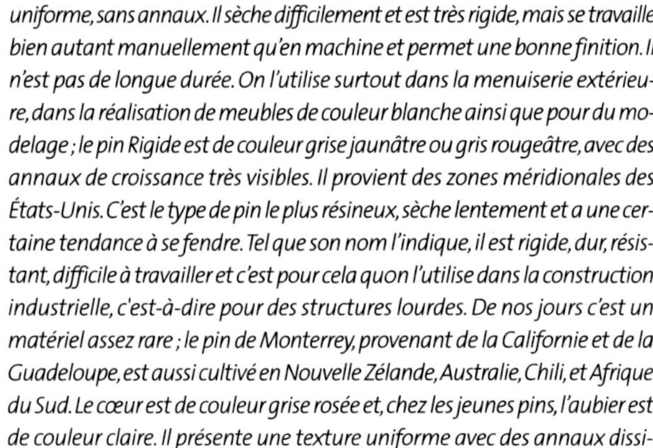

uniforme, sans annaux. Il sèche difficilement et est très rigide, mais se travaille bien autant manuellement qu'en machine et permet une bonne finition. Il n'est pas de longue durée. On l'utilise surtout dans la menuiserie extérieure, dans la réalisation de meubles de couleur blanche ainsi que pour du modelage ; le pin Rigide est de couleur grise jaunâtre ou gris rougeâtre, avec des annaux de croissance très visibles. Il provient des zones méridionales des États-Unis. C'est le type de pin le plus résineux, sèche lentement et a une certaine tendance à se fendre. Tel que son nom l'indique, il est rigide, dur, résistant, difficile à travailler et c'est pour cela quon l'utilise dans la construction industrielle, c'est-à-dire pour des structures lourdes. De nos jours c'est un matériel assez rare ; le pin de Monterrey, provenant de la Californie et de la Guadeloupe, est aussi cultivé en Nouvelle Zélande, Australie, Chili, et Afrique du Sud. Le cœur est de couleur grise rosée et, chez les jeunes pins, l'aubier est de couleur claire. Il présente une texture uniforme avec des annaux dissi-

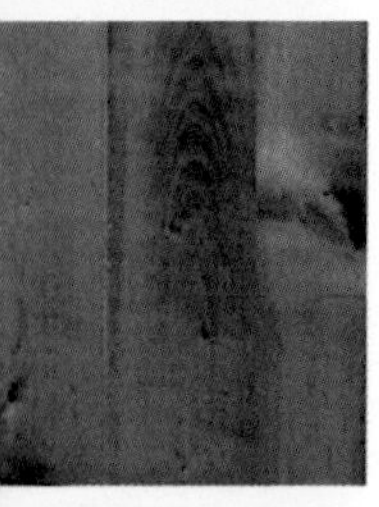

ieren. Das Splintholz des Rio-Palisanderholzes ist wie das des indischen Palisanderholzes; das Kernholz ist bräunlich und hat eine violette, bis schwarze Maserung. Die erste Spezie wächst in Ostindien, Thailand, Indonesien, Ceylon und Java; die zweite Spezie hauptsächlich in Brasilien und Argentinien. Es ist eine Holzart, die leicht trocknet und sich mechanisch gut bearbeiten läßt. Dadurch erhält man qualitativ hochwertige Furniere. Seit zweihundert Jahren wird das Palisanderholz sehr geschätzt und in der bedeutenden Kunsttischlerei für den Bau von Luxusmöbeln verwendet. Es dient auch der Herstellung von gedrechselten Gebrauchsgegenständen.

STEINEICHE. Die Steineichen wachsen in den warmen Gebieten einiger tropischer Länder und in der nördlich-mediterranen Zone Europas. Das Holz der Steineiche ist wie das der Eiche außergewöhnlich hart und beige oder hellbraun. Es trockne schwer, da es sich biegt und sich leicht spaltet. Es ist widerstandsfähig und be-

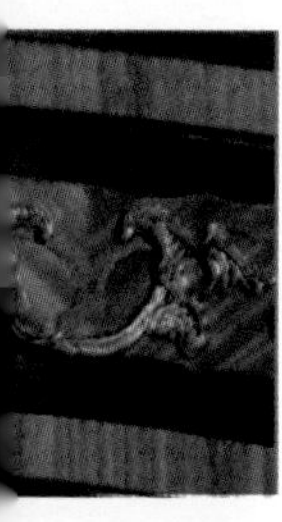

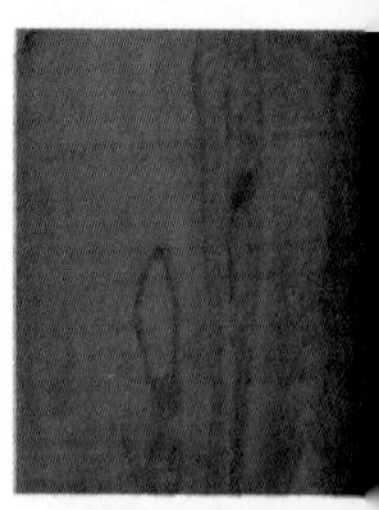

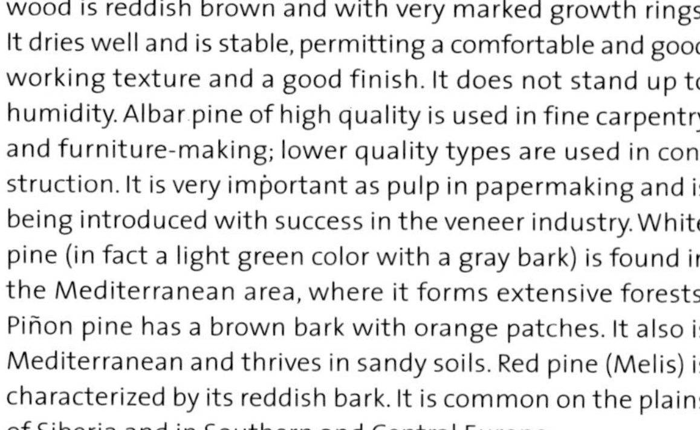

wood is reddish brown and with very marked growth rings. It dries well and is stable, permitting a comfortable and good working texture and a good finish. It does not stand up to humidity. Albar pine of high quality is used in fine carpentry and furniture-making; lower quality types are used in construction. It is very important as pulp in papermaking and is being introduced with success in the veneer industry. White pine (in fact a light green color with a gray bark) is found in the Mediterranean area, where it forms extensive forests. Piñon pine has a brown bark with orange patches. It also is Mediterranean and thrives in sandy soils. Red pine (Melis) is characterized by its reddish bark. It is common on the plains of Siberia and in Southern and Central Europe.

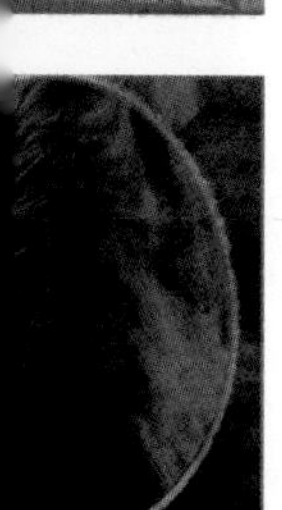

mulés et des nœuds qui le font se fendre au moment de le travailler. Il n'est pas de longue duré. On l'utilise dans la fabrication de caisses, d'emballages, de brosses et de balais, et celui de meilleure qualité permet aussi la réalisation de meubles. Le pin de Monterrey peu, en plus, s'exfolier afin d'obtenir du bois de placage ; le pin Weymouth ou canadien est un bois léger, délicat, de couleur jaune pâle ou beige, avec une petite tinte rosée. Sa texture est fine et uniforme. Il sèche sans problèmes, il est stable, peu résistant, facile à manier et obtient une excellente finition. On l'utilise pour le modelage industriel dans sa variété la plus chère et de qualité, et permet de faire des tailles avec beaucoup de détails. On l'utilise à la fois pour faire des revêtements ; le pin Albar ou sylvestre est la variété la plus commercialisée. Il pousse en Europe et Asie Centrale. Il produit un cœur de couleur gris rougeâtre. Il possède des annaux de croissance très marqués. Il sèche bien et est stable, et permet en plus un travaille facile et positif, et de bonnes finitions. Il ne ré-

---

ständig, schwer zu sägen, zu bearbeiten und abzuschleifen. Es wird im Zimmerhandwerk verwendet.

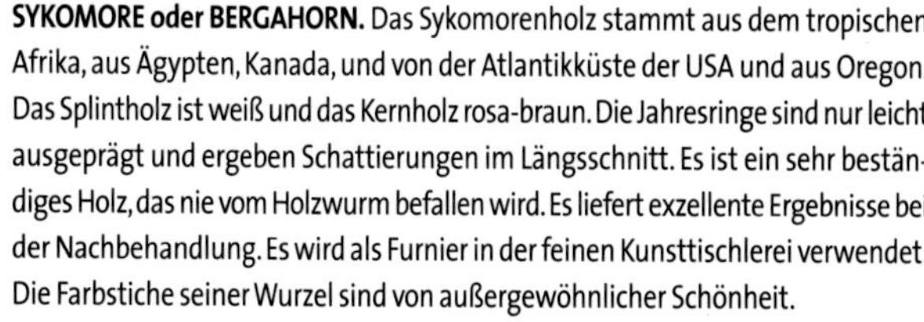

SYKOMORE oder BERGAHORN. Das Sykomorenholz stammt aus dem tropischen Afrika, aus Ägypten, Kanada, und von der Atlantikküste der USA und aus Oregon. Das Splintholz ist weiß und das Kernholz rosa-braun. Die Jahresringe sind nur leicht ausgeprägt und ergeben Schattierungen im Längsschnitt. Es ist ein sehr beständiges Holz, das nie vom Holzwurm befallen wird. Es liefert exzellente Ergebnisse bei der Nachbehandlung. Es wird als Furnier in der feinen Kunsttischlerei verwendet. Die Farbstiche seiner Wurzel sind von außergewöhnlicher Schönheit.

ULME. Die Ulme ist vor allem in Süd- und Mitteleuropa sowie in einigen Gebieten der skandinavischen Halbinsel zu Hause. Typisch für das Ulmenholz ist das auffällige Muster, das aus den Jahresringen entsteht. Seine Textur ist grob und der

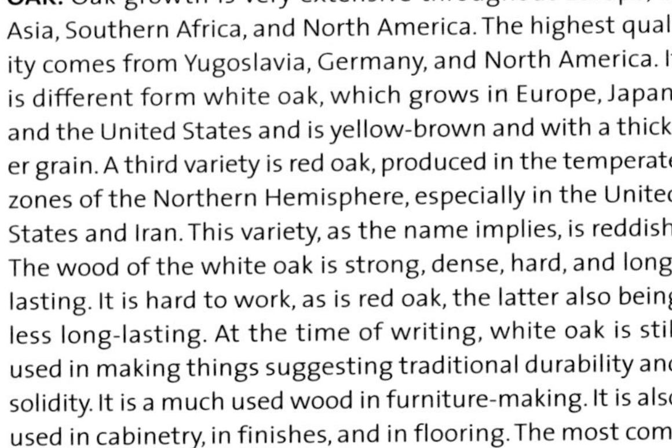

OAK. Oak growth is very extensive throughout Europe, in Asia, Southern Africa, and North America. The highest quality comes from Yugoslavia, Germany, and North America. It is different form white oak, which grows in Europe, Japan, and the United States and is yellow-brown and with a thicker grain. A third variety is red oak, produced in the temperate zones of the Northern Hemisphere, especially in the United States and Iran. This variety, as the name implies, is reddish. The wood of the white oak is strong, dense, hard, and long-lasting. It is hard to work, as is red oak, the latter also being less long-lasting. At the time of writing, white oak is still used in making things suggesting traditional durability and solidity. It is a much used wood in furniture-making. It is also used in cabinetry, in finishes, and in flooring. The most com-

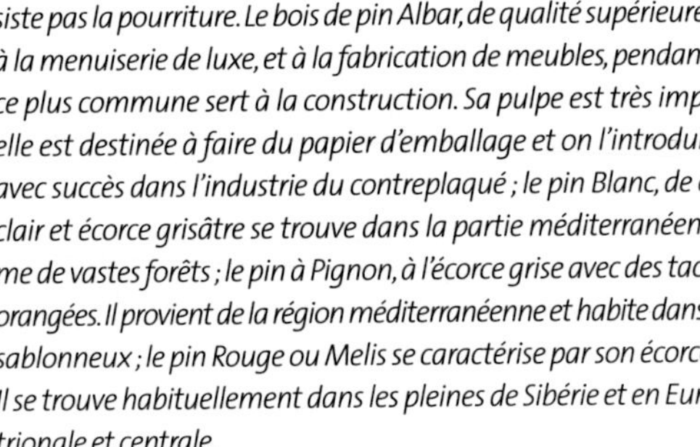

siste pas la pourriture. Le bois de pin Albar, de qualité supérieure, est destiné à la menuiserie de luxe, et à la fabrication de meubles, pendant que l'espèce plus commune sert à la construction. Sa pulpe est très importante car elle est destinée à faire du papier d'emballage et on l'introduit peu à peu avec succès dans l'industrie du contreplaqué ; le pin Blanc, de couleur vert clair et écorce grisâtre se trouve dans la partie méditerranéenne sous forme de vastes forêts ; le pin à Pignon, à l'écorce grise avec des taches marron orangées. Il provient de la région méditerranéenne et habite dans des terrains sablonneux ; le pin Rouge ou Melis se caractérise par son écorce rougeâtre. Il se trouve habituellement dans les pleines de Sibérie et en Europe septentrionale et centrale.

SYCOMORE ou ÉRABLE: *Le bois de sycomore provient d'Afrique tropicale, d'Egypte, du Canada, de la partie Atlantique des Etats-Unis et d'Oregon. L'au-*

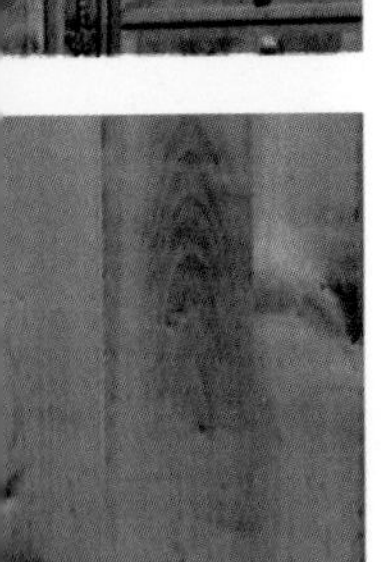

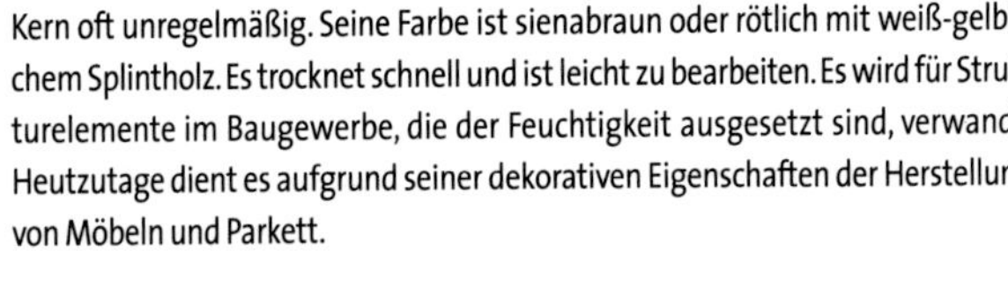

Kern oft unregelmäßig. Seine Farbe ist sienabraun oder rötlich mit weiß-gelblichem Splintholz. Es trocknet schnell und ist leicht zu bearbeiten. Es wird für Strukturelemente im Baugewerbe, die der Feuchtigkeit ausgesetzt sind, verwandt. Heutzutage dient es aufgrund seiner dekorativen Eigenschaften der Herstellung von Möbeln und Parkett.

ZEDER. Das angenehm riechende Zedernholz stammt aus Zentral- und Südamerika, aus Europa, Kleinasien (Libanon) und Afrika (Algerien). Seine Farbe gleicht der des Mahagonibaumes, aber seine Textur ist gröber, das Holz ist leichter und manchmal harzig. Es trocknet schnell, ist sehr stabil, beständig und ist schimmel- und termitenresistent. Aufgrund seiner Weichheit ist es gut zu bearbeiten. Wegen der gerade genannten Eigenschaften und seines dekorativen Aussehens wird dieses Holz sehr geschätzt und für das Verkleiden von Möbeln, Schnitzereien und lu-

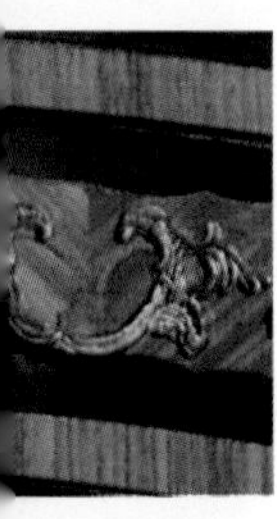

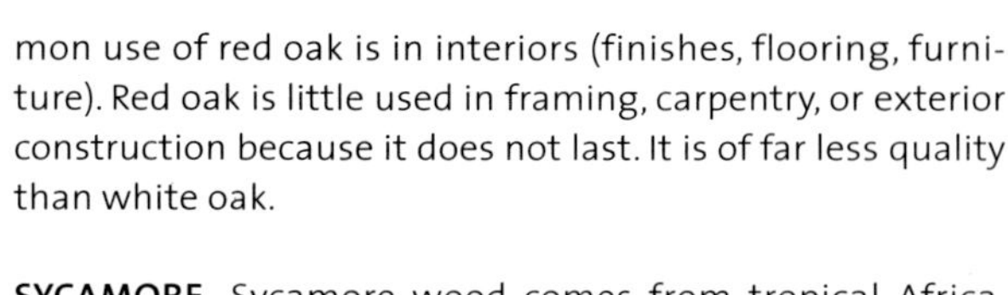

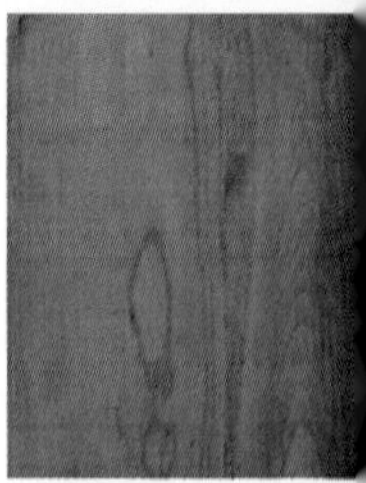

mon use of red oak is in interiors (finishes, flooring, furniture). Red oak is little used in framing, carpentry, or exterior construction because it does not last. It is of far less quality than white oak.

SYCAMORE. Sycamore wood comes from tropical Africa, Egypt, and from Canada and the Atlantic coast of the U.S.A. (it is also found in Oregon). The sapwood is white; the duramen reddish brown. The growth rings are lightly delineated and make shadowy lines longitudinally. The wood is very durable and never attacked by woodworm. It permits a good finish and is used as veneer in fine cabinetry. Maple wood has a much appreciated "bird's-eye" knotting.

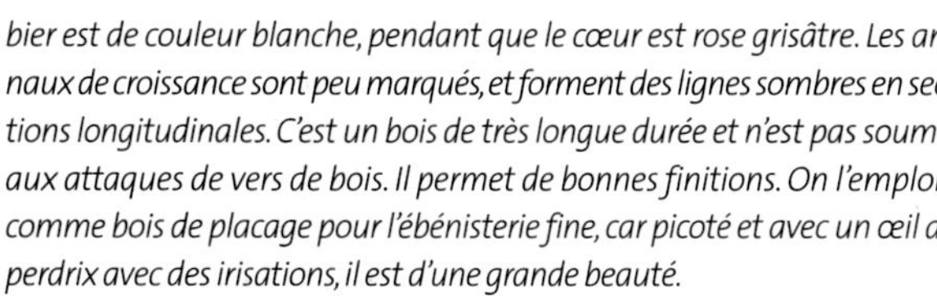

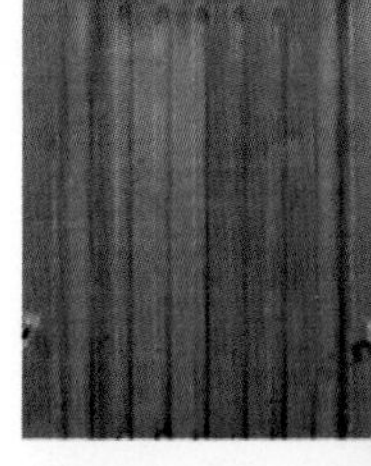

bier est de couleur blanche, pendant que le cœur est rose grisâtre. Les anaux de croissance sont peu marqués, et forment des lignes sombres en sections longitudinales. C'est un bois de très longue durée et n'est pas soumis aux attaques de vers de bois. Il permet de bonnes finitions. On l'emploie comme bois de placage pour l'ébénisterie fine, car picoté et avec un œil de perdrix avec des irisations, il est d'une grande beauté.

YEUSE: *On trouve la yeuse dans les régions chaudes de certains pays tropicaux et dans les zones méditerranéennes de l'Europe septentrionale. Le bois de yeuse est d'une dureté extraordinaire, semblable au chêne, de couleur beige ou marron clair. Il est difficile à sécher car il a tendance à se tordre et à se fendre. Il est robuste et de longue durée mais difficile scier et à travailler et présente certaines difficultés pour obtenir une finition lisse. On l'utilise pour la fabrication d'armatures en menuiserie.*

xuriöse Verkleidungen verwendet. Es ist das traditionelle Holz für die Herstellung von Zigarrenkisten.

ZITRONENBAUM. Das Holz des Zitronenbaums stammt aus Ost-Indien und Ceylon. Es hat eine bräunlich-gelbe Färbung und eine goldfarbene Maserung, so daß es ein sehr schönes Furnier ergibt. Es ist leicht zu bearbeiten. Es wird in der Möbelindustrie, in der Inneneinrichtung und bei Verkleidungen verwendet.

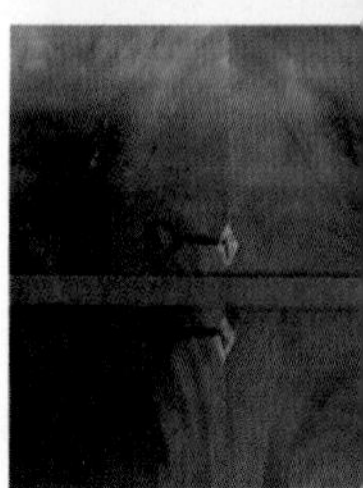

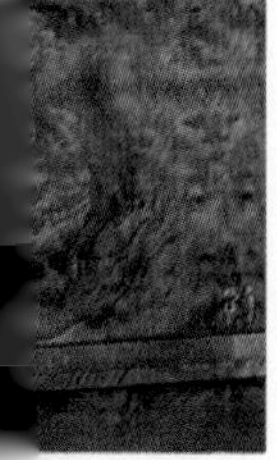

ZITRONENHOLZBAUM. Der Zitronenholzbaum wächst in Afrika und auf den Philippinen. Das Holz ist hellgelb, hart, dicht und hat gedrungene Öffnungen. Es ist leicht zu bearbeiten und zu glätten und es wird vor allem zur Herstellung von Intarsien und Furnieren verwendet.

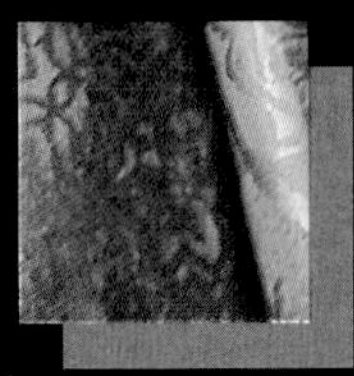

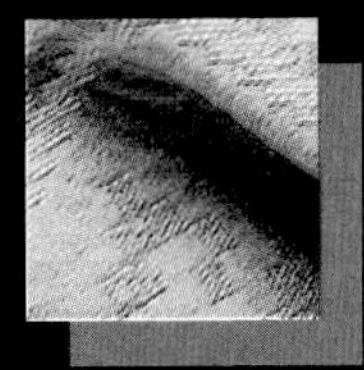

Upholstery

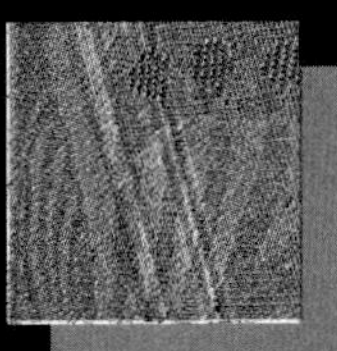

Tapisseries

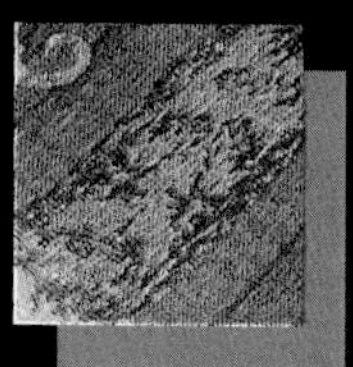

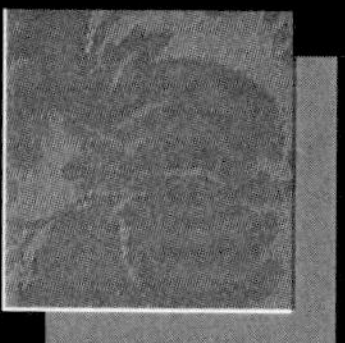

Stoffe und Bezüge

The most widely used complementary material used in decorating furniture, in the antique tradition, is without doubt fabric. The specialist manages, through the use of different fabric types, to bring about the precise finish needed. Determined pictorial scenes may be included, and the added material may be used in chair seats or cabinet furniture. There are many varieties and types of fabrics used in this way, some of the more notable ones being damask, silk, brocade, and an endless number of cottons (chintz, for example, or mercerized cottons). The following pages offer a small sample of these fabrics.

Le tissu est le matériel le plus généralement utilisé et de tradition la plus ancienne pour les meubles et la décoration. Grâce à elle, le spécialiste donne la finition précise aux pièces faites pour s'assoire dans la création d'ambiances et de scénarios déterminés, ainsi qu'aux intérieurs de meubles contenants. Il existe une grande variété de tissus utilisés dans ce but, entre lesquels ont distingue les damassés, les soies, les brocarts et une multitude de cotons -mercerisés, chintz, etc..- dont nous présentons quelques échantillons.

Ohne Zweifel ist der Stoff das am meisten verwendete Komplement. Es ist Teil der alten Tradition des Möbelbaus und der Dekoration. Mit dem Stoff vollendet der Spezialist seinen geschaffenen Raum und seine Inszenierungen, seine Sitzmöbel und die Innenauskleidungen der Möbel, die der Aufbewahrung von Gegenständen dienen. Es gibt viele Varianten und Arten von Stoffen, die zu diesem Zweck verwendet werden. Die wichtigsten Stoffe sind der Damast, die Seide, der Brokat und eine Unmenge von Baumwollarten – merzerisierte Baumwolle und Chintz - von denen wir eine kleine Auswahl vorstellen.

1.

Moirée Sauvage model, designed and produced by Esteban Figuerola.

Modèle Moiré Sauvage, créé et produit par Esteban Figuerola.

Modell Moirée Sauvage, entworfen und hergestellt von Esteban Figuerola.

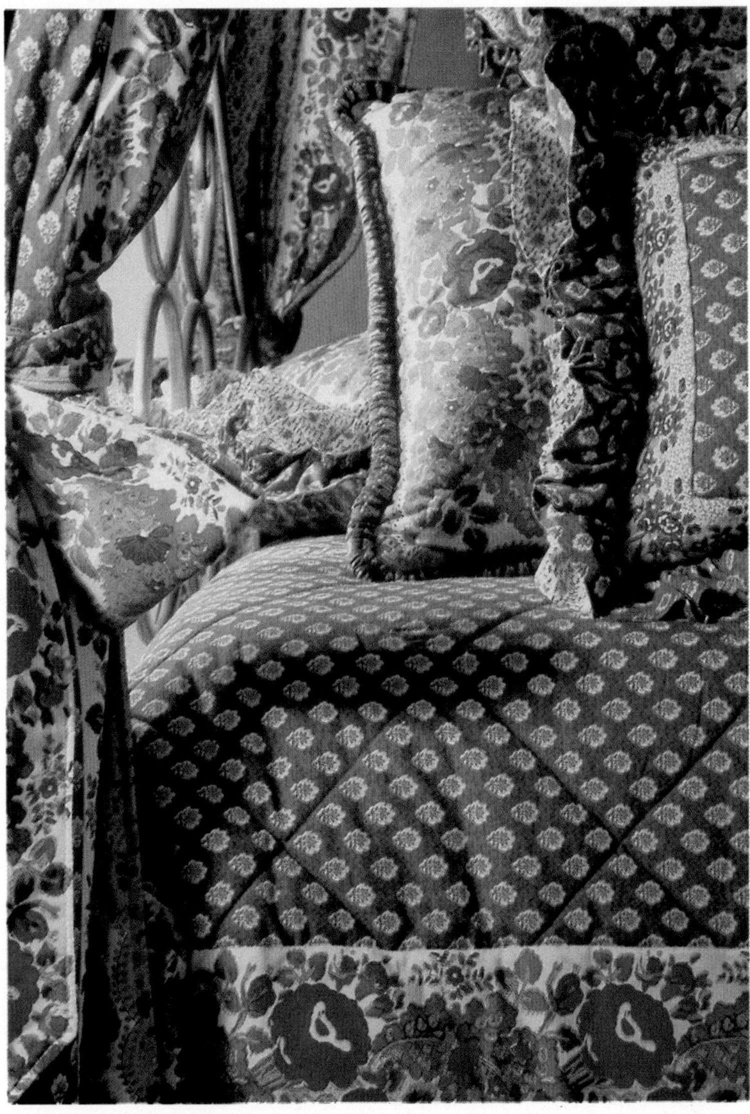

1.

Still life used in curtains, bedspread, and cushions, produced by Souleiado.

Nature morte intégrée par rideaux, dessus de lit et coussins, produits par Souleiado.

Stilleben, bestehend aus Vorhängen, Steppdecke und Kissen, hergestellt von Souleiado.

2.

Anatolia model, designed and produced by Esteban Figuerola.

Modèle Anatolia, créé et produit par Esteban Figuerola.

Modell Anatolia, entworfen und hergestellt von Esteban Figuerola.

1.

Jardino design, produced by Voghi , distributed in Spain by Alonso Mercader.

Design Jardino, produit par Voghi et distribué en Espagne par Alonso Mercader.

Design Jardino, hergestellt von Voghi. Vertrieb in Spanien durch Alonso Mercader.

2.

Cuadrado model, designed and produced by Esteban Figuerola.

Modèle Cuadrado, créé et produit par Esteban Figuerola.

Modell Cuadrado, entworfen und hergestellt von Esteban Figuerola.

1.

Patricia Wynn collection, expressly designed for Sati.

Collection Patricia Wynn créée spécialement pour Sati.

Kollektion Patricia Wynn, eigens für Sati entworfen.

2.

Senneh model, designed and produced by Esteban Figuerola.

Modèle Senneh, créé et produit par Esteban Figuerola.

Modell Senneh, entworfen und hergestellt von Esteban Figuerola.

1.

Different blue fabrics from Mayfer-Tex, porcelain vases and antique Syrian chest of drawers.

Ensemble de tissus bleus de la marque Mayfer-Tex, vases en porcelaine et commode de Syrie ancienne.

Ensemble von blauen Stoffen von Mayfer-Tex, Porzellanvasen und antike syrische Kommode.

2.

Still life of different products from Paris Shop.

Nature morte de divers produits, de Paris Shop.

Stilleben aus verschiedenen Elementen von Paris Shop.

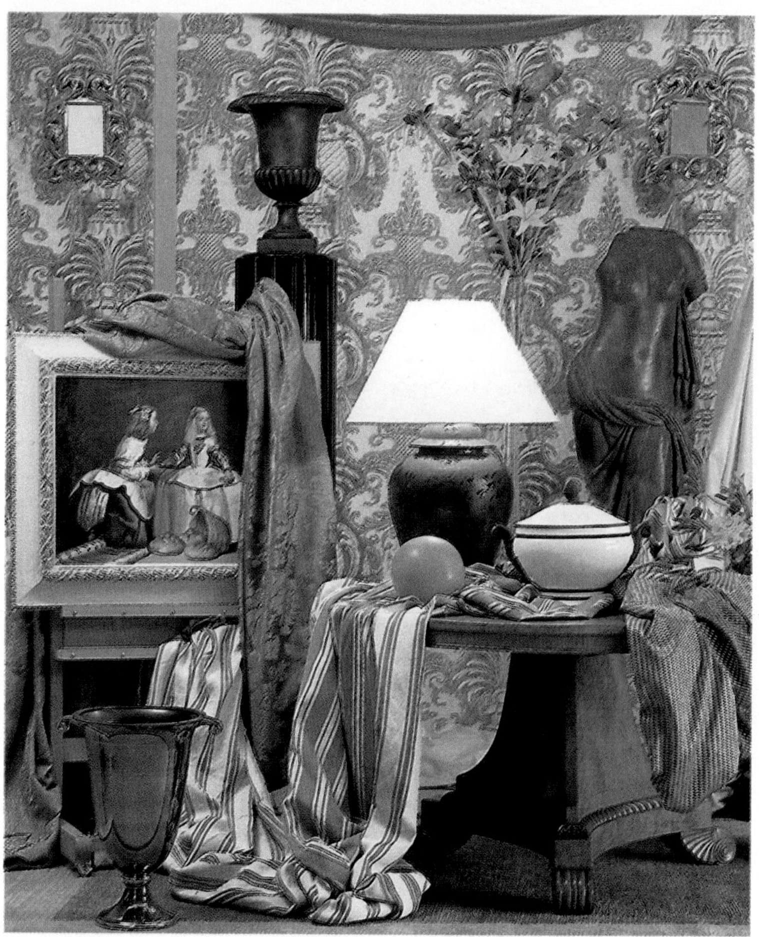

1.

Assembly of objects: table by Directorio, wooden columns in black lacquer by Enebro-Mayfer. Fabrics by Mayfer-Tex. Soup tureen and lamp by Corinto-Mayfer, cups and painting by Capitel-Mayfer.

Ensemble composé par table Directoire, colonnes de bois laquées en noir, de la marque Enebro-Mayfer. Ensemble de tissus de la marque Mayer-Tex. Soupière et lampe de Corinto-Mayfer, coupes et tableau Ménines de la marque Capitel-Mayfer

Ensemble, bestehend aus Directoire-Tisch, schwarz lackierten Holzsäulen, von der Firma Enebro-Mayfer. Ensemble von Stoffen von Mayfer-Tex. Suppenschüssel und Lampe von Corinto-Mayfer, Pokale und Bild Meninas von Capitel-Mayfer.

2.

Various prints by Gastón and Daniela.

Nature morte d'imprimés de Gaston y Daniela.

Bedrucktes Stilleben von Gastón y Daniela.

1.

Collection of English linens by Mayfer-Tex, Chippendale chair and small walnut piece by Enebro-Mayfer.

Collection de tissus de fil anglais pour la marque Mayfer-Tex, chaise Chippendale et petit meuble anglais en noyer de la marque Enebro-Mayfer.

Kollektion von englischen Stoffen für Mayfer-Tex, Chippendale Stuhl und kleines englisches Möbelstück aus Nußbaum von Enebro-Mayfer.

2.

Collection of prints on Greek patterns, marbles and onyx designed by Angelis for Mayfer-Tex.

Ensemble de tissus imprimés avec des motifs grecs, marbres et onyx créés par Angelis pour la marque Mayfer-Tex.

Ensemble von bedruckten Stoffen mit griechischen und marmorierten Motiven und Onyx, von Angelis für Mayfer-Tex entworfen.

1.

Sofa with woven upholstery of floral motifs by Mayfer-Tex. Compact marble angels by Capitel-Mayfer.

Fauteuil avec tapisserie tissée avec des motifs floraux, réalisé par Mayfer-Tex. Couple d'anges en marbre compacte de la marque Capitel-Mayfer.

Sofa mit geblümtem Stoffbezog, hergestellt von Mayfer-Tex. Engelspaar aus massivem Marmor von Capitel-Mayfer.

2.

Embajador collection of cotton fabrics, armchair, and footstool in linen print by Mayfer-Tex. Regency chest of drawers by Enebro-Mayfer. Tiffany lamb imported by Capitel-Mayfer.

Collection Embajador de tissus en coton, fauteuil et repose pieds en fil imprimé de la marque Mayfer-Tex, commode Régence de la marque Enebro-Mayfer. Sur celle-ci, lampe Tffany imprtée par Capitel-Mayfer.

Kollektion Embajador aus Baumwollstoffen, Sessel und mit bedrucktem Stoff überzogener Fußauflage von Mayfer-Tex, Régence Kommode von Enebro-Mayfer. Auf der Kommode von Capitel-Mayfer importierte Tiffany Lampe.

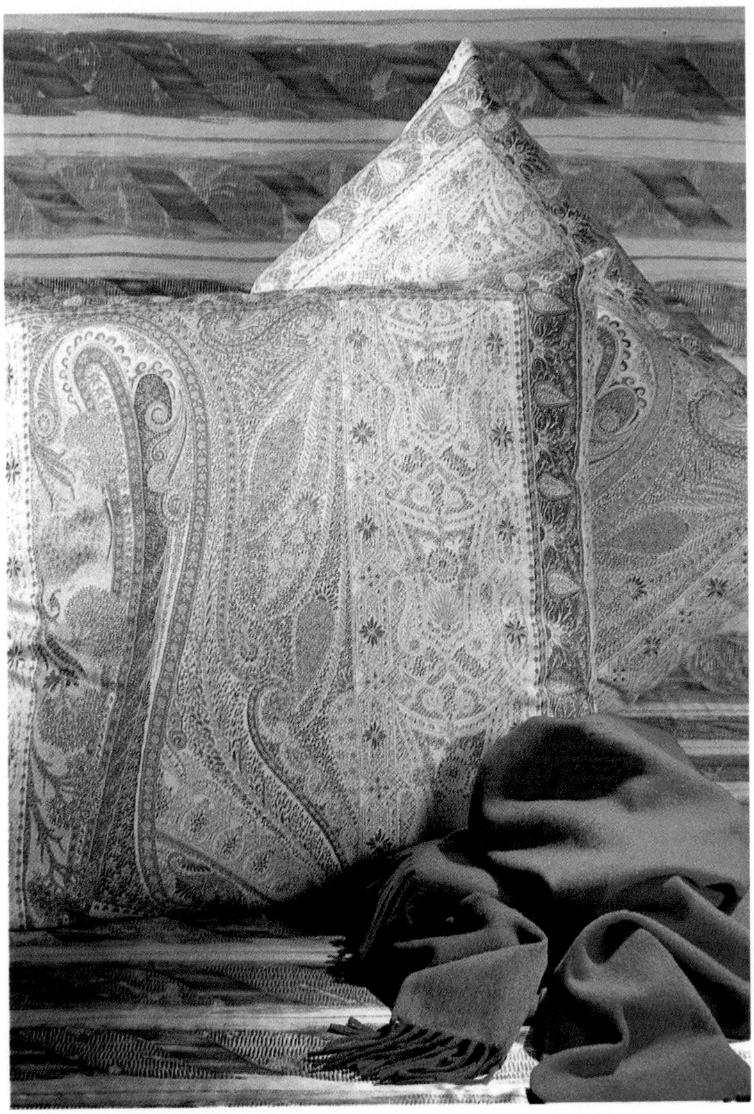

1.

Oriental cushions and striped woolen blanket by Voghi, distributed by Alonso Mercader.

Coussins d'orient et couverture de laine à rayures, de Voghi. Distribués par Alonso Mercader.

Orientkissen und gestreifte Wolldecke, von Voghi. Vertrieb durch Alonso Mercader.

2.

Two Voghi designs.

Deux design de Voghi.

Zwei Entwürfe von Voghi.

1.

Serpente blanket and Katmandu print in wool and silk by Voghi. Distributed by Alonso Mercader.

Couverture Serpente et imprimé Katmandu en laine et soie, de Voghi. Distribués par Alonso Mercader.

Decke Serpente und Druck Katmandú aus Wolle und Seide, von Voghi. Vertrieb durch Alonso Mercader.

2.

La Favorita print from the Liceo collection, designed and produced by Gastón and Daniela.

Imprimés La Favorita, de la collection Liceo, créés et produits par Gaston y Daniela.

Druck La Favorita, aus der Kollektion Liceo, entworfen und hergestellt von Gastón y Daniela.

1.

Cotton damask, designed and produced by Gastón and Daniela.

Damassé en coton. Design et production de Gaston y Daniela.

Damast aus Baumwolle. Entwurf und Herstellung von Gastón y Daniela.

2.

Tyrol model in Fibrana and cotton by Tapicerías Gancedo.

Modèle Tirol en fibranne et coton de Tapicerias Gancedo.

Modell Tirol aus Fiber und Baumwolle von Tapicerías Gancedo.

1.

Augusta design from the Reflejos de la Naturaleza collection by Manuel Romero.

Design Augusta de la collection Reflejos de la Naturaleza, de Manuel Romero.

Design Augusta aus der Kollektion Reflejos de la Naturaleza, von Manuel Romero.

2.

Caruso model by Reycol, designed by Muñoz.

Modèle Caruso de la société Reycol, créé par Muñoz.

Modell Caruso von Reycol, entworfen Muñoz.

1.

Ankara model in satin weave cotton by Coordonné.

Modèle Ankara en coton satiné, de Coordonné.

Modell Ankara aus satinierter Baumwolle, von Coordonné.

2.

Mercedes model in satin weave cotton by Coordonné.

Modèle Mercedes en coton satiné, de Coordonné.

Modell Mercedes aus satinierter Baumwolle, von Coordonné.

1.

Sofía model in satin weave cotton by Coordonné.

Modèle Sofia en coton satiné, de Coordonné.

Modell Sofía aus satinierter Baumwolle, von Coordonné.

2.

Damask in cotton and rayon by Tapicerías Gancedo.

Damassé en coton et rayon, de Tapicerias Gancedo.

Damast aus Baumwolle und Rayon, von Tapicerías Gancedo.

1.

Damask by Tapicerías Gancedo.

Damassé à rayures en coton, de Tapicerias Gancedo.

Damast mit Streifen aus Baumwolle, von Tapicerías Gancedo.

2.

Carmen print from the Liceo collection, designed and produced by Gastón and Daniela.

Imprimé Carmen, de la collection Liceo, créé et produit par Gaston y Daniele.

Druck Carmen, aus der Kollektion Liceo, entworfen und hergestellt von Gastón y Daniela.

1.

Renaissance damask in cotton and rayon by Tapicerías Gancedo.

Damassé Renaissance en coton et rayon, de Tapicerias Gancedo.

Damast Renacimiento aus Baumwolle und Rayon, von Tapicerías Gancedo.

2.

Imperio Jarroner model in rayon and cotton, by Tapicerías Gancedo.

Modèle Imperio Jarroner, en rayon et coton, de Tapicerías Gancedo.

Modell Imperio Jarroner, aus Rayon und Baumwolle, von Tapicerías Gancedo.

1.

Rayon and silk damask
by Tapicerías Gancedo.

*Damassé en rayon et soie,
de Tapicerias Gancedo.*

Damast aus Rayon und Seide,
von Tapicerías Gancedo.

2.

Ancien model in rayon and Fibrana by
Tapicerías Gancedo.

*Modèle Ancien, en rayon et fibranne, de
Tapicerias Gancedo.*

Modell Ancien, aus Rayon und Fiber,
von Tapicerías Gancedo.

1.

Thai print, from the China Imperial collection, by Gastón and Daniela.

Imprimé Thai, de la collection China Imperial, de Gaston et Daniela.

Druck Thai, aus der Kollektion China Imperial, von Gastón y Daniela.

2.

Corales y Camafeos collection, by Icíar de la Concha for Pepe Peñalver.

Collection Corales y Camafeos, de Iciar de la Concha pour Pepe Peñalver.

Kollektion Corales y Camafeos, von Icíar de la Concha für Pepe Peñalver.

2.

Marqués de Dos Aguas collection, inspired on Spanish ceramic work of the eighteenth century. Designed by Icíar de la Concha for Pepe Peñalver.

Collection Marques de Dos Aguas, inspirée de la céramique espańole du XVIII ème siècle. Créé par Iciar de la Concha pour Pepe Peñalver.

Kollektion Marqués de Dos Aguas, inspiriert von der spanischen Keramik des 18. Jh. Entworfen von Icíar de la Concha für Pepe Peñalver.

1.

Marie Antoinette model in silk and viscosa by Tapicerías Gancedo.

Modèle Ma Antonieta, en soie et viscose, de Tapicerias Gancedo.

MModell María Antonieta, aus Seide und Viskose, von Tapicerías Gancedo.

1.

Cerámicas collection, by Icíar de la Concha for Pepe Peñalver.

Collection Ceramicas, de Iciar de la Concha pour Pepe Peñalver.

Kollektion Cerámicas, von Icíar de la Concha für Pepe Peñalver.

2.

Bután collection by Icíar de la Concha for Pepe Peñalver.

Collection Butan, de Iciar de la Concha pour Pepe Peñalver.

Kollektion Bután, von Icíar de la Concha für Pepe Peñalver.

1.

Jacquard in cotton for Pepe Peñalver.

Jacquard en coton, pour Pepe Peñalver.

Jacquard aus Baumwolle, für Pepe Peñalver.

2.

Alsacia y Lorena collection designed by Icíar de la Concha for Pepe Peñalver.

Collection Alsacia et Lorena, créé par Iciar de la Concha pour Pepe Peñalver.

Kollektion Alsacia y Lorena, entworfen von Icíar de la Concha für Pepe Peñalver.

1.

Muromachi collection by Icíar de la Concha for Pepe Peñalver.

Collection Muromachi, de Iciar de la Concha pour Pepe Peñalver.

Kollektion Muromachi, von Icíar de la Concha für Pepe Peñalver.

2.

Camafeos collection by Icíar de la Concha for Pepe Peñalver.

Collection Camafeos, de Iciar de la Concha pour Pepe Peñalver.

Kollektion Camafeos, von Icíar de la Concha für Pepe Peñalver.

1.

Victoria Eugenia collection by Icíar de la Concha for Pepe Peñalver.

Collection Victoria Eugenia, de Iciar de la Concha pour Pepe Peñalver.

Kollektion Victoria Eugenia, von Icíar de la Concha für Pepe Peñalver.

2.

Camafeos collection by Icíar de la Concha for Pepe Peñalver.

Collection Camafeos, de Iciar de la Concha pour Pepe Peñalver.

Kollektion Camafeos, von Icíar de la Concha für Pepe Peñalver.

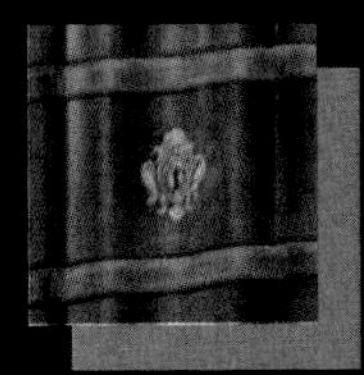

Basic Furniture Types

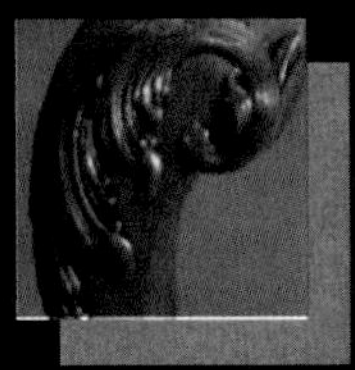

Les Meubles Basiques

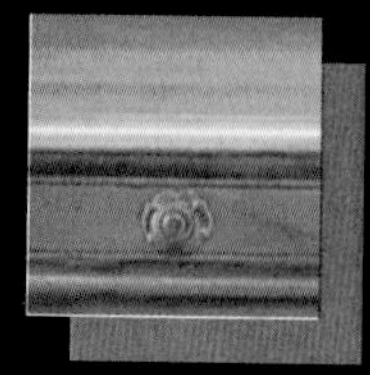

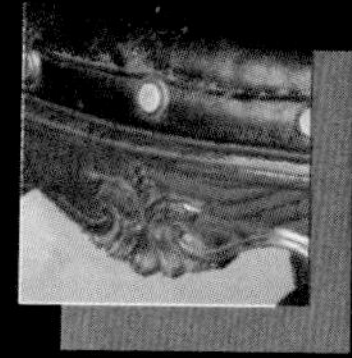

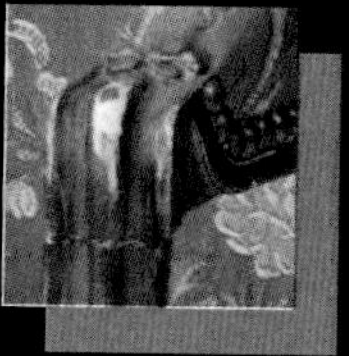

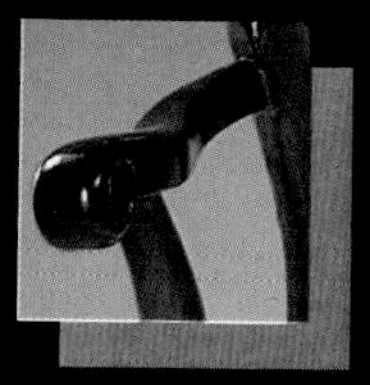

Die wichtigsten Möbelstücke

Beds

Le lit

Das Bett

With the appearance of the first civilizations, the bed appeared both as a place of rest and an element associated with death rites. With the passage of time, beds took on new meanings until it reached the contemporary restricted and concrete stage.

Many are the formal variants the bed has evolved through. Today, it is bare of the adornments of former ages. The examples presented here show the headboard as, on the one hand, an essential structural part and, on the other hand, as a stylistic reference point. Hence, the high headboard with gentle curves accentuated by capricious mold-

C'est avec l'apparition des premières civilisations qu'apparurent les lits, non seulement destinés au repos, mais aussi pour rendre culte aux morts. Avec le temps il acquit de nouvelles significations jusqu'à l'époque actuelle, où son usage est plus restreint et concret. Les variantes formelles sont nombreuses, arrivant jusqu'à la suppression totale d'éléments décoratifs. Dans ces exemplaires, la tête de lit est présentée d'un côté comme une pièce structurelle essentielle du meuble, et d'un autre, comme référence de style. C'est ainsi qu'une tête de lit en hauteur avec des courbes accentuées toute en douceur par des moulures entrelacées manifeste une

Mit dem Erscheinen der ersten Kulturen entstand das Bett, das nicht nur dem Ausruhen vorbehalten war, sondern auch für den Totenkult verwendet wurde. Mit der Zeit erhielt das Bett neue Bedeutungen, bis es die heutige begrenzte und konkrete Funktion erfüllte.

In bezug auf die Form hat es viele verschiedene Varianten gegeben, bis man schließlich heutzutage auf jegliches dekoratives Element verzichtet. In diesen Beispielen stellt das Kopfteil einerseits einen essentiellen Teil der Möbelstruktur dar, und ist andererseits ein stilistischer Bezugspunkt. So zeigt das hohe Kopfteil mit leicht geschwungenen Formen, die von den verspielten Zierleisten hervorgehoben werden, den Einfluß des Neo-Klassizismus,

1.

Bed and night table. Canaleto model, of classical inspiration (Ortolan).

Lit et table de nuit modèle Canaleto, d'inspiration classique (Ortolan).

Bett und Nachttischchen Modell Canaleto, klassisch inspiriert (Ortolan).

1

2

3

1.

Gondola bedroom suite (Zamorano).

Chambre à coucher Gondola (Zamorano).

Gondel-Schlafzimmer (Zamorano).

2.

Bedroom with bed and night tables (Muebles Picó).

Schlafzimmer, bestehend aus Bett und Nachttischchen (Muebles Picó).

Quarto composto por cama e mesinhas de cabeceira (Muebles Picó).

3.

Bedroom in sycamore wood (Mariano García).

Schlafzimmer aus Sykomorenholz (Mariano García).

Quarto em madeira de ácer (Mariano García).

4.

Sketch of bedroom 3.

Skizze Schlafzimmer 3.

Esboço do quarto de 3.

1.

Luis Felipe bedroom collection (Meubles Seguy).

Chambre à coucher Louis Philippe (Meubles Segue).

Schlafzimmer Kollektion Luis Felipe (Meubles Seguy).

2.

English style bedroom in walnut with inlaid work: headboard, four-drawer table or single drawer and doors, writing table, mirror and table (Estilo Forma).

Chambre à coucher style anglais en racine de noyer avec marqueterie, formé par tête de lit, table de nuit de quatre tiroirs ou avec tiroir et portes, commode écritoire, miroir et bureau (Estilo Forma).

Schlafzimmer im englischen Stil aus Nußbaumholz mit Intarsien, bestehend aus Kopfteil, Tischchen mit vier Schubladen bzw. Schublade und Türen, Schreibtisch-Kommode, Spiegel und Bureau (Estilo Forma).

1

ings shows Neoclassical influences, while the Luis Felipe style, with reversed underpanel and crown, is reminiscent of the gondola shape, clearly Empire-inspired.

Of minor Neoclassical inspiration, the chest of drawers on elliptical plane and with four stylized legs with brass feet is unified by the filigreed marquetry of the pilasters that sweep it harmoniously upward--as if the piece were cut from a single solid. This brings about a certain robustness that is nuanced by the ornamental delicacy of rhombic motifs livened by mother-of-

influence néoclassique, pendant que le style Louis-Philippe, avec sa tête de lit et panneau inférieur replié sur lui-même, rappelle le lit en forme de gondole, d'un style Empire évident. D'une légère inspiration néoclassique, la commode de base elliptique repose sur quatre colonnes stylisées avec des talons en laiton qui font partie de la structure verticale de la pièce, en union avec les fins piliers incrustés en ébénisterie qui prolonge harmonieusement la partie haute comme s'il s'agissait d'un meuble taillé d'une seule pièce. Ceci lui donne un certain air de solidité qui tranche bien

während das des Louis Philipp Stils, mit gewölbtem Kopfteil und gewölbtem unterem Paneel, an das Bett in Gondelform erinnert, das klar auf den Empirestil verweist. Angelehnt an den neo-klassischen Stil ruht die Kommode mit elliptischem Grundriß auf vier stilvoll gestalteten kegelstumpfförmigen Beinen mit Messingabsatz, die einen Teil der vertikalen Struktur des Möbelstückes bilden und sich so mit den dünnen, mit Intarsien verzierten Pilastern verbinden, welche harmonisch mit dem Aufbau verschlungen sind, als wenn das Möbelstück aus einem Stück geschnitzt wäre. Das verleiht dem Möbelstück eine gewisse Robust-

2

pp. 388-389.

Bedroom suite (M. Padilla).

Ensemble de chambre à coucher (M. Padilla).

Schlafzimmereinrichtung (M. Padilla).

1.

Headboard with handmade mother-of-pearl decoration (Carpanelli).

Tête de lit avec incrustations manuelles d'huître perlière (Carpanelli).

Kopfteil eines Bettes, manuell mit Perlmutt veredelt (Carpanelli).

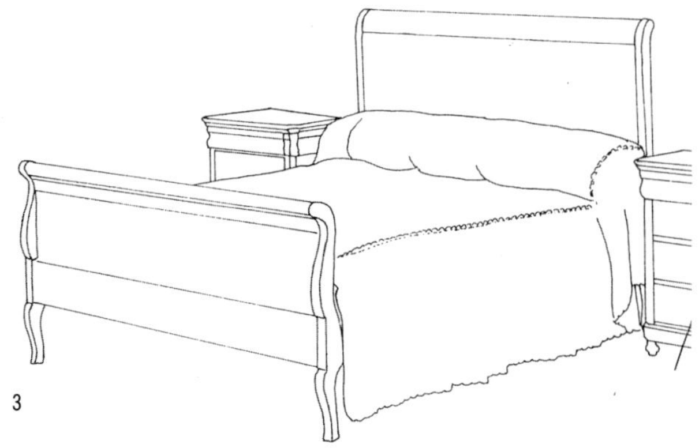

3

2.

Ship's bedroom (Zamorano).

Chambre à coucher bateau (Zamorano).

Schiff-Schlafzimmer (Zamorano).

3.

Sketch of bedroom 2.

Détail de chambre à coucher bateau 2.

Skizze Schiff-Schlafzimmer 2.

1

pp. 392-393.

Bedroom suite in walnut
(M. Padilla).

Ensemble de chambre à coucher en bois de noyer (M. Padilla).

Schlafzimmereinrichtung aus Nußbaumholz (M. Padilla).

1.

Anna model bed in brass
(Peña Vargas).

Lit modèle Anna en laiton (Peña Vargas).

Bett Modell Anna aus Messing
(Peña Vargas).

2.

Jacaranda model bedroom with headboard and foot in brass
(Peña Vargas).

Chambre à coucher modèle Jacaranda avec tête de lit et pieds en laiton (Peña Vargas).

Schlafzimmer Modell Jacaranda mit Kopfteil und Messingfuß
(Peña Vargas).

2

1

pearl circles that recur in the headboard of the bed, like an interfacing rhythm in the whole suite.

avec la délicatesse ornementale des motifs en forme de losanges, aux sommets agrémentés par des cercles en huître perlière qui apparaissent à nouveau dans la tête de lit en temps que rythme commun à tout le mobilier de la chambre à coucher.

heit, die von der Zartheit der schmückenden rhombischen Motive aufgelockert wird, die an ihrem Scheitelpunkt durch Kreise aus Perlmutt anmutig gestaltet werden. Diese Perlmuttkreise erscheinen erneut auf dem Kopfteil und finden sich auch in der gesamten Einrichtung des Schlafzimmers wieder.

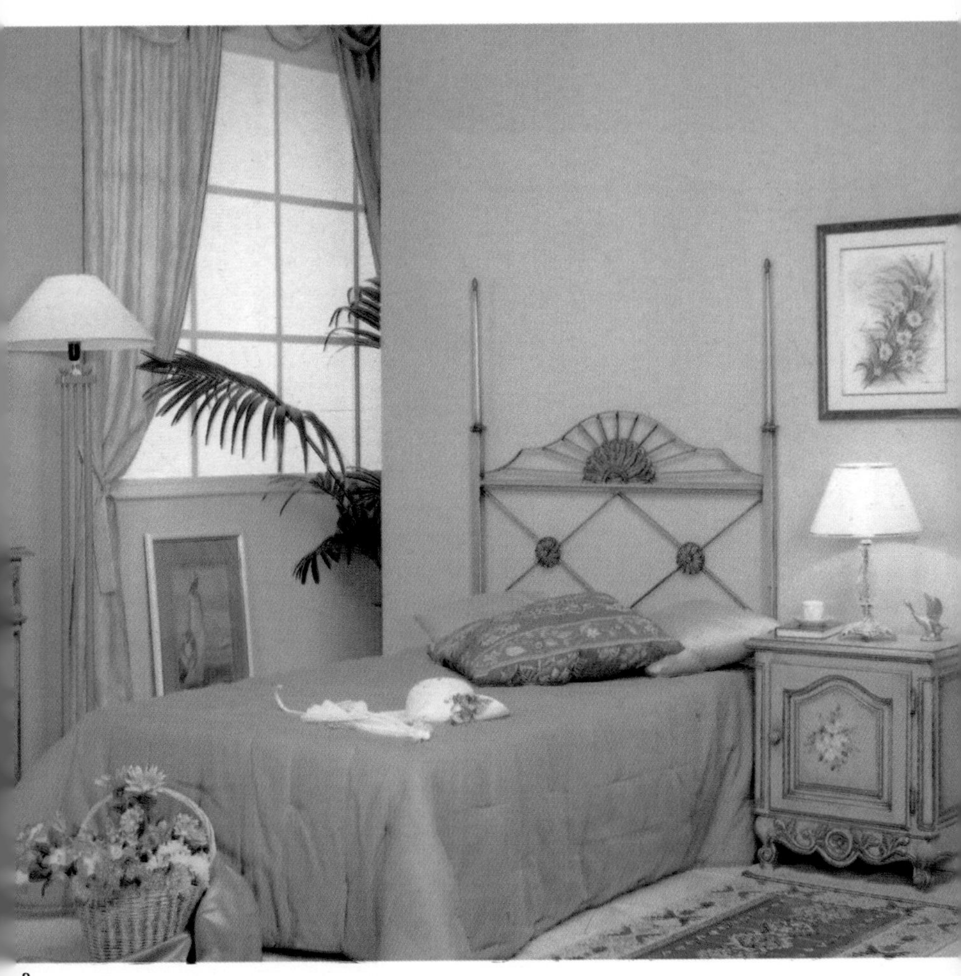

2

1.

Imola model bed in brass and silver (Peña Vargas).

Lit modèle Imola en laiton et argent (Peña Vargas).

Bett Modell Imola aus Messing und Silber (Peña Vargas).

2.

Bedroom with night table and writing desk in solid pine.

Chambre â coucher formé par table de nuit et secrétaire en bois de pin massif.

Schlafzimmer, bestehend aus Nachttischchen und Sekretär aus massiver Kiefer.

1.

Bedroom finished in antique cherry form the Europa collection (Toscano Mobil).

Schlafzimmer nachbehandelt mit Kirschbaumholz. Antiquitäten aus der Kollektion Europa, von Toscano Mobil.

Quarto com acabamento em Cerejeira Antiquário, da colecção Europa, de Toscano Mobil.

1.
Bedroom by Ebanistería Arenas.
Chambre à coucher d'Ébénisterie Arenas.
Schlafzimmer von Ebanistería Arenas.

2.
Barcones model bedroom by Artema.
Chambre à coucher Barcones, d'Artema.
Schlafzimmer Barcones, von Artema.

1.
Oncala model bedroom set by Artema.
Ensemble chambre à coucher Oncala, d'Artema.
Schlafzimmereinrichtung Oncala, von Artema.

2.
Soria model bedroom set by Artema.
Ensemble chambre à coucher Soria, d'Artema.
Mobília de quarto Soria, de Artema.

1

2

1.

Bed finished in cherry wood by JNG.

Lit avec finition en cerisier, de JNG.

Bett mit Nachbearbeitung Kirschbaumholz, von JNG.

2.

Tuscan bedroom (R. Juste Requena).

Chambre à coucher Toscano, de R. Juste Requena.

Schlafzimmer Toscano, von R. Juste Requena.

3

3.

Bed from the Mireia-99 collection by Rivera.

Lit de la collection Mireia-99, de Rivera.

Bett aus der Kollektion Mireia-99, von Rivera.

4.

Bávaro-Tirolés model canopy bed and accompanying items (R. Juste Requena).

Chambre à coucher à baldaquin Bavaro-Tiroles, de R. Juste Requena.

Bayrisch-Tirolerisches Baldachin-Schlafzimmer, von R. Juste Requena.

4

1.
Nerea collection bed, by Rivera.
Lit de la collection Nerea, de Rivera.
Bett aus der Kollektion Nerea, von Rivera.

2.
Bedroom suite and lamp (Muebles Mariner).
Chambre et lampe, de Muebles Mariner.
Schlafzimmer und Lampe, von Muebles Mariner.

The chair

La chaise

Der stuhl

Along with the bed, the chair is another piece of furniture that is essentially functional and basic. In addition to the obvious need the human body has, because of its bone structure, to be in the erect and supine positions, it must also assume intermediate positions between these two: the positions we take when we sit. Moreover, the chair is a key element in furnishing dwellings because its structure is highly complex when it comes to adapting to such human needs.

Avec le lit, la chaise est une des pièces du mobilier les plus fonctionnelles et basiques, puisque, en plus des positions debout et allongée, les personnes, à cause de leur ossature, ont besoin de la posture intermédiaire que nous adoptons en nous asseyant. La chaise est, de plus, un élément clé dans le mobilier, car il présente une grande complexité au moment d'être adapté aux nécessités motrices et fonctionnelles de l'être humain.

Pour tout cela, il a souvent été l'objet d'études tectoniques détaillées et minutieuses de la

Gemeinsam mit dem Bett ist der Stuhl eines der in erster Linie funktionellen und grundlegenden Möbelstücke; denn zusätzlich zu der aufrechten und der Rückenlage brauchen wir aufgrund unserer Knochenstruktur eine intermediäre Haltung, die wir beim Sitzen einnehmen. Der Stuhl ist andererseits ein Schlüsselelement der Möbeleinrichtung, da er eine sehr komplexe Struktur hat; denn er wird den motorischen und funktionellen Bedürfnissen des Menschen angepaßt. Aus diesen Gründen war er oft das Objekt genauer

1.

Restoration bergère (Guilles Nouailhac).

Bergère Restauration (Guilles Nouailhac).

Bergere Restauration (Guilles Nouailhac).

1

2

3

4

1.
Louis-Philippe style chair.
Chaise Louis Philippe.
Stuhl Louis Philipp.

2.
Louis-Philippe style chair.
Fauteuil Louis Philippe.
Sessel Louis Philipp.

3.
Louis-Philippe style chair.
Fauteuil Louis Philippe.
Sessel Louis Philipp.

4.
Rustic chair.
Chaise rustique.
Rustikaler Stuhl.

5

6

7

8

5.
Chair
Chaise.
Stuhl.

6.
Chair
Chaise.
Stuhl.

7.
Normanda model chair.
Chaise modèle Normanda.
Stuhl Modell Normanda.

8.
Pajizo model chair (René Hayedot).
Chaise modèle Pajizo (René Hayedot).
Stuhl Modell Pajizo (René Hayedot).

1

2

3

4

1.
Chair (René Hayedot).
Fauteuil (René Hayedot).
Sessel (René Hayedot).

2.
Chair (René Hayedot).
Chaise (René Hayedot).
Stuhl (René Hayedot).

3.
Upholstered chair (Pesmac).
Chaise tapissée (Pesmac).
Gepolsterter Stuhl (Pesmac).

5

6

4.

Louis-Philippe chair with ball feet (René Hayedot).

Chaise Louis Philippe avec pieds de boules (René Hayedot).

Louis-Philipp-Stuhl mit Kugelfüßen (René Hayedot).

5.

Brighton chair with white upholstery (Enebro).

Chaise Brighton tapissée en blanc (Enebro).

Stuhl Brighton, weiß gepolstert (Enebro).

6.

Chair with double tapestry back (Rotterdam GmbH & CoKG).

Chaise avec double dossier tapissé (Rotterdam GmbH & CoKG).

Stuhl mit zweifach gepolsterter Rückenlehne (Rotterdam GmbH & CoKG).

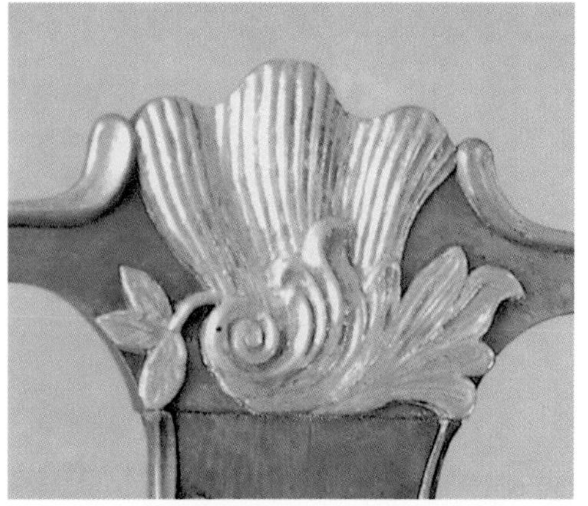

1

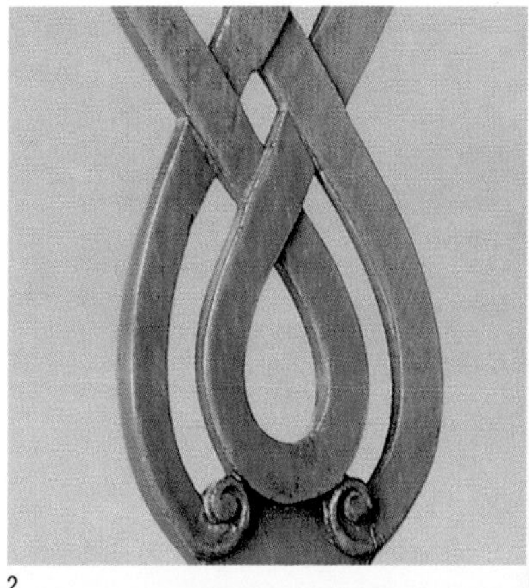

2

3

1.

Detail of the crown of chair 4: carved gilt anthemion of rococo inspiration.

Détail de sommet de la chaise 4 : frise taillée dorée d'inspiration rococo.

Ausschnitt mit obere Leiste des Stuhls 4: Geschnitztes, goldenes Blattornament, vom Rokoko inspiriert.

2.

Detail of the central upright of chair 4: carved filigree work.

Détail de pale centrale de la chaise 4 : filigrane taillée.

Ausschnitt Mittelteil Rückenlehne von Stuhl 4: geschnitzte Filigranarbeit.

3.

Detail of the upholstery of chair 4.

Détail de tapisserie du siège de la chaise 4.

Ausschnitt Stoffbezug der Sitzfläche Stuhl 4.

4.

Danish chair in different fruit tree woods. (1760: original piece held by Antigüedades Fortuny).

Chaise danoise en bois d'arbre fruitier de 1760. Pièce originale (Antiquités Foruny).

Dänischer Stuhl aus Obstbaumholz von 1760. Originalstück (Antigüedades Fortuny).

1

2

3

1.

Upholstered chair and gilt adornment (Indumoble).

Fauteuil tapissé et avec des dorures (Indumoble).

Gepolsterter Sessel mit Goldverzierungen (Indumoble).

2.

Directoire chair (Gilles Nouailhac).

Chaise Directoire (Gilles Nouailhac).

Directoire-Sessel (Gilles Nouailhac).

3 - 7.

Upholstered chair (Pesmac).

Chaise tapissée (Pesmac).

Gepolsterter Stuhl (Pesmac).

4.

Directoire consul chair (Gilles Nouailhac).

Fauteuil Directoire Consulat (Gilles Nouailhac).

Sessel Directoire-Konsular (Gilles Nouailhac).

5.

Bergère Dauphin, Restoration style (Gilles Nouailhac).

Bergère Dauphin Restauration (Gilles Nouailhac).

Bergère Dauphin Restauration (Gilles Nouailhac).

6.

Elisa model upholstered armchair (Enebro).

Fauteuil Elisa tapissé (Enebro).

Sessel Elisa, gepolstert (Enebro).

5

7

1

2

2.

Marie Antoinette Transition style salon with lacquered and gilt furniture: sofa, armchairs with woven backs (Charles Barr).

Salon style Transition Marie-Antoinette laqué et doré, formé par canapé, fauteuils avec dossier en cannage (Charles Barr).

Salon im Übergangsstil Marie Antoinette, lackiert und vergoldet, bestehend aus Sofa und Sesseln mit geflochtener Rückenlehne (Charles Barr).

1.

Upholstered armchair (Pesmac).

Fauteuil avec siège tapissé (Pesmac).

Sessel mit gepolsterter Sitzfläche (Pesmac).

Because of these considerations, the chair has often the object of highly detailed structural studies by "structure artists": architects. Since the eighteenth century, many technical advances have stimulated furniture designers to experiment with new forms and blend them daringly, in an audacious eclecticism, with older forms. The result can be

part d'artistes des structures : les architectes. Depuis le XVIII ème siècle, les avances techniques stimulent les créateurs de meubles à expérimenter avec de nouvelles formes et les conjuguer avec audace, dans un élan d'éclectisme, avec d'autres passées, tout en essayant de récupérer les points les plus significatifs des styles antérieurs. Suivant ce nouveau chemin, le

und manischer tektonischer Studien der Strukturkünstler: der Architekten. Seit dem 18. Jh. regen die technischen Fortschritte die Möbelschaffenden dazu an, neue Formen auszuprobieren und sie wagemutig in einem Anzeichen von Eklektizismus mit anderen vergangenen Formen in Einklang zu bringen, indem sie versuchen, die bedeutsamsten Punkte der vor-

1

2

1.

Canterbury armchair (Enebro).

Fauteuil Canterbury (Enebro).

Sessel Canterbury (Enebro).

2.

George III armchair in oak. Original piece (Antigüedades Fortuny).

Fauteuil en chêne George III. Pièce originale(Antiquités Fortuny).

Sessel aus Eiche Georg III. Originalstück (Antigüedades Fortuny).

3.

Chair and armchair (Charles Barr).

Chaise et fauteuil (Charles Barr).

Stuhl und Sessel (Charles Barr).

3

the recovery of those features that meant most to the earlier styles.

Following this new trace, modern design almost always finds a different ergonomic pathway. At the same time, perhaps there are as many designers who enjoy the creation of new potentials as those who enjoy adapting popular types to the demands of pluralism in our new world.

design moderne tente presque toujours de conjuguer commodité et ergonomie, bien que beaucoup de créateurs préfèrent réaliser des œuvres d'art en puissance et beaucoup d'autres préfèrent innover en adaptant quelques types populaires aux exigences de la pluralité et des activités concrètes du nouveau monde.

angegangenen Stilrichtungen wiederaufzunehmen. Das moderne Design folgt dieser neuen Richtung und versucht fast immer, Bequemlichkeit und Ergonomie zu verbinden; obwohl es viele Designer gibt, die gerne potentielle Kunstwerke schaffen, und viele andere, die Neuheiten hervorbringen, indem sie einige populäre Modelle den Forderungen der Mehrheit und den tatsächlichen Aktivitäten unserer neuen alltäglichen Welt anpassen.

1

1.

Chair and armchair with quadrangular back (Heinrich Rotterdam GmbH & CoKG).

Chaise et fauteuil avec dossier quadrangulaire (Heinrich Rotterdam GmH & CoKG).

Stuhl und Sessel mit quadratischer Rückenlehne (Heinrich Rotterdam GmbH & CoKG).

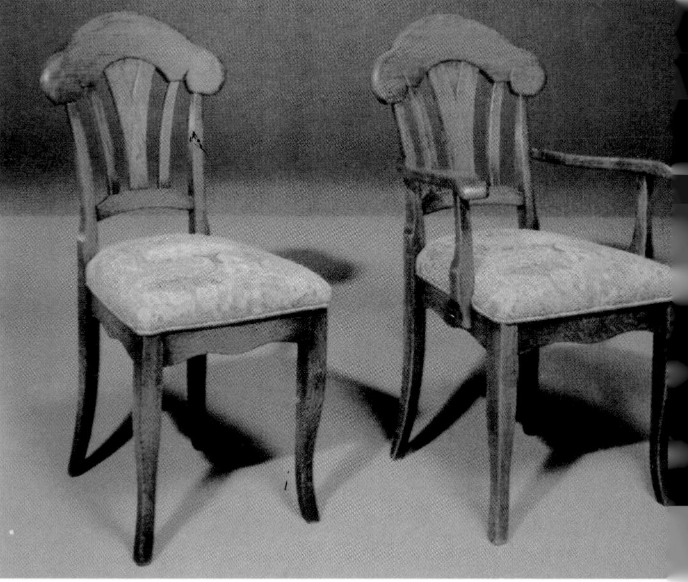

2

2.

Chair and armchair with quadrangular back and curved crown (Heinrich Rotterdam GmbH & CoKG).

Chaise et fauteuil avec dossier quadrangulaire et sommet courbé (Heinrich Rotterdam GmbH & CoKG).

Stuhl und Sessel mit quadratischer Rückenlehne und abgerundeter oberer Leiste (Heinrich Rotterdam GmbH & CoKG).

3.

Chair and armchair with quadrangular back and wave-form crown (Heinrich Rotterdam GmbH & CoKG).

Chaise et fauteuil avec dossier quadrangulaire et sommet ondulé (Heinrich Rotterdam GmbH & CoKG).

Stuhl und Sessel mit quadratischer Rückenlehne und wellenförmiger oberer Leister (Heinrich Rotterdam GmbH & CoKG).

3

4

4.

Chair and armchair with upholstered back (Heinrich Rotterdam GmbH & CoKG).

Chaise et fauteuil avec dossier tapissé (Heinrich Rotterdam GmbH & CoKG).

Stuhl und Sessel mit gepolsterter Rückenlehne (Heinrich Rotterdam GmbH & CoKG).

1

2

3

4

1.

Armchair with upholstered and studded wings (René Hayedot).

Fauteuil avec oreilles, recouvert de cuir et cloué.

Ohrensessel mit Leder überzogen und mit Nägeln beschlagen.

2.

Armchair with half back and revealed legs.

Fauteuil au dossier moyen avec pattes apparentes.

Sessel mit halbhoher Rückenlehne und sichtbaren Sesselfüßen.

3.

Armchair with upholstered and studded back.

fauteuil avec dossier carré recouvert de cuir et cloué.

Sessel mit viereckiger Rückenlehne, mit Leder überzogen und Nägeln beschlagen.

5

5.

Armchair with high covered back and wings (Royal Antique Leather).

Fauteuil recouvert de cuir avec dossier en hauteur et oreilles (Royal Antique leather).

Ohrensessel mit hoher Rückenlehne, mit Leder überzogen (Royal Antique Leather).

4.

Armchair with upholstered wings and revealed legs.

Fauteuil avec oreilles recouvert de cuir avec pattes apparentes.

Ohrensessel, mit Leder überzogen und sichtbaren Sesselfüßen.

1

2

3

4

1.

Armchair with fallen back and revealed legs.

Fauteuil avec dossier tombant et pattes apparentes.

Sessel mit geneigter Rückenlehne und sichtbaren Sesselfüßen.

2.

Armchair with wings and overlap.

Fauteuil à basques avec oreilles.

Ohrensessel mit Schürze.

3.

Armchair with wings and revealed legs.

Fauteuil avec oreilles et pattes apparentes.

Ohrensessel mit sichtbaren Sesselfüßen.

5

4.

Armchair with high, square, wave-shaped back.

Fauteuil avec dossier carré et sommet ondulé.

Sessel mit viereckiger Rückenlehne
und wellenförmigem oberem Teil.

5.

Armchair with semi-circular back (Royal Antique Leather).

Fauteuil avec dossier demi circulaire (Royal Antique Leather).

Sessel mit halbkreisförmiger Rückenlehne
(Royal Antique Leather).

1.
Velilla armchair by Artema.
Fauteuil Velilla, D'Artema.
Sessel Velilla, von Artema.

2.
Lumias chair by Artema.
Chaise Lumias, d'Artema.
Stuhl Lumias, von Artema.

1

2

3

1.

Queen Anne style chair by Rosewood.

Chaise Reine Anne, de Rosewood.

Queen-Ann-Stuhl, von Rosewood.

2.

Queen Victoria style chair by Rosewood.

Chaise Reine Vistoire, de Rosewood.

Stuhl Königin Viktoria, von Rosewood.

3.

Bedroom settee by Rosewood.

Fauteuil de chambre à coucher, de Rosewood.

Lehnsessel, von Rosewood.

4

5

4.

German model chair by Rosewood.

Chaise German, de Rosewood.

Stuhl German, von Rosewood.

5.

Cristian model chair by Rosewood.

Chaise Christian, de Rosewood.

Stuhl Cristian, von Rosewood.

1

2

1.

Table and chairs by Anticuario Ocejo.
Table et chaises, d'Anticuario Ocejo.
Tisch und Stühle, von Anticuario Ocejo.

2.

Ander model armchair by Rosewood.
Fauteuil Ander, de Rosewood.
Sessel Ander, von Rosewood.

The Table

La Table

Der Tisch

Table furniture was first invented as a simple plank that rested directly on the legs or knees of the user, who could then continue to work while seated on the ground.

From the fourteenth and fifteenth centuries, the table was used for different activities. Aside from being the place where meals were taken, tables developed into forms better adapted to sedentary work, desks for example, or other versions, like console tables, which are largely ornamental, the center table, or the great variety of multi-use versions. The table is always based on two basic elements: the work surface (a plane) and

Aux premiers temps, la table était représentée par une simple planche d'appui soutenue directement sur les genoux de l'usager, qui à son tour, continuait à développer ses activités en contacte avec le sol.

A partir du XIV ème et XV ème siècle, la table assuma peu à peu différentes fonctions, à partir desquelles se développèrent de nouvelles formes dérivées de ses nouvelles exigences. À part les tables à repas, apparurent les tables adaptées au travail sédentaire, comme l'écritoire, ou bien d'autres modèles comme les consoles (table adossée au mur), dont la fonction est principalement ornementale, la table de centre ou celle de multiples usages.

Anfangs war der Tisch ein einfaches Stützbrett, das direkt auf die Knie des Benutzers gelegt wurde, der für gewöhnlich seine Tätigkeiten in direktem Kontakt mit dem Boden ausübte.

Ab dem 14. und 15. Jh. wurden dem Tisch verschiedene Funktionen zuteil, aus denen spezische Formen entstanden, die den diversen Anforderungen gerecht wurden. Außer dem Eßtisch entstanden der sitzenden Tätigkeit angepaßte Formen wie der Schreibtisch oder weitere Modelle, wie die Konsoltische (an der Wand angebrachtes, tischartiges Möbel), deren Funktion rein dekorativ ist, der Wohnzimmertisch

1

1.

Room with different types of auxiliary tables (Enebro).

Salon présenté avec plusieurs types de tables auxiliaires (Enebro).

Wohnzimmer, bestehend aus verschiedenartigen Beistelltischen (Enebro).

1

2

3

4

5

1.

Council table (Enebro).

Table de conseil (Enebro).

Ratstisch (Enebro).

2.

Detail of table 1.

Détail de table 1.

Ausschnitt Tisch 1.

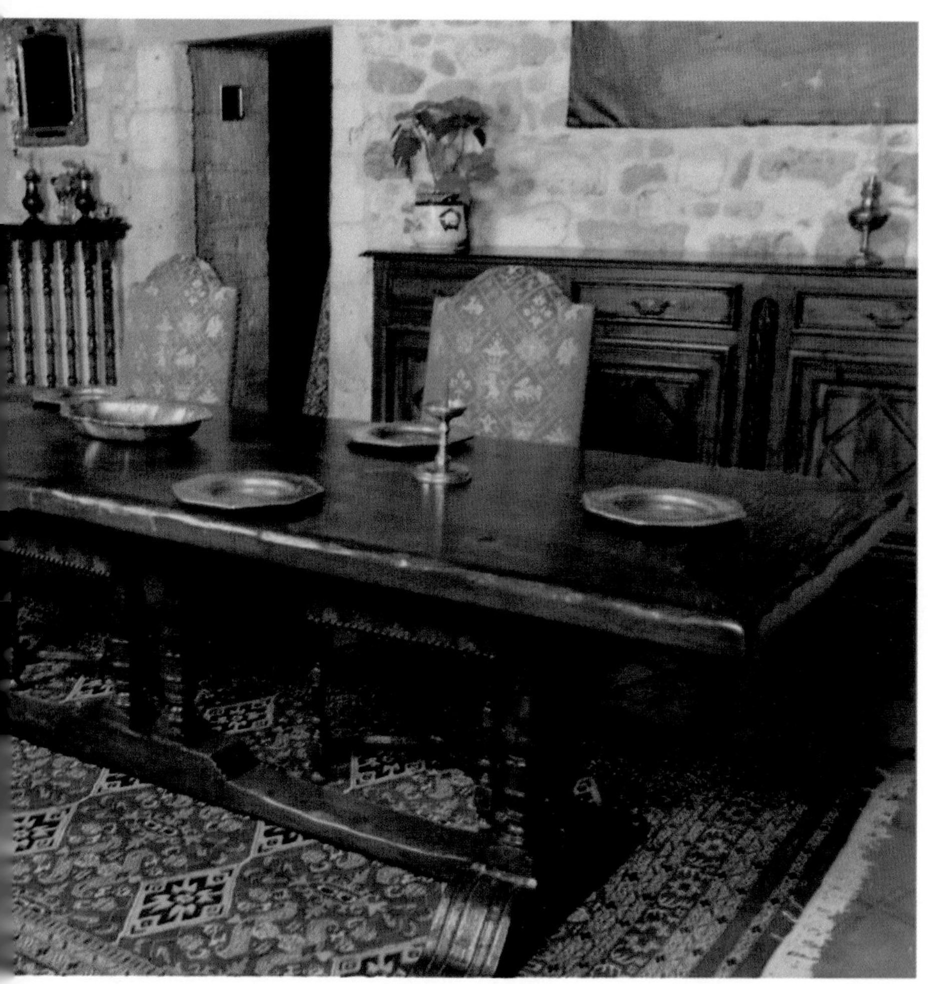

3.

Detail, table 4 (Enebro).

Détail de table 4.

Ausschnitt Tisch 4.

4.

Rectangular table (Zamorano).

Table rectangulaire (Zamorano).

Reckteckiger Tisch (Zamorano).

5.

Refectory table, Saint Remy model in oak (Faïsse et Plata).

Table de réfectoire Saint Rémy en chêne (Faïsse et Plata).

Refektoriumstisch Saint Remy aus Eiche (Faïsse et Plata).

1

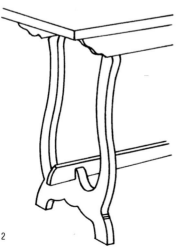

2

1.

Extendible monk's table of wood, of Tuscan and Venetian influence, eighteenth and nineteenth centuries (Vecchio Stile).

Table extensible de moine en bois d'influence toscane et vénitienne (XVIII ème et XIX ème siècle) (Vecchio Stile).

Ausziehbarer Ordenstisch aus Holz, toskanischer und venezianischer Einfluß (18. und 19. Jh.) (Vecchio Stile).

2.

Sketch of beveled joints in legs of 1 and 3.

Détail d'union de pattes et chambranles 1 et 3.

Skizze Verbindung Tischbeine und Horizontalsteg 1 und 3.

3.

Extendible monk's table.

Tavola allungabile da frate.

Ausgezogener Ordenstisch.

3

the support structure (a column or columns).

While the support system greatly varies in form and number of elements, table tops, from antiquity, have retained the most restricted shape--square, rectangular, circular, oval--but have been made of many materials, among which wood and marble are the most classical.

La table est toujours formée par les éléments de base : la planche et la structure qui sert de support.

Pendant que cette dernière présente diverses possibilités dans les formes et numéros de pièces qui la composent, les dessus, de longue date, présentent une typologie de formes plus réduites –carrée, rectangulaires, rondes ou ovales–, mais permettent être réalisés dans une grande variété de matériels, entre lesquels ont trouve surtout du bois et du marbre comme les plus classiques.

oder der Mehrzwecktisch. Der Tisch besteht immer aus zwei Elementen: der Tischplatte und der tragenden Struktur. Während letztere verschiedene Formen annehmen und in der Anzahl seiner Elemente variieren kann, ist der obere Teil seit jeher in seiner Form eingeschränkter – viereckig, rechteckig, rund und oval – aber das Material kann stark variieren. Die am häufigsten vorkommenden und klassischsten Materialien sind das Holz und der Marmor.

1

1.

Extendible oval-shaped table in old wood, of eighteenth- and nineteenth-century Tuscan and Venetian influence (Vecchio Stile).

Table ovale extensible en bois ancienne d'influence toscane et vénitienne (XVIII ème et XIX ème siècle) (Vecchio Stile).

Ausziehbarer ovaler Tisch aus antikem Holz, toskanischer und venezianischer Einfluß (18. und 19. Jh.) (Vecchio Stile).

2.

Extendible dining table (Heinrich Rotterdam GmbH & CoKG).

Table de salle à manger extensible (Heinrich Rotterdam GbmH & CoKG).

Ausziehbarer Eßtisch (Heinrich Rotterdam GmbH & CoKG).

3 - 4.

Detail of table 2.

Détail table 2

Ausschnitt Tisch 2.

2

3

4

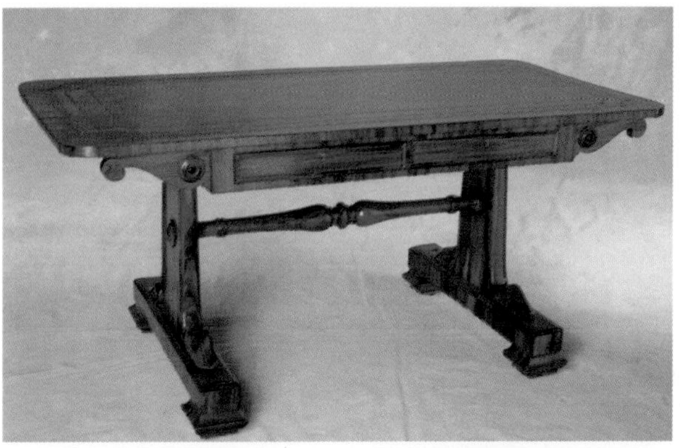
1

2

3

4

5

6

1.

William IV office table in acacia wood. Original piece from 1830 (Antigüedades Fortuny).

Table de bureau anglais Guillaume IV de 1830 en bois d'acacia. Pièce originale (Antigüedades Fortuny).

Englischer Büro-Schreibtisch Wilhelm IV. von 1830 aus Akazienholz. Originalstück. (Antigüedades Fortuny).

2 - 5.

Details of table 1.

Détail de table 1.

Ausschnitt Tisch 1.

6.
Dining room table (Heinrich GmbH & CoKG).
Table de salle à manger (Heinrich Rotterdam GmbH & CoKG).
Eßtisch (Heinrich Rotterdam GmbH & CoKG).

1

2

1.

William IV dining room table in mahogany. Original piece from 1830. (Antigüedades Fortuny).

Table de salle à manger anglaise Guillaume IV de 1830 en acajou. Pièce originale (Antigüedades Fortuny).

Englischer Eßtisch Wilhelm IV. von 1830 aus Mahagoni. Originalstück (Antigüedades Fortuny).

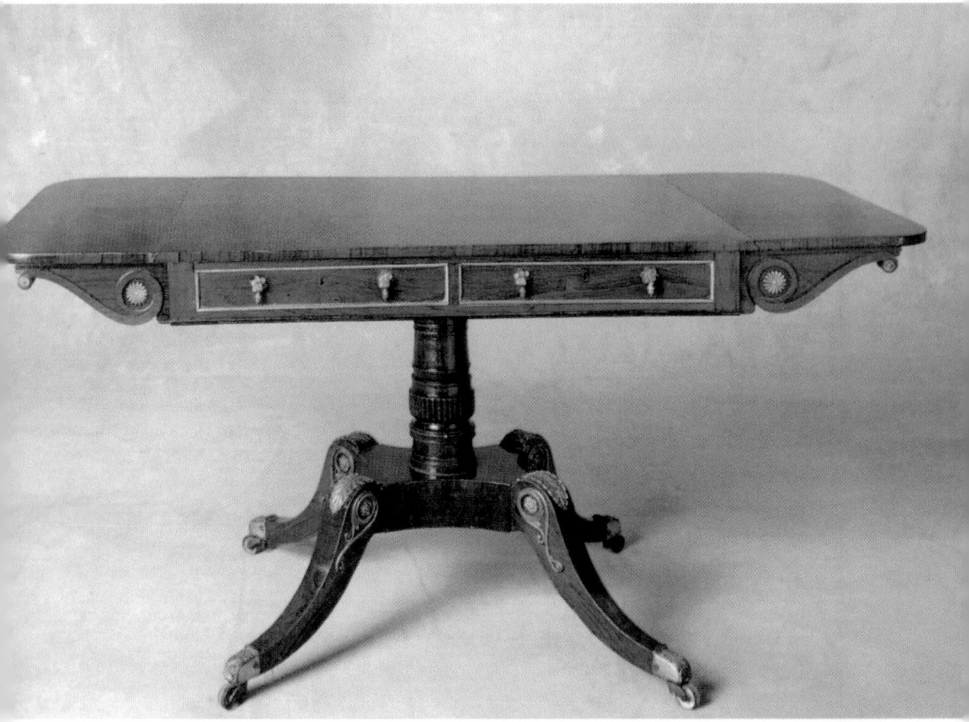

3

2.

William IV dining room table in lignum vitae. Original piece dated 1830. (Antigüedades Fortuny).

Table de salle à manger anglaise Guillaume IV de 1830 en bois saint. Pièce originale (Antigüedades Fortuny).

Englischer Eßtisch Wilhelm IV. von 1830 aus Guajakholz. Originalstück (Antigüedades Fortuny).

3.

Regency library table, 1820, in lignum vitae. Original piece (Antigüedades Fortuny).

Table de bibliothèque Régence de 1820 en bois saint. Pièce originale (Antigüedades Fortuny).

Régence Bibliothekstisch von 1820 aus Guajakholz. Originalstück (Antigüedades Fortuny).

4.

Detail of the ornamental garlands on the legs of the table.

Détail de guirlande ornementale des pattes de la table.

Ausschnitt Verzierungen der Tischbeine.

4

1

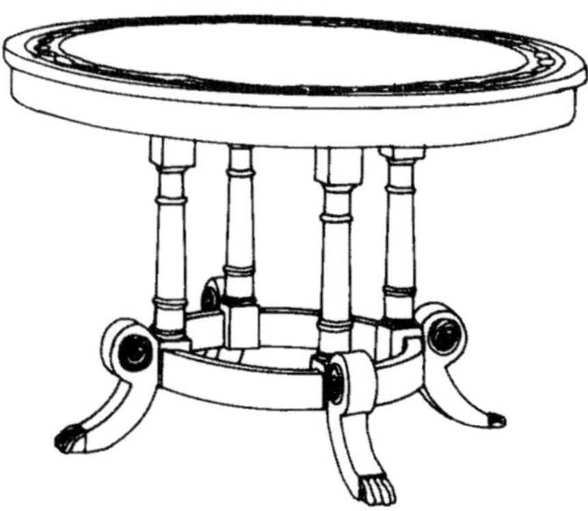

2

1.

Greek dinner tables. (Enebro).

Table à repas lisérée (Enebro).

Eßtisch mit Mäander (Enebro).

2.

Sketch of Greek dinner tables.

Détail de table à repas lisérée.

Skizze Eßtisch mit Mäander.

3

3.

Greek dinner table top (Enebro).).

Dessus de table à manger lisérée. (Enebro).

Oberfläche des Eßtisches mit Mäander (Enebro).

1

2

1.

Extendible table with round top in solid walnut and wild cherry wood. (Tradition).

Table ronde extensible en noyer massif et cerisier sylvestre (Tradition).

Runder ausziehbarer Tisch aus massivem Nußbaum und Wildkirschbaumholz (Tradition).

2.

Eighteenth-century Dutch dressing table in walnut with marquetry. Original piece (Antigüedades Fortuny).

Table boudoir hollandaise du XVIII ème siècle en acajou et marqueterie. Pièce originale (Antigüedades Fortuny).

Holländischer Frisiertisch des 18. Jh. aus Mahagoni mit Intarsien. Originalstück. (Antigüedades Fortuny).

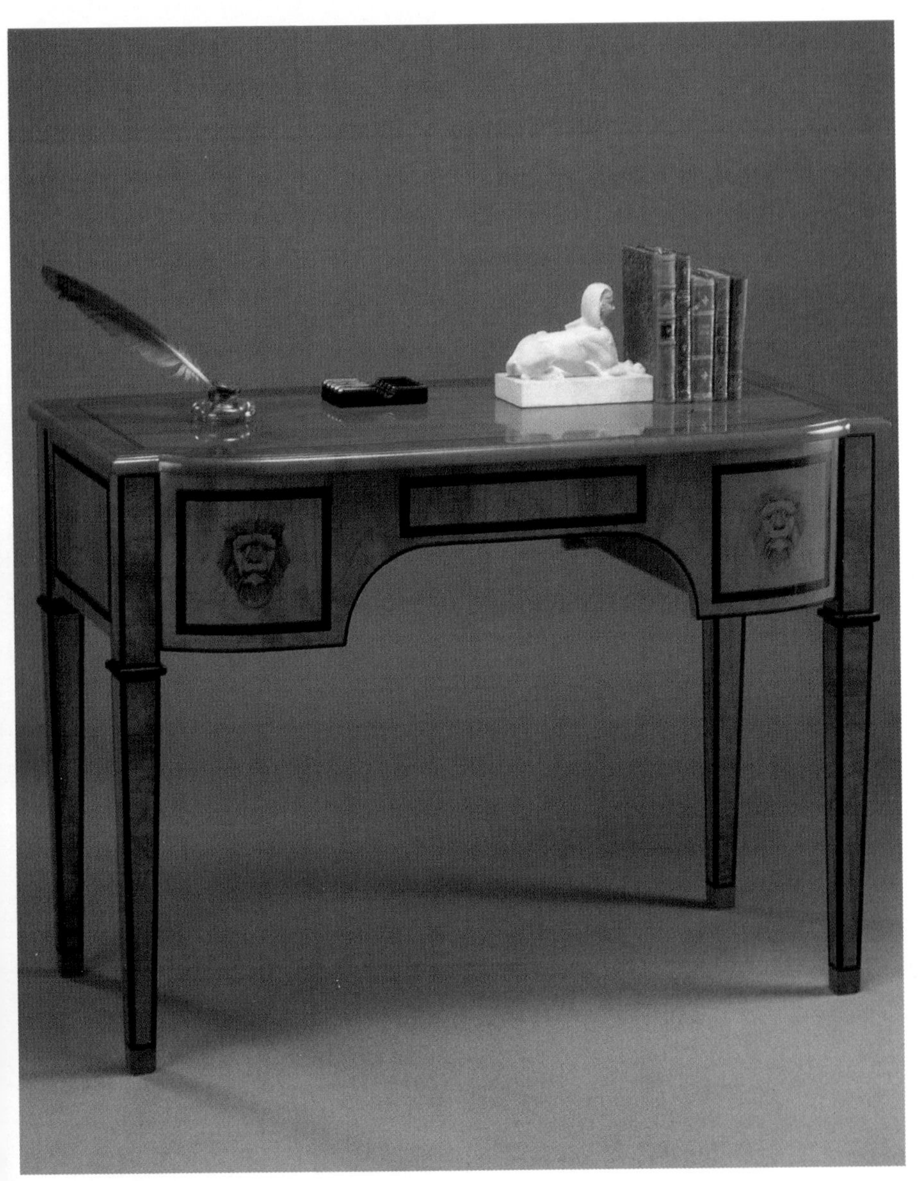

3.
Nelson console table.(Enebro).
Console Nelson (Enebro).
Konsoltisch Nelson (Enebro).

1

1.

Tall auxiliary table (Meubles Bufflier).

Petite table haute (Meubles Bufflier).

Hohes Tischchen (Meubles Bufflier).

2.

Writing table. (Caler Tol).

Table à rabats écritoire (Caler Tol).

Schreibtisch mit Flügeln (Caler Tol).

2

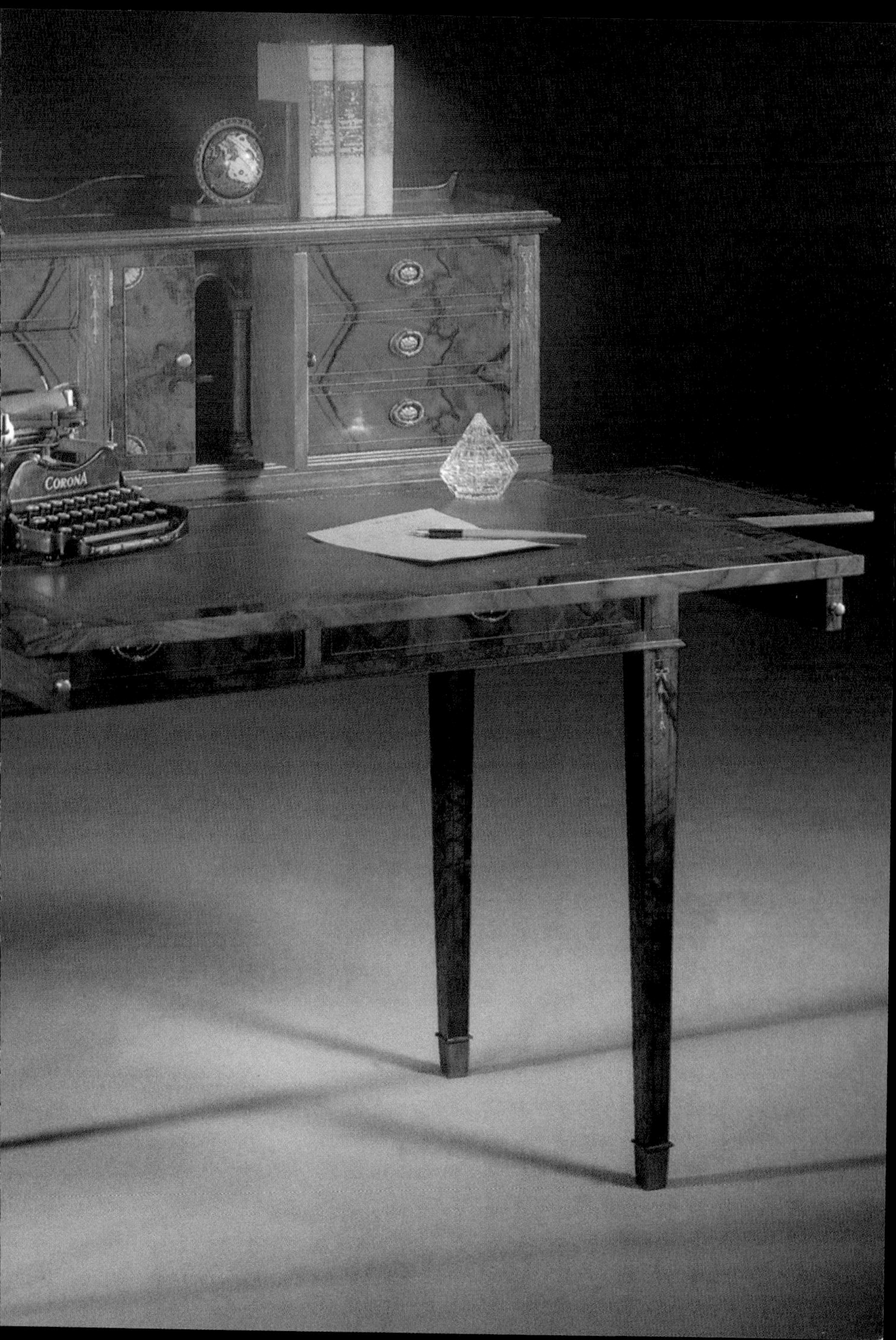
CORONA

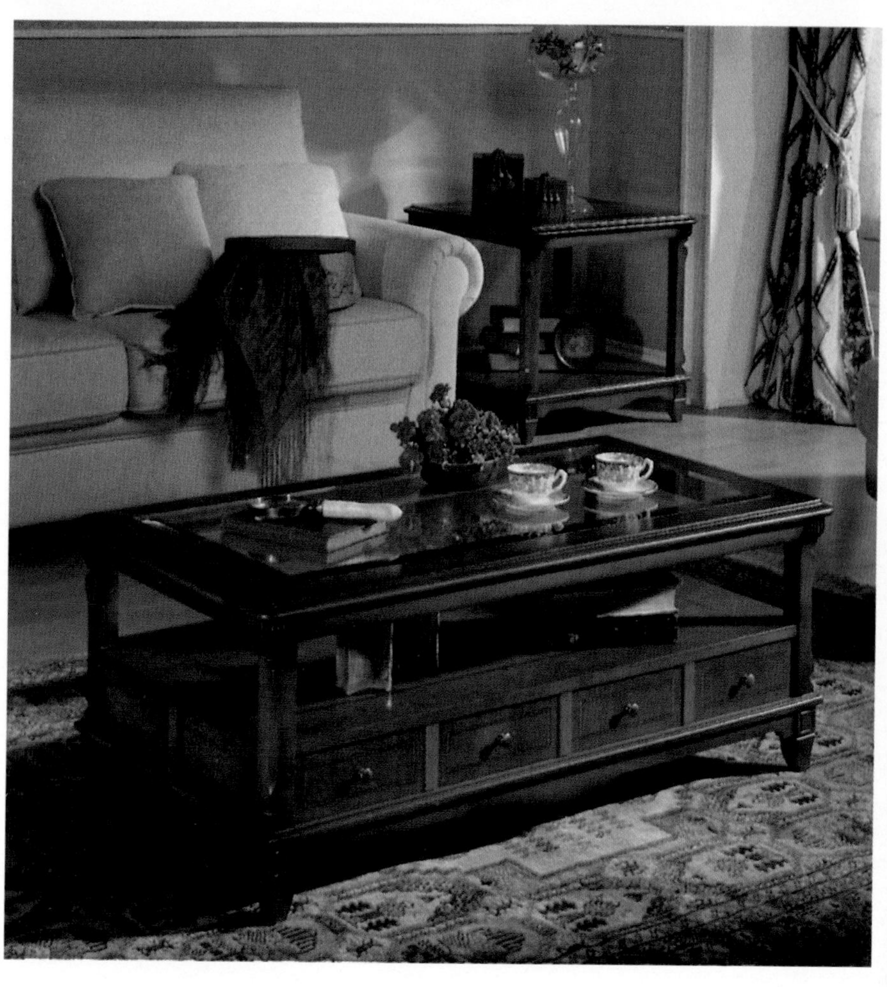

1.
Center table. (Mobles Larvi).
Table de centre, de Meubles Larvi.
Wohnzimmertisch, von Mobles Larvi.

2.

Center table. (Mobles Larvi).

Table de centre, de Mobles Larvi.

Wohnzimmertisch, von Mobles Larvi.

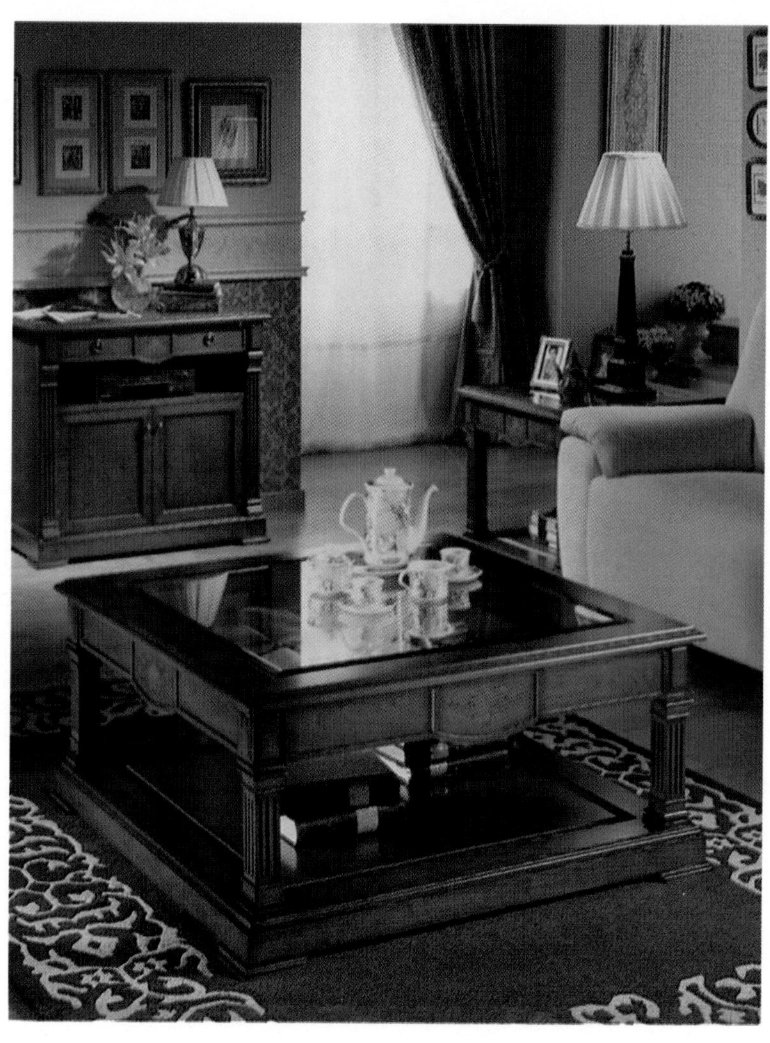

1.

Center table (Qualitat Mobles).

Table de centre, de Qualitat Mobles.

Wohnzimmertisch, von Qualitat Mobles.

2.

Siglo XXI collection auxiliary table, by Techni Nova.

Table auxiliaire de la collection Siècle XXI, de Tecni Nova.

Beistelltisch aus der Kollektion Siglo XXI, von Tecni Nova.

1.
Dining room, by Mogart.
Salle à manger, de Mogart.
Eßzimmer, von Mogart.

2.
Dining room, by Mogart.
Salle à manger, de Mogart.
Eßzimmer, von Mogart.

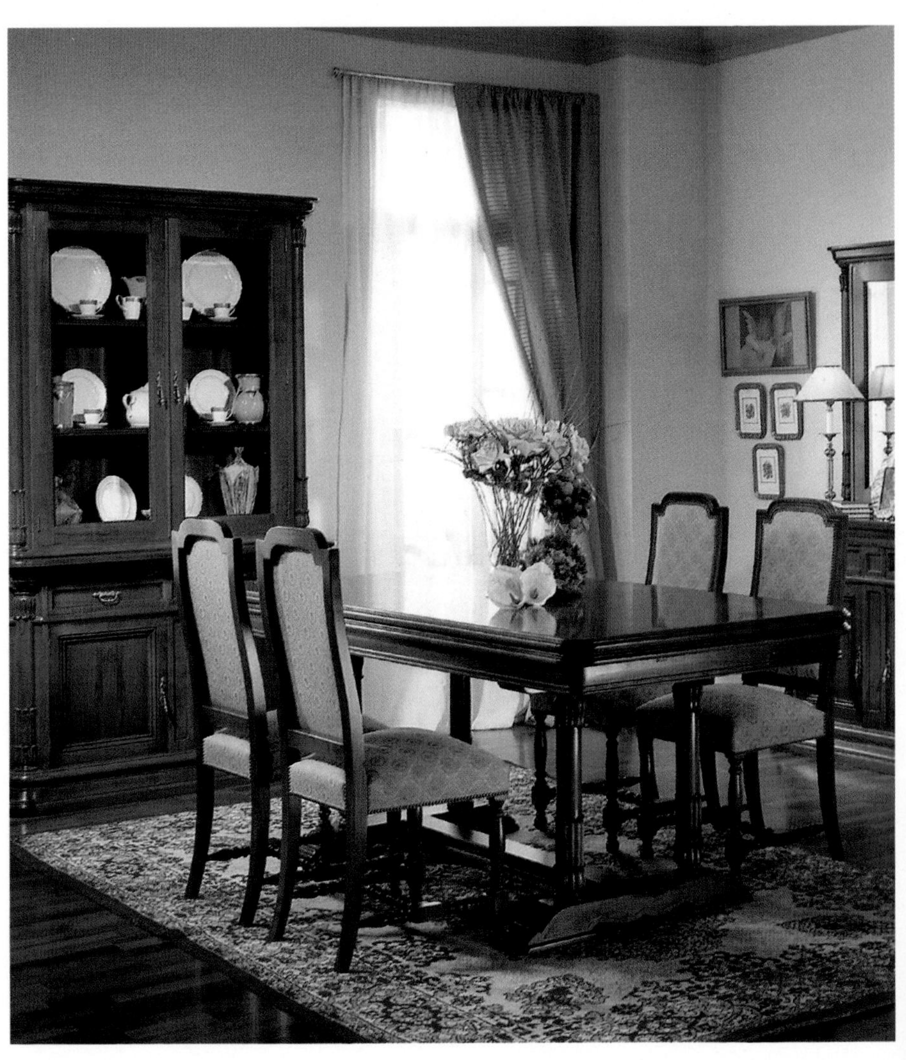

1.

Dining room table, Berlanga model, by Artema.

Table à manger Berlanga, d'Artema.

Eßtisch Berlanga, von Artema.

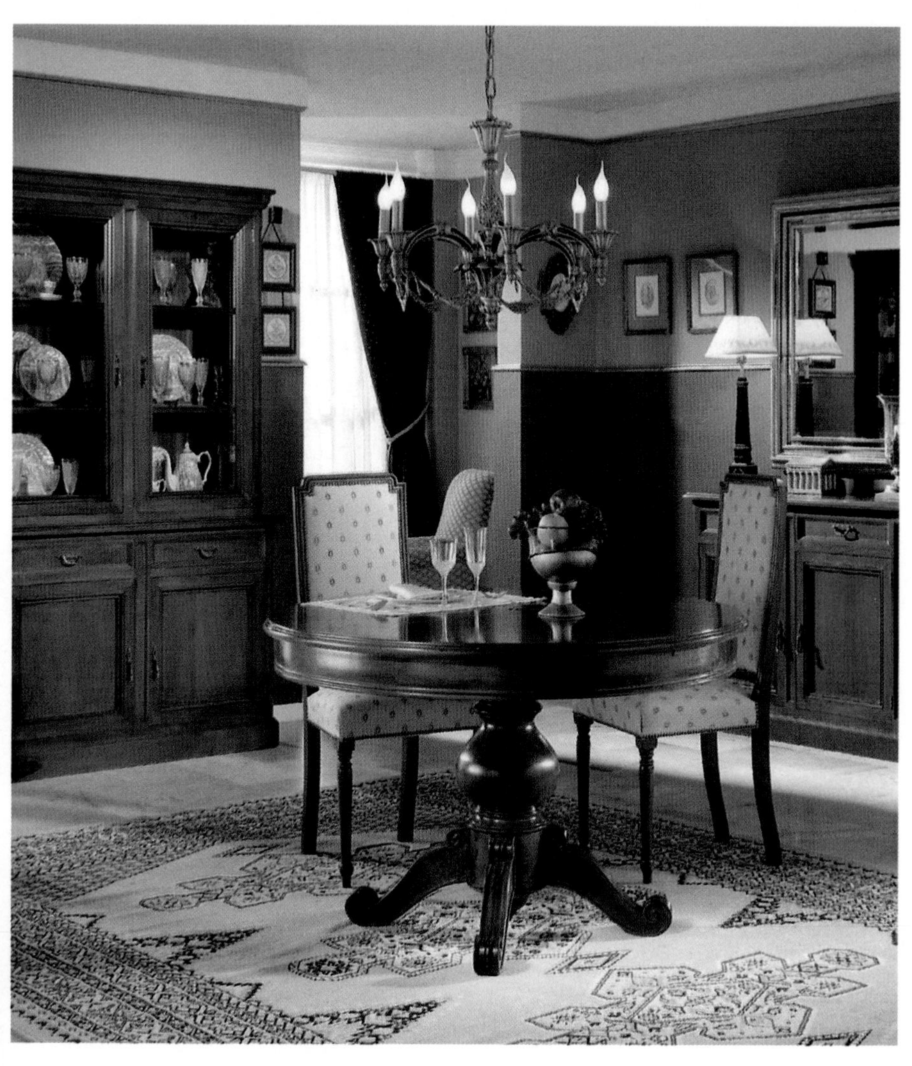

2.
Extendible dining room table, Agreda model by Artema.
table à repas extensible Agreda, d'Artema.
Ausziehbarer Eßtisch Agreda, von Artema.

pp. 460-461

Table, settees, and office bookcases, from Ofifran.

Table, fauteuils et librairie de bureau, d'Ofifran.

Tisch, Lehnsessel und Bücherschränke, von Ofifran.

1.

Dining room collection from Toscano Mobil.

Salle à manger de la collection Veronna, de Toscano Mobil.

Eßzimmer der Kollektion Veronna, von Toscano Mobil.

1

2

1.

Neoclassical dining room collection, Georgian model from Mariner.

Salle à manger néoclassique de la collection Georgia, de Mariner.

Neo-klassisches Eßzimmer der Kollektion Georgia, von Mariner.

2.

Eighteenth-century table from Colombo Mobili.

Table du XVIII ème siècle, de Colombo Mobili.

Tisch des 18. Jh., von Colombo Mobili.

3

3.

Office from the Versailles collection by Mariner..

Bureau de la collection Versailles, de Mariner.

Büro aus der Kollektion Versalles, von Mariner.

4.

Office table by Picó Muebles.

Table de bureau, de Pico Muebles.

Schreibtisch, von Picó Muebles.

4

1

2

1.
Small center table by Yondar.
Petite table de centre, de Yondar.
Wohnzimmertischchen, von Yondar.

2.
Pedestal table by Mobles Morellá.
Guéridon, de meubles Morella.
Tischchen, von Mobles Morellá.

3.
Table and bookcase by Picó Muebles.
Table et vitrine, de Pico Muebles.
Tisch und Vitrine, von Picó Muebles.

3

1.

Extendible dining room table, Olvega model by Artema.

Table à repas extensible Olvega, d'Artema.

Ausziehbarer Eßtisch Olvega, von Artema.

2.

Dining room table, Abejar model by Artema.

Table à repas Abejar, d'Artema.

Eßtisch Abejar, von Artema.

1.

Dining room table, Almenar model by Artema.

Table à repas Almenar, d'Artema.

Eßtisch Almenar, von Artema.

2.
Office table, Burgo model by Artema.
Table de bureau Burgo, d'Artema.
Schreibtisch Burgo, von Artema.

1

2

1.

Dining room table, by Dis-Arte.

Table à repas, de Dis-Arte.

Eßtisch, von Dis-Arte.

2.

Center table, by Mogart.

Table de centre, de Mogart.

Wohnzimmertisch, von Mogart.

3

3.

Center table, by Mogart.

Table de centre, de Mogart.

Wohnzimmertisch, von Mogart.

1.

Center table from the Basilea collection by Toscano Mobil.

Table de centre de la collection Basilea, de Toscano Mobil.

Wohnzimmertisch aus der Kollektion Basilea, von Toscano Mobil.

2.

Dining room by Mariner.

Salle à manger, de Mariner.

Eßzimmer, von Mariner.

1.

Neoclassical style dining room table by Colombo Mobili.

Table à repas de style Néoclassique, de Colombo Mobili.

Eßtisch im neo-klassischen Stil, von Colombo Mobili.

2.
Dining room by Mogart.
Salle à manger, de Mogart.
Eßzimmer, von Mogart.

1

2

3

1.

Center table by Mudeva.

Table de centre, de Mudeva.

Wohnzimmertisch, von Mudeva.

2.

Center table, from the Europa collection by Toscano Mobil.

Table de centre de la collection Europa, de Toscano Mobil.

Wohnzimmertisch aus der Kollektion Europa, von Toscano Mobil.

3.

Center table, from the Veronna collection by Toscano Mobil..

Table de centre de la collection Veronna, de Toscano Mobil.

Wohnzimmertisch aus der Kollektion Veronna, von Toscano Mobil.

Cabinet furniture

Les Meubles Contenants

Aufbewahrungsmöbel

The last furniture structure that we consider basic in human culture is the cabinet. The origin of cabinet furniture is in the chest, trunk, or medieval hall seat. These are pieces that later evolved into their many other obvious forms.

One rudimentary container is the trunk, which in its most basic form is a section of tree trunk hollowed out, often with one part used as a cover. The top soon added hinges, thus turning into a piece that was so hardy and functional that it kept on being constructed until the seventeenth century (and of course is still manufactured synthetically).

Slowly, the next creative instinct was to decorate the

La dernière des structures mobilières considérées comme basiques dans l'espace et destiné à l'hêtre humain est le meuble contenant, dont l'origine se trouve dans le coffre, bahut ou le banc coffret médiéval, pièces qui à l'époque offrait déjà une multitudes d'usages.

Le meuble contenant le plus rudimentaire et le bahut, qui est en fait un tronc d'arbre coupé, vidé et dont on utilise la partie supérieure comme couvercle.

On rajoutât part la suite des charnières et de gons, obtenant ainsi une pièce robuste et fonctionnelle qui continuât à se fabriquer jusqu'au XVII ème siècle. Peu à peu l'imagination de l'homme permit, d'un côté la décoration des coffres et d'un

Das letzte grundlegende Möbelstück, das der Mensch entwikkelte und an seine Bedürfnisse anpaßte, ist das Aufbewahrungsmöbel, dessen Ursprung in den mittelalterlichen Kästen, Truhen und Kastenbänken zu suchen ist, die zu ihrer damaligen Zeit dem Benutzer eine Vielfalt von Gebrauchsmöglichkeiten boten.

Das rudimentärste Aufbewahrungmöbel ist die Truhe, die daraus entstand, daß man einen Baumstamm zerteilte, ihn aushöhlte und den zuvor abgetrennten Teil als Deckel verwendete. Dieser Deckel wurde bald mit Hilfe von Scharnieren und Gelenken befestigt, so daß ein robustes und funktionales Möbelstück entstand, daß bis ins 17. Jh. gebaut

1.

Spanish bureau in solid walnut (Eduardo Terrádez).

Cabinet español en noyer massif (Eduardo Terradez).

Spanischer Sekretär aus massivem Nußbaum (Eduardo Terrádez).

1

2

3

1.

Writing table-bookcase (Heinrich Rotterdam & CoKG).

Bureau bas librairie (Heirich Rotterdam & CoKG.

Canterano-Bücherschrank (Heinrich Rotterdam & CoKG).

2.

Detail, upper door elements of 1.

Détail de la tige de porte supérieure du bureau bas 1.

Ausschnitt Gestänge der oberen Tür des Canterano 1.

3.

Detail, carved ornamental elements and lower door of 1.

Détail de tailles ornementales montantes et porte inférieure 1.

Ausschnitt Ornament-Schnitzereien und untere Tür 1.

4

5

6

4.

Detail, top of cabinet in 6.

Détail de sommet d'armoire 6.

Ausschnitt Sims Schrank 6.

5.

Detail, ornamental foot of cabinet in 6.

Détail d'ornementation de patte d'armoire 6.

Ausschnitt Ornament Fuß von Schrank 6.

6.

Cabinet (Heinrich Rotterdam & CoKG).

Armoire (Heinrich Rotterdam & CoKG).

Schrank (Heinrich Rotterdam & CoKG).

1

2

3

1.

Display case in antique wood, inspired on Tuscan and Venetian furniture (eighteenth and nineteenth centuries, Vecchio Stile).

Vitrine en bois ancien d'inspiration toscane et venitienne (XVIII ème et XIX ème siècle) (Vecchio Stile).

Vitrine aus antikem Holz, toskanisch und venezianisch inspiriert (18. und 19. Jh.) (Vecchio Stile).

2.

Cabinet (Atelier du Vendelais).

Schrank (Atelier du Vendelais).

Armário (Atelier du Vendelais)

3.

Detail, cabinet 2.

Détail d'armoire 2.

Ausschnitt Schrank 2.

4

5

4.

Display case in antique wood, inspired on Tuscan and Venetian furniture (eighteenth and nineteenth centuries, Vecchio Stile).

Vitrine en bois ancien d'influence toscane et vénitienne (XVIII ème et XIX ème siècle) (Vecchio Stile).

Vitrine aus antikem Holz mit toskanischem und venezianischem Einfluß (18. und 19. Jh.) (Vecchio Stile).

5.

Sketch of cabinet in 3.

Détail de vitrine 3.

Skizze Vitrine 3.

p. 486.

Bordelais cabinet from the "Les armoires de prestige" collection in wild cherry wood (René Trotel).

Armoire Bordelais de la collection " Les Armoires de Prestige " en cerisier sauvage (René Trotel).

Schrank Bordelais aus der Kollektion "Les Armoires de Prestige" aus Wildkirschbaumholz (René Trotel).

p. 487.

Coletais cabinet from the collection "Les armoires de prestige" in wild cherry wood (René Trotel).

Armoire Chotelais de la collection " Les armoires de Prestige " en cerisier sauvage (René Trorel).

Schrank Choletais aus der Kollektion "Les Armoires de Prestige" aus Wildkirschbaumholz (René Trotel).

1.

Sketch of cabinet.

Détail d'armoire.

Skizze Schrank.

2.

Sketch of cabinet.

Détail d'armoire.

Skizze Schrank.

3

3.

Dressing table in antique wood, inspired on Tuscan and Venetian furniture (eighteenth and nineteenth centuries, Vecchio Stile).

Commode en bois ancien d'influence toscane et vénitienne (XVIII ème et XIX ème siècle).

Kommode aus antikem Holz mit toskanischem und venezianischem Einfluß (18. und 19. Jh.) (Vecchio Stile).

1

2

2.

Credence table in antique wood, inspired on Tuscan and Venetian furniture (eighteenth and nineteenth centuries, Vecchio Stile).

Crédence en bois ancien d'inspiration toscane et vénitienne (XVIII ème et XIX ème siècle) (Vecchio Stile).

Kredenz aus antikem Holz, toskanische und venezianische Inspiration (18. und 19. Jh.) (Vecchio Stile).

1.

Barcelonette model bedside lamp (Atelier du Vendelais).

Chever Barcelonnette (Atelier du Vendelais).

Chevet Barcelonnette (Atelier du Vendelais).

3.

Sketch of 2.

Détail de crédence 2.

Skizze Kredenz 2.

3

1.

Credence table with center drawers in antique wood, inspired on Tuscan and Venetian furniture (eighteenth and nineteenth centuries, Vecchio Stile).

Crédence avec tiroirs centraux en bois ancien d'inspiration toscane et vénitienne (XVIII ème et XIX ème siècle) (Vecchio Stile).

Kredenz mit Schubladen im mittleren Teil aus antikem Holz, toskanisch und venezianisch inspiriert (18. und 19. Jh.) (Vecchio Stile).

2.

Bureau in walnut with lemon wood marquetry. The finish is a wax coating on authentic tortoise shell enamel (Faïsse et Plata).

Cabinet español en noyer, revêtu de citronnier, ciré et émaillé avec de la véritable écaille de tortue (Faïsse et Argent).

Bargueño aus Nußbaumholz, mit Citronierholz getäfelt, wachsnachbehandelt und mit echtem Schildpatt emailliert (Faïsse et Plata).

1

2

chest, then to make more complex forms by the addition of hinged doors and drawers. From then on, the three requirements needed to create all kinds of variations gave cabinet furniture a full-fledged position alongside the table and chair. If the chest raised off the floor adds two doors, the credence table comes into being; turned to a vertical position, the chest becomes a prototypical cabinet or cupboard; the chest of drawers or dresser follows when drawers are added; the desk becomes a simple matter when the top surface is used for writing.

autre, le compliquer dans sa forme en lui rajoutant des portes, des charnières et des tiroirs. À partir de là, les coordonnées nécessaires à la création de toutes les variations de meubles contenants. C'est ainsi que si nous surélevons un coffre et nous lui ajoutons deux portes, nous obtenons une crédence ; si nous disposons le coffre en hauteur nous avons le prototype d'armoire classique et si nous lui ajoutons des tiroirs, des gavettes et des éléments de séparation, nous obtenons un secrétaire.

wurde. Nach und nach ermöglichte es der Erfindergeist des Menschen, die Truhen einerseits zu dekorieren und andererseits die Form weiterzuentwickeln, indem er Türen, Scharniere und Schubladen hinzufügte. Von da ab entwickelten sich die drei wichtigsten Bestandteile, die erforderlich sind, um jegliche Variante von Aufbewahrungsmöbeln herzustellen. Stattet man also eine erhöhte Truhe mit zwei Türen aus, entsteht so eine Kredenz. Stellt man eine Truhe vertikal auf, erhält man den Prototyp des Schrankes. Wenn wir diesen Letzteren mit Schubladen, Schubfächern und Trennelementen versehen, entsteht ein Sekretär.

3

pp. 494-495.

1.

Reproduction of a nineteenth-century bureau (Bargueños y Muebles de Estilo).

Reproduction d'un cabinet español du XVIII ème siècle (Bargueños y Muebles de Estilo).

Reproduktion eine Bargueños des 18. Jh. (Bargueños y Muebles de Estilo).

2.

Nineteenth-century bureau (Bargueños y Muebles de Estilo).

Cabinet español du XVIII ème siècle (Bargueños y Muebles de EStilo).

Bargueño des 18. Jh. (Bargueños y Muebles de Estilo).

3.

Closed writing table (Eduardo Terrádez).

Cabinet español fermé (Eduardo Terradez).

Bargueño, geschlossen (Eduardo Terrádez).

1.

Display-credence, Heidelberg model (Heinrich Rotterdam GmbH & CoKG).

Crédence vitrine modèle Heidelberg (Heinrich Rotterdam and GmbH & CoKG).

Kredenz-Vitrine Modell Heidelberg (Heinrich Rotterdam GmbH & CoKG).

1.

Display case, Strasbourg model (Heinrich Rotterdam GmbH & CoKG).

Vitrine modèle Strasbourg (Heinrich Rotterdam and GmbH & COKG.

Vitrine Modell Strasbourg (Heinrich Rotterdam GmbH & CoKG).

2.

Toulouse model display case (Heinrich Rotterdam and GmbH & CoKG).

Vitrine Toulouse (Heinrich Rotterdam and GmbH & CoKG).

Vitrine Toulouse (Heinrich Rotterdam GmbH & CoKG).

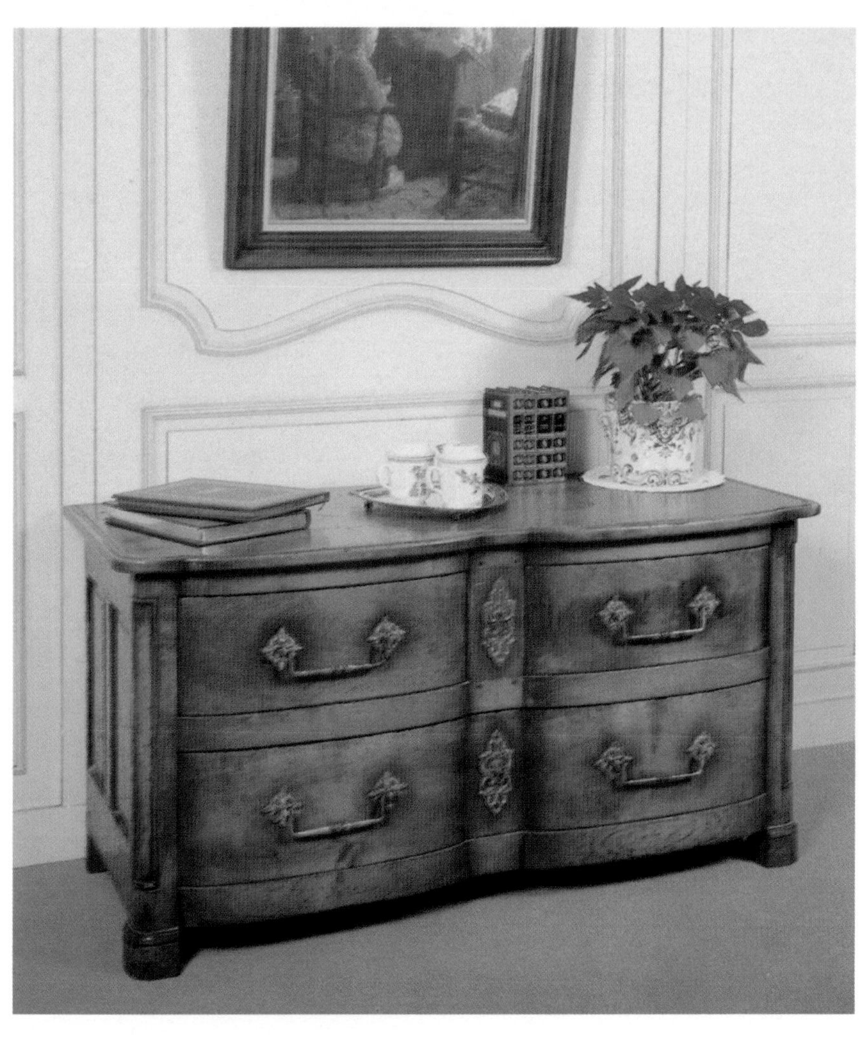

1.

Ermitage model seventeenth-century chest of drawers (Atelier du Vendelais).

Commode Ermitage du XVII ème siècle (Atelier du Vendelais).

Kommode Ermitage des 17. Jh. (Atelier du Vendelais).

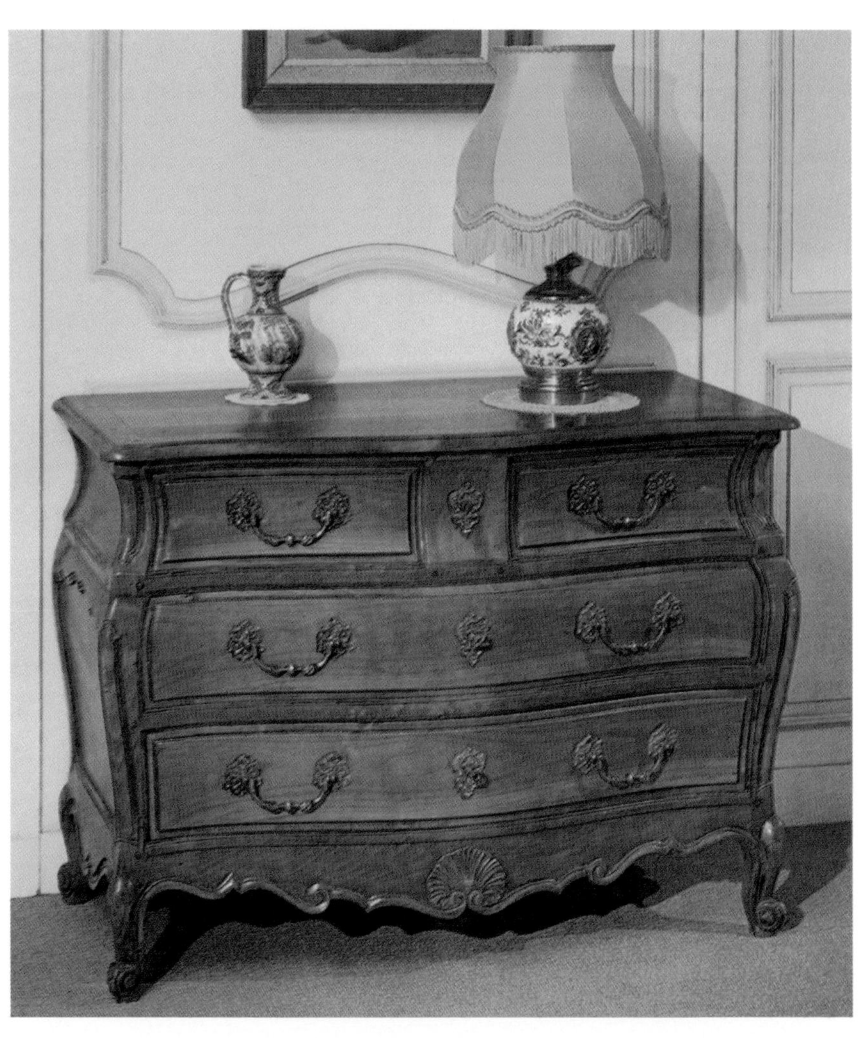

2.
Chest of drawers from Bordeaux (Atelier du Vendelais).
Commode de Bordeaux (Atelier du Vendelais).
Kommode aus Bordeaux (Atelier du Vendelais).

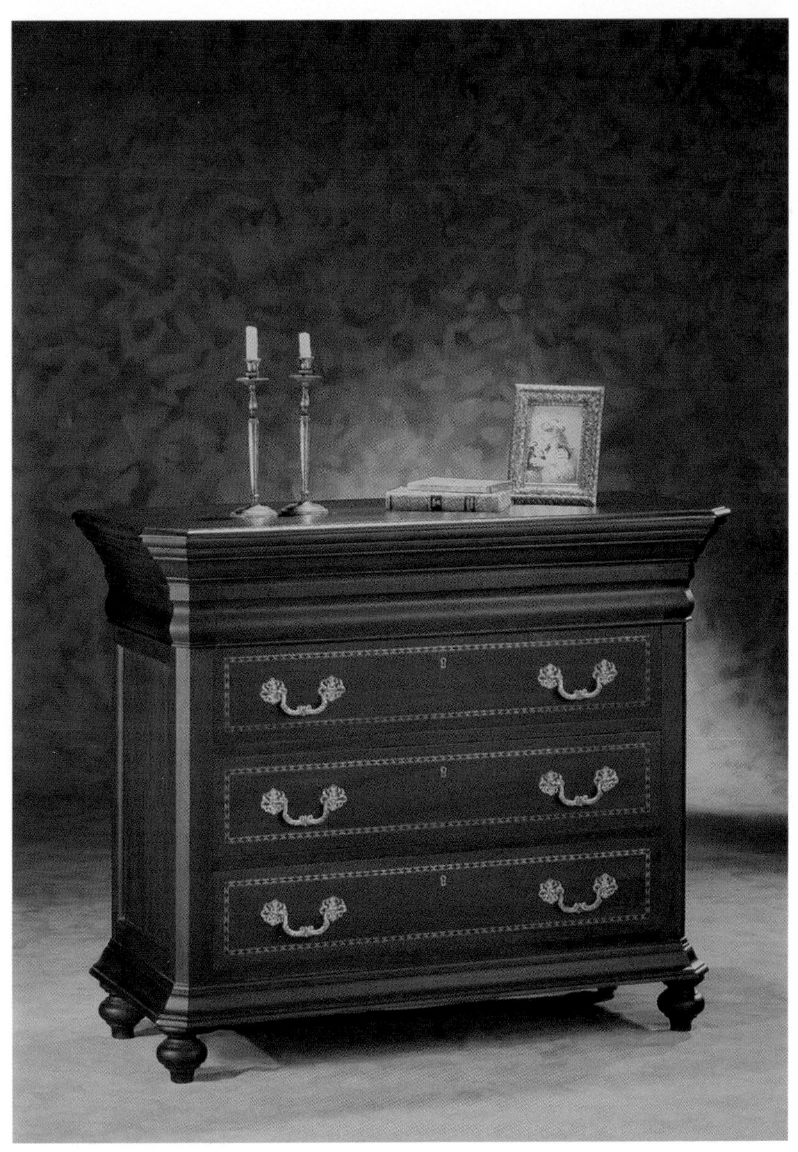

1.
Josefina chest of drawers (Zamorano).
Commode Joséphine (Zamorano).
Kommode Josefina (Zamorano).

2.
Art Deco Chest of drawers in olive (Enebro).
Commode Art Déco en olivier (Enebro).
Art Deco Kommode, Olivenbaumholz (Enebro).

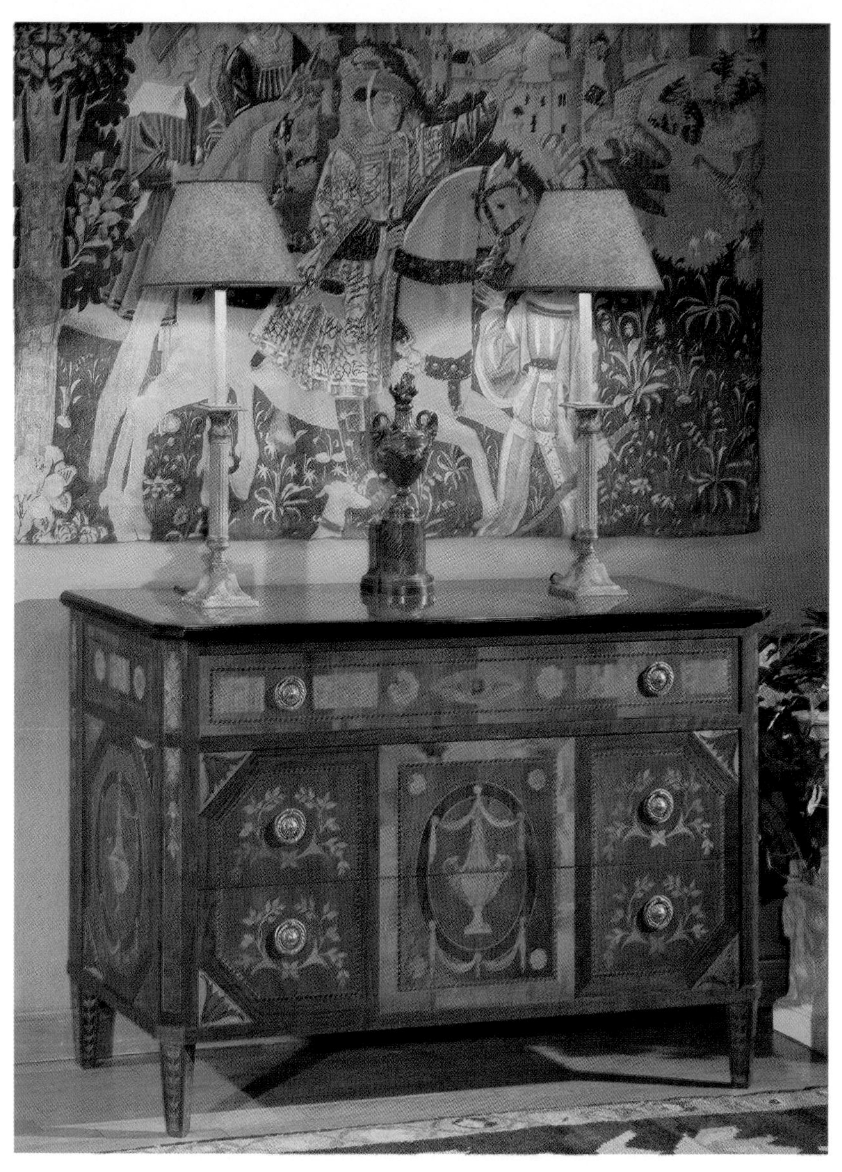

1.
Carlos IV chest of drawers (Enebro).
Commode Charles IV (Enebro).
Kommode Karl IV. (Enebro).

2.

Regency chest of drawers in solid wild cherry (Styl Mueble).

Commode Régence en cerisier sylvestre massif (Style Mueble).

Régence Kommode aus Wildkirschbaumholz (Styl Mueble).

1.
Sotherby curved chest (Enebro).
Commode courbée Sotherby (Enebro).
Halbrunde Kommode Sotherby (Enebro).

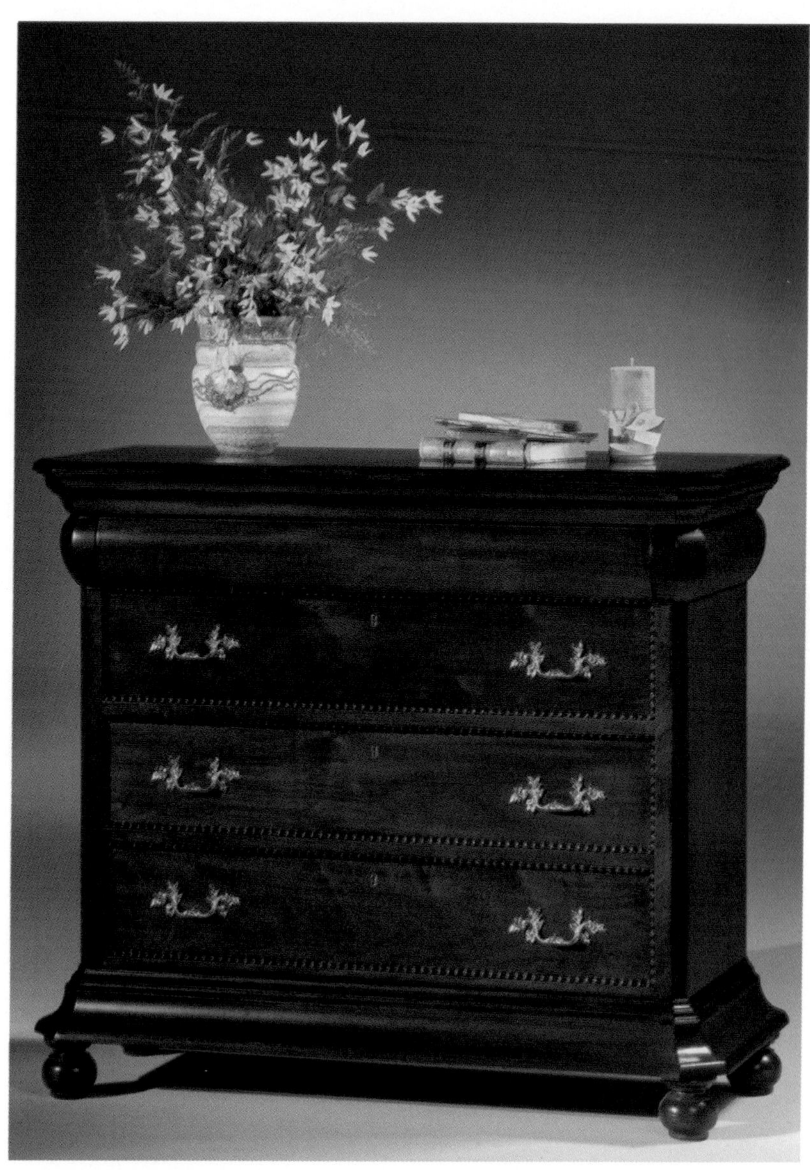

2.
Ana Cristina chest of drawers (Zamorano).
Commode Anne Christine (Zamorano).
Kommode Ana Cristina (Zamorano).

2.

Chest of drawers and mirror from the Veronna collection of Toscano Mobil.

Commode avec tiroir et miroir de la collection Veronna, de Toscano Mobil.

Kommode mit Schubladen und Spiegel aus der Kollektion Veronna, von Toscano Mobil.

1.

Bookcase by Mobles Larvi.

Librairie, de Mobles Larvi.

Bücherregal, von Mobles Larvi.

1.
Writing table by Mobles Larvi.
Bureau, de Mobles Larvi.
Bureau, von Mobles Larvi.

2.
Shoe box by Mobles Larvi.
Armoire à chaussures, de Mobles Larvi.
Schuhschrank, von Mobles Larvi.

1

2

1.

Caltojar writing table by Artema.

Écritoire Caltojar, d'Artema.

Schreibtisch Caltojar, von Artema.

2.

Calatañazor writing table by Artema.

Écritoire Calatañazor, d'Artema.

Schreibtisch Calatañazor, von Artema.

3.

Rachelle model console table and mirror from the Basilea collection by Toscano Mobil.

Console et miroir Rachelle, de la collection Basilea, de Toscano Mobil.

Konsoltisch und Spiegel Rachelle, aus der Kollektion Basilea, von Toscano Mobil.

1

2

1.

Viana model halltree by Artema.

" Gabanero " Viana, d'Artema.

Garderobe Viana, von Artema.

2.

Chest of drawers by Solís.

Commode, de Solís.

Kommode, von Solís.

3.

Console table and mirror in distressed cherry and gild carving. From the Adria collection by Toscano Mobil.

Console et miroir en cerisier vieilli et taille en or de la collection Adria, de Toscano Mobil.

Konsoltisch und Spiegel aus altgemachtem Wildkirschbaumholz mit Schnitzerei aus Gold, aus der Kollektion Adria, von Toscano Mobil.

3

1.
Display case by Mobles Larvi.
Vitrine, de Mobles Larvi.
Vitrine, von Mobles Larvi.

2.
Impresionante model display case by Canella.
Impressionnante vitrine , de Canella.
Beeindruckende Vitrine, von Canella.

1.
Chest of drawers by Esmor.
Commode, d'Esmor.
Kommode, von Esmor.

2.
Auxiliary piece by Blanch's International House.
Meuble auxiliaire, de Blanch's Internacional House.
Beistellmöbel, von Blanch's Internacional House.

1

2

1.

Display case by Yondar.

Vitrine, de Yondar.

Vitrine, von Yondar.

2.

Display case by Picó Muebles.

Vitrine, von Picó Muebles.

Vitrina, de Picó Muebles.

3.

Display case, Disarte.

Vitrine, de Disarte.

Vitrine, von Disarte.

3

1.
Ash veneer boisserie, Versalles model (Orells e Hijos).
Boiserie plaquée en frêne, modèle Versailles, d'Ortells e Hijos.
Boiserie mit Esche furniert, Modell Versalles, von Ortells e Hijos.

2.
Elena collection display case (Lanpas).
Vitrine de la collection Elena, de Lampas.
Vitrine aus der Kollektion Elena, von Lanpas.

1

2

1.

Bookcase with two-door compartment by Rosewood.

Librairie avec secrétaire à deux portes, de Rosewood.

Bücherschrank mit zweitürigem Sekretär, von Rosewood.

2.

Sidebar, by Mudeva.

Meuble bar, de Mudeva.

Barmöbel, von Mudeva.

3.

Console table (Acanto).

Console, d'Acanto.

Konsoltisch, von Acanto.

1

2

1.

Tron model cabinet (Cenedese).

Armoire, modèle Tron, de Cenedese.

Schrank, Modell Tron, von Cenedese.

2.

Mireia-99 collection cabinet by Rivera.

Armoire de la collection Mireia-99, de Rivera.

Schrank aus der Kollektion Mireia-99, von Rivera.

3

4

3.
Querini model cabinet (Cenedese).
Armoire, modèle Querini, de Cenedese.
Schrank, Modell Querini, von Cenedese.

4.
Nerea collection cabinet by Rivera.
Armoire de la collection Nerea, deRivera.
Schrank aus der Kollektion Nerea, von Rivera.

1

2

1.

Cabinet finished in ash (JNG).

Armoire avec finition en frêne, de JNG.

Schrank mit Esche nachbehandelt, von JNG.

2.

Auxiliary table by Alcores Diseño.

Meuble auxiliaire de Alcores Diseño.

Beistellmöbel von Alcores Diseño.

p. 530.

Sideboard with two doors, mirror frame, in cherry and walnut veneers. Bolonia collection by Ortells e Hijos.

Buffet à deux portes et cadre de miroir, plaqués en cerisier et noyer. Collection Bolonia, d'Ortells e Hijos.

Anrichte mit zwei Türen und Spiegelrahmen, furniert mit Wildkirsche und Nußbaum. Kollektion Bolonia, von Ortells e Hijos.

p. 531

Chest of drawers by Línea Stil.

Commode, de Linea Stil.

Kommode, von Línea Stil.

1.

Combination piece by Mudeva.

Commode armoire à vêtements et à chaussures, de Mudeva.

Kommode für Kleidung und Schuhe, von Mudeva.

2.

Chest of drawers by Jiménez.

Commode, de Jimenez.

Kommode, von Jiménez.

1.

Low cabinet from the Louis Philippe series by Alpuch.

Vitrine basse de la série Louis Philippe, d'Alpuch.

Niedrige Vitrine aus der Serie Louis Philipp, von Alpuch.

2.

Cabinet in cherry veneer, Sirer model for Ortells e Hijos.

Buffet plaqué en cerisier, modèle Sirer d'Ortells e Hijos.

Anrichte, Furnier aus Wildkirschbaumholz, Modell Sirer für Ortells e Hijos.

Comfort pieces

Les meubles de confort

Sitz- und Liegemöbel

In terms of comfort furniture, the bench is, without the least doubt, the basic model from which other more complex models developed.

Throughout the Renaissance, the bench scarcely modified its forms and complements. But from the seventeenth century, under the reign of Louis XIV, new forms were generated such as the canapé or the divan. Here, while the first type kept some of the structural pieces in combination with new upholstery, the second opted for still more comfort.

When the European mercantile bourgeoisie began to increase its political and economic power, other parallels came

Quant aux meubles de confort, le banc est certainement le modèle de base à partir duquel se développèrent d'autres formes plus complexes et confortables.

Durant la Renaissance, cette pièce du mobilier changea peu de forme et de compléments, mais à partir du XVII ème siècle, sous le reine de Louis XIV, apparurent de nouvelles formes telles que le canapé et le divan, où le premier combinait quelques pièces apparentes de sa structure avec d'autres tapissées, pendant que le second se caractérisait par son confort.

Quand la bourgeoisie européenne commença à augmenter son pouvoir politique et économique grâce au commerce, apparu une autre en parallèle, ab-

In Bezug auf die Sitz- und Liegemöbel ist die Bank mit großer Sicherheit das Grundmöbelstück, aus dem sich komplexere und bequemere Formen entwickelten.

Während der Renaissance erfuhren die Formen und Komplemente dieses Möbelstückes wenige Veränderungen. Aber ab dem 17. Jh., unter der Herrschaft Louis XIV., entstanden neue Formen, wie z. B. das Canapé oder der Diwan. Beim Canapé waren einige Strukturelemente sichtbar, andere hingegen überzogen. Beim Diwan lag das Gewicht auf der Bequemlichkeit. Als die europäische Handelsbourgeosie ihre politische und wirtschaftliche Macht ausbaute, schlug

1.
Prague upholstered sofa (Enebro).
Sofa Praga tapissé (Enebro).
Sofa Praga, gepolstert (Enebro).

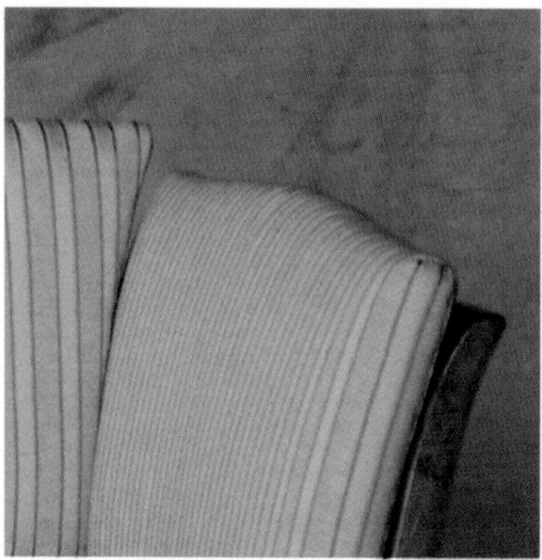
1

2

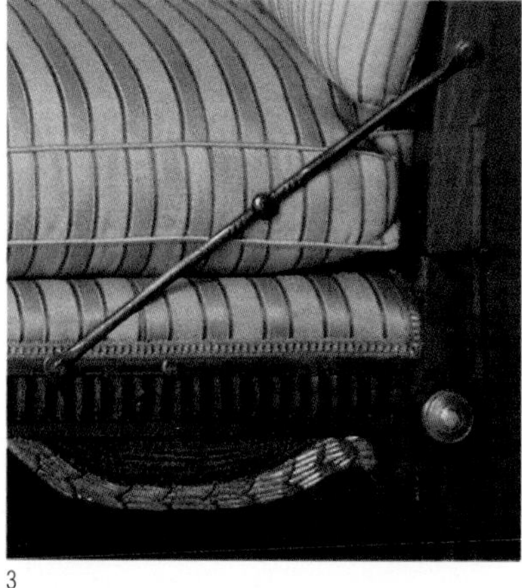
3

4

1.

Detail of the junction between back and arm of sofa 4.

Détail d'union dossier-accoudoir sofa 4.

Ausschnitt Verbindung Rücken- und Armlehne von Sofa 4.

2.

Detail legs and ornamental festoons of sofa 4.

Détail pattes et festons ornementaux sofa 4.

Ausschnitt Fuß und Ornament-Festons Sofa 4.

3.

Detail of the stretcher piece in reclinable sofa 4.

Détail baguette de soutient du bras inclinable sofa 4.

Ausschnitt Stützgestänge der ausklappbaren Armlehne Sofa 4.

4.

Danish sofa in fruit tree woods, 1770. Original piece (Antigüedades Fortuny).

Sofa danois en bois d'arbre fruitier de 1770. Pièce originale (Antigüedades Fortuny).

Dänisches Sofa aus Obstbaumholz von 1770. Originalstück (Antigüedades Fortuny).

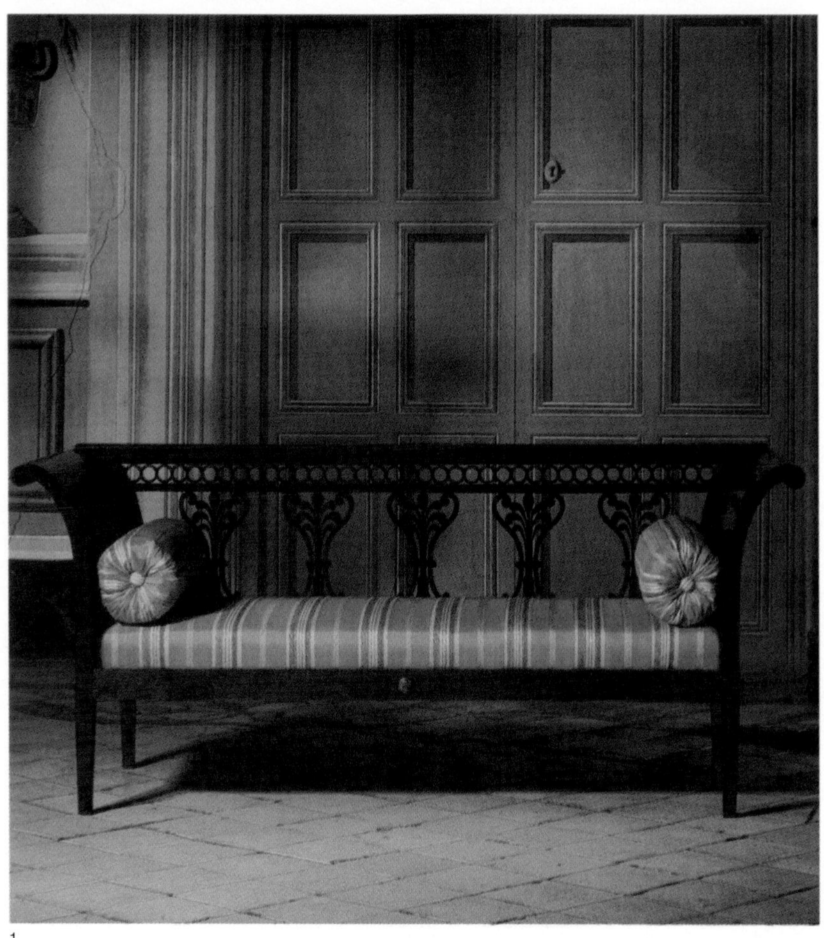

1

1.

Torla sofa. Reproduction of an original piece in Fernandino style (Acanto).

Sofa Torla. Reproduction d'une pièce originale de style Fernand VII (Acanto).

Sofa Torla. Reproduktion eines Originalstückes im Ferdinand-Stil (Acanto).

2.

Peñalara sofa. Reproduction of an original piece in Fernandino style (Acanto).

Sofa Peñalara. Reproduction d'une pièce originale de style Fernand VII (Acanto).

Sofa Peñalara. Reproduktion eines Originalstückes im Ferdinand-Stil (Acanto).

2

about. These were absolutely differentiated and became the driving force in generating new models of furniture, particularly in the first decades of the eighteenth-century. Hence, the rigid, bulky Renaissance and baroque armchairs began to be replaced by the first upholstered couches, made in England and in France.

solument différente, qui provoqua la parution de nouveaux modèles de mobilier, en particulier durant les premières décennies du XVIII ème siècle. C'est ainsi qu'en contre position aux grands et rigides fauteuils de la Renaissance et du Baroque, apparurent les premiers canapés matelassés, réalisés en Angleterre et en France.

man weitere Parallelen vor, die das Erscheinen neuer Möbelarten förderten. Dies geschah vor allem in den ersten Jahrzehnten des 18. Jh. So begann man, den strengen und großen Sesseln der Renaissance und des Barocks die ersten gepolsterten Lehnsessel entgegenzustellen, die in England und Frankreich hergestellt wurden.

1

1.

Tebas bench in polychrome olive, upholstered in striped material (Enebro).

Banquette Tebas d'olivier polychromé et tapissée à rayures (Enebro).

Bänkchen Tebas, mehrfarbiges Olivenholz und mit gestreiftem Stoff überzogen (Enebro).

2.

Tebas bench in olive, upholstered in white (Enebro).

Banquette Tebas d'olivier tapissée en blanc (Enebro).

Bänkchen Tebas, Olivenholz, mit weißem Stoff überzogen (Enebro).

3.

Tebas bench in polychrome olive, upholstered in flower print material (Enebro).

Banquette tapissée avec des motifs floraux (Enebro).

Bänkchen, mit geblümtem Stoff überzogen (Enebro).

2

3

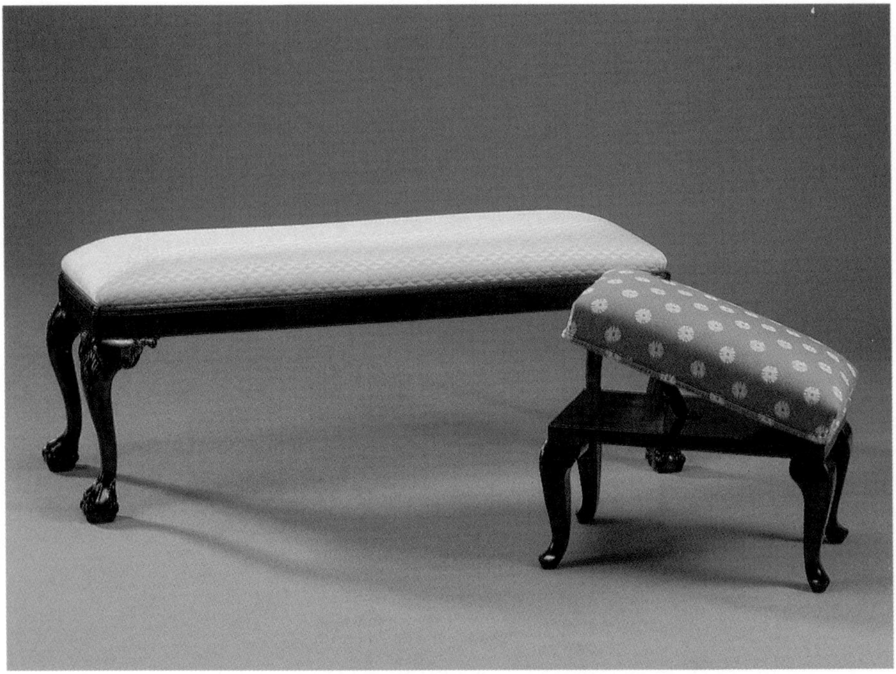

1

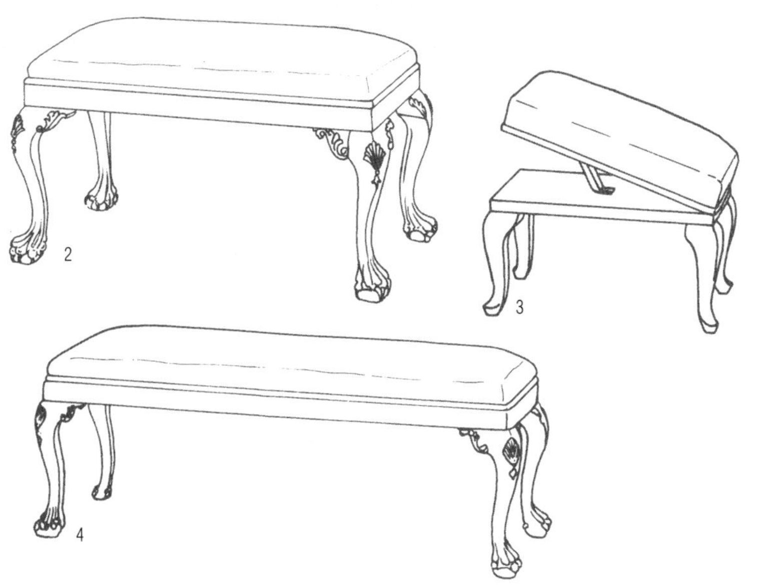

5

1.

Collection of bench at the foot of the bed in white upholstery and footrest in flower print upholstery (Enebro).

Ensemble de banquette pied de lit tapissée en blanc et repose pied tapissé avec des motifs floraux sur fond lisse (Enebro).

Bänkchen eines Bettendes, mit weißem Stoff überzogen, und Fußbänkchen mit Stoff überzogen, Blumenmotive auf einfarbigem Untergrund (Enebro).

2.

Sketch of upholstered bench.

Détail banquette tapissée.

Skizze mit Stoff überzogenes Bänkchen.

3.

Upholstered footrest.

Repose pied tapissé.

Mit Stoff überzogenes Fußbänkchen.

4.

Apunte banqueta pie de cama.

Détail banquette de pied de lit.

Skizze Bänkchen eines Bettendes.

5.

Tebas bench in polychrome, upholstered in brocade (Enebro).

Banquette Tebas polychromée et tapissée avec tissu broquart (Enebro).

Bänkchen Tebas, mehrfarbig und mit Brokatstoff überzogen (Enebro).

1

1.

Sofa, armchair, and center table (Ofifran).

Sofa, fauteuil et table de centre, d'Ofifran.

Sofa, Sessel und Wohnzimmertisch, von Ofifran.

2

3

2.

Armchair and small table by Rosewood.

Canapé avec petite table, de Rosewood.

Lehnsessel mit Tischchen, von Rosewood.

3.

Andrea model sofa (Rosewood).

Sofa Andrea, de Rosewood.

Sofa Andrea, von Rosewood.

Basic glossary

Glossaire de base

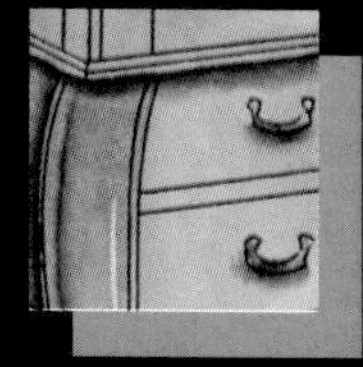

Grundbegriffe

A

A la reina. Oval back much used in the Plateresque style.

Abacus. Molded slab that crowns the capital of a column.

Altar piece. Decorative scenes on the frontal of an altar. A bench with retable.

Anthemion. Ornament using stylized honeysuckle, somewhat similar to the palmette and other nature themes.

Arabesque. Geometrical and complicated vegetal decoration of complex interwoven patterns. Of Arabic origin, it is used in friezes, soccles, and borders of pieces of furniture.

Arch, archway. Arches or series of arches making up a decorative whole.

Architrave.. The lowest section of the entablature, resting directly on the abaci of columns or on a panel.

Astragal. A small molding, semi-circular in shape. Roundel.

A

Abaque: *Partie supérieure du chapiteau des colonnes, en forme de damier.*

A la Reine: *Dossier ovale très utilisé dans le style Isabelle II.*

Âme: *Partie intérieure du bois contreplaqué formé par de fines couches qui lui donne de la consistance et qui est ensuite revêtue par d'autres couches qui composent les parois extérieures.*

Angelot: *Genre de décoration de taille exubérante et de caractère populaire, avec des motifs floraux ou d'animaux, mais surtout des figures humaines, telles que des enfants bien gras. Ornementation qui imite les formes de la nature.*

Arabesque: *Ornementation aux combinaisons géométriques ou végétales très variées d'origine arabe, qui s'emploi dans les frises, socles ou franges de meubles.*

Araser: *Rendre plane et lisse la superficie d'un meuble, sans aucune moulure entrante ou saillante.*

Arcatures: *Série d'arcs qui composent un ensemble décoratif.*

Architrave: *Partie principale de l'entablement entre la frise et le chapiteau.*

Armature: *Pièce ou ensemble de pièces en bois ou en fer unies les unes aux autres, dans le but de soutenir ou renforcer des éléments d'un meuble.*

Astragale: *Petite moulure demi circulaire convexe.*

A

À la reine. Ovale Rückenlehne, die oft im isabelinischen Stil verwandt wurde.

Abakus. Ausgekehltes Stück in Form einer Säulenplatte, die den oberen Abschluß eines Kapitells bildet.

Abgleichen. Die Oberfläche eines Möbelstückes ebnen und glätten, ohne daß Vorsprünge oder Öffnungen übrigbleiben.

Anfänger. Schräg geschnittener Quaderstein, aus dem ein Stichbogen oder Flachbogen entspringt.

Angelot. Populäres üppiges Dekorationselement mit Blumen- oder Tiermotiven, aber im allgemeinen mit menschlichen Figuren, wie z. B. dralle Kinder.

Atlante. Atlante. Heroic male figure used as a column or as a corbel element. Cf. caryatide.

Attic. Ático. A story of a building over the principal entablature. It may crown the building's façade.

B

Baluster. Balaustre. A vertical element, usually turned and circular in section, or else prismatic or pyramidal, highly varied in profile.

Balustrade. Balaustrada. A parapet formed by a row of balusters, often circular in section and with arched moldings. The balusters are regularly spaced and held in place between a base and a rail or coping.

Banquette. Banqueta. A raised part of a wall or parapet. or trench.

Assemblage: *Union, joint, ou montage de pièces en bois à travers des sections spéciales en faisant coïncider les parties saillantes des unes avec les parties entrantes des autres. Particulièrement, assembler à tenon et mortaise, queue de milan, lacet, tenaille, demi bois, entaille, fausse entaille, languette, boîtes en épis, lacets perdus, etc...*

Attique: *Élément d'architecture placé sur la corniche d'un immeuble comme terminaison de la façade.*

Atlante: *Figure d'homme supportant une corniche ou une tribune.*

B

Baldaquin: *Sorte de dossier ou pavillon qui couvre en partie ou entièrement le lit ; il est soutenu par des colonnes qui sont la continuation des pattes du lit ; d'autres*

Anteme. Verzierung, die Naturformen imitiert.

Arabeske. Ornament aus kombinierten, sehr variierten geometrischen Formen oder Abbildungen von Pflanzen, arabischer Herkunft, das man bei Täfelungen, Sockeln und Einfassungen der Möbel anwendet.

Architrav. Unterer Teil des Simswerkes, das auf Säulen oder einem Paneel ruht.

Arkaden. Anreihung von Bögen, die eine dekorative Einheit ergeben.

Armierung. Ein oder mehrere Teile aus Holz oder Eisen, die miteinander verbunden sind und dazu dienen, Elemente eines Möbels zu stützen oder zu verstärken.

Astragal. Kleines, halbrundes, konvexes Rundprofil. Torus.

Atlant. Tragendes Element in Gestalt einer Männerfigur anstelle einer Säule oder eines Pfeilers. Karyatide.

Attika. Architektonischer Körper, der auf das Obersims eines Gebäudes als Abschluß der Fassade aufgesetzt wird.

B

Baldachin. Art von Betthimmel oder Zeltdach, das teilweise oder ganz das Bett bedeckt; Es wird von Säulen getragen, die den Fortsatz der Beine des Bettes bilden; in anderen Fällen ist er an der Decke oder der Wand angebracht.

Balken. Element, das als Verstärkung oder Stütze dient.

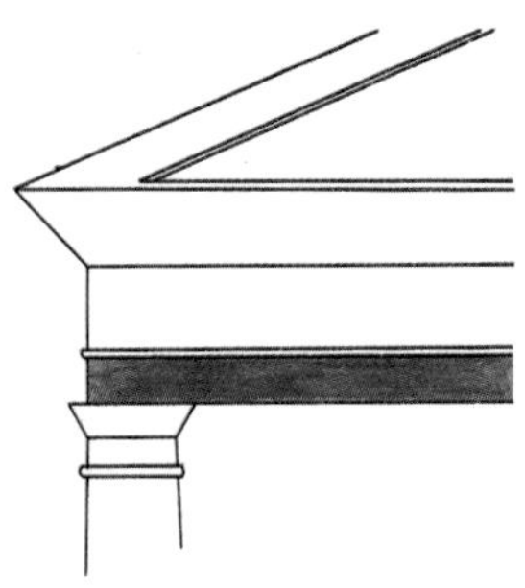

Base. Basa. Pedestal on which a column, statue, or other element is seated.

Bergère. Bergère. An upholstered French armchair of wide proportions. It has an exposed wood frame and loose seat cushion.

Boiserie (Fr). Wood finishing for walls. Wainscot. Paneling.

Bonheur-du-jour (Fr). A small writing desk with a drawered or pigeonholed section. It may be closed by a folding, hinged cover. The piece may also include a small cabinet in the lower part. Mid-eighteenth-century French origin.

Border. Cenefa. A piece of material around the edges or along the upper edge of a piece. If decorated, the design or motif repeats itself indefinitely.

Boudoir. A sitting room or toilette for the woman of the house, originating toward the middle of the eighteenth century in France.

fois, il est suspendu du plafond ou du mur.

Balustre: *Élément vertical, habituellement taillé, en forme de prisme ou de pyramide, à la silhouette très variée.*

Balustrade: *Barrière architectonique formée par une rangée de colonnes de section circulaire et moulures arrondies, et unies par une base et un architrave continu.*

Banquette: *Petit renfoncement qui se forme au long d'un mur quand celui-ci change d'épaisseur en hauteur.*

Base:*Socle ou piédestal sur lequel repose la colonne ou la statue, ou n'importe quel élément.*

Bergère: *Fauteuil incrusté, avec des accoudoirs, dont la forme tendait à envelopper le corps de l'usager et à le protéger ; le dossier est concave, avec deux côtés tapissés unis à celui-ci ; il a un coussin à part sur le siège: Son utilisation commence vers la moitié du XVIII ème siècle en France.*

Bosel: *Moulure de forme cylindrique convexe. Cordon.*

Boiserie: *Revêtement de bois pour les murs. Lambris. Panneaux.*

Bonheur *du jour: Petit écritoire secrétaire pour dames, pourvu d'un petit cabinet avec des petits tiroirs, rayons et départements, généralement fermé par un couvercle abattable et uni à la partie postérieure de l'écritoire et pourvu, dans sa partie inférieure, d'une armoire ou petite étagère ; son utilisation*

Baluster. Vertikales Element, einfach gedreht, prismatisch oder pyramidenförmig. Die Silhouette kann stark variieren.

Balustrade. Architektonische Brüstung, bestehend aus einer Reihe von kleinen Säulen mit runder Schnittfläche und bogenförmigem Gesims, in gleichmäßigen Abständen angeordnet und mit durchgehendem Unterbau und Architrav verbunden.

Bankett. Kleine Zwischenebene, die längs an einer Wand angebracht wird, wenn diese die Stärke in ihrer Höhe ändert.

Bargueño. Typisch spanisches Möbel maurischen Ursprungs, in Form eines quadratischen Schrankes mit Griffen an den Seiten und herunterklappbarem Deckel; er bezeichnet eine Art Schreibtisch mit Schubladen und Schubfächern im Innenteil.

Basis. Fundament oder Sockel, auf dem die Säule, Statue oder ein anderes Element ruht.

Bekrönung. Zierde, die der Vollendung eines Möbels dient.

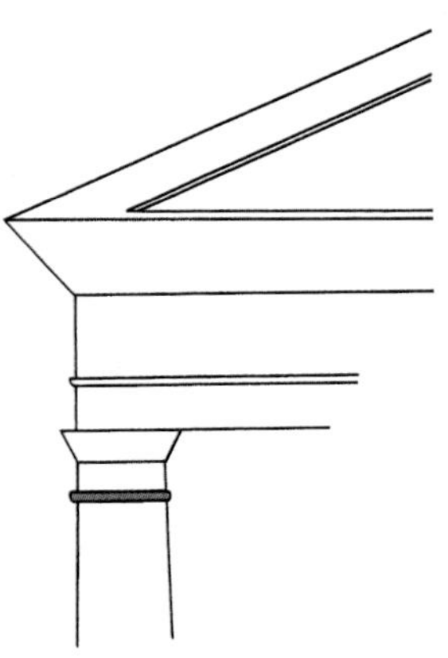

Brocade. Brocado. A rich silk cloth with raised patterns interwoven in silk and gold thread.

Bun. Cebolla. A sphere, sometimes flattened, with a shape something like an onion, that serves as the foot of a piece of furniture. It may be smooth, with molding, or it may include a talon. Lattice window. Celosía. A window made of interwoven strips. The material used varies (iron, wood, reed), but the object is to let air into the space being protected.

Bureau. Arquimesa. A writing desk with many compartments. A low chest of drawers. Both types are often used in bedrooms.

Bureau. Bargueño. The word may denote either writing desk with many compartments or a low chest of drawers. One eminently Spanish version, of morisco origin, is in the form of a chest with handles on the sides and a folding top.

Bureau. Bureau. See desk.

commença vers la moitié du XVIII ème siècle en France.

Boudoir: *Coiffeuse ou toilette de dames. Son utilisation commence vers la moitié du XVIII ème en France.*

Buffet: *Crédence pourvue d'étagères où on place les aliments, la vaisselle, le linge de maison et tout ce qui est nécessaire pour parer un table.*

Bureau: *Meuble écritoire qui doit son nom à la bure, une grosse étoffe en laine ou en lin (XII ème siècle), avec laquelle on recouvrait les tables ou les écritoires du clergé.*

C

Cabinet: *Petite armoire ou crédence utilisée pour placer, souvent à portée de la vue, des objets de tous genres.*

Cabinet español: *Meuble éminemment español d'origine arabe, en forme de coffre quadrangulaire avec des anses sur les côtés et un couvercle abattable ; il représente un genre d'écritoire avec des tiroirs et des gavettes intérieures.*

Cabriolé: *Forme de patte caractéristique du XVIII ème siècle, intro-*

Bergere (frz.). Mit Intarsien verzierter Lehnstuhl, mit Armlehnen, in dessen Form der Körper des Sitzenden versinkt; die Rückenlehne ist konkav und hat zwei mit der Lehne verbundene, gepolsterte Seitenteile; das Polsterkissen liegt lose auf der Sitzfläche. Sie tauchte Mitte des 18. Jh. in Frankreich auf.

Beschlag. Eisenteile, mit denen ein Möbel verziert wird und mit dem dieses auf einfache Art und Weise verstärkt wird. Teile, die das Öffnen und Schließen von Türen oder Fenstern sichern und erleichtern.

Boiserie (frz.). Wandverkleidung aus Holz. Wandtäfelung. Vertäfelung.

Bonheur-du-jour (frz.). Kleiner Schrei-btisch-Sekretär für Damen mit einem kleinen Schubfach mit Schublädchen, Füllfächern oder Abtrennungen, der im allgemeinen mit einem klappbaren Deckel verschlossen wurde, welcher an der Vorderseite des Schreibtisches angebracht war. Im unteren Teil befand sich ein Schrank oder ein kleines Regal. Er tauchte ab Mitte des 18. Jh. in Frankreich auf.

Bord. Brett aus beliebigem Material, das horizontal an einer Wand befestigt wird oder Teil eines Schrankes oder eines anderen Möbels ist. Es dient der Ablage. Regalbrett. Gestell.

Borte. Zierstreifen an der Kante eines Möbels.

Boudoir (frz.). Frisier- oder Toilettentisch für Damen. Er taucht Mitte des 18. Jh. in Frankreich auf.

Brokat. Seidenstoff mit scheinbar gestickten Mustern, in den Gold- oder Silberfäden eingewebt werden.

C

Cabinet. Cabinet. Small storage space with compartments and which may be open or fitted with doors. Cabinets, sometimes in the form of the credence type, are used to display decorative objects or to store different types of objects.

Cabinet. Entredós. An element used in bedrooms generally, with a rather large inner compartment and, often, a drawer over it, generally with a marble top. Favorite locations are between balconies and windows.

Cabinetmaker. Ebanista. A skilled worker in wood, especially precious, exotic woods, who makes fine furniture.

Cabriole leg. Cabriolé. A type of furniture leg characteristic of the eighteenth century, introduced into Europe at the end of the seventeenth century from China. The long S-shaped curve moves outward from the edge of the seat of the chair, then returns inward and the leg tapers toward the foot, which is ornamented as a club, clog, talon, bun, volute or ball. Also, the concave, curved back of chairs.

Canopy. Baldaquino. A kind of covering or pavilion over all or part of a bed. Canopies are supported by columns that are the continuation of the foot and the headboard, although they may also be atta-

duite en Europe à la fin du XVII ème siècle, originaire de Chine ; la silhouette en forme de S allongée se courbe vers l'extérieur au-delà du bord du siège de la chaise, pour, par la suite, descendre en une contre courbe fuselée dans l'intérieur, qui diminue graduellement et se termine par un petit pied en forme de bâton, sabot, griffe, bosse, volute, ou boule. Dossier de chaise courbé et concave.

Canapé: *Meuble de siège continu avec des accoudoirs dont le numéro de places est déterminé par le dossier.*

Cannage: *Ouvrage fait de tiges ou fibres de certaines plantes entrelacées qui sert de siège de chaises, fauteuil basculant, etc...*

« Canterano »: *Nom donné en Catalogne à la commode écritoire avec couvercle incliné. C'est un meuble avec beaucoup de tiroirs, transformation de l'ancien coffre auquel on rajouta des tiroirs au XVI ème siècle, au début à la base du meuble et par la suite au XVI*

Buffet (frz.). Kredenz mit Regalen für Lebensmittel, Geschirr, Tischdecken und alle Gegenstände, die zum Anrichten eines Tisches dienen.

Bureau (frz.). Schreibtischmöbel, dessen Name auf den Stoff Burre zurükkgeht, ein grober Woll- oder Leinenstoff (13. Jh.), mit dem der Tisch oder Schreibtisch der Geistlichen bedeckt wurde.

C

Cabinet (frz.). Kleiner Schrank oder Kredenz, der zur meist sichtbaren Aufbewahrung von diversen Gegenständen jeglicher Art diente.

Cabriolé (frz.). Form der Tisch- oder Stuhlbeine, charakteristisch für das 18. Jh. Ursprünglich aus China, in Europa verwendet ab dem Ende des 17. Jh. Die verlängerte Silhouette des S wölbt sich nach außen über die Kante der Sitzfläche des Stuhls hinaus, um dann nach unten fortlaufend eine nach innen gewölbte Gegenbewegung zu beschreiben, die stufenweise kleiner wird und in einem kleinen Ornament am Fuß des Beines endet. Dieses Or-

ched to the ceiling or to the wall.

Cartouche. Cartela. A painted or sculpted decorative representation used as a tablet or frame for inscriptions and in th form of a scroll or curling piece of parchment. A modillion like this, especially one with an S-shaped curve.

Carving. Talla. Artistic technique consisting in cutting a surface (sometimes on a piece of furniture) to create figures, decorative motifs, etc. The surface may be of wood, marble, etc., and the figures vary in depth of relief.

Caryatid. Cariátide. Heroic male figure used as a column or as a corbel element.

Cathedra. Cátedra. A bishop's chair. A chair used by Roman women, like the Greek klismos.

Coffer. Arca. Box or chest with a closing top, often kept apart and containing valuables.

ème et au XVII ème siècle dans tout le meuble ; au début du XVIII ème siècle, le « Canterano » ou bureau bas substitua définitivement l'ancien coffre Coffre: Caisse, coffret, bahut fermé par un couvercle et généralement situé dans un lieu à part.

***Cariatide:** Motif architectonique utilisé aussi dans la structure des meubles , spécialement dans les montants, en bronze, en forme de figure féminine debout, sculptée de forme arrondie, faisant la fonction de colonne ou de pilier.*

***Cartisane:** Représentation en peinture ou sculptée d'un parchemin à moitié déroulé, généralement avec des inscriptions, utilisé dans un but ornemental. Motif décoratif, en carton ou papier, généralement en forme de carte et dont les rebords se retordent en volutes et autres éléments, selon le style employé. Élément saillant en forme de S qui soutient un corps émergeant.*

***Chaire:** Ample siège massif avec dossier surélevé, réservé généralement aux personnages représentatifs, qui confère de la majesté. Siège de la femme romaine, semblable aux « klismes » grecs.*

nament hat die Form eines Stockes, Holzschuhes, einer Klaue, eines Kegels, einer Schnecke oder einer Kugel. Die Rückenlehne ist gewölbt und konkav.

Canapé (frz.). Möbelstück mit fortlaufender Sitzfläche und Armlehnen. Auf der Rückenlehne kann man die Anzahl der Sitzplätze erkennen.

Canterano. Name, mit dem in Katalonien die Kommode mit Schreibtisch und geneigtem Deckel bezeichnet wird; es ist ein Möbel mit vielen Schubladen, eine Abwandlung der antiken Truhe, die im 16. Jh. mit Schubladen ausgestattet wurde; dies anfangs im unteren Teil und später, im Laufe des 16. und 17. Jh. am ganzen Möbel. Zu Beginn des 18. Jh. ersetzte der Canterano oder die Kommode endgültig die alte Truhe.

Chaise-longue (frz.). Stuhl mit sehr langer Sitzfläche, um die Beine auszustrecken. Sie kann an der Fußseite eine kleine Lehne haben.

Chiffonnier (frz.). Hohes und schmales Möbel mit vielen Schubladen, typisch für das Ende des 18. und das gesamte 19. Jh.

Coiffeuse (frz.). Toilettentischchen, an dem man sich kämmte; ähnlich der Poudreuse.

D

Die Holme waren mit Voluten, Palmetten, Fadenalgen oder anderen Motiven verziert.

Diwan. Bankähnlicher Sitz, lang und weich, von ausreichender Breite und Länge für mehrere Personen oder um sich hinzulegen. Die Struktur ist aus Holz oder Metall, eher niedrig, nor-

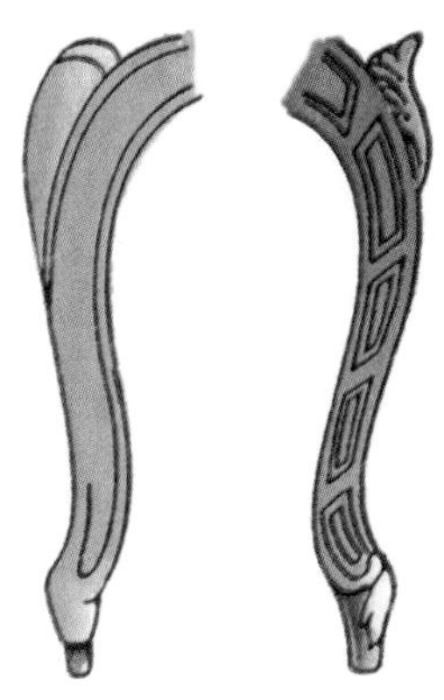

Column. Columna. A pillar, usually circular on plane. Columns consist of a base, a shaft, and a capital. In trabeation, columns support arches, ceilings, beams, etc. Their form is very often used to define the style of architecture or furniture in which they occur. Some of the names used are: Tuscan, Dorian, Ionic, Corinthian, Composite, Attic, Solomonic, Gothic, Fluted, etc.

Console table. Consola. A table attached to or resting against a wall, its top further supported by consoles or front legs. Also, an ornamental bracket that serves to support another piece, such as a cornice. Ancone.

Corbel. Zapata. A projecting element used to support another.

Core. Alma. The innermost material, often of sawed lumber, used to strengthen plywood. The more decorative veneer strips are glued onto the outer surfaces of the core.

Chaise-longue: Chaise au siège très allongé pour reposer les jambes ; il peu avoir un dossier sous les pieds.

Chambranle: *Pièce horizontale qui uni les pattes des tables et des chaises ; elle peut être continue (l'une à continuation de l'autre de forme périphérique), en H (une de chaque côté et unies entre elles par une traverse centrale) ou en croix (croisant la première avec la troisième et la seconde avec la quatrième). Clôture ornementale d'un creux (porte, fenêtre ou cheminée).*

Chanfrein: *Dans les corps qui en possède, petite surface qui se forme en abattant une arête par un plan proche ou parallèle à elle.*

Chiffonnier: *Meuble haut et étroit avec beaucoup de tiroirs, caractéristique de la fin du XVIII ème et de tout le XIX ème siècle.*

Coffre banc: *Meuble en bois en forme de coffre rectangulaire, creux, pourvut d'un couvercle soutenu par des charnières, qui s'utilise comme meuble contenant.*

Coffre table: *Meuble formé par un corps vertical avec beaucoup de tiroirs et une tablette qui peut s'escamoter ou s'extraire selon la nécessité.*

Coiffeuse: *Petite table de toilette qui, avec la poudreuse, servait pour s'arranger les cheveux.*

Colonne: *Élément architecturale qui consiste en une pièce haute et mince, de section ronde habituellement, qui soutient un arc, un*

malerweise ohne Rückenlehne und mit aufgelegten Sitzkissen. Der Diwan wurde in Europa im 18. Jh. bekannt und wurde im folgenden Jh. größtenteils durch das bequemere Sofa ersetzt.

Drechseln. Technik, die einem prismatischen Holzstück beim Schleifen und Abrunden Form verleiht; das Holzstück wird auf eine horizontale Platte gelegt, die sich um ein vertikales Brett dreht, bis es die Form eines Fußes mit runder Schnittfläche und dem erforderlichen Umriß erreicht.

Dressoir (frz.). Anrichte, ursprünglich aus dem Burgund, ähnlich einer Truhe mit hohen Beinen, mit auf dem Deckel aufgesetzter Stufenreihe, deren Abschluß eine Art Baldachin bildet.

E

Einbauschrank. Hohlraum in der Wand mit Türen und Querbrettern,

Cornice. Cornisa. A generally horizontal projection with moldings of wood, stone, or other materials that crowns another piece, especially an entablature, wall, or opening. The cornice is an ornamental and protective piece. Each architectural style has its characteristic cornice, with variants and adequate proportions for each distinct order of Classical and Renaissance architecture.

Cornucopia. Cornucopia. Motif consisting in a wide curved goat's horn overflowing with flowers and fruits and used as a symbol of abundance.

Credence (credence table). Credencia. A small table or dresser used to store plate. A similar piece where the bread and wine used in the mass rest before consecration.

Crest. Crestería. The ornamental finishing which crowns the upper part of a piece of furniture.

Crosspiece. Aldaba. Rung, slat, or spindle-shaped piece placed horizontally to join the upright pieces of a chair or armchair. (See stretcher.)

Crosspiece. Travesaño. See stretcher.

Crown. Copete. Top part of a piece of furniture. The upper part of an ornamented gable.

toit, une poutre, etc... ;sa forme définit le style architecturale et le meuble ; la nomenclature les plus courantes est: toscane, dorique, ionique, corinthienne ou composée, attique, exempte, adossée, salomonique ou en flambeau, gotique, en tambours, cannelée ou striée, corollaire.

***Commode:** Banc appuyé sur des pattes hautes et de ce fait confortable, destiné à garder des objets et pourvus de tiroirs dans toute sa hauteur, avec un damier horizontal dans la partie supérieure.*

***Confidente:** Canapé sur lequel ne peuvent s'asseoir uniquement que deux personnes.*

***Console:** Table de décoration, faite pour s'appuyer contre le mur, sur laquelle on expose des objets d'ornement, tels qu'une horloge, des candélabres ou des vases. Piè-*

der als Schrank genutzt wird. Nachfolger ist der Schrank.

Einlegearbeiten. Eingelegte Arbeit in Holz, Metall oder Stein; für Dekorationszwecke.

Enjuta. Raum der 4 Flächen, die übrigbleiben, wenn man einen Kreis in ein Quadrat einfügt.

F

Facette. An Körpern mit Kanten oder Ecken, diejenige Seite, die eine von diesen nahe der Kante und parallel zur Kante schneidet.

Feston. Jegliche Verzierung oder Abschlußstück in Form einer Welle, Spitze etc., in die Kante eines Möbels oder in eines seiner Elemente eingearbeitet.

Filet. Langes und schmales Muster oder Relief, von gleichmäßiger Breite, das als Teil eines Elementes oder zusätzlich als Verzierung angebracht wird.

Filigranarbeit. Jegliche feine und zierliche Verzierung, die ein hohlsaumartiges Muster ergibt.

Fries. Dekoratives architektonisches Element, bestehend aus einem Bandgesims, im allgemeinen horizontal, in das Figuren oder Ornamentmotive eingemeißelt werden; es ist Teil des Simses in den klassischen Baustilen. Ornamentales Bandgesims, das als Dekoration auf Objekte aufgesetzt wird, mit Motiven wie Kränzen, Festons, Trophähen und ähnlichem.

Frontispiz. Fassade oder Vorderseite eines Hauses, oder analog beim Möbel.

Crown. Coronamiento. The upper part of a building or part of a building and, by extension, of a piece of furniture or any of its parts.

Cupboard, closet. Alacena. Recessed space in a wall with doors and shelves used for storage.

Chaise-longue (Fr). A long reclining chair. It may have a low back.

Chamfer. Chaflán. A pared off angle or arris.

Checkerboard. Escaqueado. Work done in two different materials or two different colors in a pattern like a chessboard.

Cherub (cupid, etc.). Angelote. Popular name given to denote the technical term putto (plural, putti). Putti are figures of infant boys, usually represented as chubby and healthy, much used in Renaissance art.

ce émergeante qui sert de support à une corniche.

***Contreplaqué:** Planche formée par une ou plusieurs feuilles de bois encollées avec les veines croisées ; cette construction évite les torsions, les mouvements, les fissures et les contractions ou dilatations, et les problèmes que subissent les bois massifs tels que la chaleur ou l'humidité.*

***Coquille:** Triangle courbé entre les arcs d'une arcade.*

***Coquille** Saint-Jacques: Ornement qui reproduit la coquille demi circulaire caractéristique du pèlerin.*

***Corne d'abondance:** Motif d'ornement qui consiste en une corne large pleine de fleurs et de fruits qui s'utilise comme symbole de l'abondance. Cadre doré, large, taillé parfois avec un support pour des bougis, avec un petit miroir, employé en décoration.*

***Corniche:** Membre saillant généralement horizontal et avec des*

Fronton. Architektonische Bekrönung in Form eines kleinen gleichschenkligen Dreieckes, das den oberen Abschluß von Möbelstücken, Schränken, Bücherschränken etc. bildet. Er ähnelt der Bekrönung der griechischen Tempel; er kann einfach, gebogen oder gebrochen sein. In letzterem Fall wird er durch eine Volute abgeschlossen und hat normalerweise in der Mitte einen Kelch.

Füllhorn. Ziermotiv, bestehend aus einem breiten Horn, das mit Blumen und Früchten überfüllt ist und als Symbol des Überflusses gilt.

Fundamentbasis. Horizontales Stück auf oder unter einem geraden Fuß, um diesen zu stützen oder sein ausgedehntes Gewicht zu beschweren und das obere Gewicht besser zu verteilen.

Furnier. Platte, die aus einer oder mehreren verleimten dünnen Holzplatten besteht, wobei die Maserung kreuzförmig übereinandergelegt wird. Diese Konstruktion vermeidet

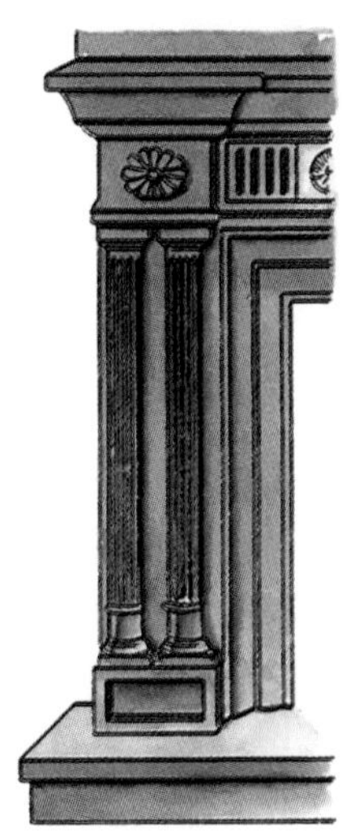

Chest of drawers. Cómoda. A chest, often on high legs and thus of comfortable height--it is also called a commode--used to keep objects in its many drawers. It has a finished panel on top.

Chest. Arquibanco. Piece of furniture made of wood, rectangular in shape and hollow. Chests have a hinged top and are used as storage containers.

Chiffonier. Chiffonnier. A high chest of drawers, usually narrow, characteristic of the end of the eighteenth century and all of the nineteenth century.

D

Dado. Dado. The central piece of the body of a pedestal or plinth of a column, without moldings. Also called a die.

moulures en bois, en pierre ou en un autre matériel, qui sert de couronnement pour ornementer ou protéger ; chaque style architecturale a sa propre corniche caractéristique, avec les variations et proportions adéquat aux besoins de son ordre esthétique ou utilitaire ; dans les cinq ordres de l'architecture classique, la corniche est la partie supérieure des trois qui composent l'ensemble des corniches et occupe la deux cinquième partie de sa hauteur..

Couronnement: *Ornement qui termine un meuble.*

Crédence: *Meuble aux dimensions similaires à une commode, en forme d'armoire pourvu de deux ou plusieurs portes, avec des tiroirs ou sans, pour garder la vaisselle, le linge de maison et les aliments ; il présente parfois des étagères pour exposer la vaisselle.*

Crête: *Ornement continu, généralement ajouré, qui couronne la partie supérieure des meubles.*

Verkrümmungen, Verrutschen, Risse und Kontraktionen oder Ausdehnungen - Defekte die Massivholz bei Wärme- oder Feuchtigkeitseinwirkung erleidet.

Furnieren. Von den Kunsttischlern angewandte Technik zur Verzierung, die darin besteht, die Oberfläche mit für Möbel und Gegenstände typischem Holz zu verkleiden. Verwendet werden qualitativ bessere dünne Platten mit einer Dicke von 0,5 bis 2 mm, je nach Art der geplanten Dekoration, die aus feinem Holz oder Schildpatt, Perlmutt oder Elfenbein bestehen kann.

G

Galbe (frz.). Leicht gebogenes Möbelbein.

Galerie. Abschluß aus Säulchen und Bögen am oberen Teil eines Möbels.

Geflecht. Arbeit, bei der Stile oder Fasern von bestimmten Pflanzen verflochten werden; es wird verwendet für die Herstellung der Sitzflächen von Stühlen, Schaukelstühlen, etc.

Dais, platform. Tarima. A raised structure, sometimes with a set of stairs, on which a throne or armchairs may be arranged, offering a certain authority to those seated.

Desk, writing table. Bufete. A table used for writing and fitted with drawers. In Britain, the word bureau is used, especially when describing slant-top or roll-top desks.

Divan. Diván. A large couch or bench wide and long enough to accommodate several people or to allow someone to recline. The framework may be of wood or metal. Divans tend to be low and without a backrest, and often use loose cushions. The divan was widely used in Europe in the eighteenth century. In the nineteenth, it was substituted in large part by the more comfortable sofa.

Dresser. Dressoir (Fr). Side table of Burgundian origin. It is

D

***Damassé:** Tissu en soie avec des dessins qui paraissent brodés, où se mêlent les fils d'or et d'argent.*

***Dé:** Pièce centrale d'un piédestal d'une colonne sans moulures, nette. Pierre carrée et plane qui couronne le chapiteau d'une colonne. Abaque.*

***Demi tige:** Moulure concave, dont le profil est habituellement un demi cercle. Gavette.*

***Divan:** Siège qui sert de banc, long et molletonné, de longueur et largeur suffisante pour accommoder plusieurs personnes, ou s'allonger, avec des structures en bois ou métal, plutôt bas, habituellement sans dossier, et avec des coussins amovibles. Le divan apparut en Europe durant le XVIII ème siècle, et fut remplacé par la suite par un sofa plus confortable.*

***Dressoir:** Buffet d'origine bourguignonne, semblable à un coffret haut sur pattes, avec des tri-*

Gesimsband. Verzierung aus einem Reliefband mit verschiedenen Umrissen und manchmal mit Elementen wie aufeinanderfolgenden Eiern oder Blättern; die wichtigsten Arten sind: konkav (Trochilus, Echinus); konvex (Torus und Wulst); verschiedene (Karnies, Kehlleiste).

Giebelband. Verzierung oder Dekoration, die den vorderen Teil eines Möbels bildet oder den vorderen Teil bedeckt.

Goldplättchen. Extrem dünnes Blatt aus Gold, für dekorative Verkleidungen verwendet.

Gondel. Sessel mit sehr konkavem und halbrundem Rückenteil, der mit den Armlehnen verbunden ist; er wird so genannt wegen seiner Ähnlichkeit mit den venezianischen Booten des 18. Jh. Bett mit Eigenschaften, die den genannten Booten ähnlich sind.

Guéridon (frz.). Kleinerer runder Tisch mit einem Mittelfuß oder Sockel, der im 17. und 18. Jh. zum Aufstellen von Kerzenhaltern, Spielen, Gläsern, etc. diente.

H

Hängezwickel. Abgerundetes Dreieck zwischen den Bögen einer Arkade.

Hohlkehle. Ausgesparte oder gerillte Riefe, die normalerweise in einige Säulen oder Pilaster von oben nach unten eingearbeitet wird.

Holm. Vertikales Element der Struktur eines Möbels, das mit den Querbalken oder horizontalen Elementen verzapft wird, um ein Gestell zu bilden.

basically a chest on high legs with architectural forms on the top, sometimes crowned by a kind of canopy.

Dressing table. Coiffeuse (Fr). Small toilette table used, along with the poudreuse, for arranging dress, hair, etc.

E

Emboss. Repujar. To raise or carve in relief on metal, leather, etc., using a hammer.

Entablature. Entablamiento. Cornisamento. In Classical architecture, the superstructure of an order. It consists of the architrave, frieze, and cornice. The terminology also applies to the parts of a piece of furniture using columns.

F

Festoon. Festón. Any design or ornament in the form of a wave, S-curve, etc., on the edge of a piece of furniture on one of its elements.

Filigree. Filigrana. Any ornamental work of fine delicate design, especially openwork.

Fillet. Filete. A small narrow band used as a part of a molding or between moldings. Listel. It can also encircle a column (annulet). Such adornment pieces may have relief designs.

Finishing. Acabado. Any operation executed on a completed object with the aim of making its outer surface agreeable to the eye, especially in

bunes couronnées sur le couvercle, et terminé par une espèce de dais.

E

Ébéniste: *Artisan qui travaille les bois précieux et en particulier l'ébène.*

Echiquier: *Œuvre réalisée avec deux matériaux différents, par exemple en pierre et en brique, formant des dés, ou avec du carrelage en noir et blanc semblable á un damier.*

Écosse: *Moulure concave, plus saillante dans la partie inférieure, située généralement entre deux bosels. Moulure généralement courbée qui enlace le mur avec le plafond.*

Écritoire: *Table avec des tiroirs sur laquelle on écrit. Bureau. Spécialement les cylindriques qui se ferment avec des volets.*

Embasement: *Espace entre les quatre restants entre un carré et le cercle inscrit en son intérieur.*

Entablement: *Corniches. Ensemble de moulures qui couronnent la façade d'un édifice classique ou d'un meuble supportées par des colonnes ; il se divise en trois parties: l'architrave, la corniche et la frise.*

Entre deux: *Meuble de salon, avec armoire et un tiroir au-dessus, généralement avec la partie supérieure en marbre, qui se place entre les fenêtres et les balcons.*

Entretoise: *Traverse horizontale qui uni les barres des fauteuils et des chaises dans le dossier.*

I

Imbrikation. Architektonische Verzierung, bei der kleine vieleckige Zacken aneinander und übereinander gelegt werden, wobei kleine leere Flächen entstehen, oder auch bogenförmige Motive, die die Schuppen der Fische nachahmen.

Intarsien. Dekorative Einlegearbeiten, dem Holzmosaik sehr ähnlich, in die Struktur des Möbels eingearbeitet; bestehend aus feinen Stücken aus Holz oder anderem organischen Material, wie Knochen oder Elfenbein, oder auch Mineral, die so angeordnet werden, daß sie ein Mosaik mit Blumenmotiven, Arabesken und malerischen Szenen ergeben. Einlegearbeit. Holzmosaik.

J

Jalousie. Durchbrochene oder gitterförmige Struktur aus verschiedenen gekreuzten und parallelen Elementen, die an den Fenstern oder an anderen Orten angebracht wird, um das Innere oder das, was sich auf der anderen Seite befindet, zu verdecken und dabei Luft und Licht hindurchzulassen

K

Kannelierung. Aufeinanderfolge von

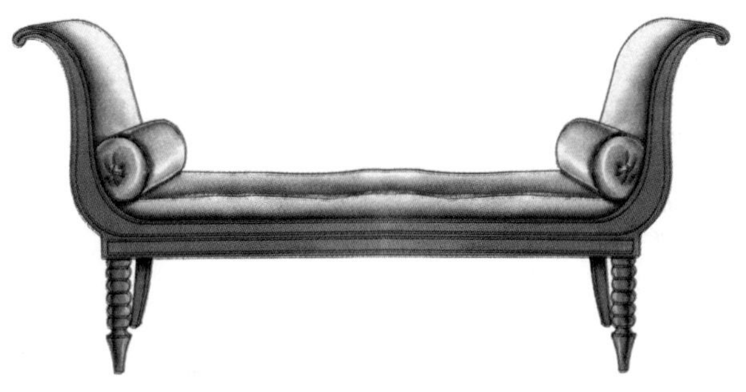

regard to coats of paint, varnish, lacquer, etc. The final polish or coating given a wall.

Fleur-de-lys. Lis. Stylization, in heraldry, of the lily (used since the Middle Ages).

Fluting, flute. Estría. The hollow channels cut into the shafts of Classical columns and, by extension, in different parts of pieces of furniture, especially the legs.

F**rame, framework.** Armadura. The (usually) wooden or iron structure of a piece of furniture bearing the weight or serving as reinforcement.

Fret, fretwork. Greca. Fillets at right angles one to another, arranged in bands and in geometric repetition.

Frieze. Friso. The middle division of the entablature. It is composed of a band, generally horizontal, and may include relief figures or designs. Also, an ornamental band with garlands, festoons, trophies, and other motifs used to decorate art objects.

Estrade: *Plancher surélevé, parfois avec des gradins sur lequel on place des trônes et des sièges, pour donner plus d'autorité à celui qui s'y assoit.*

Étagère: *table ou planche de n'importe quel matériel adossé horizontalement au mur ou appartenant à une armoire ou autre meuble, qui sert à soutenir des choses. Rayon.*

Etayé: *Technique qui consiste à tailler ou arrondir une pièce en bois fixée sur une plateforme horizontale qui tourne autour d'une planche verticale, jusqu'à obtenir la forme d'une patte de section circulaire et du profil désiré.*

F

Feston: *N'importe quel ornement ou achèvement en forme d'onde, pointe, etc...réalisé sur le bord d'un meuble ou d'un de ces éléments.*

Filet: *Genre de moulure, la plus fine de toutes, qui représente une rayure longue et mince.*

Filigrane: *N'importe quel ornement fin et délicat avec lequel on forme un dessin semblable à une broderie.*

Hohlkehlen in Form eines verlängerten S.

Kargstein. Massiver Teil eines Werkes oder der Sockel einer Mauer, Wand oder eines anderen Konstruktionselementes, der mehr als der Rest hervorsteht.

Karnies. Vorspringendes Element, im allgemeinen horizontal und mit Zierleisten aus Holz, Stein oder anderem Material, das als Aufsatz dient, um ein anderes Element zu verzieren oder zu bedecken; jeder architektonsiche Stil hat ein charakteristisches Karnies mit den entsprechenden Varianten und Größenverhältnissen, die auf die Äshetik des Stils oder den Nutzen abgestimmt sind. In den fünf Baustilen der klassischen Architektur stellt das Karnies den oberen Teil der drei Elemente dar, die zusammen das Simswerk bilden, wobei das Karnies zwei Fünftel der Höhe einnimmt.

Karyatide. Architektonisches Motiv, das auch im Möbelbau verwendet wird; vor allem bei Zwischenpfeilern verwendet; aus Bronze, in Form von aufgerichteter Frauenfigur, aus Stein gehauene runde Büste. Sie hat die Funktion einer Säule oder eines Pilaster.

Kastenbank. Truhenartiges, rechteckiges Möbelstück aus Holz, hohl, versehen mit einem mit Scharnieren ausgestatteten Deckel, der der Aufbewahrung von Gegenständen dient.

Kathederstuhl. Breitflächiger massiver Sitz mit erhöhter Rückenlehne, im allgemeinen Personen mit repräsentativen Funktionen vorbehalten, um majestätischen Glanz auszudrücken. Sitz der römischen Frau, ähnlich dem griechischen Klismos.

Front, façade. Frontis. The main side of a house and, by analogy, of a piece of furniture.

Frontal. Frontal. The antependium in front of an altar or the decoration on the front of a piece of furniture.

Fronton. Frontón. A pediment, i.e., loosely, the triangular space forming the gable of a low roof in classical architecture. By extension, any such triangular structure of adornment on furniture.

G

Galbe (Fr). A gently curved leg on a piece of furniture.

Gallery. Galería. Ornamental element of little columns and arches on the upper part of a piece of furniture.

Gold leaf. Pan de oro. Microthin gold used in decorative facings.

Gondola chair. Góndola. Armchair with very concave back attached to the arms. Wooden sidechair with very concave sidepieces that may serve as arms. Bed shaped like the Italian boat of the same name.

H

Half round. Media caña. A molding or torus that is semicircular in section.

Handle. Tirador. Bar, strap, knob, etc. used to open and

Finition: *Opération exécutée afin d'apporter une dernière touche à un ouvrage, particulièrement à la peinture.*

Frange: *Frange d'ornementation posée sur le bord d'un meuble.*

Frise: *Élément décoratif architecturale, composé par une bande, généralement horizontale, où sont sculptés des figures ou des motifs ornementaux ; il forme partie de l'entablement dans les ordres classiques. Bande ornementale avec des motifs de guirlandes, festons, trophées et d'autres, appliquée aux objets pou les décorer.*

Frontale: *Ornementation ou décoration qui forme ou couvre la partie de devant d'un meuble.*

Frontispice: *Façade ou partie antérieure d'une maison ou, par analogie, d'un meuble.*

Kegelstumpfförmig. Pilaster in Form einer umgekehrten kegelstumpfförmigen Pyramide, mit dem kleineren Sockel nach unten zeigend; Dieser Typ von Tisch- und Stuhlbein wurde im neo-klassischen Stil und im Empire-Stil häufig verwendet.

Keilsteg. Horizontales Stück, das die Beine von Stühlen oder Tischen miteinander verbindet; Es kann durchgehend sein (ineinanderübergehend und sich am Rande berührend), in Form eines H (auf jeder Seite eines, und durch eine zentrale Querverbindung miteinander verbunden) oder in Form eines Kreuzes (der erste überkreuzt sich mit dem dritten und der zweite mit dem vierten). Ornamenteinfassung einer Spannweite (Tür, Fenster oder Kamin).

Kliné (gr.). Modell des griechischen Bettes, das in der romanischen Epoche und später im Empire-Stil verbreitet war, bestehend aus einem einfachen rechteckigen Gestell, das auf

close a drawer, door, window, etc.

Headboard. Cabecera. A surface, often decorative, forming the head of a bed or sofa.

I

Imbricated tracery. Imbricación. A pattern that mimics the superimposition of tiles on a roof.

Inlaid work. Incrustación. Ornamentation embedded in the surface of a material.

Ironwork. Herraje. Decorative work in wrought iron or other metal decorating or reinforcing a piece of furniture. The grille made of similar materials on doors, windows, balconies, etc.

J

Jamb. Jamba. The side pieces of an aperture such as a door or window.

Fronton: *Couronnement architecturale en forme de petits triangles isocèles qui terminent les meubles, armoires, librairies, etc...semblable au couronnement des temples grecs ; il peut être simple, courbé ou fendillé ; dans ce dernier cas, il se termine avec des volutes et il porte habituellement une coupe en son centre.*

Fuselé: *Se dit d'une colonne ou d'un support taillés en forme de fuseau.*

Fustet: ***Partie de la colonne qui se*** *trouve entre le chapiteau et la base.*

G

Galbe*: Patte légèrement recourbée.*

Galerie: *Terminaison de petites colonnes et arcs dans la partie supérieure d'un meuble.*

Gondole: *Fauteuil avec dossier de forme concave et demi circulaire, uni aux accoudoirs ; dénommé ainsi par sa ressemblance avec l'embarcation vénitienne du XVIII ème siècle. Lit aux caractéristiques semblables à l'embarcation précédemment citée.*

Grecque: *Ornementation qui consiste en une bande plus ou moins large qui répète la même combinaison d'éléments décoratifs de forme géométrique.*

Guéridon: *Table circulaire de taille réduite, avec un pied central ou piédestal, que l'on utilisait au XVII ème et au XVIII ème siècle pour soutenir des candélabres, des jeux, des vases, etc...*

Füße in Form von Adlern, Löwen, Greifen, geflügelten Pferden etc. gestellt wurde.

Klismos (gr.). Griechischer sehr leichter Stuhl, gehalten von vier doppelt gebogenen Stuhlbeinen, deren abgerundete Enden über die Kante der Sitzfläche hinausragten; die Verlängerung der hinteren Stuhlbeine bildete eine entgegengesetzte Krümmung und endete in einer gebogenen Holzleiste, die als Rückenlehne diente.

Knauf. Henkel oder Griff, an dem man zieht, um eine Schublade, Tür, etc. zu öffnen oder zu schließen.

Kommode. Kastenbank, die auf hohe Beine gestellt wird und daher kommod ist. Sie dient der Aufbewahrung von Gegenständen, hat auf die gesamte Höhe verteilte Schubladen und am oberen Ende eine horizontale Platte.

Konsole. Element der Architektur, der Dekoration oder des Mobiliars, das an eine Wand angebaut wird, und aus dieser herausragt, um als Stütze für etwas zu dienen; im allgemeinen hat

Joint, junction. Ensamble. The union of different pieces (of wood, etc.) by means of special cuts to fit them together. Particularly, tongue-and-groove joints, or mortise-and-tenon joints, miter, chevron or herringbone, etc.

K

Keyhole. Bocallave. The open part of a lock where the key is fitted, often decorated with plates of worked or etched steel or brass.

Kliné (Gr). A Greek bed, also used in ancient Roman times and later in the Empire style. It is a simple rectangular surface on legs in the form of eagles, lions, griffins, horses, etc., and with long decorative volutes, palmettes, ovals, and other designs.

Klismos (Gr). A chair, light and elegant, developed by the

I

Incrustation: *Garnir ou engager dans une surface de bois avec des matériaux nobles tels que du bois, de l'huître perlière, des écailles,etc...en composant des figures et des motifs ornementaux.*

J

Jalousie: *Ajour ou treillage d'éléments divers et parallèles qui se pose devant les fenêtres entre autres, pour celer l'intérieur ou ce qu'il y a de l'autre côté afin de laisser passer l'air et la lumière.*

Jambage: *Chacune des pièces latérales qui forment un creux .*

K

« Kliné »: *Modèle de lit grec, utilisé à l'époque romaine et postérieurement durant l'Empire, constitué par un simple châssis rectangulaire surélevé du sol par des pattes en forme d'aigle, lion, robinet, cheval ailé, etc... et avec des traverses décorées avec des vo-*

sie die Form einer Volute, die am oberen Ende das Bord stützt und sich am unteren Ende gegen die Wand stützt oder, insofern es sich um ein Möbel handelt, gegen das Stück, das hinter ihm liegt.

Konsoltischchen/Konsole. Ziertisch, der an die Wand gestellt wird, auf dem Ziergegenstände aufgestellt werden, wie z. B. eine Uhr, Kerzenhalter oder Krüge. Vorprung, der als Stütze für ein Karnies dient.

Kopfteil. Oberer Teil des Bettes.

Kredenz. Möbelstück mit ähnlichen Maßen wie die Kommode, in Form eines Schrankes mit zwei oder mehreren Türen, mit oder ohne Schubladen für Geschirr, Tischdecken und Lebensmittel; manchmal verfügt sie über zusätzliche Regale für das Ausstellen von Geschirr.

Kunsttischler. Künstler, der Edelhölzer verarbeitet, vor allem Ebenholz.

L

Lit de repos (frz.). Bett-Sofa zum Ausruhen mit mittelhoher Rückenlehne und einer einzigen Armlehne.

M

Mäander. Verzierung, bestehend aus einem mehr oder weniger breiten Bandgesims, in dem sich die gleiche Kombination geometrischer dekorativer Elemente wiederholt.

Maßwerk. Architektonische Dekoration, bestehend aus Kombinationen von geometrischen Figuren.

Medaillon. Dekoratives kreisförmiges, ovales oder elliptisches Element, das im allgemeinen figürliche Motive einrahmt, aber auch Landschaf-

ancient Greeks. It had four curving legs and a double curve to the back.

L

Lit de repos (Fr). Sofa-bed with a half-back and a single arm.

Lobe of an arch. Lóbulo. The foil(s), or small arc(s) of a Gothic arch.

Loveseat.,Confidente. Canapé or settee for two people.

M

Marquetry, inlay. Taracea. Ornamentation embedded in the surface of a material, especially fine substances like

hardwoods, mother-of-pearl, shells, etc.

Marquetry. Marquetería. Decorative inlaid work, something like tracery, set into the surface of different parts of a piece of furniture. Marquetry or inlays may be of wood or other materials, such as bone, ivory, stone, metal. The designs are in the form of mosaics or tracery using floral *lutes, palmes, oeufs et autres dessins.*

« Klismos »: *Chaise grecque très légère, soutenue par quatre pattes à double courbure, qui saillissent du plan du siège avec les extrémités arrondies ; la prolongation des pattes postérieures, formant une contre courbe, est terminée par une frange de bois courbé qui sert de dossier.*

L

Lambris: *Revêtement d'un mur avec une décoration en bois. Lambris d'appui. Boiserie.*

Lambris d'appui: *Revêtement en bois ou autre matériel qui couvre et protège la partie inférieure des murs d'une pièce.*

Lit de repos: *Canapé- lit pour le repos avec un demi dossier et un seul accoudoir.*

Liséré: *Dessin d'ornementation, qui peu être placé sur le bord de quelque chose , consistant en un motif ou un dessin répété indéfiniment.*

Listel: *Dessin ou relief large et étroit, de largeur uniforme, qui est placé sur quelque chose, comme élément ou comme ornement.*

Lobe: *Chacune des ondes et arcs en cercle qui décorent généralement l'entre deux des arcs, principalement dans le style gotique et arabe.*

Lys: *Stylisation héraldique du lys depuis le Moyen âge.*

ten, heraldische und andere Wappen, gemeißelt, gemalt, mit metallischen Applikationen auf Hoch- und Flachrelief.

Méridienne (frz.). Art Canapé, deren eine Seite höher als die andere ist; die Struktur hat eine geschwunge Form, aus dem französischen Empire-Stil.

Mosaik. Dekoration, bei der pflanzliche Materialen (Hölzer verschiedener Farben), Tiermaterialien (Knochen, Elfenbein, Muscheln) oder Minerale (Marmor, Hartstein) in die Möbelstruktur eingefaßt werden. Intarsien. Einlegearbeiten.

N

Nachbearbeitung. Jeglicher Arbeitsvorgang, der an einem bereits fertigen Objekt ausgeführt wird, um ihm ein schönes Aussehen zu verleihen – vor allem der Anstrich. Letztes Schleifen einer Wand. Polieren.

O

Or moulu (frz.). Gemisch aus Gold und Quecksilber, das für die Dekoration der französischen Bronzefiguren

patterns, arabesques, and pictorial scenes.

Medallion. Medallón. A tablet in square, circular, oval or elliptic shape bearing low relief figures or busts.

Mensula. Ménsula. Modillion: projecting console brakkets.

Meridienne sofa. Méridienne (Fr). A kind of canapé or settee with a back that is high at one end and low at the other, of curved structure, popular in the French Empire style.

Molding. Moldura. Adornment in the form of a contour piece used on the angles or different features of a building or piece of funiture. There are many different types, e.g., half round, torus, cable, edge roll, running dog (Vitruvian scroll), etc.

Montant. Montante. An upright element in the frame of a structure. Also, sometimes used to refer to a transom in a window.

O

Orle. Orla. A fillet in a capital or on a piece of furniture.

Ormolu. Ormoulu. Golden or gilded brass or bronze decorations used in eighteenth- and nineteenth-century pieces.

Oval. Oval. Egg-shaped in section.

M

Manette: *Anse, poignée, duquel on tire pour ouvrir ou fermer un tiroir, une porte etc...*

Marqueterie: *Placage décoratif, très semblable à l'incrustation, appliqué à la structure du meuble et composé par de fins morceaux de bois ou autre matériel organique, tel que de l'ivoire et de l'os, ou bien minéral, disposés de telle manière qu'ils forment un mosaïque aux motifs floraux, arabesques et scènes pictorialistes. Incrustation.*

Marteler: *Travailler une planche métallique ou autre matériel comme le cuir à coups de marteau pour lui donner du relief.*

Médaillon: *Élément décoratif de forme circulaire, ovale ou elliptique ; généralement il encadre des motifs figurés, mais aussi des paysages, des écussons héraldiques ou autres, sculptés, peints, avec des applications métalliques en relief ou bas relief.*

Méridienne: *Espèce de canapé qui présent un côté plus haut que l'autre et de structure courbée, de style Empire français.*

Montant: *Élément vertical de la structure d'un meuble pour assembler les traverses, ou éléments horizontaux dans le but de former le châssis. Fenêtre ou creux au-dessus d'une porte*

.Moulure: *Ornement consistant en une bande en relief avec différents profils et parfois avec des éléments tels que des ovules, des feuilles répétés de façon successive ; les principaux sont: concaves*

des 18. und 19. Jh. verwendet wurde. Zu feinstem Pulver gemahlenes Gold zum Kolorieren.

Oval. Eine dem Ei ähnliche Form. Ellipse.

P

Paneele. Die glatten Einheiten, die durch Kehlleisten, Säulen, etc. begrenzt sind; auf Türblättern, großen Möbeloberflächen und Wandverkleidungen. Gerahmte Umrandung, oft mit Schnitzereien im Innenteil, Intarsien und Malereien, um die Komposition zweckmäßig zu gestalten.

Papyrusrolle. Gemalte oder gemeißelte Darstellung einer nicht ganz aufgerollten Papierrolle, im allgemeinen mit Inschriften, die als Ornament verwendet wird. Dekoratives Motiv, wie aus Karton oder Papier, im allgemeinen in Form einer Karte, deren Ränder sich zu Schnecken drehen und anderen Elementen, je nach angewandtem Stil.

Paß. Jede einzelne der Wellen und runden Bögen, die im allgemeinen die Leibung der Bögen verzieren, hauptsächlich im gotischen und arabischen Stil.

Piedestal. Relativ niedriger Pilaster mit Sockel und Karnies, der eine Säule, eine Statue oder ein anderes Ornament stützt. Säulenunterbau.

Pilaster. Quadratische oder halbrunde Säule, die an der Vorderseite eines Gebäudes oder eines Möbels befestigt ist.

Pilgermuschel. Zierrat, der die halbrunde Muschel mit zwei Hälften abbildet, charakteristisch für den Pilgerer. Jakobsmuschel.

P

Panel. Panel. Different plane parts, often surrounded by moldings or delimited by columns, in a door or in the large sections of pieces of furniture and the walls of buildings.

Paneled. Panelado. Framed section with internal decorations in marquetry, painting, etc., to rationally organize a composition.

Paneling. Empanelado. Wood (such as wainscot) used as finishing on a wall.

Pedestal table. Guéridon (Fr). Small circular table with a central foot or pedestal, used in the seventeenth and eighteenth centuries to hold candelabra, games, vases, etc.

Pedestal. Estípite. Base in the form of an inverse truncated pyramid. It is a type of leg or support much used in the Neo-classical and Imperial styles.

Pedestal. Pilastra. The base that supports a statue or other decorative element.

Pilaster. Pilastra. A shallow column that conforms with a specific order used and is engaged with a wall of a building or the surface of a piece of furniture. Pilasters may be squared or semi-circular.

Plane. Enrasar. To make smooth or even, especially the

(demi tige, cavette, équine) ; convexe (bosel) ; variés (froncé, nette, frange et écosse).

O

***Onde:** Ornementation architectonique en forme de S.*

***Orbe:** Sphère, parfois aplatie, en forme d'oignon, qui sert de pied de meuble. Il peu être lisse, avec des moulures, des griffes ou bosselé.*

***Or moulu:** Amalgame d'or et de mercure employé pour décorer les bronzes français du XVII ème et XIX ème siècle. Or moulu en une poudre extrêmement fine pour illuminer.*

***Ovale:** Se dit d'un objet avec une forme semblable à celle d'un œuf ou à son profil. Ellipse.*

P

***Pain d'or:** Lamelle extrêmement fine d'or employée pour des revêtements décoratifs.*

Plaudersofa. Canapé, auf dem nur zwei Personen Platz finden.

Podium. Erhöhung, manchmal mit mehreren Stufen versehen, auf den man die Thröne oder Lehnsessel stellt, um dem Sitzenden mehr Autorität zu verleihen. Erhöhter Unterbau für ein Bauwerk.

Poudreuse (frz.). Kleiner Toilettentisch, der im 17. Jh. dazu diente, sich zu pudern und die Perücken zu kämmen.

Predella. Bank oder Schemel eines Retabel oder eines ähnlichen Möbelstückes, normalerweise mit mehreren Abteilungen, in denen Szenen abgebildet sind, die im Zusammenhang mit denen des oberen Teiles stehen; unterer Teil von dieser.

Punzen. Mit Hammerschlägen eine Metallplatte oder andere Materialien, wie das Leder, bearbeiten, wobei Figuren auf dem Relief gebildet werden.

Putti (it). Dekoratives Motiv mit Kindern. Angelot.

Q

Querstrebe. Querverbindung, die das Gestänge der Rückenlehnen von Sesseln und Stühlen horizontal verbindet.

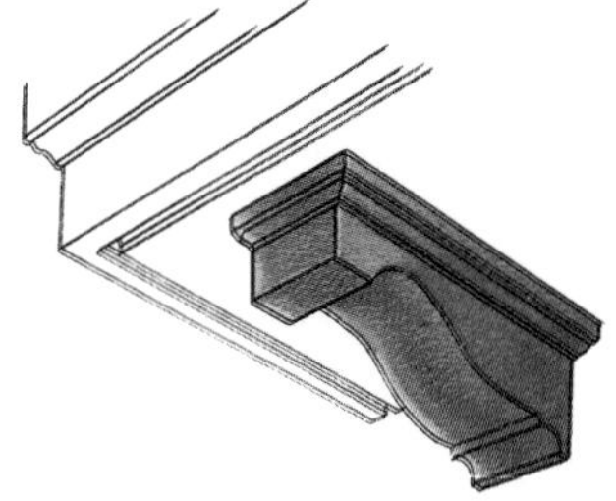

wooden surface of a piece of furniture.

Plywood. Contrachapado. A material used in construction and carpentry made of sheets of wood glued together. The grains of the wood used are usually arranged at right angles in each adjacent layer to avoid warping or slippage as well as cracks, contraction, expansion, etc. Solid wood pieces are often subject due to heat or humidity.

Poudreuse. Poudreuse. Small toilette table used in the seventeenth century to powder the face and arrange wigs.

Profile. Perfil. A vertical section of a body; the silhouette or outline. Any of the long thin lines made by painters or decorators to outline ornamentation

Projection. Repisa. A part jettying out from, projecting from, or forming a cantilever of a structure.

Putti (It). Figures of infant boys, usually represented as chubby and healthy, much used in Renaissance art. The

Panel: *Encadrement , souvent avec des décorations internes sous forme de tailles, incrustations ou peintures, pour organiser rationnellement la composition.*

Panneau: *Chacune des portions lisses, limitées par des moulures, piliers, etc..., dans un pan de porte, dans les grandes surfaces de meubles et les revêtements de murs .*

Piédestal: *Pilastre relativement bas, avec base et corniche, qui supporte une colonne, une statue ou autre motif ornemental. Contre base.*

Pilastre: *Colonne carrée ou demi circulaire adossée à un parement ou front d'un édifice ou d'un meuble.*

Placard: *Creux taillé dans un mur et fermé par des portes avec des étagères qui sert d'armoire. Par extension, armoire.*

Plaquage: *Technique utilisée par les ébénistes dans un but ornementale, qui consiste à revêtir la superficie de bois communs de meubles et objets, par des plaques de meilleur qualité d'une épaisseur de 0,5 à 2 mm., selon le type de motif décoratif qui va le composer, en bois fin, écaille de tortue, huître perlière ou ivoire.*

R

Randverzierung. Ornament, das am Rand von etwas angebracht wird und das aus Motiven oder sich unendlich wiederholenden Mustern besteht.

Regula. Unterer Umriß des hervorstehenden Teils eines Karnies oder eines anderen architektonischen Elementes, oder eines hervorstehenden Holzwerkes.

Rocaille (frz.). Dekorationselement aus Steinchen und Muscheln, charakteristisch für den Louis-quinze und den Rokoko.

S

Sable (frz.). Art gebogenes Stuhlbein, mit quadratischer Schnittfläche, in der zweiten Hälfte des 18. Jh. verbreitet.

Salomonisch. Säulenschaft mit runder Schnittfläche, schraubenförmig verwunden.

Säule. Architektonisches Element, das aus einem hohen und schlanken Teil besteht, normalerweise rund, das einen Bogen, ein Dach oder einen Balken sützt; ihre Form definiert für gewöhnlich den Architektur- oder Möbelstil; die häufigsten Bezeichnungen sind: toskanisch, dorisch, ionisch, korinthisch oder zusammengesetzt, athenisch, freistehend, angelehnt, gewunden, gotisch, mit Tambour, kanneliert oder streifenförmig.

Säulenfuß. Mittelstück des Säulensockels ohne Sims. Ebener und quadratischer Stein, der das Kapitell einer Säule krönt. Abakus.

Säulenschaft. Teil der Säule, der sich zwischen dem Kapitell und dem Säulenfuß befindet.

singular is putto. Loosely, cherub.

Q

Quatrefoil. Cuadrifolio. Ornamental motif representing a flower with four petals or a leaf with four leaflets.

R

Ressault. Retranqueado. Recess of one member in relation to another.

Rocaille. Rocalla, rocaille, rococó. Type of building using rocks or pebbles in different decorative elements, characteristic of Louis XV and rococo styles.

S

Sable (Fr). Curved leg of a piece of furniture, square in plane. The sable leg was much

Plafond: *Plan inférieur de la saillie d'une corniche ou autre élément d'architecture ou de menuiserie sous forme de rebord. Ornement qui se place dans la partie centrale du plafond d'une pièce, dans le centre duquel on suspend habituellement une lampe.*

Plinthe: *Corps inférieur lise ou avec des moulures d'un meuble, qui le termine et le sépare du sol.*

Poudreuse: *Petite table de toilette utilisée au XVII ème siècle pour se poudrer le nez et se peigner la perruque.*

Prédelle: *Banc ou banquette d'un retable ou meuble similaire, généralement divisé en petits compartiments où sont représentés des scènes en relation avec la partie supérieure ; partie inférieure horizontale de celle-ci.*

Profil: *Contour d'une figure plane. Ligne qui dessine n'importe quelle figure taillée par un plan vertical. Chacun des tracés longs et minces que font les peintres ou les décorateurs pour marquer les ornements.*

« Putti »: *Motif décoratif en forme de petits enfants. Angelets.*

Q

Quatre feuilles: *Motif ornementale de style roman ou gotique qui forme un espace vide imitant le contour d'une fleur à quatre feuilles, appliqué aux balustrades en pierre, rosaces et tracés de fenêtres.*

R

Ressaut: *Pièce d'architecture, de décoration ou de mobilier adossée*

Schachbrett. Aus zwei verschiedenen Materialien hergestelltes Werk, z. B. Stein und Ziegelstein, die Würfel bilden, oder mit weißen und schwarzen Fliesen, die einem Schachbrett ähneln.

Schlüsselloch. Sichtbarer Teil des Verschlusses; mit durchbrochenen Eisenbeschlägen, Zisilierarbeiten oder Bronze verziert.

Schmalleiste. Der feinste Teil der Kehlleiste, in Form eines langen und schmalen Streifens.

Schnitzerei. Kunsttechnik, die darin besteht, Figuren, Motive und Ornamentverzierungen in Hoch- oder Flachreliefs auf der Holzoberfläche eines Möbels, der Oberfläche eines Objektes, Hartsteins, oder Marmors, etc. einzuarbeiten.

Schnitzwerk. Durchgehendes Ornament, das den oberen Teil der Möbel krönt.

Schreibschrank. Möbelstück, bestehend aus einem vertikalen Körper mit

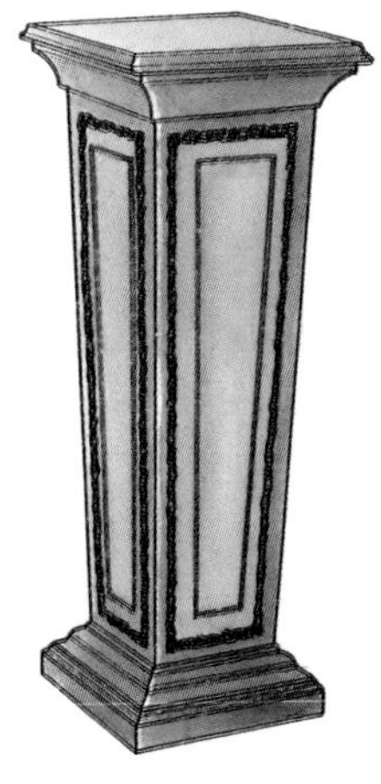

used in the second half of the eighteenth century.

Scallop. Enjuta. An ornament resembling a scallop shell.

Scallop. Venera. An ornament resembling a scallop shell.

Scotia. Escocia. A concave molding at the base of a column, generally situated between two torus moldings. A molding that is generally curved that joins wall to ceiling.

Scroll, Vitruvian scroll. Onda. An adornment in the shape of an S.

Secrétaire (Fr). An enclosed writing desk with compartments in the upper part.

Settee, sofa. Canapé. A seat of some length with a back or a medium-size backed sofa.

Shaft, support. Astil. A column- or beam-like piece giving support.

Shaft. Fuste. The long part of a column between the capital.

Shelf. Anaquel. Planking or boards of any kind of material set horizontally against or between walls to carry objects. Shelves are also used in cupboards, cabinets, and closets, etc.

Sideboard. Buffet. A sideboard or buffet is a piece of dining-room furniture with drawers and/or shelves where

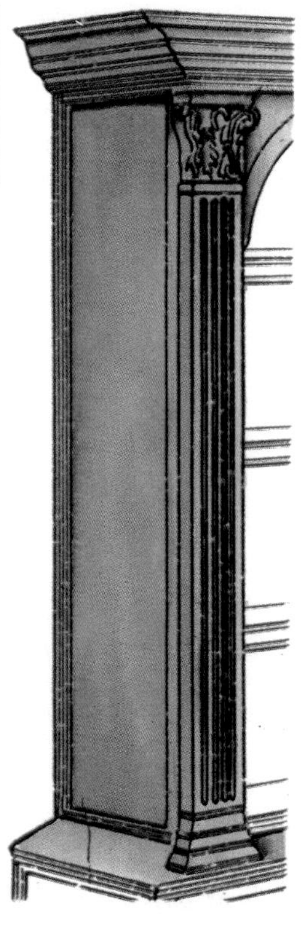

au mur et saillante qui sert d'appui à quelque chose ; il a généralement la forme d'un volute qui soutient par l'extrémité supérieure une tablette et repose sur le mur par la partie inférieure, et si c'est un meuble, sur la pièce postérieure à lui.

Retondre: *Contourner les moulures, toutes les parties entrantes et saillantes de la surface en suivant les changements de direction.*

Retrait: *Recul total ou partiel du front d'un meuble.*

vielen Schubladen und einer Platte, die als Tisch ausgeklappt werden kann.

Sécrétaire (frz.). Schreibtisch mit Schubladen. Bureau. Besonders die zylindrischen, die mit Rolladen verschlossen werden.

Sekretär. Schreibtisch oder Schreibmöbel, in dessen Schublädchen und Schubfächern man Geheimnisse oder Papiere verstecken und aufbewahren kann.

Simswerk. Karnies. Bestehend aus Simsen, die die Fassade eines klassischen Gebäudes oder eines auf Säulen getragenen Möbels krönen; man unterscheidet drei Teile: Architrav, Karnies und Fries.

Sockel. Stütze, Fuß, Vorsprung oder Plattform, auf die ein Bildnis, eine Figur, ein Bild oder etwas anderes gestellt wird.

Spindelförmig. Bezogen auf Säulen oder Stützen, die spindelförmig geschnitzt sind.

Stipo (it.). Nicht allzu großes Möbelstück, ausgestattet mit Schublädchen und geschlossenen Fächern, mit zwei oder mehr Fensterchen; es wurde normalerweise auf einen Tisch, einen Konsoltisch oder einen Sockel gestellt; charakteristisch für das 16. und 17. Jh.

Strebe. Jeglicher Stab, Leiste oder Teil, aus Holz oder einem anderen Material, das zwei sich gegenüberliegende Teile eines Gegenstandes miteinander verbindet, wie die Tischbeine, Stuhlbeine, etc. Traverse.

T

Tabouret (frz.). Hocker mit festen

vertikalen Hockerbeinen, normalerweise rechteckig und Sitz mit Intarsien.

Toilette (frz.). Frisiertisch.

Tripus. Dreifuß

Trochilus. Konkave Kehlleiste, die an der unteren Seite mehr herausragt und im allgemeinen zwischen zwei Tori plaziert wird. Im allgemeinen runde Kehlleiste, die Wand und Decke verbindet.

Trochilus. Konkave Voute, deren Umriß normalerwe ein Halbkreis ist. Hohlkehle.

Truhe. Kiste, Kasten oder Kästchen, das mit einem Deckel verschlossen wird und normalerweise alleine steht.

tableware is stored and from which meals may be served to the table.

Soccle. Zócalo. Smooth block or molding on a piece used as part of the finish and to separate it from wall or floor.

Soffit. Plafón. A ceiling. Also, the lower surface of an arch or the under surface of a corona of a cornice. In general, the underside of any part of a building.

Solomonic. Salomónico. Used to describe a column, a twisted or helical shape.

Spindle shaped. Ahusado. Term used to describe columns or supports in a tapering shape.

Rocaille, rococo. Type *de décoration à base de petites pierres et de coquillages, caractéristique du style Louis XV et du Rococo.*

S

Sable: *Type de patte de chaise courbée, de section carrée, apparue dans la seconde moitié du XVIIème siècle.*

Saillie: *Massif de maçonnerie ou base de mur, ou autre élément de construction, qui saillit un peu plus qu le reste.*

Salmer: *Bloc de pierre coupé sur un plan incliné, d'où part un arc en forme de linteau.*

Salomonique: *Dans une colonne, partie centrale de section circulaire en forme d'hélice ou de torche.*

Trumeau (frz.). Kommode mit Aufbau. Dekoration einer Wand oder

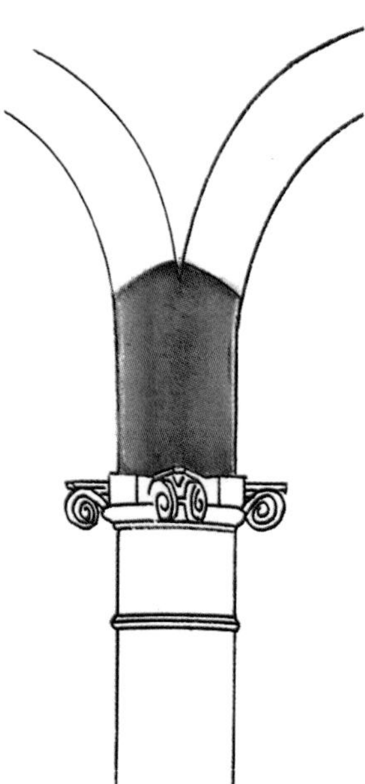

Stipo (It). Small writing table with closed compartments. (See desk).

Stretcher. Chambrana. Travesaño. A horizontal rod or bar joining the legs of chairs and tables.

Striae. Estrígiles. Succession of fillets, sometimes in long S-shapes.

T

Tabouret. (Fr). A cylinder-shaped seat with no back or arms.

Toilette table. Toilette. Small table used in the boudoir, etc.

Torus. Bocel. Convex molding at the base of a column. Cordon.

Tracery. Tracería. The intersection of elements in screens, windows, panels, etc. to form geometric figures.

Tripod. Trípode. A three-legged support.

Trumeau (Fr). A decorative mirror on a dresser or console table.

Turned. Torneado. Turned objects are those worked on a lathe. They have a rounded form that varies in profile and may, of course, be tapered.

V

Veneer. Chapeado. An overlay or plate. As a verb, it denotes the technique of using these thin sheets in cabinetry

Secrétaire: *Écritoire ou meuble pour écrire où l'on peut cacher et maintenir des secrets dans des gavettes ou des petits tiroirs.*

Serrurerie: *Ensemble de pièces en fer avec lesquelles ont garni un meuble et avec lesquelles on le renforçait autrefois. Ensemble de pièces qui assurent et facilitent l'ouverture des portes et fenêtres.*

Socle: *Pied qui sert de support ou d'appui.*

Sommet: *Partie la plus élevée d'un meuble. Partie supérieure d'une basque brisée.*

Soubassement: *Pièce horizontale au-dessus ou au-dessous d'un pied droit, pour soutenir ou charger le poids et répartir mieux la charge supérieure.*

Stipo: *Meuble aux dimensions réduites, pourvu de petits tiroirs et de compartiments fermés, avec deux petites fenêtres ou plus, audessus d'une table ou d'une console ou sur un socle ; il est caractéristique du XVI ème et du XVII ème siècle.*

Strie: *Demi tige creusée ou rainurée, que l'on cisèle dans certaines colonnes ou piliers de haut en bas.*

Strigiles: *Succession de stries en forme de S allongé.*

Styptique: *Pilier en forme de pyramide tronquée invertie, avec la base plus étroite vers le bas ; c'est un type de patte très utilisé dans les styles Néoclassique et Empire.*

Wandverkleidung mit einem Spiegel über einem Kamin oder einem Konsoltischchen.

U

Umriß. Profil einer flachen Figur. Linie, die jegliche geschnittene Figur auf vertikaler Ebene zeichnet. Lange und dünne Striche, die die Maler oder Dekorateure zeichnen, um die Ornamente zu umreißen.

Unterbau. Unteres Element eines Möbels, glatt oder gekehlt, das es abschließt und vom Boden trennt.

Untergrund. Innerer Teil von Holzfurnieren, der aus dünnen Holzplatten zusammengesetzt ist, welche ihm Konsistenz verleihen, und der dann mit weiteren Platten überzogen wird, die die Außenseite bilden.

V

Verdrehen. Das Drehen der Leisten, sowohl herausragende als auch nach innen gehende, wobei die Richtung beibehalten wird.

for ornamental or finishing purposes. Veneer varies in width from 0.5 to 2 mm, according to the type of decorative motif or finish desired. The material also varies, and includes wood, tortoise shell, mother-of-pearl, ivory, etc.

Violonné (Fr). Used to refer to the form of the backs of chairs. Violin-shaped.

Volute. Voluta. A spiral scroll on the Ionic capital, also called a helix. The form is also used in furniture.

Voussoir. Salmer. In an arch, a stone in the shape of a wedge.

Voyeuse (Fr). Chair used at gaming tables, allowing the player's companion to lean on the back, and thus easily see (voir) the game.

W

Wainscot. Arrimadero. Timber lining or paneling of walls or ceilings.

Woven work. Rejilla. Interlaced fibers of certain plants used in the seats of chairs or

Support: *Appui, pied, support, plateforme sur lequel on place une effigie, une figure, une image ou autre chose.*

T

Tabouret: *Siège avec des pattes verticales fixes, généralement de forme rectangulaire.*

Taille: *Technique artistique qui consiste à réaliser sur la surface du bois d'un meuble ou objet, pierre dure, marbres, etc...des figures, motifs, et décorations ornementales en bas ou haut relief.*

Tête de lit: *Pièce supérieurequi limite le lit.*

Tarsier: *Décorer en incrustant du matériel végétal (bois de différentes couleurs), des animaux (os, ivoire, écaille), ou minéral (Marbre, pierres dures) sur la structure en bois du meuble. Incrustation. Marqueterie.*

Toilette: *Table de la coiffeuse.*

Tracement: *Décoration architecturale consistant à combiner des figures géométriques.*

Traverse: *N'importe quelle barre, montant ou pièce, en bois ou n'-importe quel matériel, qui uni deux parties opposées d'un chose, comme les pattes de tables, de chaises, etc... Chambranle.*

Trépied: *À trois pattes.*

Trou de serrure: *Partie à la vue du pertuis de la serrure ; il est décoré avec des plaques en fer ajouré ou martelé, ou en bronze.*

Verzapfen. Verbindung, Aneinanderpassen oder Angleichen von Holzstücken, indem hervorstehende Teile eines Holzstückes in die Öffnungen des zweiten Stückes eingepaßt werden. Im besonderen Spunden, Schwalbenschwanz, Schlaufe, Beisszange, im Winkelverband fügen, Verbindungszunge, Zusam-menblatten, Verdübeln, etc.

Vierblatt. Ornamentmotiv des romanischen oder gotischen Stils, das eine leere Fläche bildet und den Umriß einer vierblättrigen Blume imitiert; es wird für Steingeländer, Rosetten und Kirchenfenster verwendet.

Violonné (frz.). Form der Stuhlrükkenlehne, in der Mitte abgeschnürt, wie eine Violine.

Volute. Spiralförmige Einrollung am Kapitell ionischer Säulen und außerdem Ornament bei Möbelstücken.

Voyeuse (frz.). Stuhl zum Spielen, auf den man sich im Reitersitz setzt und die Arme auf den oberen gepolsterten Teil der Rückenlehne stützt.

Wandschränkchen. Wohnzimmermöbel, mit Schrank und über diesem ein Kasten, der obere Teil im allgemeinen aus Marmor; es wird zwischen Balkone und Fenster gestellt.

Wandtäfelung. Verkleiden einer Wand mit Holz. Täfelwerk. Boiserie.

Wandtäfelung. Verkleidung aus Holz oder anderem Material, die den unteren Teil der Zimmerwände bedeckt oder schützt.

Wappenlilie. Heraldische Stilisierung der Lilie seit dem Mittelalter.

other parts of furniture pieces.

Writing table. Canterano. See desk. The name canterano is given in Catalonia to the type of writing table that has an inclined top. It always denotes a piece with many drawers, a transformation of the chest, to which such drawers were added in the sixteenth century. These were first and addition to the base, later, over the course of the sixteenth and seventeenth centuries, to the entire piece. At the beginning of the eighteenth century, the canterano as a table of this type, with a writing surface, had definitively substituted the old chest.

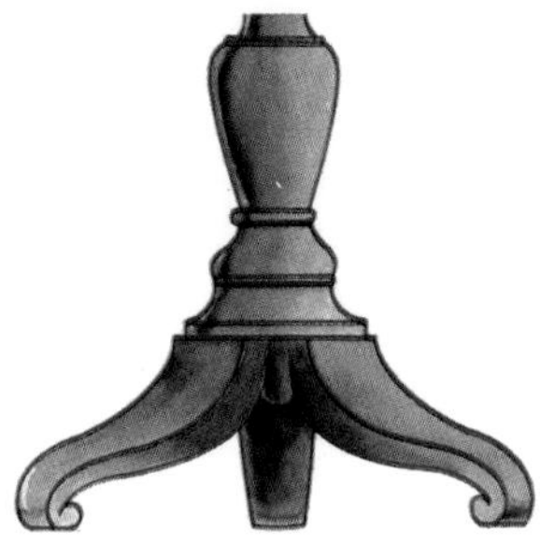

Trumeau: *Commode en hauteur. Décoration d'un mur ou étagère avec un miroir, au-dessus d'une cheminée ou d'une console.*

V

Violoné: *Forme de dossier de chaises, étranglé dans le centre, comme les violons.*

Volute: *Ornement en forme de spirale que l'on place dans les chapiteaux de l'ordre ionique et que l'on trouve par conséquence dans certaines pièces du mobilier.*

Voyeuse: *Chaise de jeu pour s'asseoir à cheval en appuyant les bras sur le haut tapissé du dossier.*

Welle. Architektonische Verzierung in S-Form.

Widerlager. Alle seitlichen Teile, die eine Nische bilden.

Wulst. Zylinderförmiges konvexes Gesims. Rundstab. Torus.

Z

Zurücksetzung. Völliges oder teilweises Zurücksetzen der Vorderseite eines Möbels.

Zwiebel. Kugel, manchmal zusammengedrückt, in Form einer Zwiebel, als Fuß eines Möbels verwendet. Sie kann glatt oder gekehlt sein, eingedreht oder mit Klaue.